NEWGRANGE

AND THE

BEND OF THE BOYNE

Geraldine Stout

CORK UNIVERSITY PRESS

Irish Rural Landscapes: Volume I
Newgrange and the Bend of the Boyne

General Editors:
F.H.A. Aalen,
Kevin Whelan
Matthew Stout

First Published by
Cork University Press,
Crawford Business Park,
Crosses Green,
Cork,
Ireland

British Library Cataloguing in Publication Data
A CIP catalogue record for this book is available from the British
Library.

ISBN 1 85918 341 7

Colour Reproduction by Phototype-Set Ltd., Dublin
Printed in China. Through Phoenix Offset

Dedicated to the memory of my dear friends
Caitlín Bean Uí Chairbre and Leo Swan

FROM THE EDITORS OF *IRISH RURAL LANDSCAPES*

The *Atlas of the Irish Rural Landscape* was published in 1997 with the aim of accelerating awareness of the landscape as a central component of national heritage, to show its relevance in environmental, educational and public policy issues, to reveal its historic underpinnings, and to deepen aesthetic appreciation of the landscape as a shared creation of the myriad generations of Irish people. One of the *Atlas* sections comprised short case studies of a series of distinct regions in Ireland – the Hook, Lecale, the Burren, The Bend of the Boyne, the Ring of Gullion and Connemara. In this new series of ancillary studies entitled *Irish Rural Landscapes*, some of these case studies will be expanded to full-length monographs, modelled on the original *Atlas* format. We hope the publication of this first volume will also inspire intensive landscape studies in additional areas. The critical and popular reception of the original volume (reprinted several times since 1997) indicated a growing appreciation of both the importance and the fragility of the landscape at a period of momentous transformation in Irish life.

This series develops at greater length the themes of the original atlas – the landscape as a reciprocal relationship between nature and culture, the variety of regional landscapes as a reflection of cultural complexity and natural diversity, the challenge to landscape legacy by potent forces of change, the need for change to be channelled in sympathy with inherited landscape features. The pervasive 'Tiger economy' has accelerated these challenges in the five years since 1997: now more than ever, we need to widen our understanding of how landscape works, and to develop policies decisively tempered by concern for landscape qualities.

In her exciting study of the Bend of the Boyne, Geraldine Stout shows what can achieved in landscape studies by carefully integrating field work, the archival record, archaeology and an overwhelming passion for an intimate place. While the mighty megaliths of the Boyne Valley loom deservedly large, her exemplary study pays equally careful attention to every phase of the Valley's rich history, from the Mesolithic to the modern. Second World War pill boxes, Parnell cottages, field boundaries are treated in loving detail as well as the most magnificent collection of megalithic art in Europe. The extra-ordinary is set within the ordinary, and new contexts and interpretative vistas are constantly opened. The Bend of the Boyne was declared a World Heritage Site in 1993. This well-informed study shows us why: it is an outstanding contribution to our understanding of the Irish rural landscape in all it historic depth, beauty and fragility.

F. H. A. Aalen
Kevin Whelan
Matthew Stout

CONTENTS

PREFACE AND ACKNOWLEDGEMENTS

In 1993 Newgrange and the Bend of the Boyne, also known as Brú na Bóinne, were declared a World Heritage Site by UNESCO. This listing affirms the international importance of Newgrange and the pre-eminence of the passage tomb culture in the Boyne Valley. The World Heritage Site status was also designated to the Bend of the Boyne in recognition of the continuity of settlement in the area, evident in its wide range of archaeological monuments of prehistoric and historic date. It is a multilayered landscape with many stories to tell. This book is a broad, personal exploration of Newgrange and its environs, gained from years of reading and interpreting its field evidence. Each discovery, however small, has been a source of personal pleasure. This book seeks to increase appreciation for, and public enjoyment of, this prized landscape.

I first came to the Boyne Valley as a first-year archaeology student in 1976 to work for George Eogan of the Department of Archaeology at University College Dublin on his excavations at Knowth, and spent the remainder of my undergraduate summers at the site. This was the experience of a lifetime. I worked alongside Meath men, many of them local sheep or cattle farmers, and students from Europe, America and Australia. In those years the mound was a hive of activity, with rough paving stones of Early Christian houses being exposed on one side, soil-stained sockets of smaller passage tombs appearing on the other, the mixed debris of Early Bronze Age Beaker settlements around the back, and the mortared walls of a medieval stone building being revealed on the top. Strip by strip the site was trowelled back and forward and as each tantalising pit or stone setting appeared it was brushed clean, surveyed using line, bubble level and tapes and recorded in the utmost detail.

At the end of each day trays of finds would be brought into the finds hut for registering and numbering. They would contain a range of artefacts from different eras: bronze pins, flint scrapers, glazed pottery or perhaps a spindle whorl or corroded iron knife from one of the houses. The site had witnessed many transformations over five millennia, and it reflected in microcosm the prehistory and history of the Boyne Valley, indeed of Ireland itself. All was painstakingly recorded so that one day an accurate interpretation of this site could be presented to the public. In 2002, after forty years of excavation and research, Knowth passage tomb is open to the public and guides tell the stories that revealed themselves to us over those years.

Drawing on the disciplines of archaeology and historical geography, this book documents the evolution of this unique Irish landscape. It explores natural and cultural elements of its make-up, and considers the issues involved in its protection. This study complements the *Atlas of the Irish Rural Landscape*, published in 1997, and will be one of a Landscape Series that will look in detail at different regions in Ireland.

I wish to record my thanks to many individuals, organisations, friends and family for their assistance in preparing this publication: Professor George Eogan, University College Dublin, for allowing me to assist on his excavations at Knowth as an undergraduate; the late Leo Swan, who introduced me to the delights of henge monuments and copper-fastened my links with the Boyne; and the Cairbre family, who have given me a great deal of encouragement and help over many a pint in their justly famous Drogheda hostelry. I trust that the late Caitlín Bean Uí Chairbre would have been pleased with this publication.

Thanks to all my colleagues at Dúchas, the Heritage Service, for their encouragement and financial support: in particular David Sweetman, Chief Archaeologist, for allowing me to assist on his excavations at Newgrange and approving the career break necessary to complete this work; Dave Fadden, Martin Luby and Eugene Keane for their support; archaeologists including Con Manning, Victor Buckley, Michael Moore, Eamonn Cody, Paul Walsh, Finbar Moore, Barry O'Reilly and Michael Higginbottom (architect), the last two of whom advised on vernacular architecture; Senior Architect Willie Cumming, who advised on conservation; archaeologist and editor Tom Condit; Muiris de Butléir and Rob Obbington in GIS; and librarian Valerie Ingram and her staff. I am greatly indebted to the staff of the Photographic Section in Dúchas, especially Senior Photographer Con Brogan for his wonderful photographs which are a major contribution to this publication; John Scarry for photographing archival material; and Anthony Roche, photo-archivist, for his endless patience and generosity. Tom Byrne also generously supplied his photography.

I would like to acknowledge the assistance of staff in numerous institutions: the National Library; the National Museum, especially Mary Cahill and Valerie Dowling of its Photographic Section; the National Archive, especially Aideen Ireland; the Royal Irish Academy, especially Siobháin Ó Rafferty and Peter Harbison; the Royal Society of Antiquaries of Ireland; the Traditional Music Archive;

the Farm Development Service, Navan, County Meath; the County Louth Museum, Dundalk, especially Martin Clarke, museum technician; Drogheda Public Library; Jane Beattie of the James Adams Salesrooms; David Byrne, Eastern Regional Fisheries Board; and Matthew Parks of the Geological Survey of Ireland for providing access to the wonderfully indexed collection of fossils. Thanks to Michael Lynam and the ever-friendly staff at Photo-Typeset for work of such high standard.

My warmest thanks to my many friends in the Boyne Valley for their help and hospitality: in particular Clive Ó Gibne, who showed me how to make a Boyne Coracle, his wife Sinéad and his brothers Gearóid and Brian; Séan and Pauline Fullham of Stalleen for their hospitality; Breda Tuite of Tullyallen for helpful discussions on the Battle of the Boyne; Barry Flood of Rossin Anglers, who accompanied me on a tour of the Boyne fish weirs; Hugh Gough MMCC for local history on Rossnaree; my old friend and colleague Kieran Campbell for much valuable information and photographs; local poet Susan Connolly; Anne-Marie Moroney for many discussions on Dowth; local artists Ray Balfe and Richard Moore; Sean Corcoran and Gerry Cullen for information on local songs; Elizabeth Addison of Glebe House; and Michael 'Munich' O'Reilly of Drogheda, who assisted in the survey of pillboxes along the Boyne and shares his wonderful enthusiasm for the Boyne with all he comes in contact with. I would especially like to thank Claire Tuffy, Manager of the Brú na Bóinne Visitor Centre, who has made a reality of the centre's name by putting it at the core of activities organised in the Bend of the Boyne. Thanks also to Leonsha Lenehan and Pauline Moore in the Brú na Bóinne Visitor Centre for their warm hospitality.

Thanks to fellow researchers who make the pursuit of knowledge a pursuit of fun and friendship as well: Cristóir Mac Cárthaigh, Department of Folklore, and Gabriel Cooney, Department of Archaeology, University College Dublin; Liam Mac Mathúna, St Patrick's College, Drumcondra who advised on Dindshenchas Érenn; Micheál Ó Siochrú, Department of History, University of Aberdeen; Mark Clinton; Lianda D'Auria; Anthony Lynch, who assisted me with translations of Latin sources; Billy Colfer for helpful discussions on Cistercian settlement and watercolouring of drawings; Petra Coffey for information on the Du Noyer drawings; William Nolan, Department of Geography, for providing access to unpublished research at University College Dublin; William Jenkinson, who allowed me to consult his unpublished research on the Boyne valley; Hugh Carey, who gave me access to his unpublished thesis on Norman Meath; and Magda Loeber and Rolf Loeber for their regular parcels of valuable information and support. Thanks to Paul Kerrigan for drawings of Dowth towerhouse and advice on pillboxes. I would like to thank the staff in the Department of Geography, Trinity College Dublin, where I presented the thesis which was the basis of this book: especially Eileen Russell, Secretary Emeritus; Richard Haworth, Freeman Librarian; Terry Dunne; and Mark Hennessy. Thanks also to Declan Burke, Department of Geology, Trinity College Dublin, for photographing the fossils; and Bernard Meehan, the Keeper of Manuscripts. The index was expertly compiled by Yann Kelly.

My extended family suffered great neglect during the preparation of this publication and I am deeply grateful to them for their patience. Thanks in particular to my sister Marian and her family who have taken such good care of my children, and to my sister Loretto Lacey who provided much needed funding. I would especially like to thank my husband Matthew and daughters Nóra and Helen for their great tolerance. Matthew also designed the book, edited and typeset the text, and prepared the maps and illustrations.

I would like to especially acknowledge the help of my mentor and friend Kevin Whelan, director of the Keough-Notre Dame Centre, who critically read and reread drafts of this publication. His encouragement was indispensable. I am also extremely grateful to my doctoral supervisor, F.H.A. Aalen, Department of Geography, Trinity College Dublin, for his years of support for this project. His enthusiasm for landscape conservation has been a great inspiration to my own research. Finally I would like to thank my publisher Cork University Press, in particular Sara Wilbourne for her faith in me and the Boyne Valley.

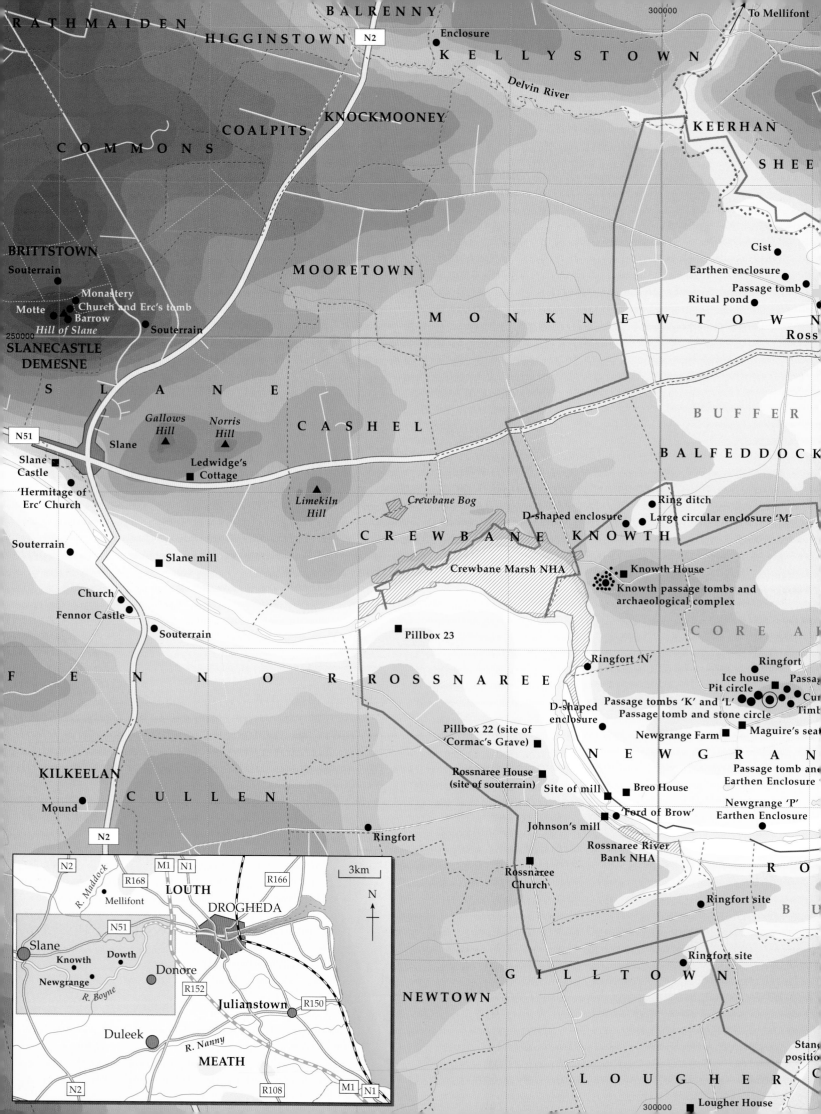

THE BEND OF THE BOYNE

A cultural landscape such as the Bend of the Boyne is the product of dynamic interaction between cultural components and the natural environment. Geological, climatic and biological processes have given the area its unique regional character and physical resources. Physical geography has, in turn, had a significant impact on the seven millennia of human land use in the valley, particularly on agriculture, communications and local industries. All the sites on which its archaeological monuments occur were chosen as a result of their shape, size, and position in the landscape.[1]

The Bend of the Boyne lies in the lower Boyne Valley in the Central Lowland region of Ireland, a landscape characterised by its undulating drift-covered relief. This region is comprised of prosperous, medium-to-large-sized farms of meadow, pasture and arable, with deciduous woodland occurring in demesnes and steep river valleys.[2] For the most part, it is an area of heavy grassland soils which traditionally, and in modern times, have been part of a cattle-fattening belt.[3] The lower Boyne Valley opens onto an area of the coastline where the near-continuous upland perimeter of the island is absent; here the lowlands reach the Irish Sea and the Boyne Valley provides one of the few easy avenues of access to Ireland's eastern interior. Moreover, this area also lies within the 'eastern triangle', a part of Ireland which receives less rain and contains less bog and mountain than any other compact area of similar size in the country.[4] Accessibility and environmental resources combined to make the area attractive to a succession of groups and conducive to striking indigenous cultural developments.

BRADY, SHIPMAN AND MARTIN

Fig. 1 Low-level aerial coverage shows the Bend of the Boyne in 2000. The 'bend' respects a geological obstruction in the course of the Boyne, downriver from the village of Slane in county Meath. Here, the river abruptly changes direction and runs southwards below an elevated ridge. The river flows parallel to the ridge for some distance until it twists northwards through a glacial gorge, eventually resuming its eastward course to the Irish Sea. This bend cradles a region which has been at the forefront of settlement history for more than five thousand years.

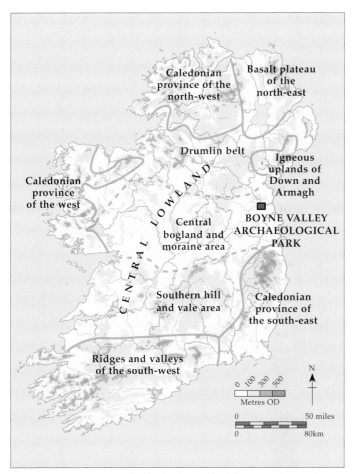

Fig. 2   Physical regions of Ireland. The Bend of the Boyne lies to the east of the Central Lowland, a region dominated by low-lying glacial features.

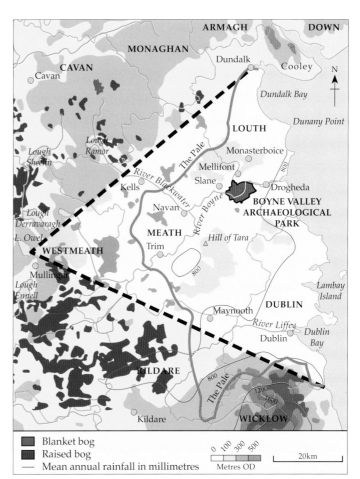

Fig. 3   The 'eastern triangle' in general, and the Boyne Valley in particular, represent the traditional geopolitical focus of Ireland.[8]

GEOLOGY

The Boyne landscape has developed on ancient rocks influenced by the folding and faulting of the Caledonian mountain building phase and largely blanketed by drift deposits derived from the last Ice Age.[5] The oldest rock types in the area are the Lower Palaeozoic rocks (slates) which form an east/west ridge on the northern edge of the valley, dominating its northern prospect; they lie close to the north bank of the Mattock River and extend northwards as far as Nobber in north-west Meath. They make contact with Carboniferous limestones to the north of the Boyne on a fault line running through the townlands of Monknewtown and Littlegrange. They are strongly folded and consist of steeply dipping beds of green quartzites or greywackes, hard greenish-grey and buff mudstones, slates and black-brown slates.[6] Lead and zinc can often be deposited at these contact points and exploration licences have been taken out in these areas.[7]

Lying stratigraphically above the Lower Palaeozoic rocks are the Carboniferous rocks. The lower Boyne Valley is essentially a Carboniferous syncline with a dominant north-east/south-west axis reflected in the local topography.[9] The core of this syncline is formed of Namurian shales and sandstones. The Carboniferous shales in the area lie stratigraphically above the limestone.

The Platin limestone is the best exposed of all the Carboniferous limestone in the area. In general it is thick-bedded, medium- to coarse-grained limestone that is mainly pale. The top of the Platin limestone is found at Mullaghcrone House quarry where the limestone is exposed. Near Duleek, the Platin limestone is obscured by marshy river flats but reappears near Newtown Bridge. There is a still younger limestone in the area which consists of well-bedded limestones with some cherty bands. Most are dark and fine grained. It outcrops in two places, the north of Newgrange and Dowth, and also in a north-east to south-west belt from Oldbridge to as far south as Cruicerath.[10]

The presence of limestone is mirrored in the building stone used locally and in the names of houses such as Whiterock House near Duleek and Rock House at Stalleen. The Carboniferous rock formation is similar to that at Fennor, which was used in the building of the church and fortified house. There were building-stone quarries at Sheephouse and Oldbridge which provided the ashlar limestone for the front of the present church at Donore opened in 1838, the parochial house built in 1860 and many of the stone houses in Donore village and churches in Drogheda.[11] Between 1866 and 1884, four churches were built in Drogheda, all using Sheephouse stone.[12] The Boyne viaduct was also constructed with this stone in the 1850s.[13] In the eighteenth and

nineteenth centuries, there were additional quarries at Cashel, Dowth, Proudfootstown and Slane.

Fossil-rich deposits are recorded in this Carboniferous limestone in a number of locations in the Bend of the Boyne: in a quarry east of Slane, Sheephouse quarry, Cruicerath, a limestone cave at 'Corragubbin' near the

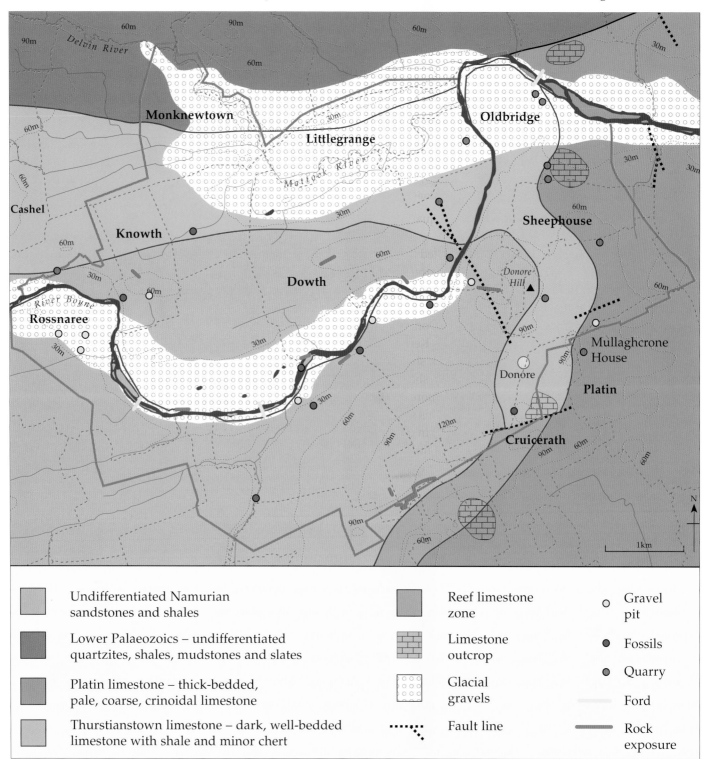

Fig. 4   Geological map of the Bend of the Boyne. The area consists mainly of rocks of Carboniferous age and lies between two inliers of Lower Palaeozoic rock, the Louth massif to the north and the Balbriggan massif to the south.

DÚCHAS/CON BROGAN

Fig. 5   Platin quarry exploits Carboniferous limestone which lies in a belt stretching from the southwest near Duleek, through Platin Cement Works and Sheephouse, to Oldbridge in the north. All the limestone north of the Boyne also appears to be of this type. It is exposed as limestone outcrop with low crags and hollows visible north of Duleek and at Cruicerath.[14]

boundary of Corballis and Newtown, and in quarries one mile east of Platin House.

North of the River Boyne lies an elongated ridge of Carboniferous shale, overlying the earlier Carboniferous limestone. The shales form the core of the south-west plunging syncline. On the south side of the river, this shale forms a still higher rock ridge between Donore and Redmountain and stretches south-west as far as Kentstown. The Redmountain shale group consists of black shales and massive sandstones. A shale group of black shales and minor beds of limestone is found south of Glenmore.

Fossil-rich deposits have been recorded in this shale: on the north side of the river near Knowth House; in a quarry in junction beds between shale and limestone a little east of Rossnaree House; on the north side of the river east of the lock south of Newgrange House; on the south side of the

DÚCHAS/CON BROGAN

Fig. 7   The eastern extremity of the Carboniferous shales is being quarried at Donore Hill by Irish Cement.

river in a cutting for the road to Duleek at Roughgrange; on the south side of the Navan–Drogheda road about a quarter of a mile east of the preceding site; on the south side of the river close to the 'cottage' at Stalleen; on a road-cutting half a mile south-west of Donore; and on the banks of a stream in Sheephouse.[16]

DÚCHAS/CON BROGAN

DÚCHAS/CON BROGAN

Fig. 6   The disused quarry at Cruicerath. The reef of limestone here is remarkable in the number and quality of fossils, with over seventy species recorded from this single locality.[15]

Fig. 8   Exposure of shale is mainly confined to stream beds and banks, such as this example beside Rock House opposite the Brú na Bóinne Visitor Centre.

BOYNE VALLEY FOSSILS

Fossils form when organisms are buried in rock where sediment is accumulating. The types of organisms most likely to become a fossil are those with a hard, external skeleton and small size, such as shellfish. Different geological deposits produce different varieties of fossil. These reflect the varying nature of their former habitats. Thus it is possible to reconstruct the earliest landscapes from a study of the fossil content of their rocks.

Brachiopods from *c.* two miles north of Duleek at Cruicerath. Shown actual size.

FOSSILS FROM LOCAL CARBONIFEROUS LIMESTONE

The boss of limestone at Cruicerath, near Donore, is remarkable for the number of fossil species it has yielded and the state of preservation in which the fossils have been found. The fossils illustrated in this section are a group known as brachiopods. Amongst their diagnostic features is the presence of a fleshy stalk, which they generally used to attach themselves to sediment. Evidence for the former presence of this stalk is often visible as a protruding opening on the fossil. Brachiopods sit at or very close to the sea floor and would have been part of a diverse habitat. They are typical of limestone fossils and reflect a period more than 300,000 million years ago when the Cruicerath area was a tropical seabed.

FOSSILS FROM LOCAL SHALE DEPOSITS

Different geological deposits produce a different spectrum of fossils. Those found in shale formed originally in mud. The fossils illustrated in this section are a fossil group known as bivalves. Bivalves are the common shells on a beach, which include cockles, mussels, scallops and razor shells. As molluscs, they are related to squids, octopuses, ammonites and snails. They are thin-shelled and free-swimming rather than confined to the seabed. They are mainly filter-feeders, but many groups live in burrows and are tolerant of a range of conditions. The orthocones are like today's squid. The presence of teeth in the collection indicates that there may have been shark present.

Molluscs (bivalve) from north side of River Boyne near Knowth House.

All fossils shown actual size.

Molluscs (bivalve) from north side of River Boyne near Knowth House.

Molluscs (bivalve) from exposure by north side of River Boyne, a little east of the fortieth lock and south of Newgrange House.

Molluscs (orthocone) found by the riverside near Knowth House.

Molluscs (orthocone) found south of River Boyne at Stalleen.

Molluscs (orthocone) found south of River Boyne at Stalleen.

Copper resources occur in the lower Boyne Valley.[17] Deposits of coal and copper ore were exploited to a limited extent near the Boyne in the eighteenth and nineteenth centuries. Isaac Butler, visiting Slane in 1744, was told of a deep and dry copper mine in the townland of Cashel, known as the Golden Spot, the site of which has not been clearly identified.[18] There are also lead and copper deposits west of Oldbridge.[19]

GLACIAL HISTORY

The surface landforms of the lower Boyne Valley have been moulded by relatively recent geological events during the last Ice Age. The glacial deposits were laid down mainly during the most recent glaciation when the area was smothered by ice, and these vary in form and sedimentology. The pattern of glacial movement and deposition in the area can be interpreted from these geomorphological and geological features.[20] The area was influenced by ice coming from two sources: the North-central Midlands and the Irish Sea basin. The Drogheda till is the oldest glacial deposit known in the area. A sizeable ice sheet built up somewhere to the north-west of the area in central and northern Ireland – which subsequently moved over the valley in a north-west to south-eastward direction over the Drogheda region. Indirect evidence for this glaciation occurs at Monknewtown in the Mattock valley where distinctive erratics of inland provenance are found in a till underlying the Tullyallen deposits.[21] The Drogheda ice withdrew inland immediately prior to the main south-westward advance of the ice sheet which deposited the Tullyallen till deposits; this is associated with the ice sheet in the Irish Sea basin. There are some erratics of volcanic rock from the Mourne Mountains in the gravel pits at Oldbridge associated with this glaciation.[22] Inland penetration of the Tullyallen ice was restricted by the presence of the Drogheda ice sheet to the west of Slane. The inland Drogheda ice sheet and the Tullyallen ice sheet were roughly coeval during the maximum stage of the Tullyallen glaciation.[23] Subsequently, sea level fell 100m and a major re-advance of ice from a source in the Irish Midlands took place. This laid down the Newgrange moraine. Detailed field mapping and laboratory analysis of till deposits demonstrates that there was a withdrawal of inland ice to the Boyne. The effects of this retreating ice sheet can now be detected in the landscape by the presence of the Sheephouse and Proudfootstown moraines.[24]

Glacial debris was frequently deposited at the ice margin as accumulations of tills, gravels, sands and silts, in the form of ridges called moraines. In the valley of the

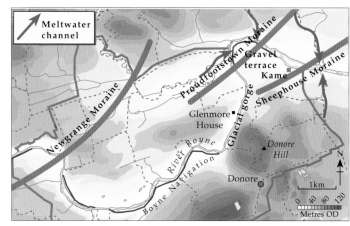

Fig. 9   Glacial features in the Bend of the Boyne. The moraines which straddle the Boyne are aligned south-west to north-east, indicating that the ice margin was orientated in this direction during its retreat.

lower Boyne, the association of moraines and outwash terraces influenced by rising sea level is particularly clear.[25] Between Slane and the coast, there are three terraces – at Newgrange, Proudfootstown and Sheephouse – associated with glacial outwash from a particular morainic stage of the ice sheet. Their presence suggests that sea level was initially rising as the ice margin receded up the Boyne Valley but it then fell as the ice margin receded further.[26] The gradient of the lower outwash terraces indicates that the sea level fell rapidly while the ice front still lay stationary at Proudfootstown. A well-developed, flat-topped terrace is visible to the south of the bridge at Oldbridge. This terrace represents the river flood plain during deglaciation. Since deglaciation, the river has cut its way down to the modern flood plain. At Oldbridge there are mounds (or kames) which were deposited by the ice.[27]

Fig. 10   The ice sheet stood still at Sheephouse creating a moraine; subsequently it withdrew to Proudfootstown where it left morainic drift straddling the townlands of Proudfootstown and Drybridge. At Oldbridge there are hummocks or kames which were deposited by the melting ice during the last Ice Age.

DRAINAGE

The development of the modern fluvial system was largely controlled by the pre-existing glacial landscape. Meltwater erosion cut spectacular channels in the area, which now house streams much smaller than would be expected. The floors of these valleys take the form of alluvial flood plains. The very steep flanks of the Boyne channel itself reflect this glacio-fluvial erosion during deglaciation. The 'bend' in the Boyne was formed at the end of the Ice Age *c.*12,000 years ago. As the ice sheet retreated to the north-west, it left a mantle of glacial till. The Boyne incised itself into this glacial plain and wound a course dictated by a fault line in the underlying shale. East of Crewbane, the river abruptly changes direction and runs southwards below an elevated ridge. Subsequently, the river flows parallel to the shale

ridge for some distance until it twists northwards through a glacial gorge, thus completing the Bend of the Boyne. Near King William's Glen, at the point on the river where the Delvin and the Mattock join the Boyne, the river resumes its eastward course to the Irish Sea.

The Boyne in its lower reaches trends generally slightly north of east and flows across rocks of Carboniferous age, chiefly limestone buried by glacial deposits. The trench is largely floored by glacial outwash gravels rich in limestone. In places the gravels have a more morainic character. The valley of the Mattock is similarly incised and choked with gravels. Gravel pits line the south side of the river at Rossnaree, Roughgrange and Stalleen, taking advantage of this resource. The Boyne is joined from the north by several large streams which originate in the Louth massif, the largest of which is the Mattock River.

There are five drainage systems in the area. At Roughgrange an extensive stream system drains an escarpment and flows through the wetland below. There is a high water table on much of this escarpment which, in the Battle of the Boyne, impeded an engagement between Williamite and Jacobite forces. The second system is also at Roughgrange and consists of a series of short drainage channels created in the floodable callows of the Boyne. North of the river at Knowth, a system of streams drains into the Mattock. This system has created a marshy area

Fig. 11 Before the Ice Age the ridge of black shale north of the river continued southward to the present village of Donore, but today it is cut by a glacial gorge running south-west from the Boyne. At some stage in the Ice Age, large quantities of meltwater spilled across the ridge and cut a narrow gorge through the rock along the course that the river now takes. This event created a dramatic, deep and narrow ravine at Oldbridge. Glenmore, an eighteenth-century estate house, was erected overlooking the chasm. The presence of estuarine material as far inland as Glenmore shows that the tide had once flowed freely to this point.[28]

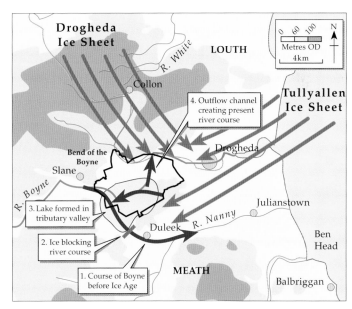

Fig. 12 Before the Ice Age the Boyne flowed southeast towards Duleek and followed the course of the Nanny to the Irish Sea. A small tributary of the Boyne started in the vicinity of Donore and flowed westward on the south side of the shale ridge, before joining the Boyne below Knowth. At some late stage in the Ice Age, ice occupied the area and blocked the course of the Boyne flowing into the Nanny Valley. A lake formed in the valley of this small tributary river. The lake eventually overflowed by cutting a new channel through the shale ridge that joined Donore Hill to Dowth, not following the blocked-up tributary valley, thus escaping into the Mattock River valley.

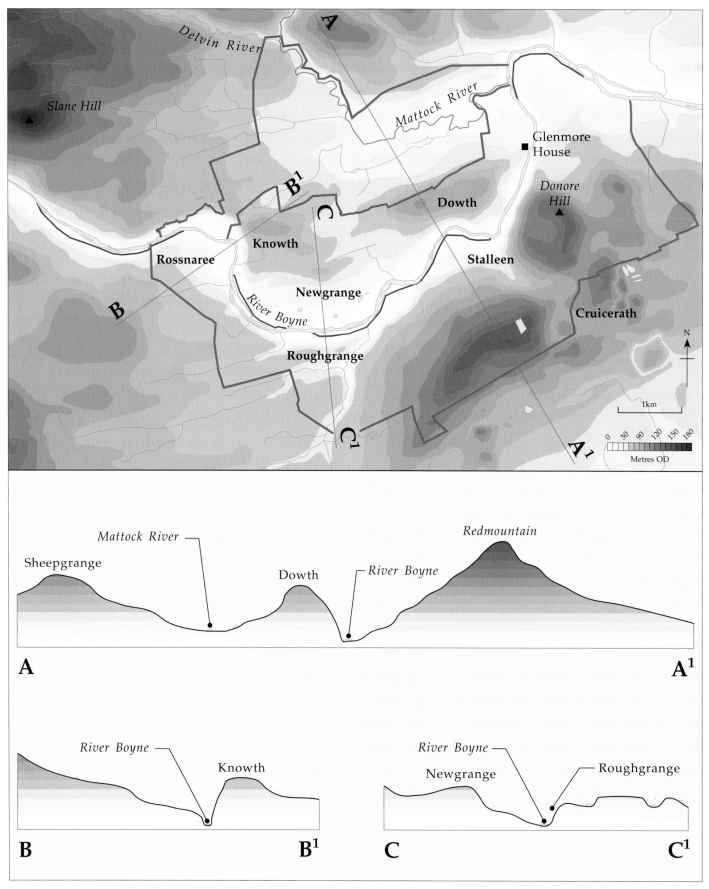

Fig. 13   Topography and elevations in the Bend of the Boyne.

Fig. 14 A) The wide flood plain of the River Boyne below Newgrange. B) The Boyne formerly occupied a higher elevation, as is evidenced by the steep flanks of the Boyne channel, a striking feature between Oldbridge and Slane.[29]

between Newgrange and Dowth. Two of the streams flow north/south and drain into floodable land adjoining the Boyne. One forms a townland boundary, the other runs east to west between Newgrange and Dowth. The fifth stream system in the area flows from Donore Hill. Further underground drainage has been suggested in the limestone areas, but the only direct evidence for this is a dry stream valley with caves which may follow a fault east of Sheephouse, opposite Drybridge.[30]

Five and a half thousand years ago, the sea was four metres above its present level and was tidal at least as far as Glenmore.[31] The Boyne is now tidal as far upstream as Oldbridge at the junction of the Mattock and Boyne rivers. Shallows formed where rivers cut through glacial ridges. They were particularly favoured as fords because the glacial ridges formed natural routeways over the landscape. Fords, depending on how they are used, may constitute either aids to river crossings or barriers to river travel. Rivers functioned as territorial boundaries, and,

being places where tribal territories meet, fords were often places of strategic importance and conflict. When many Irish rivers were dredged in arterial drainage schemes of the late nineteenth and early twentieth centuries, fords were disturbed and large bodies of archaeological material discovered, thereby emphasising their strategic importance.[32]

SOILS

In this lowland area, the dominant action of the ice was the deposition of drift sheets on which the productive soils of the Bend of the Boyne subsequently developed. Two parent materials contribute to these glacial deposits: an eastern component from the Irish Sea basin, rich in clay

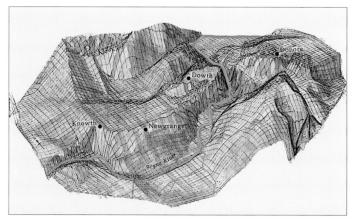

Fig. 15 Isometric representation of the Bend of the Boyne. The ridge at Knowth presents a barrier to the eastward progress of the Boyne. The steep high ground in Donore contrasts with the stepped rise at Newgrange.

Fig. 16 There are two deep feeder meltwater channels on the south side of the river at Roughgrange which were cut by powerful flows of meltwater during the deglaciation of the last Ice Age.[33]

Fig. 17 Shallows in the Boyne were used as fording points: one between Tullyallen and Oldbridge, as shown in this photograph, and two between Roughgrange and Newgrange.

with a high content of calcium carbonate, and a less rich western component. The calcareous drift in this area is technically referred to as 'Tullyallen Till'.[34] The soils derived from this drift of limestone and shales consist mainly of grey brown podzolics. Flint occurs sporadically in this material. The soil profile is very deep, tending to be slightly shallower on the hill slopes.

The dominant soil type in the Bend of the Boyne is a fertile, grey-brown podzolic.[35] It is a medium to heavy clay loam with a wide range of uses but in the Boyne valley it is largely devoted to grassland. It occurs in a

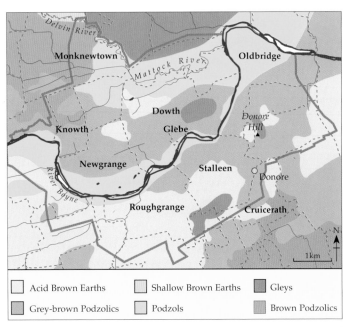

Fig. 18 The National Soil Survey of Ireland has completed a detailed soil survey of County Meath to provide basic information for land-use planning.[36] The soils within the Bend of the Boyne have a wide range of uses and are suitable to both pasture and tillage.

broad band across the north side of the river, in the townlands of Knowth, Newgrange, Dowth and Glebe, and south-east of the Boyne in the townlands of Oldbridge, Sheephouse, Donore, Stalleen and part of Roughgrange and Cruicerath.[37] Brown earths have developed on the first glacio-fluvial terrace to the south of Newgrange and continue west along the south side of the river to Rossnaree and east to Oldbridge.[38] These soils are moderately deep and well drained with a gravelly loam texture that is easy to cultivate. They have a 'moderately wide' to 'wide' use-range and are suited to pasture and tillage. At present much of these areas are in tillage. An organic regosol covers the low-lying floodable lands adjoining the Boyne's north and south banks and along

Fig. 19 Land under tillage and pasture at Newgrange. Most farmers in the Boyne valley keep cattle and grow crops.

the Mattock edges.[39] These are notoriously susceptible to poaching and are used largely for summer pasture because of flash flooding. North of the shale ridge sloping down to the Mattock Valley, the land has a northerly aspect with areas of ill-drained and heavy gley soils and is liable to flooding. The areas more suitable to arable farming lie west and south of Monknewtown church and south of Townley Hall. There are pockets of heavy gley soils in the area north of Newgrange and Ballyboy in Dowth townland and this soil type predominates within the area south of the river, forming heavy textured clay loams, predominantly used for pasture.[40]

CLIMATE

The Bend of the Boyne climate has been described as oceanic, with relatively mild, moist winters and cool cloudy summers.[41] This maritime climate is associated with the Gulf Stream which helps to moderate temperatures; the average humidity is high and the prevailing winds are south-westerly to north-westerly.[42] Because of its coastal position this area enjoys higher air temperatures in winter than inland areas.[43] The stations which record temperature closest to the Bend of the Boyne are at Dublin airport and Warrenstown Agricultural College.[44] For the period 1931–60, the mean air temperature in January was 4.7°C (Dublin) and 3.8°C (Warrenstown). Temperatures rise to 15.0°C (Dublin) and 14.8°C (Warrenstown) for July and August. It rains most in December, least in February and March.[45] However, the average annual rainfall figure (1951–68) for Slane, county Meath is just 875mm.[46] This places the area within one of the driest parts of the country.[47] This favourable climate provided few obstacles to agriculture and settlement from Neolithic times onwards.

WILDLIFE

The edge of the river attracts kingfishers and herons to the minnows or pinkeens that collect there. There is a large otter community on the river islands and the south bank of the river at Rossnaree. Since the passing of the Wildlife Act

Fig. 21   The Boyne is a popular fishing ground for anglers from both home and abroad. It is a designated salmon river under an EU Freshwater Fish Directive, given effect in an Irish law passed in 1988.[48]

in 1976, the otter has been a fully protected species. This species of otter (*Lutra lutra*) has a range that stretches from the Atlantic coastline across Europe and Asia. Because their numbers are declining in Western Europe, Ireland's otter population is of international importance.[49]

In the winter, the flood plains of the lower Boyne are home to migrating water fowl populations, particularly the whooper swans that come to the callows below Newgrange every year. These have inspired many legends associated with the Boyne Valley. Unfortunately, their numbers have decreased considerably at Newgrange over the last few years due to aggressive farming practices.

The submerged banks of fine gravel and silt provide a habitat for the mayfly, a great gift to the Boyne anglers. Accordingly, the Boyne has always been an important river for salmon, if not the best in the country. The Boyne salmon is short for its size, deep-shouldered and shaped like a bow. It is exceptionally strong – 'as strong as a horse

Fig. 20   A cormorant (*Corvus marinus*) resting by the river's edge at Oldbridge.

Fig. 22   The whooper swans (*Cygnus cygnus*) have their breeding grounds in Iceland and are distinguished among the northern swans by their yellow bills and trumpet-like call; in their wintering areas, they consume aquatic plants such as pondweeds, but they can also graze on winter wheat, waste grain, turnips and potatoes.[50]

Fig. 23 A large herd of red deer (*Cervus elaphus*) grazes on Dowth Demesne. They are descended from the herd established in the eighteenth-century deerpark.

and never out of season' it is said locally. Many myths have given prominence to it. It is featured in local traditional stories relating to Fionn Mhic Cumhaill who was said to have gained his wisdom upon tasting a magic salmon taken from the Boyne. Amongst the traditional *buadha* (prescriptions) of the High King of Ireland for a good life without misfortune was the salmon of the Boyne, consumed at the annual festival of Lughnasa. The great and wise King Cormac Mac Airt died of an obstruction of the throat caused by a salmon bone.[51]

Wild salmon fishing on the Boyne is a seasonal activity running from February to September. The salmon swim up the Boyne to spawn in August, September and October, as the floods favour. Once spent, the exhausted kelts drift downstream to the sea where they may feed again. Their predators include eels, kingfishers, herons and mink (an unfortunate recent escapee into the area). The salmon's

Fig. 24 A badger (*Meles meles*) found refuge in Newgrange when it was closed to the public duing the 2001 outbreak of foot and mouth disease.

main feeding grounds are in Greenland; the female fish returns there towards the end of December. The fry are conducted to the sea by the male and reach the estuary as smolts. The smolt goes to sea for a year and then returns to the river where it was spawned.

Since the early nineteenth century, Atlantic salmon stocks have come under increasing pressure from industrial and commercial sources. Today, most salmon is caught within drift nets offshore (68%), with inshore drift nets (28%) and anglers (7%) taking a smaller share. The traditional quality of the Boyne salmon fishery was badly degraded by an ill-advised destructive arterial drainage scheme commencing in the late 1960s and continuing into the mid-1980s, but has largely recovered subsequently.[52]

NATURAL HERITAGE AREAS

The catchment area of the Bend of the Boyne provides varied habitats for vegetation, especially on the flood plain of the river. The Boyne wetlands harbour many forms of wildlife. Seasonal floodwaters cover this area in the winter and coarse vegetation traps enriching silt and encourages accretion. In summer it dries out sufficiently to allow grazing, while its ditches support a diverse aquatic and avian life. Green algae and mosses are a natural feature of the river.

Crewbane Marsh (NHA 00553) is a small area of freshwater marsh which occurs on a very wet alluvial flood plain along the north bank of the river. It contains one of the last remaining examples of flood plain marsh on the banks of the Boyne. The main habitat is the freshwater marsh dominated by yellow flag, creeping bent, reed grass, marsh bedstraw and water forget-me-not. In the wetter areas of the marsh, common meadow rue is found. Between the marsh and river, there is a drier elevated area

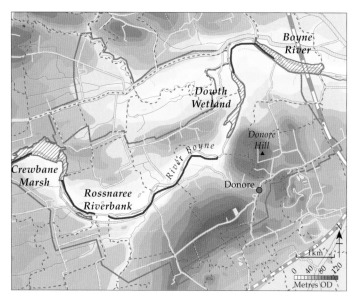

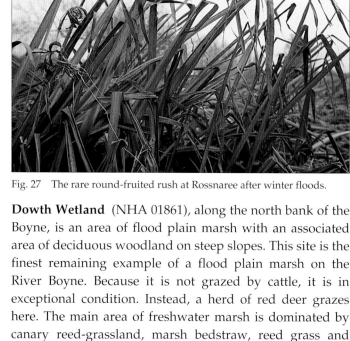

Fig. 25 The National Parks and Wildlife Service (NPWS), Department of Arts, Heritage, Gaeltacht and the Islands, is charged with the preservation and maintenance of habitat sites here. Along this stretch of the river, they have designated four areas of scientific value as Natural Heritage Areas.[53]

Fig. 27 The rare round-fruited rush at Rossnaree after winter floods.

with wet grassland. The south-facing slope above the marsh is covered by deciduous woodland dominated by ash, sycamore, hawthorn, blackthorn and elder. This area of deciduous woodland is one of the best examples in the Boyne Valley. Animal life in the woodland is relatively rich, with fox, badger, stoat, red squirrel and grey squirrel. Rare pine marten and otter have also been recorded.

Rossnaree Riverbank (NHA 01589) is a small site on the banks of the Boyne. It is of national scientific interest due to the presence of round-fruited rush. This rare plant is only found in three counties in Ireland and was first recorded in Ireland at Rossnaree. It is found in alluvial pasture with yellow flag, creeping buttercup and perennial ryegrass.

Dowth Wetland (NHA 01861), along the north bank of the Boyne, is an area of flood plain marsh with an associated area of deciduous woodland on steep slopes. This site is the finest remaining example of a flood plain marsh on the River Boyne. Because it is not grazed by cattle, it is in exceptional condition. Instead, a herd of red deer grazes here. The main area of freshwater marsh is dominated by canary reed-grassland, marsh bedstraw, reed grass and meadowsweet. Sedges are common. Fen bedstraw, a rare species, is also found here.

The Boyne River Islands (NHA 01862) is another area where species rare in Ireland are found. They are a small chain of three islands formed by the build-up of alluvial sediment in this sluggish part of the river. The islands are covered by dense thickets of wet, willow woodland

Fig. 26 A) Crewbane Marsh, below Knowth passage tomb, is a nationally important habitat for flora and fauna containing some of the last remaining examples of flood plain marsh on the banks of the Boyne, and the best deciduous woodland in the valley. B) In early placelore these woods provided the blood-red nuts for Oengus and his band (see chapter 3).

composed of the following species: willow, osier, crack willow, white willow, purple willow and grey willow. The Boyne island willow has been used for basket, mat and coracle making in the Oldbridge area. This type of alluvial woodland is scarce in the country. It is notable for its natural, unmodified condition and diversity of willow species. The site includes an area of wet grassland found along the river bank to the north of the islands. This grassland is dominated by soft rush and hard rush with

creeping buttercup, red fescue, creeping bent and marsh thistle. In places, this wet grassland grades into freshwater marsh, which supports a diverse assemblage of sedge. At the water's edge, there are tall plants such as reeds (in gravelly areas), horsetail and common clubrush which are used in rushwork. Between the reed swamp and dry land, sedge and purple loosestrife flourish. In summer, birds such as coot, mallard, water hens and swans disappear into these reed swamps.

Fig. 28 The main canopy species at Dowth Wetland include the woodland ash, sycamore, hazel, lime, beech, cherry laurel and bird cherry.

Fig. 29 The National Parks and Wildlife Service is responsible for identifying Special Areas of Conservation (SACS) under European Habitats Directive (92/43/EEC) and the Boyne River Islands have been so designated. These islands preserve nationally significant ecosystems. A) This photograph captured a view which is now obstructed by the new Motorway Bridge. B) Designation did not save them from encroachment encouraged by the National Roads Authority.

THE PREHISTORIC LANDSCAPE

During the Neolithic period, the Bend of the Boyne stood foremost amongst the ritual centres of Northern Europe. Communities united by a religious belief and a spiritual identity that had taken hold of much of the western fringes of Europe chose to settle this fertile valley on the east coast of Ireland. They built massive tombs of earth and stone, which in their art and in scientific achievement are unparalleled in Europe and established this valley as a religious mecca for succeeding millennia. These prehistoric tombs are the oldest surviving monuments in the Boyne Valley. Their large, round, stone-kerbed mounds still dominate the surrounding countryside. Newgrange is undoubtedly the most famous of the tombs, largely because of its unique roof box which allows the sun to penetrate deep into the chamber during the winter solstice. Visitors from all over the world come to wonder at this creation.

The international significance of the area has been gradually revealed through a process of discovery and research which began over three hundred years ago, making the Bend of the Boyne one of the most intensively excavated areas in rural Ireland. A programme of major scientific excavations began at Knowth in the 1940s and George Eogan has been working there since 1962. M. J. O'Kelly undertook excavations at Newgrange between 1962 and 1975. These excavations have highlighted the pre-eminence of the passage tomb culture in the Boyne Valley and illuminated the lives of the people who built the tombs.

David Sweetman's excavations at Monknewtown in the 1970s and the environs of Newgrange in the 1980s have identified a significant concentration of Late Neolithic/Early Bronze Age ceremonial enclosures. This work has shown that even with the decline of its passage tomb culture, the area remained the focus for ritual activity. The prehistoric enclosures in the Bend of the Boyne form one of the most significant concentrations of the monuments to be found in Britain and Ireland.

DÚCHAS/CON BROGAN

Fig. 1 The prehistoric component of the Boyne Valley landscape has a high public profile and has been the subject of intensive research over the last fifty years, focused on a selection of internationally famous sites including Knowth and Newgrange. The Bend of the Boyne is the most extensively excavated area in Ireland. Knowledge of prehistoric land use in the Boyne Valley has increased dramatically as a result, and the excavations have highlighted the international value of its archaeological monuments, resulting in the designation of the area as a World Heritage Site in 1993.

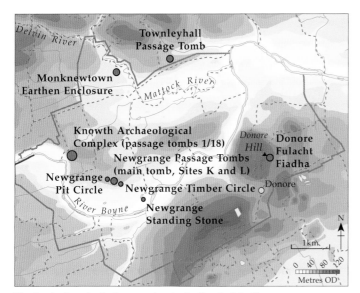

Fig. 2   Archaeological excavation in the Bend of the Boyne.

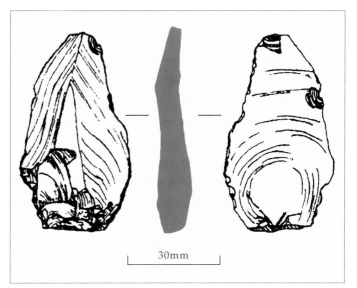

Fig. 3   Bann flake from Newgrange. This culturally diagnostic tool has long been associated with pre-farming communities in the valley of the Bann in county Derry, where they were used as fishing, cutting, sawing and whittling tools in Later Mesolithic times.[4]

-MESOLITHIC SETTLEMENT

The earliest evidence for a human presence in the Bend of the Boyne was identified in the finds from the excavation of the Late Neolithic/Beaker levels at Newgrange. Amongst this assemblage, archaeologist Daragh Lehane identified Bann flakes, leaf-shaped flint flakes that have been trimmed at the butt. Lehane also noted the possible survival of Mesolithic flint-working techniques in some of the Late Neolithic/Early Bronze Age stone tools from Newgrange, especially microlithic forms and borers thought to have been used for piercing some comparatively soft substance.[1] These tools had been made from flint pebbles collected locally in the flint-rich glacial drift which covers much of the Bend of the Boyne.

Although this evidence for Later Mesolithic activity from Newgrange was not considered conclusive at the time by the wider archaeological community, there is every reason to believe that there was a sizeable hunter-gathering community in the Bend of the Boyne, given the area's rich natural resources, its proximity to other Mesolithic coastal communities in neighbouring Louth and Dublin, and some promising results from a recent field-walking project.[2] These areas had a rich and diverse annual food supply. The Boyne was able to supply salmon and eels – an important component in the diet of the first hunter-gathering communities, given the limited range of mammals then present in Ireland. Excavations of Mesolithic settlements at Mount Sandel established that fish loomed large in the diet of this early community as a resource that could be exploited for much of the year. Many Later Mesolithic artefacts were probably wood-working tools used for making traps, particularly those used in fishing.[3]

Fig. 4   The lower Boyne Valley is typical of locations chosen by these early communities: proximity to water – in coastal, lakeside or riverine settings – is a locational feature of 72% of the Mesolithic sites in Ireland.[5]

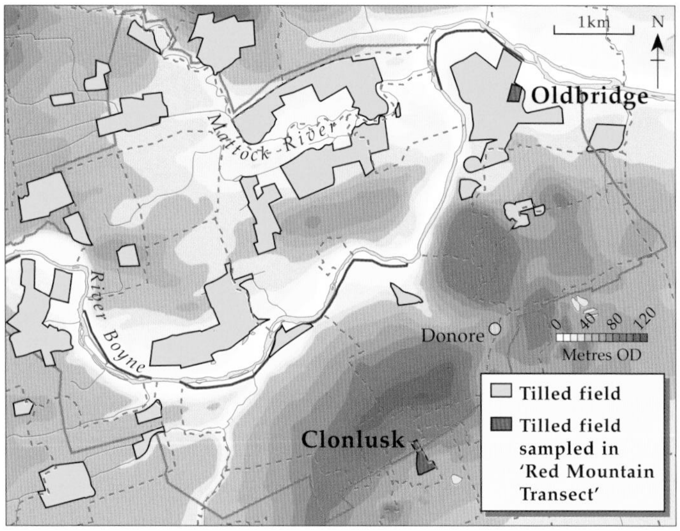

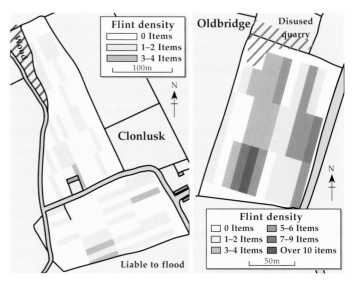

Fig. 5   Because substantial areas within and around the Bend of the Boyne are under tillage, systematic field survey could be used to identify lithic evidence for Mesolithic communities in the plough zone. Non-systematic field walking in the Boyne Valley has uncovered significant quantities of prehistoric material.[6]

Pollen and seed analysis from soil samples removed from the Knowth excavations indicates that the Bend of the Boyne was a heavily forested area during the Mesolithic period. Oak and elm on the higher ground were flanked by hazel, with birch and alder in the valley bottom.[7] The river banks presented a break in this heavily forested landscape. Further, the presence of water and adjacent vegetation in the Boyne valley attracted mammals out of the forest cover. Analysis of animal bones from the 1963–77 excavations at the perimeter of Newgrange revealed the presence of red deer, the most important game animal on Irish Mesolithic sites.[8] Within a ten kilometre radius of Newgrange, one hundred red deer could have been killed annually.[9] Other species in this animal bone collection from the old ground level at Newgrange included brown bear, hare, possibly a wild boar, wild cat and fox. Evidence from other Mesolithic sites indicates that hare and wild cat were occasionally hunted, but they did not constitute a regular food resource and may have been hunted for their skins. A wide variety of birds was also represented, including goshawk, a wild bird of prey usually found in deciduous woodland which may have bred in the Boyne Valley in prehistoric times; the water rail, a resident or winter visitor which haunts swampy places; the woodcock, a winter visitor; and the pied wagtail.[10] The presence of older dog bones at Newgrange suggests that dogs were used in hunting.[11]

The most prominent aspect of Mesolithic culture is technical mastery in the production of stone tools. The prehistoric lithic material contained in the plough soil of the Boyne Valley offers our best guide to understanding the extent of Mesolithic settlement in this intensively

Fig. 6   In spring 1997, a pilot field-walking survey evaluated the potential of ploughzone archaeology in the Boyne Valley area.[12] The study area formed a transect across the Boyne river, incorporating part of the Bend of the Boyne. Within this 'Red Mountain Transect', thirteen fields were sampled, including four fields in the townlands of Clonlusk and Oldbridge.[13] The methodology used was to systematically sample the surface of the plough zone. The range of material from each field was broken down into separate types which were then grouped according to their probable date. All the walked fields produced evidence for prehistoric stone-working in varying densities.

farmed area. Systematic field walking of ploughed field surfaces is widely recognised internationally as an essential archaeological technique in the location of prehistoric settlements.[14] In the Boyne Valley, a 1997 pilot field-walking survey recovered a wide range of stone artefacts. The lithic material collected included debris resulting from the preparation and production of flint tools together with a range of finished examples, including a hollow-based

NATIONAL MUSEUM OF IRELAND

Fig. 7   A large struck flint flake from Mell, near Drogheda, which may date to the Palaeolithic c.8000BC. Although it is generally believed that settlement in Ireland began in Mesolitic times (c.7000BC) this artefact may suggest an earlier human presence. However, this find may have been carried from Britain through natural glacial processes. It has been a source of controversy since its discovery by Frank Mitchell in the 1980s.

Fig. 8 At Knowth, pre-tomb Neolithic settlement was extensive and prolonged.[15] Five houses were found, the homesteads of the first farming communities to settle in the Bend of the Boyne.

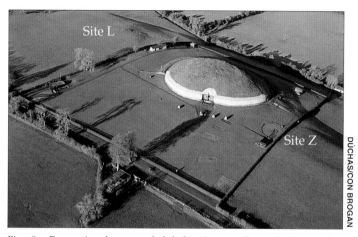

Fig. 9 Excavation has revealed habitations underneath the smaller passage tombs (Sites L and Z) either side of Newgrange. Stone tools and pottery have been found within these houses.

arrowhead, scrapers, blades and a perforator. These diagnostic tools indicate that this activity spanned at least the Later Mesolithic, the Neolithic and the Early Bronze Age. There was no evidence of any surviving, upstanding traces of prehistoric sites in any of the fields walked. However, flint concentrations were noted, which could be tested in future fieldwork for settlement remains. Gabriel Cooney has recommended that the cultural material in the plough zone be treated as an important archaeological resource: any developments in the area involving the removal of the top soil should be assessed for archaeological deposits to militate against their loss.[16] Not to do so would surely inhibit our understanding of the Mesolithic in this area.

PRE-TOMB WESTERN NEOLITHIC

The earliest *conclusive* evidence for human activity recorded in the Bend of the Boyne is derived from the ridge on the north bank of the Boyne, focused at Knowth and Newgrange where there has been a programme of excavations for the last fifty years. This settlement evidence had been fortuitously sealed when the passage tombs at these sites were built. The pre-tomb settlements have been dated to a distinct phase of human activity in the Bend of the Boyne – the earlier Neolithic period – between 3900BC and 3500BC.[17] The presence of sheep and cattle bones and cereal grains indicates that the occupants practised mixed farming in the environs of their homes. These remains represent the homesteads of the first farming communities to settle permanently in this part of the Boyne Valley.

Two phases of pre-tomb building have been identified at Knowth, differentiated by archaeologists on the basis of pottery styles; the earliest are the remains of three houses built around 3900BC, two of which extended beneath the mound of the main tomb. These timber houses had a simple rectangular ground plan and a single entrance. The occupants used flint tools and undecorated pottery.[18] Hazelnut shells and charred remains of emmer wheat, barley and oat were found in the foundation trenches of one house.[19] The second stage of house building at Knowth took place around 3500BC. Two houses were found in the western area of the main passage tomb, one beneath a smaller satellite tomb, the other underlying the passage of the western tomb of the main mound.[20] The latter, which was recently found to the rear of the entrance stone, was sealed with a thick natural sod layer. This layer was contemporary with the original ground level on which the large tomb was built. The stratigraphical sequence therefore showed that this house had been abandoned for a considerable time before the tomb was built. A range of stone tools (flint scrapers, blades) and decorated, shouldered bowls were found amongst the remains of this house. These houses were protected in prehistoric times by a large timber-palisaded corral.

The second focus for pre-tomb activity in the Bend of the Boyne was again on the summit of this ridge but further east at Newgrange. Removal of the smaller passage grave mound (Site L) immediately west of the main tomb exposed habitation material that was sealed by and extended beyond the mound. A stake hole and areas of burning indicated a probable cooking pit. Hollow scrapers and undecorated shouldered bowls were found at the site.[21] The pottery was similar to that found at the neighbouring houses in Knowth. Excavations of a small passage tomb (Site Z) east of the main mound at Newgrange also revealed pre-tomb activity comprising a hearth, a setting of cobbles, several postholes associated with flint chips, a hollow-based arrowhead, scrapers, a stone axe and animal bone.[22]

Clusters of timber houses and evidence for agriculture suggest a permanency about this early farming settlement.

Fig. 10   Pre-tomb activity of a slightly later date than at Knowth and Newgrange has been identified at Townleyhall. Circular stake-built houses were found with domestic utensils. Finds from Townleyhall: A) Flint hollow-scrapers. B) Remains of a broad-rimmed, handmade pot.

This is all the more striking when placed in the context of the beginning of farming in Ireland, the dates for which have been established at c.4200BC.[23] These early pioneering communities successfully exploited the rich soils of their immediate environment and took advantage of the long, benign, grass-growing season to rear their cattle and sheep. The local forests provided the hardwoods needed for their house building and palisades. These pre-tomb settlements in the Bend of the Boyne are also strikingly similar to structures and cultural assemblages from other Neolithic domestic sites recently discovered in county Meath (at Newtown, near Nobber) and in other parts of the country.[24] This growing evidence substantiates the development of a 'mosaic' landscape in early Neolithic Ireland made up of dispersed yet contemporary pioneering communities.[25] Indeed the cultural traits of these early farming communities have been identified further afield in Great Britain and Europe, suggesting a broad Atlantic culture. The new species of cereals and animal stock are non-native to the Bend of the Boyne and had to be brought into the country, either from the western shores of Britain or directly from Atlantic Europe. The similarity in cultural traits suggests that the earliest communities probably came from Britain: the pottery is of a style that has been identified there.[26] Despite the influx of people and animals, Mesolithic flint-working techniques and tools in later tool assemblages suggest some continuity with the Mesolithic population.

THE PASSAGE TOMB BUILDERS

During the Neolithic, a group of people settled in the Boyne valley who were united by a religious belief and a spiritual vitality that had taken hold of much of the western fringes of Atlantic Europe. Their ideological identity was expressed in their mortuary ritual, a tomb architecture embellished with art, and a particular set of grave goods deposited with the burials which indicated a hierarchical society. Their burial tombs are the oldest surviving monuments in the Boyne Valley today. These round, stone-kerbed mounds dominate the ridge top and south-facing slopes which run between the Boyne and Mattock rivers.[27] Thirty-one definite and nine possible passage tomb sites can be identified in the Bend of the Boyne.[28]

Architecture   A long history of field survey in the Boyne valley allows a detailed insight into the architecture of these tombs and more minute

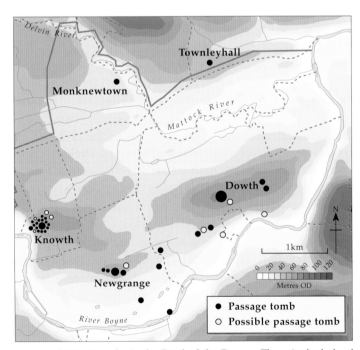

Fig. 11   Passage tombs in the Bend of the Boyne. These 'cathedrals of the megalithic religion' have had a more profound impact on the landscape than any other ideological force in the history of this valley, creating a 'sacred landscape' which still attracts an international audience five thousand years after they were built.[29]

DÚCHAS/CON BROGAN

Fig. 12   Passage tombs are found throughout the Bend of the Boyne and there is a sense of order and formality in their arrangement in the landscape. They appear in clusters or cemeteries built on the most prominent knolls, with the smaller mounds arranged around the three largest sites; a circular pattern exists at Knowth, a linear one at Newgrange, and a dispersed one at Dowth. Their tightest concentration is around the main mound at Knowth at the western edge of the ridge, as shown above.

constructional detail is available for the twenty-five excavated tombs at Newgrange, Knowth and Townley-hall. The excavation reports reveal the care taken by the builders in every aspect of the tombs' construction, which followed a prescribed pattern leading to a general morphological similarity. Burial chambers are entered off passages under a mound. The mounds are usually rounded but the larger sites at Knowth and Newgrange have a flattened profile. The mounds are delimited by a series of kerbstones placed end to end set directly on the ground, their bases propped by packing stones. At Dowth and Newgrange Site E, a level space or berm occurs between the edge of the mound and kerbstones.[30] This berm can indicate the presence of a construction ditch like the one discovered at Newgrange Site K.[31] The passages and chamber are constructed using large stones placed in an upright position.

The passages are roofed with lintels; a corbelling technique was used to construct the roofs of those with beehive chambers. It was very important for the tomb builders to seal the chamber area and keep it dry: at Newgrange Site 1, a core of water-rolled stones covered the chamber; the joints had been caulked and water grooves were incised into the stones to allow water to run off.[32] At Knowth Site 1, the area around the chamber of the eastern tomb was consolidated with a pile of stones, then covered by a thin spread of small flat stones, thus sealing the chamber.[33] At Newgrange Site L, a core of sand, covered by stone-capped turves, sealed the chamber. At Knowth Site 12, the tomb was enclosed in a oval-shaped core of stones.[34] At Knowth Site 15, a large core consisting of sods was built around the tomb retained by a stone setting.[35] Again, Townleyhall had this 'protective crust' which kept the chamber dry.[36]

DÚCHAS/CON BROGAN

Fig. 13   At Newgrange Site E the presence of a berm indicates a construction ditch inside the kerbstones. This feature is also found at Newgrange Site K and at Dowth.

DÚCHAS/DAVID SWEETMAN

Fig. 15   Layered turves, shown here at Knowth, were used to retain the completed mound or phases of tomb construction. The turves are an important source of pollen used to reconstruct the Neolithic environment.

DÚCHAS/CON BROGAN

Fig. 14   The corbelled roof inside the burial chamber at Newgrange. Although the roof was constructed over 5,000 years ago, it is still watertight and supports an estimated 200,000 tonnes of cairn material. Horizontal courses of large slabs, each partly resting on the one below, were laid until the vault could be closed by a single massive capstone 6m above the floor of the chamber. The roof slabs tilt slightly to allow the water to drain through the cairn, along channels cut into the upper surfaces of some of the slabs.

This inner core sealing the tomb chamber was then covered by a layered mound, comprising turves interspersed with boulder clay, shale and water-rolled stones in varying combinations. The exposed hollow in the mound at Dowth shows that it is made up of angular quarried stones rather than water-rolled stones as at Newgrange.[37] The layers of turves visible at Knowth and Newgrange were used to retain the completed mound or a particular phase in tomb construction. This was also true at Newgrange Site Z.[38] At Newgrange Site 1, turves retained the cairn stones at certain stages, and seem to represent interruptions in the construction of the mound.[39]

Stone settings within the make-up of the tomb are present in a large number of the excavated tombs, particularly in the Knowth cemetery. Townleyhall demonstrates the most impressive example of this structural feature. Lines of boulders were used to retain

DÚCHAS/CON BROGAN

Fig. 16   At Dowth and Newgrange the sides of the mounds were thought by M. J. O'Kelly to have been nearly vertical.[40] This flattened profile may have been maintained by a retaining wall as indicated at Newgrange where the cairn above the kerb had been retained by means of a drystone wall.[41]

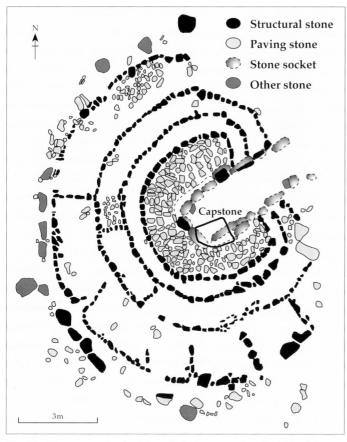

Structural stone
Paving stone
Stone socket
Other stone

Capstone

N

3m

0

Fig. 17   The passage tomb at Townleyhall was enclosed within elaborate rings of stone settings, the ends of which fitted neatly to the walls of the tomb on each side. This 'cellular planning' may have been laid out to form guidelines for the builders, to prevent the cairns from spreading or as a means of dividing up the site to share the work between different groups of workers.[42]

sections of the main mound at Knowth Site 1.[43] At Knowth Site 4, there were stone settings in the mound but no evidence suggested that they formed an edging to the layered mound of boulder clay and shale.[44] At Knowth Sites 9 and 16, the tombs are partially surrounded by a series of stone settings in the form of arcs.[45]

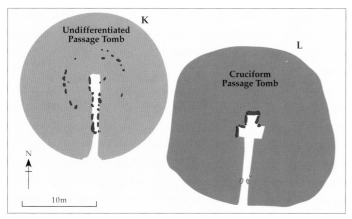

Undifferentiated Passage Tomb

K

L

Cruciform Passage Tomb

N

10m

Fig. 18   The juxtaposition of Newgrange Sites K and L demonstrates that both plan types (*undifferentiated* and *cruciform*) were in use at the same time by the tomb builders.

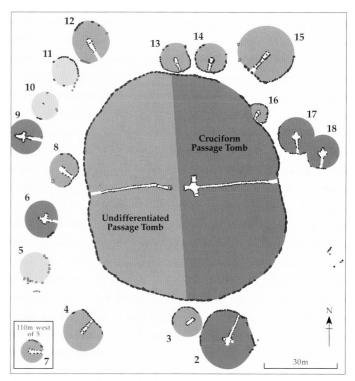

Cruciform Passage Tomb

Undifferentiated Passage Tomb

110m west of 5

30m

N

Fig. 19   At Knowth, where both types occur in a cemetery arrangement, the undifferentiated sites focus on the hilltop whereas the cruciform tombs have a different focus on an area southeast of the main tomb.[46] The smaller Knowth tombs face between northeast and southwest. There may have been some key point on the hilltop which served as a focus for their entrances.[47]

Two plans are followed in the construction of the inner burial area: the *undifferentiated* form with a passage widening inwards from entrance to interior, and *cruciform* with a parallel-sided passage and cruciform-shaped chamber, the right-hand recess usually being the largest. The undifferentiated plan is more common and is the earliest type found at Knowth.[48] Knowth has the greatest concentration of undifferentiated tombs in Ireland,[49] of a type which have an earlier manifestation in Atlantic Europe. Therefore the ultimate origins for the Boyne tomb types lie in Continental Europe. Outside the Boyne Valley, the cruciform plan is more common.[50] The juxtaposition of both plan types under one mound at both Dowth and Knowth indicates that the two forms were in use simultaneously.

Both types vary considerably in size; the undifferentiated tombs vary in length, from 6.5m at Newgrange Site K to 34.2m for the western tomb at Knowth Site 1.[51] The passages of cruciform sites vary from 4m at Knowth Site 17 to 40.4m at the eastern tomb of Knowth's main mound.[52] There is no apparent difference in the pattern of decoration used on the cruciform and undifferentiated tombs.[53] Basin stones appear in both types, i.e. Newgrange Site Z and the western tomb at Knowth Site 1.[54] Within cemeteries, tombs of a particular plan tend to repeat an orientation or to share a similar focus. This is a feature of tombs outside the Boyne

Table 1
Passage tombs in the Bend of the Boyne

Passage tomb		SMR No.
Dowth	Main mound with cruciform and undifferentiated chambers	20:16
Dowth E	Round mound with berm and outer kerb	19:43
Dowth F	Circular mound	19:42
Dowth G	Possible site, elongated mound	19:41
Dowth H	Circular, kerbed mound	19:40
Dowth I	Kerbed mound	20:12
Dowth J	Chambered round mound	20:13
Dowth	Site, no precise location	Wilde 1847
Dowth	Possible site, round mound	20:23
Dowth	Site	20:09
Dowth	Possible site	C. O'Kelly 1979
Knowth 1	Main mound with cruciform and undifferentiated chambers	19:30
Knowth 2	Partial remains	19:30
Knowth 3	Possible site	19:30
Knowth 4	Partial remains with undifferentiated chamber	19:30
Knowth 5	Possible site	19:30
Knowth 6	Partial remains with cruciform chamber	19:30
Knowth 7	Reconstructed with undifferentiated chamber	19:30
Knowth 8	Partial remains with undifferentiated chamber	19:30
Knowth 9	Partial remains with cruciform chamber	19:30
Knowth 10	Partial remains with undifferentiated chamber	19:30
Knowth 11	Site	19:30
Knowth 12	Partial remains with undifferentiated chamber	19:30
Knowth 13	Reconstructed with undifferentiated chamber	19:30
Knowth 14	Reconstructed with undifferentiated chamber	19:30
Knowth 15	Undifferentiated chamber	19:30
Knowth 16	Reconstructed with undifferentiated chamber	19:30
Knowth 17	Reconstructed with cruciform chamber	19:30
Knowth 18	Reconstructed with cruciform chamber	19:30
Knowth	Possible site	Herity 1967
Knowth	Possible site	Eogan 1986
Newgrange 1	Main mound, reconstructed with cruciform chamber	19:45
Newgrange A	Circular, flat-topped mound	19:49
Newgrange B	Circular mound	19:58
Newgrange K	Partial remains with undifferentiated chamber	19:46
Newgrange L	Partial remains with cruciform chamber	19:46
Newgrange U	Kerbed mound	19:51
Newgrange Z	Partial remains with undifferentiated chamber	19:44
Newgrange Z1	Possible site, circular mound	19:44
Monknewtown	Round mound	19:17
Townleyhall	Round mound, with undifferentiated chamber	LH24:08

setting sun lights the northern chamber. Astronomic observation may have been an aspect of ceremonial activity at Knowth; one of the stone carvings is possibly a 'map' of lunar features.[56]

Art   A major aesthetic component of this cultural group within the Boyne Valley is the concentration of funerary art on the structural stones of their tombs and grave goods including pottery and pendants, the most dramatic example being the ceremonial macehead from the eastern tomb at Knowth.[57] This art and the degree of ritual in their burial behaviour distinguish these passage tomb builders from the other tomb-building communities in Ireland. The art reflects an ornamental tradition present in a restricted coastal area along the western edge of Europe during the Later Neolithic/Early Bronze Age, whose origins possibly lay in south-east Europe.[58] There are key concentrations of decorated tombs in western Iberia and on the Gulf of Morbihan (near Carnac in Brittany) but the Boyne is pre-eminent. Over 600 decorated stones in the Boyne represent two-thirds of the megalithic art of Europe and more than four-fifths of the decorated passage tomb stones in Ireland.[59]

Technically, the art is characterised by carved and picked designs that are non-representational. The earlier style is based on a standard geometric vocabulary of circles, spirals, triangles, zig-zags and serpentine forms. Confined to the outer faces of the kerbstones and the inner faces of the orthostats, it was designed to be seen. The art was applied through incision or picking. Incision is often used in guidelines for the layout, but picking or pocking is the main technique used. At Knowth this was produced using a chisel stone and punch.[60] Each tomb in the valley had a repertoire unique to itself: lozenges and zig-zags are most common at Newgrange, while angular art is the art *par excellence* at Knowth. Spirals are positioned on the most prominent stones at both tombs. The spiral, which has become a trademark motif for Irish heritage, is only common in Ireland. In some cases, the art occurs on surfaces that were later hidden. Area picking or dressing, added when the stones were in place, is only found in the Boyne Valley. By applying art to the stones, the passage tomb builders may have been making visually permanent a part of their ideology, like the bibical scenes on the high crosses of the Early Christian period.

The larger tombs took so long to build that an indigenous style of art had emerged between the time they were initiated and completed. Some of the more dramatic ornamentation of the later plastic style in Newgrange and Knowth was added after the tomb was built. This stylistic

valley as well. In Newgrange, the main site and smaller tombs face south. At Knowth, the two tomb types have different orientations.

The discovery of the solstice orientation at Newgrange established the fact that an understanding of the calendar and of the movement of the sun must have preceded the construction of the passage tomb.[55] The two Dowth tombs face west. During the winter solstice, the

wgrange from the River Boyne.

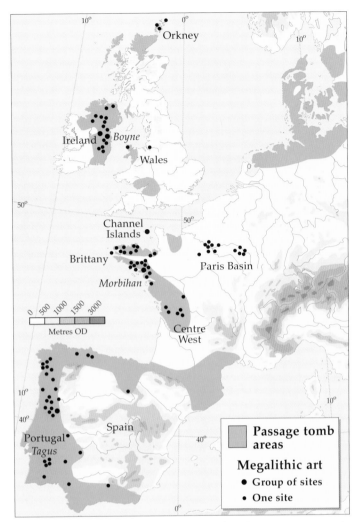

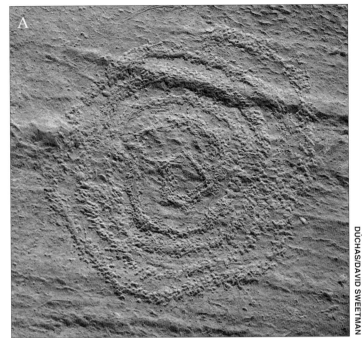

DÚCHAS/DAVID SWEETMAN

Fig. 20 Western European megalithic art is found on passage graves in Iberia, western France, Ireland and Britain. Passage grave art can be found on tomb orthostats, lintels and kerbstones.

revolution took place when a distinctive school emerged on a grander scale with a 'boldness of expression and simplicity of design that concentrated on the visual impact'.[61] The artists adopted a sculptural approach and appeared more inspired by the shape of the structural stones. This 'school' reached a pinnacle at Knowth. The 'plastic style' overlies the earlier style/symbolism and shows a revolutionary disregard for it. The art became visually dramatic and functional as artist and architect became one. Stones bearing specific motifs were consciously positioned at the entrance of the large mounds, for example, which are marked by a long stone with a central vertical line, a functional motif at Knowth and Newgrange.[62] The largest and most highly decorated stones occur in the kerb closest to the entrance.[63] Angular spiral styles are positioned at different heights to draw one's attention inward, usually appearing on decorated roof stones. This is seen at Newgrange where the capstone of the roof box was decorated in an angular style.

DÚCHAS/DAVID SWEETMAN

Fig. 21 The structural stones of the passage tombs acted as surfaces on which geometric elements were applied. This art occurs externally and internally, and is both seen and unseen, with decoration applied to the naturally smooth, cleaved surfaces. A) The spiral on a stone at Newgrange is a typical motif of the earlier incised art style. B) Lozenges in false relief are executed in the more sculpted or plastic style on this stone from Newgrange.

Of twenty-five passage tombs that were excavated at Knowth, Newgrange and Townleyhall, all but three (badly damaged) produced evidence for burial. The numbers of buried individuals varied from one to as many as sixteen at Knowth Site 16.[64] One hundred individuals were recovered in the large eastern tomb at Knowth, representing both sexes and various age groups; children and young adults were frequently present.[65] Cremation before deposition predominated, although unburnt human remains were found at Newgrange Site 1 and accompanied cremated remains in the stone basin at Newgrange Site Z.[66] The human remains appear to have been burnt in a pyre elsewhere and then deposited in the tombs. The pyre material was included with the human remains at Newgrange Site L.[67] Animal bones were deposited in a large number of the sites.

Various methods for the deposition of human remains were employed but they were usually confined to the chamber area (which the builders made every effort to seal)

Fig. 23 Human remains were accompanied by grave goods, often of a spectacular nature. This ceremonial macehead was found at the entrance to the right-hand recess in the cruciform chamber at Knowth.

and in the recesses of the cruciform tombs. In the eastern tomb at Knowth Site 1, they were placed in little stone compartments in the left recess.[68] At Knowth Site 16, they were placed on or under a flagstone before the chamber was roofed.[69] The most elaborate containers were the stone basins at Newgrange Site Z and the eastern tomb of Knowth Site 1.

The human remains were usually accompanied by grave goods which varied in quantity and quality: stems of bracken with flint chips and decorated pottery at Knowth Site 9;[70] pestle pendants, mushroom-headed pins, skewer-type pins and maceheads at the eastern tomb of Knowth Site 1.[71] Grave goods at the other sites included bone pendants, chalk marbles, a range of pins made from bone and antler including mushroom-headed and skewer-type pins, and stone beads. Carrowkeel pottery was the funerary vessel used.

The construction of these monuments involved extensive exploitation of the natural resources of the immediate countryside to such an extent that their make-up embodies the prehistoric environment. Some glacial erratics from the drift cover were used in the kerbstones of

Fig. 22 The deposition of human remains was usually confined to chamber areas. They were laid in stone basins like this impressive example from the passage tomb at Dowth.

DÚCHAS/CON BROGAN

Fig. 24   The megaliths were most likely transported for short distances using logs and ropes, as suggested in this reconstruction from the Brú na Bóinne Visitor Centre. The passage tomb builders selected local sandstones and limestones for the structural stones, probably from natural outcrops where the stratification of the bedrock would have facilitated simple quarrying. Some may have been transported from as far away as Clogher Head on the coast north of Drogheda.[72]

the smaller tombs. The kerbstones of the passage tombs at Knowth were undressed. Their origin appears local; some were glacial erratics. Better-quality stone was used for the orthostats of the chamber. At Newgrange, the majority of the stones, including most of the kerbstones, were Lower Palaezoic greywacke, a green coarse slate that outcrops to the north of Newgrange. This type of rock weathers well and provides a good surface for decorating; it is the favoured stone type of the tomb builders.[73]

Given the quantity of stone used (c.200,000 tonnes) there must have been organised extraction of this material. Recent research suggests that the greywacke was quarried. Similar stone has been identified in the Lower Palaeozoic Silurian zone which runs between counties Longford and Down and extends to within five kilometres of the area. The precise location of these prehistoric quarries has yet to be discovered. The maximum depth of these deposits does not exceed three metres, so exploitation of many sites would have been necessary. Primitive quarries, if back-filled, would not be easily noticed today.[74]

In France much research has taken place on the prehistoric quarries used by megalithic tomb builders. At Bougon in Deux-Sèvres quarries were discovered – using resistivity survey techniques – close to tumuli. The rock was extracted from conical pits, c.3m deep. They were almost completely filled in after use. Quarrying tools, including several picks of deer antler, were used to scrape away the split layers of rocky bands to expose blocks of

RICHARD MOORE

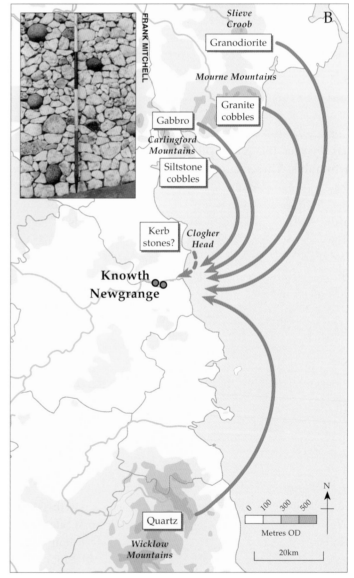

FRANK MITCHELL

Fig. 25   A) Artist Richard Moore and, more recently, a team of geologists have identified Clogher Head as a likely location for the megaliths used in the Boyne Valley tombs. B) The tomb builders used different types of stones to embellish the entrance facades at Knowth and Newgrange. White quartz was brought from Wicklow and dark granite from the Mournes.

Fig. 26   The material for the cairn of Newgrange possibly came from the figure-of-eight-shaped pond on the lowest terrace of the river.[75]

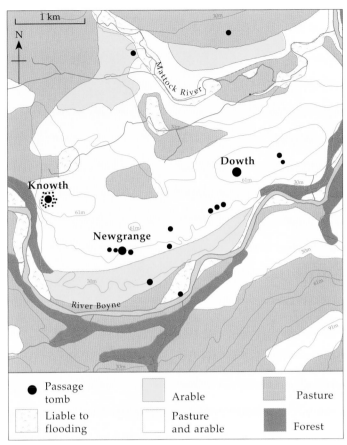

●	Passage tomb		Arable		Pasture
	Liable to flooding		Pasture and arable		Forest

Fig. 27 A pattern of Neolithic land use in the vicinity of the passage tomb cemeteries has been reconstructed by Gabriel Cooney, combining the evidence of excavation with the geomorphology, geology and the modern soil pattern. The soil in the main cemetery area is a grey-brown podzolic suitable for pasture and tillage. The upper terrace below Newgrange is a deep, well-drained soil more suited to cereal cultivation; the lower terrace was probably used for pasture because of the danger of flooding. Heavy gley soils in the valley of the Mattock River were also likely areas of cattle rearing.

solid rock. These were then loosened with axe hammers. Stones extracted in this way (without the use of fire) are fairly regular and parallel-sided. They can be used to form kerbs both inside and outside the mound. Excavation of the Champ-Chalon monument at Benon in Charente-Maritime has revealed the quarry pit that supplied the small slabs for a tumulus. These had been transported using ropes, tree trunks and human muscle.[76]

The Boyne tombs were covered by mounds composed of the local boulder clay interspersed with sods removed from nearby fields. The stones used are water-rolled (taken from the riverbed and local drift) or local shale. Some of the stones used, especially at Dowth, were quarried and could be a by-product from quarrying for the kerbstones.

Five types of non-local 'collectable cobbles' were used to embellish the tombs at Newgrange and Knowth.[77] Quartz occurs in large quantities near the main entrance to Newgrange and in smaller quantities at Newgrange Site Z. It is flecked with white mica, a prominent mineral in the granite of the Wicklow Mountains. During the Ice Age there was no movement of ice from south to north, so quartz was not transported naturally to the Boyne Valley. It would have been brought there manually, probably carried by boat. Dark, oval, naturally rounded cobbles of grandiorite were also found around the entrance to Newgrange Site 1, Newgrange Site Z and Knowth Site 1. Well-rounded cobbles of granite at Newgrange Site 1 and Newgrange Site Z are from the Mourne Mountains. The gabbro cobbles used are from the Carlingford Mountains, the most likely source being a stretch of shore of Dundalk Bay, between Giles Quay and Rathcor.[78] The presence of these 'imports' highlights the extent of communications with regions outside the valley.

Neolithic funerary ritual was expressed in tomb architecture, landscape positioning of the monuments, orientation of the entrances and positioning of the art on the structural stones. The largest and most elaborate stones are found nearest the entrance. At the western tomb at Knowth, there were settings, standing stones and a spread of exotic stones around the entrance. Non-local stones were found at the entrance of a number of sites. Ritual practices are also apparent in the placement of the burials and accompanying grave goods.

Economy   These monuments were designed to be seen and to dominate the landscape, and their conspicuous position along the ridge above the Boyne indicates considerable clearance of the native forest in their environs. This fact is confirmed by archaeological excavation. The environmental evidence provided by the excavations at Knowth, Newgrange and Townleyhall offers a profound insight into the economic foundation of these early

Fig. 28 Artist's reconstruction of Newgrange and its environs during the Neolithic. The illustration shows a cluster of houses whose occupants raised crops and kept livestock.

communities.[79] The environmental evidence from the excavations at Knowth, Newgrange and Townleyhall shows that the passage tombs were built on open farmland cleared during the five centuries preceding their construction. The mounds incorporate part of that early farmed landscape in their make-up, in the form of turves, cereal grains and macroscopic plant remains, together with water-rolled stones from the river bed and stone from local quarries. Pollen, seed and macro-fossil analysis from Knowth and Newgrange, and the evidence for a large number and variety of herbs, shows that this was an open landscape, strongly influenced by herding activity.[80] The presence of *cerealis* pollen grains in the make-up of the Newgrange mound demonstrates that the tomb builders also worked their crop fields in the vicinity, probably on the higher flanks of the Boyne. The turves used in the mound came from damp meadows rich in buttercups and blackberry and crab apple, probably from the lower terraces of the river.[81] This mixed pastoral and tillage economy, still common today, was practised from the earliest Neolithic levels; charred wheat grains came from the timber palisade that enclosed the earliest houses and from hearth material in the houses at Knowth. Oats have been tentatively recognised, again associated with the circular houses.[82] Domesticated cattle, sheep and pig were also introduced. The animal bone remains from the Neolithic levels in Knowth indicate a predominance of cattle over pig, with sheep/goat also present.[83]

The environment around Townleyhall passage tomb also indicates considerable forest clearance. The remains of fires show that the wood used did not come from a high forest but from scrub that may have invaded former cultivation patches.[84] The trees included a low percentage of oak and elder and a much higher percentage of undershrubs, notably hazel, willow, hawthorn and elderberry. The habitation site under the passage tomb produced carbonised cereal grains of wheat and barley, and hazelnut shells.[85] This accumulated environmental evidence further suggests that this was a structured landscape with fields enclosing tillage and pasture.[86] The making of fields was an integral part of this activity, probably using bramble and crab apple as hedging material. However, this area's successful farming tradition has dictated that the physical evidence for the early organisation of agriculture has been substantially removed. There is clear evidence of a farming system capable of sustaining a major monument-building project.

Settlement In sharp contrast to the major investment in their funerary monuments and the richness of the accompanying grave goods, the houses of this community were insubstantial constructions which have left no visible impact on today's landscape. Their houses have been described as 'adequate' and 'mundane', 'requiring no great skill'.[87] Unlike the tombs, the houses were not built to withstand the ravages of time. Evidence for the homes of the passage tomb builders comes from under the tombs at Knowth: clusters of stake holes, all that remains of circular or oval houses. Traces of at least ten and as many as fourteen houses were found at Knowth.[88] The stake holes suggest that some of the houses were substantial structures, with straw or rush conical roofs supported on a ring of upright posts. Wood was the main building material. Evidence for hearths and pits was found within or close to these houses. The

Fig. 29 Reconstruction from Brú na Bóinne Visitor Centre. It depicts a Neolithic family involved in producing the range of household goods, tools and weapons needed to sustain life.

DÚCHAS/CON BROGAN

Fig. 30 Unlike the tombs, Neolithic houses were fragile. This reconstruction in the Brú na Bóinne Visitor Centre is modelled on a house uncovered at Knowth.

organisation of the domestic space – they were not divided internally – suggests sufficient room for five to ten individuals. The size range does exhibit a wide variation, perhaps an indication of family size, function or status.[89] A basic range of features, including a fireplace and storage or refuse pits, was present. The houses were not enclosed, suggesting no preconceived threat from outside. The superimposition of six houses in one area at Knowth indicates a longevity of settlement.[90] The finds from these houses demonstrate no specialised use, but there were very few scrapers relative to more common cutting implements.[91] Decorated Carrowkeel pottery and broad-rimmed pottery were found together in the houses just as they were together in the tombs.

Similar timber structures were located under a mound at Townleyhall, enclosed by a bank and ditch.[92] At Townleyhall, 142 stake holes and nine hearths were uncovered, with hazelnut shells and cereal grains of wheat and barley. There was considerable industrial activity on the site, with a wide range of finished implements including hollow scrapers, end scrapers and flint artefacts known as 'petit tranchet derivatives' (triangular flint tools hafted to a shaft with the cutting edge disposed obliquely to form a single barbed harpoon). At Townleyhall I, a settlement site east of the passage tomb, domestic features, including stone-lined storage bins and small pits, were exposed, associated with hollow scrapers, convex scrapers and retouched blades. Traces of domestic settlement appeared during excavations west of the entrance at Newgrange. Here, a house foundation associated with a stone bowl and a hollow scraper was regarded as being contemporary or nearly so with the building of the tomb.[93]

It is not known why this magnificent Neolithic civilisation came to an end. The people who created the

tombs in the Bend of the Boyne were not conquered by a superior force, nor is there evidence that the construction of the tombs led to a marked degradation of the landscape. Most probably, the societal energy which resulted in the unprecedented outpouring of construction and artistic endeavour simply could not be sustained. The tombs, or the massive artificial mounds with the strange symbol-decorated stones as they would have been known to subsequent peoples, continued to exude a magic which maintained this area as a focus for ritual activity.

LATE NEOLITHIC/EARLY BRONZE AGE LAND USE

Within a few centuries of the building of the passage tombs, there was a renewed phase of monument building in the Bend of the Boyne. The peripheries of the larger passage tombs (in particular their entrances) again became a focus for intense outdoor ritual activity. Large ceremonial enclosures were constructed from stone, timber and earth for great public assemblies. Remains of great fires were revealed around the entrance of Newgrange. Deep pits were dug to receive votive offerings of burnt animals (pig in particular), perhaps during significant solar events.[94] A similar Late Neolithic/Early Bronze Age revival is evidenced at Knowth. Here a timber circle was placed near the entrance of the eastern tomb.[95]

A ceremonial avenue or cursus was constructed across the ridge top immediately east of Newgrange. This marked the route of a ritual procession through the landscape. Located c.100m east of the main passage tomb at Newgrange, it consists of two parallel banks c.20m apart, the southern end terminating on the summit of the ridge in a U shape. It extends for c.100m and its original position

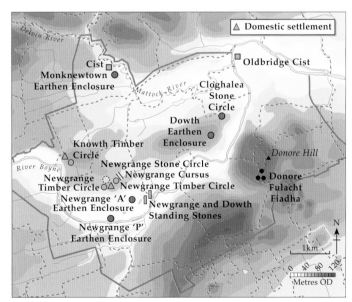

Fig. 31 Late Neolithic/Early Bronze Age sites in the Bend of the Boyne.

DÚCHAS/CON BROGAN

Fig. 32 Ritual monuments constructed during the Late Neolithic at Newgrange include a timber circle (or 'woodhenge') to its south-east, a smaller, possibly roofed timber circle to the west, and a free-standing stone circle which encircled the actual passage tomb.[96]

further north is indicated by a narrow enclosed field which runs on the same axis to the north.[97]

During this stage in the area's history, earthen embanked enclosures (commonly termed henges) were built on the terraces below Newgrange and elsewhere in the valley. The four earthen embanked enclosures within the Bend of the Boyne form part of a well-defined group of thirteen embanked ceremonial enclosures within the lowland river valleys of county Meath.[98] The term *henge*, coined as an archaeological term after the typesite of Stonehenge in Britain, is used to cover a wide variety of ceremonial sites of Late Neolithic/Early Bronze Age date, including embanked enclosures, pit circles and pit and post circles.[99]

The earthen henges in the Bend of the Boyne area are characteristically circular or oval in plan and are defined by a high, flat-topped bank. Banks range from 10m to 14m in width but survive to a height of only 1.2m to 2.5m. Dowth is unique in the group in having a well-preserved bank width of *c*.20m, rising to an average height of 4m. They

GILLIAN BARRETT

Fig. 33 The ploughed-out remains of a still impressive henge monument (Site P) at the edge of the Boyne below Newgrange passage tomb cemetery, and a second henge on a higher terrace enclosing a small passage tomb. The 'Boyne type' henges have their own regional characteristics. With broad, flat-topped banks, they are circular to oval in shape with a domed or hollowed profile (depending on whether material for the bank was scraped from the centre or the perimeter of the interior). Diameters exceed one hundred metres. These henges are inward looking, and usually have only one entrance, orientated towards the east or west/south-west.

often exceed one hundred metres in diameter. Many have a domed or hollowed interior, artificially created by scraping the material away from the whole interior of the smaller enclosures and the internal perimeter of the larger sites to use as material for the bank. This method of construction was confirmed during the excavation at Monknewtown.[100] The builders avoided digging construction ditches, a standard feature of the British sites, thereby creating an open, inward-looking monument. Usually a single entrance opens downslope. There is a distinct preference for an east, west or south-west entrance. An aerial photograph of Newgrange Site P suggests opposing entrances. The eastern opening at this site is visible on the ground, but the opening in the west is narrower and can only be detected from an aerial photograph.[101] Internal features exist in two of the sites in the Bend of the Boyne: Newgrange A and Monknewtown. A flat-topped circular mound, probably a passage tomb, is eccentrically located within the enclosure at Newgrange Site A. A linear feature, 5m wide, running in line with the bank core, was identified by a resistivity survey. Prior to excavation, the interior of the

Table 2
Late Neolithic – Bronze Age sites in the Boyne Valley Archaeological Park

Townland		SMR No.
Dowth	Earthen enclosure (henge)	20:10
Knowth	Timber circle, site of	19:30
Monknewtown	Cist burial	19:14
Monknewtown	Earthen enclosure (henge), partial remains	19:1601
Newgrange	Cursus, partial remains	19:4401
Newgrange A	Earthen enclosure (henge) ploughed	19:45
Newgrange P	Earthen enclosure (henge) ploughed	26:06
Newgrange	Standing stone	26:55
Newgrange	Stone circle	19:45
Newgrange	Timber circle, partial remains	19:4402
Oldbridge	Cist burials	20:02
Sheephouse	Fulachta fiadh, sites	20:2901

DÚCHAS/CON BROGAN

DÚCHAS/CON BROGAN

Fig. 34 An aerial view of Dowth henge, an earthen amphitheatre built 4,000 years ago for community worship. Labour input into the construction of these open enclosures was immense, almost on a par with the earlier passage tombs.

Monknewtown henge was considered to be featureless. However, a rescue excavation revealed a pit cemetery, habitation site and a ring ditch within the interior. Eleven pits were found in the interior near the bank edge, two containing cist-like structures and a cremation in a Carrowkeel bowl. Six of the pits contained cremations, in one instance contained in a bucket-shaped pot.[102]

There is a close physical, chronological and artefactual relationship between these earthen henges and the passage tombs in the Boyne valley. A passage tomb was incorporated into an embanked enclosure on a terrace south of Newgrange. This juxtaposition is also evident in its timber versions of henge monuments. The pit circle on the ridge east of Newgrange incorporates the passage tomb

DÚCHAS/CON BROGAN

Fig. 35 A passage tomb lies to the east of the henge at Monknewtown. The Carrowkeel bowl found in the henge is a type of ware used by the passage tomb builders, evidence for some overlap between the passage tomb and henge-building cultures.

Fig. 36 South of Newgrange, excavations revealed a ritual site. It comprises a large circle of mainly clay-lined pits c.100m in external diameter, originally enclosed by free-standing timber posts. This structure was built around 2000BC.[103] The pits contained quantities of burnt and unburnt animal bones from pig (the vast majority of bones), cattle, deer, sheep and/or goat, and two breeds of dog.[104] These were placed as votive offerings. The interior of the 'woodhenge' contained remains of stake holes from a temporary habitation which produced flint flakes and Beaker pottery. Note also the stone circle which surrounds the passage tomb and cuts through the earlier pit circle.

Newgrange Site Z. There is an obvious desire to locate ritual activities in an area of pre-established ritual significance.[105] This continuity of place and pottery styles and a desire to incorporate the earlier tombs into later ritual suggest a continuity of population linked to the passage tomb past.

The timber circles around the periphery of Newgrange and Knowth are part of this Late Neolithic/ Early Bronze Age ritual activity. Downslope from the tomb entrance at Newgrange are the preserved remains of a monument revealed by excavations in 1982 when the Office of Public Works were attempting to dig found-ations for a new visitor facility. A standing stone was discovered immediately outside the circle of pits at the south-south-west. These features compare with henge sites in England and have also been compared with the tapering shafts found at Maumbury Rings, Dorchester, and the Aubrey Holes at Stonehenge, Wiltshire.[106]

A smaller pit and post circle, interpreted by archaeol-ogists as a place of public assembly, was discovered west of Newgrange in 1984 when sod removal for a new roadway revealed the remains of prehistoric activity.[107] Excavations exposed the remains of a circle of pits and post holes c.20m in diameter. Here a number of pits had deliberate deposits of burnt flint. Similarly, 12m east of the entrance to the eastern passage at Knowth, a substantial circular wooden structure was built. The nature of the finds suggested a temple or sacred place.[108] This structure was defined by a ring of thirty-five wooden posts, the only

Fig. 37   Major Charles Vallancey's (1776) survey of Newgrange shows a triangular shaped standing stone opposite the entrance to the tomb and inside the line of the Great Stone Circle. Recent astronomical investigations by Frank Prendergast indicate a pivotal relationship between the entrance stone of the passage tomb at Newgrange and the positioning of the stones of the great circle.[109]

surviving evidence being the post shafts in which they had stood. The entrance was defined by four large posts which were more substantial and provided a porch-like feature. Finds included grooved ware, flint tools and stone axes, deliberately deposited in the post pits at the time of construction. The Irish grooved ware pottery is related to a special kind of ware usually found during the excavation of ceremonial earthen enclosures (frequently enclosing stone circles and/or pits) in Great Britain.

A stone circle surrounds Newgrange passage tomb but the two are not concentric. The stones vary from 6m to 18m away from the perimeter of the cairn.[110] Only twelve standing stones survive, none of which are decorated. They are irregularly spaced except for the three opposite the entrance: these are the largest, standing, on average, 2.5m high. They are inserted into foundation sockets lined with packing stones which have maintained their original position despite cairn collapse. Excavations of the pit circle east of Newgrange showed that the stone circle was built later than the circle of pits and was associated with the

Beaker settlement, and not pre-passage tomb activity as had been previously argued.[111]

Technology   This Late Neolithic/Early Bronze Age phase in the Boyne Valley is still a stone-using economy, if a somewhat unimpressive one. It had a conservative stone-tool industry where earlier flint-working techniques and tools, particularly scrapers used in the dressing of skins, combined with some new tool types, especially barbed and tanged arrowheads. These are found in the Late Neolithic/Early Bronze Age assemblages from Knowth and Newgrange. One of the characteristics of the flint industry of Newgrange at this time is the high proportion of scrapers to other implements.[112] Stone tools from the timber circle at Knowth include those made from flint, pebble and chalk. There was little evidence for the finished tools used, as the majority of the finds are un-utilised blades and flakes.[113]

Evidence for the use of metal by these communities is quite meagre. The Beaker settlement at Newgrange

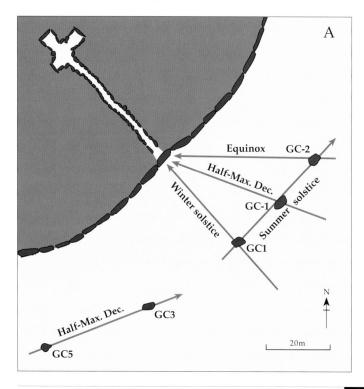

Fig. 38   Twelve standing stones of a great circle of stones surround the base of the earlier passage tomb at Newgrange. A) A computer simulation of the movement of the sun for the period c.2000BC has demonstrated that these stones throw shadows on the decorated entrance stone of Newgrange during such key times in the year as the winter and summer solstices and equinoxes, thus suggesting their use as a ritual calendar. This suggests a need for this agricultural society to divide the year and highlights once again the desire to incorporate the earlier monuments into later practices. B) Stones GC1, GC-1 and GC-2 of the Great Stone Circle.

ROYAL IRISH ACADEMY

Fig. 39   A drawing by Gabriel Beranger (1775) shows the remains of a stone circle enclosed by a low bank which stands at the brink of a quarry at Dowth. Cloghalea, as it was marked on the first edition OS maps, was removed by subsequent quarrying, although some of the enclosing bank may yet be present.

produced a number of stone objects that may have been used by a metal worker and a thin-butted bronze axe head.[114] The builders of the embanked enclosures may have had an interest in the copper resources of the Boyne region as their distribution coincides with a concentration of copper in the eastern half of Meath.[115] Pottery was locally made, using local raw materials (logically enough) but exotic styles. At Newgrange an actual pottery workshop was identified by the presence of prepared or accidentally fired unshaped clay.[116] However, the presence of local clays cannot be used as evidence against an influx of a new population in the Late Neolithic/Early Bronze Age, as has sometimes been argued.[117]

Economy   A much greater degree of continuity in agricultural practice between the Neolithic and Bronze Ages has been identified.[118] This is particularly true if the faunal collections from the Bronze Age at Knowth and Newgrange (where pig bones outnumbered cattle bones) are viewed as ritually selective rather than being representative of the farm stock in general.[119] Despite the presence of arrowheads of various types, hunting was of negligible importance. The keeping of sheep and goats was

also a peripheral activity.[120] A mixed farming economy is indicated by grains of wheat, barley and oat in the post pits of the timber circle at Knowth.[121] The Early Bronze Age 'Beaker' concentration at Knowth produced small quantities of wheat and barley grains, hazelnut shells, blackberry and elderberry seeds, vetch, dock, sloe, goosefoot, mint, bracken, hazel, alder, elm and oak, indicating little change in vegetation in the post–Passage tomb period.[122]

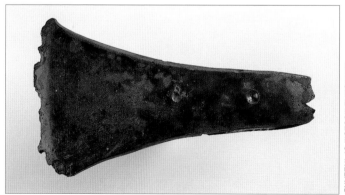

NATIIONAL MUSEUM OF IRELAND

Fig. 40   This Early Bronze Age axe from the Boyne is an example of the earliest metal axes used in the valley. It is very similar to the stone version which it replaced.

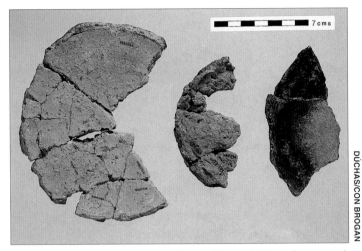

Fig. 41   Flint and pottery from the Late Neolithic levels at Knowth. As the use of metal became more common, flint-working techniques degenerated. Working is concentrated on the edges of the flint cores and little effort was made to remove the outer cortex.

This renewed phase of monument building in the Boyne region heralded an impressive change in the ritual landscape of the area. It coincided with a decline in the fabric of the passage tombs, resulting in cairn collapse at Newgrange.[123] It is associated with the adoption of new pottery styles (Beaker and grooved ware) and a simpler burial tradition. Similar trends emerged in Late Neolithic/Early Bronze Age Britain from c.2,500BC. In Britain there was a similar decline in monumental tombs; traditional pottery styles were replaced by new types; flint working techniques degenerated; single grave burial was adopted; large-scale enclosures or henges for burial and ritual practice were constructed. These changes affected both north and south Britain and are seen as largely indigenous in origin. They have been interpreted as the emergence of a stratified society with a focus on the individual rather than the community.[124] In Ireland the stimulus for Late Neolithic/Early Bronze Age changes was probably exogenous and the arrival of new populations presumably from Britain cannot be ruled out.

MIDDLE BRONZE AGE SETTLEMENT

There were permanent communities south of the river Boyne in the Middle Bronze Age. Two cist burials (burials in stone-lined boxes) have been discovered at Oldbridge. The most tantalising indication of a human presence in the valley during the Middle Bronze Age is the recent discovery of fulachta fiadh – mounds of burnt stones with

Fig. 42   Cist burial on the grounds of Oldbridge House. A) These stone-lined boxes are typical of the funerary ritual of the Early and Late Bronze Ages. They are manifestly less monumental tombs than the great passage graves which preceded them. B) Spider nests hang from the cap stone of the cist.

Fig. 43 Fulachta fiadh were recently discovered south of the Boyne at Sheephouse. These cooking sites were used by communities who came to settle in the valley *c*.3,500 years ago. A) When topsoil was removed in advance of a quarry, concentrations of burnt stone were exposed. B) The burnt stones covered a charcoal-filled cooking pit.

pits that are the remains of ancient cooking sites. These were located in a natural basin high above the south bank of the Boyne at Sheephouse. A small community may have lived here three and a half thousand years ago (*c*.1,400BC). There are some Late Bronze Age finds from Newgrange but by this time the burial mounds here and at Knowth had collapsed to cover over all traces of the earlier settlement. The entrance to Newgrange remained hidden for thousands of years.

NEW DISCOVERIES

The accepted interpretation of prehistoric settlement in the Boyne Valley will have to be re-evaluated in the light of the many new discoveries that have been made during the construction of the Northern Motorway (M1 Drogheda By Pass). A stretch of new motorway *c*.17km long between the River Nanny and Monasterboice has produced evidence for human activity throughout its length.[125] These sites have all been identified from sub-surface remains after the topsoil was removed by mechanical digger. Full publication of numerous excavations are still pending, but preliminary results indicate a high density of prehistoric remains; occupation sites, cooking areas, and ceremonial pit and timber circles. Discoveries range from isolated pits (containing cremated bone, flint or pottery) to large prehistoric enclosures. These finds highlight, once again, the exceptional nature of the archaeology in the Boyne Valley. The density of archaeological sites south of the river in the lowlands of Donore and Rathmullan is significant, given the absence of upstanding monuments there. Three of Rathmullan's sites are known to be prehistoric. One of these sites produced 'poly pod' vessels, a rare form of pottery which has previously only been found in Newgrange in this region.[126]

KIERAN CAMPBELL

KIERAN CAMPBELL

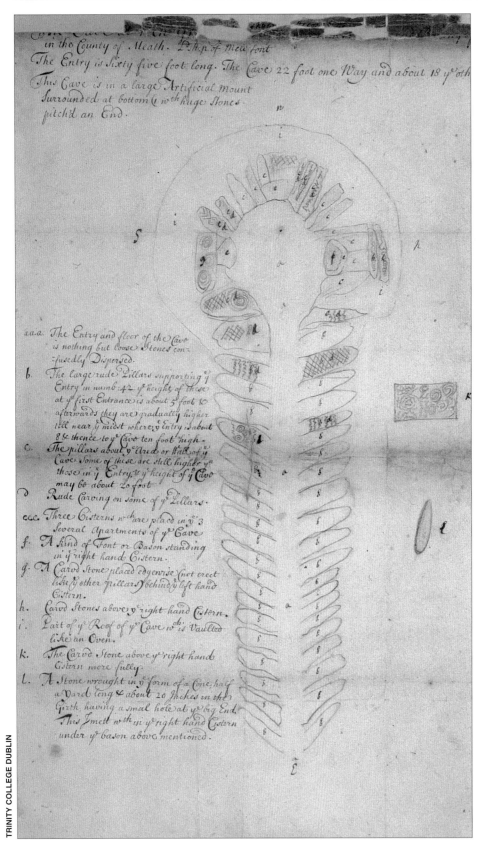

Fig. 1 Lhwyd's survey of Newgrange, the first known plan of the tomb.

NEWGRANGE DISCOVERED

Edward Lhwyd, the Welsh antiquary visited, Newgrange during his tour of Ireland in 1699. He witnessed the entrance to Newgrange being robbed for stone by the local landowner, Charles Campbell. Nonetheless, the tumulus at Newgrange considerably impressed him.[1] In several letters he gives an account of the discovery of the entrance passage, the state of the monument at the time, the finds in the chamber, and the former presence of a standing stone on the top of the mound. Lhwyd's letter of 15 December 1699 reports:

> The gentleman of the village observing that under the green turf this mount was wholly composed of stones, and having occasion for some, employed his servants to carry off a considerable parcel of them; till they came at last to a very broad flat stone rudely carved, and placed edgewise at the bottom of the mount. This they discovered to be the door of a cave, which had a long entry into it.[2]

From its discovery, Newgrange attracted great antiquarian interest

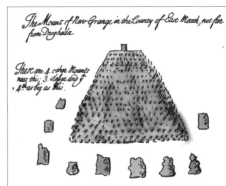

Fig. 2   John Antis (1699–1745) travelled to Ireland recording ancient monuments. He visited Newgrange and his manuscript account has a crude illustration which shows the standing stone on top of the mound first mentioned by Lhwyd.

Fig. 3 Gabriel Beranger's watercolour of Newgrange in 1775. It shows a heap of stones in front of the entrance.

and we are fortunate to have a large number of early illustrations of the

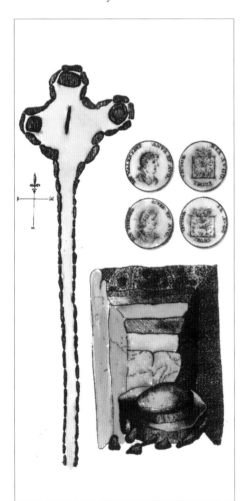

Fig. 4 Thomas Molyneaux's plan, illustrates a 'pyramidal shaped stone' in the middle of the chamber, which no longer exists, and he described human remains on the floor.[6] The detail of the east recess shows megalithic art. Roman coins found at the site are also shown.

monument. Many show features which are no longer extant. Antiquarian thought varied as to the purpose of the passage tomb. Edward Ledwich, in his *Antiquities of Ireland* (1790), was convinced that this was a Christian-era monument built by the Vikings for a 'principal commander dying at Newgrange'.[3] Colt Hoare, in his 1806 *Journal*, was the first to compare Newgrange with sites in Britain such as the Wessex long barrows,[4] a view still endorsed by archaeologists. The first 'modern' archaeological treatment of the monument and its art was George Coffey's 1911 *Newgrange*.[5]

Fig. 5 Pownall's detailed plans from 1773. These are the first accurate sections of the tomb produced by a local land surveyor.[7]

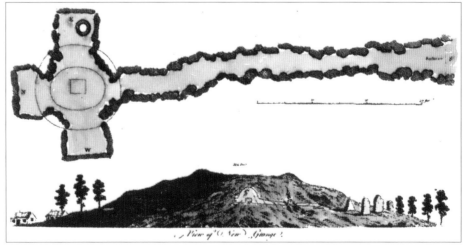

Fig. 6 Charles Vallancey's 1776 survey of the Newgrange tomb shows a triangular stone opposite the entrance and inside the line of the stone circle.[8] Excavations around the tomb entrance may have exposed the socket of this stone.

Fig. 7 Engraving from Ledwich's *Antiquities of Ireland* (1790). It also shows the triangular shaped stone which originally stood outside the engrance to Newgrange. This picturesque view would not have been greatly altered until excavations began in the 1960s.

EXCAVATION

In the late nineteenth century the Board of Works began exposing kerbstones, thus creating the present bank and ditch effect which is visible to the rear of the site. R. A. S. Macalister, Robert Lloyd Praeger and Harold Leask continued this work in the 1930s by exposing a further fifty-four kerbstones. Trial excavations by Ó Ríordáin and Ó hEochaidhe in 1956 in the outer stone circle produced some archaeological finds and information on the sockets of the missing stones. Around the same time, Paddy Hartnett discovered flints and an adze south of the entrance during the laying down of electricity cable to provide light in the tomb. As Archaeological Officer in Bord Fáilte, the Irish Tourist Board, Hartnett instigated the excavations at

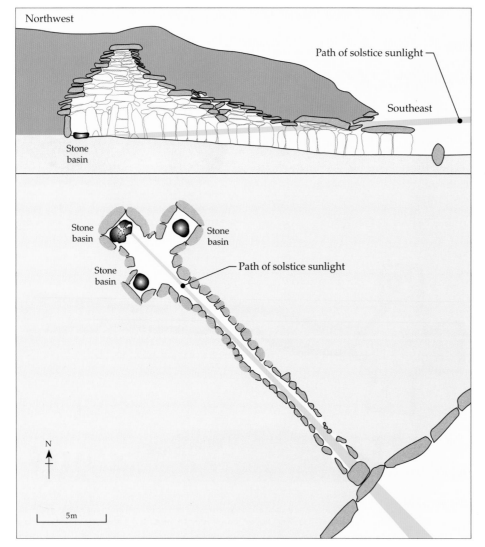

Northwest

Path of solstice sunlight

Southeast

Stone basin

Stone basin

Stone basin

Stone basin

Path of solstice sunlight

N

5m

NATIONAL MUSEUM OF IRELAND

Fig. 9 Fragment of a stone bowl found in the foundations of a hut in front of Newgrange. It is made from andesite, a type of igneous rock which is found in the locality of Newgrange.

NATIONAL MUSEUM OF IRELAND

Fig. 10 A bone point, chisel and waste flint from the grave deposits from the chamber at Newgrange.

Fig. 8 Plan and section of Newgrange after excavation.

Fig. 11 Grave deposits found in the burial chamber of Newgrange include: a dumb-bell shaped bead cut out of a piece of chalk with a polished surface; three marbles made from Antrim chalk; two hammer pendants made of pottery; a barrel-shaped bead of pottery; a pendant made from fused pottery marbles; and a bone disc-bead.

roofbox, after reconstruction, channelled the mid-winter sun into the back of the chamber. This is a unique feature of Newgrange and unknown in the megalithic tomb architecture of Western Europe. Modern excavation provided the first reliable Carbon 14 dates (*c.*3200BC) for the construction at Newgrange.

NEWGRANGE TODAY

Newgrange lies on the summit of an elongated ridge north of the River Boyne. It is the largest tomb within a cemetery that extends east, west and south. The main tomb at Newgrange has a passage and chamber, built of large stones, and opens to the southeast in the direction of the midwinter solstice. It is topped by an ovoid-shaped, grass-covered cairn. The cairn is flat-topped. Excavations

Newgrange which were undertaken by M. J. O'Kelly. Between 1962 and 1975 one-third of the mound was excavated and a number of breath-taking discoveries were made. Foremost of these discoveries was the way the

Fig. 12 The entrance stone at Newgrange is decorated with this great free-flowing curvilinear design which has a strong sculptural quality A vertical channel divides the upper half of the decorated surface. A similar feature occurs diametrically opposite on the kerbstone to the rear of the mound. This enigmatic line is also a feature of the entrance stone in the western passage tomb at Knowth.

DÚCHAS/CON BROGAN

Fig. 13 Aerial photograph of Newgrange following conservation. The site, as presented to the public, is clinical and closely cropped. The white quartz wall has a glaringly modern appearance. Although it was justified on the basis of an engineer's analysis of the cairn collapse, it is difficult to imagine that the monument could ever have appeared like this in prehistoric times. Its construction has to be understood in the context of late 1960s fashions in restoration. Many have argued for its removal.

have shown that the cairn had a layered structure and that sods were used to secure the stones at certain places and during phases of construction. Some of the cairn stones had picked decoration. O'Kelly believed that the cairn collapse indicated that the cairn had a near-vertical face. A highly controversial wall was erected at the entrance to Newgrange designed according to this hypothesis. The wall is made up of quartz and granite cobbles found during the excavation. O'Kelly believed that the builders used selected boulders to build a revetment on top of the kerbstones creating a drum-like shape. It is highly unlikely that such a steep profile was ever maintained using a quartz revetment.

Ninety-seven kerbstones surround the base of the cairn, which is broadest to the south and has a pointed part to the north. Despite the varying size and shape of the surrounding kerbstones, the tomb builders consciously created a finished, even top line by setting some of them in boulder-packed sockets whilst others were raised up on boulders. Some flint objects were found behind the kerbstones during excavations. The slab now set upright to the right of the passage mouth is the original closing slab or door to the tomb. It has been demonstrated that when the curved end of this large slab is placed on the ground and the straight one uppermost, it closes the entrance to the passage exactly.

Above the entrance to the passage is a roof box. In 1963 O'Kelly discovered, that at the time of the winter solstice the rays of the rising sun directly passed through this opening and illuminated the chamber within. Newgrange is the oldest astronomically aligned structure in the world, predating the first phase of Stonehenge by 1,000 years and the Egyptian pyramids by c.400 years. The winter solstice illumination at Newgrange was first recorded by O'Kelly in 1969. The alignment of the roof box to the solstice was deliberate and shows that the builders were familiar with basic astronomical cycles. This roof box – as an integral feature of the tomb's design – is unparalleled in Europe. However, while the Newgrange roof box may be unique in its detail, a comparable effect is achieved in the chamber at Maes Howe in Orkney by light passing through the main entrance, an arrangement which has recently been paralleled at Crantit chambered tomb, also in Orkney.

The roof box rests partly on the first and second roof slabs. The front lintel is highly decorated. The passage and chamber occupy only one-third of the diameter of the cairn. Passage stones were placed in two parallel rows in sockets dug into the old ground surface. It had been constructed as a free-standing structure. There is a kink in the passage halfway along where it weaves to the southwest and then northeast. It also rises in height from the opening to the chamber. The tomb builders filled the gaps between the passage roof stones with burnt soil and sea sand to keep the passage dry.

The chamber is roughly cruciform in plan, containing three recesses or side chambers, the eastern one being the largest. The central chamber is roofed with a corbelled vault, which rises and narrows gradually until it is closed by a single capstone. It is the finest of its kind in Western Europe. There are four carved stone basins in the burial chamber. The basin stone in the west is sub-circular in shape whilst (unfortunately) that in the north is in fragments. There are two basin stones in the east recess; the upper is a very fine granite example which was worked all over and has two circular depressions on its upper surface. The

DÚCHAS/CON BROGAN

Fig. 14 The chamber and passage at Newgrange when viewed from the end recess.

DÚCHAS/CON BROGAN

Fig. 15 The triple spiral used so effectively by the artists at Newgrange has lately been adopted as a symbol of ancient 'Celtic' spirituality.

chamber had been disturbed by humans and animals in the distant past, and basins have been moved or broken. Centuries of disturbance have removed most of the original archaeological deposits. Nonetheless, in the chamber a layer of soil with broken stones contained the burnt and unburnt remains of five persons. They were found with their original grave deposits of pendants, beads, clay marbles and bone objects.

ART

At Newgrange the megalithic art is geometrical and non-representational. There are two main styles of megalithic art; an earlier incised geometric style and the later, more dramatic, 'plastic' or sculptured style. Lozenge and chevron are the most common motifs. Spirals, though less common, are prominently displayed. Some of the stones such as the entrance stone, lintel of the roof box and Kerbstone 52 (at the back of the mound directly opposite the entrance)

are highly-accomplished pieces of sculpture. Art is present on hidden surfaces particularly motifs such as dot radials and dot-in-circles. Many of the stones were carved before being inserted into position but some, in particular the entrance stone, was carved in situ. The ornament stops at a

horizontal line which represents the original ground level.

The motifs were picked on the surface of the stones by making a series of small pits, using a sharp point of flint or quartz. A line of these pits was used to trace out the design. The artist sometimes rubbed these with a stone to create a grooved line, or an area was solidly picked. Alternatively, the surface of the stone was picked, leaving an unpicked area, which created the motif. Guidelines were usually scratched or incised into the stone before carving began. Many of the stones were given a further overall dressing once they were positioned.

DÚCHAS/CON BROGAN

Fig. 16 This spectacular decoration appears on the underside of a roofstone in the east recess. Some of the art is hidden by the enclosing cairn. The motifs include chevrons, concentric circles, spirals and zigzag lines.

DÚCHAS/CON BROGAN

Fig. 17 One of the megaliths forming the passage which is decorated with spirals and zigzag lines. The spirals are arranged around a lozenge. The surface of the stone above and below these motifs has been pick-dressed.

DÚCHAS/CON BROGAN

Fig. 18 Positioned directly opposite the entrance stone to the rear of the mound, this stone contains an ambitious composition, which harmonises with the varying contours of the stone. Although the presence of a vertical channel on a stone usually indicates the entrance to a passage tomb, excavation has failed to identify another passage on this side of the mound. The motifs on the left-hand side of this kerbstone are picked out to create a false relief, which contrasts with the free-flowing spirals on the right hand side.

DÚCHAS/CON BROGAN

Fig. 19 This dramatically decorated stone stands guard at the mouth of the chamber. Broad shallow grooves were picked across the surface of the stone creating this striking ribbed effect. Its upper edge has this cluster of chevrons picked into the stone.

ter solstice at Newgrange passage tomb

KNOWTH PASSAGE TOMB

KNOWTH DISCOVERED

In 1725 Thomas Molyneaux reported the discovery of a stone urn in a mound at Knowth found with burnt bones in a 'cist' (a stone box).[1] Later, an eighteenth-century estate map showed the site with one of the passages possibly indicated. In the mid-nineteenth century the first detailed accounts of Knowth were published.[2] Knowth is shown as a mound by Wakeman, and described as having 'an abrupt hemispherical mound with rather a flattened top, rising out of the sloping hill' by Wilde.[3] In 1912 Coffey wrote that it was less dilapidated than Newgrange or Dowth.[4] At that time, no kerbstones were visible except for some stones that protruded from the northern side of the mound: Coffey believed that these marked the entrance to the tomb. The top of the mound had a

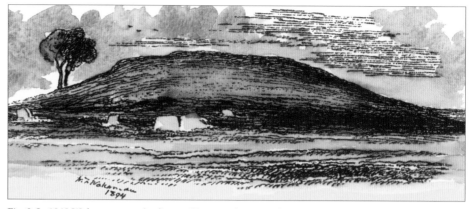

Fig. 2 In 1848 Wakeman was the first to illustrate the mound at Knowth.[6]

considerable depression in the centre that gave the appearance of a rampart around the margin.

EXCAVATION

Excavations by R. A. S. Macalister in 1941 exposed half of the outer kerbstones of the main mound, a souterrain and the burial chamber of one of the satellite tombs.[7] In 1962 George Eogan began his excavations at Knowth with the original intention of assessing only the presence or

Fig. 4 Stone urn from Knowth now in the National Museum of Ireland.

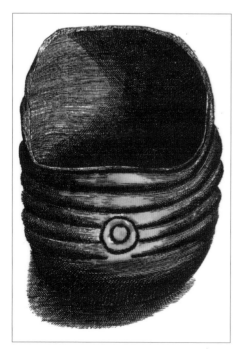

Fig. 1 Thomas Molyneaux's illustration of a stone urn 'found enclosed in a square stone box, about five foot long and four foot broad, made of four rude large flag stones set together edgeways', found at Knowth in the early eighteenth century.[5] This is a rare object to come from a megalithic tomb in Ireland.

Fig. 3 One of the small satellite tombs at Knowth (Site 16). The southern portion of this tomb was removed by the builders of the large mound and an alternate entrance constructed at right angles to the original passage. The small mound is D-shaped in plan. Cremated remains of adults and children were found in the chamber and passage of this tomb with grave goods, including a pin made from the leg of a bird.

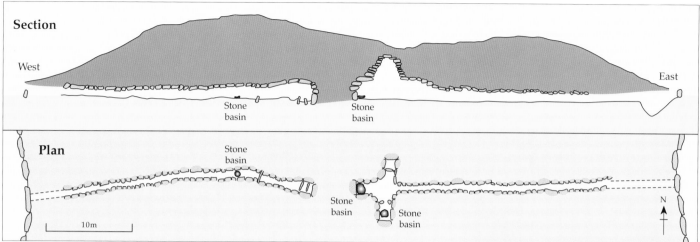

Fig. 5 Plan and section of the passage tomb at Knowth.

absence of satellite tombs. Eogan dedicated the next four decades to exploring and explaining the most amazing archaeological complex in Western Europe. He discovered that the main mound at Knowth covered two passage tombs, placed back to back. The western undifferentiated tomb was found in 1967. The eastern cruciform tomb was discovered in 1968. A total of nineteen satellite tombs were also discovered and completely excavated. Evidence from all periods of Irish prehistory and history were revealed at this one remarkable site.

KNOWTH TODAY

Knowth lies to the west of Newgrange on the western edge of a shale ridge overlooking the Boyne. The large mound covers two passage tombs, placed back to back. Today Knowth is open to the public after almost forty years of excavation and reconstruction. Whereas a century ago, only the main

Fig. 6 Aerial photograph of Knowth taken at the completion of excavations and while conservation was in progress. A number of the smaller tombs have subsequently been restored.

Fig. 7 A phallus-shaped stone object found at the entrance to the western tomb at Knowth.

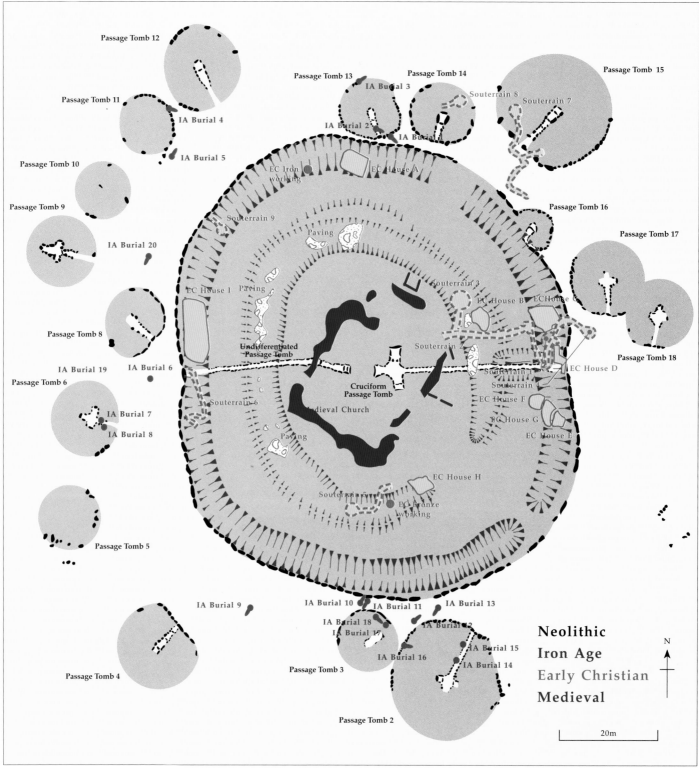

Passage Tomb 12

Passage Tomb 11

Passage Tomb 13

Passage Tomb 14

Passage Tomb 15

IA Burial 4

IA Burial 3

Souterrain 8

Souterrain 7

Passage Tomb 10

IA Burial 5

IA Burial 2

IA Burial

Passage Tomb 9

EC Iron working

EC House A

Souterrain 9

Passage Tomb 16

IA Burial 20

Paving

Passage Tomb 17

EC House 1

Paving

Souterrain 3

EC House B

EC House

Passage Tomb 8

Undifferentiated Passage Tomb

Souterrain 2

Passage Tomb 18

IA Burial 19

IA Burial 6

Souterrain

EC House D

Cruciform Passage Tomb

Souterrain 4

Passage Tomb 6

Souterrain 6

EC House F

IA Burial 7

Medieval Church

EC House G

IA Burial 8

EC House E

Paving

Passage Tomb 5

EC House H

Souterrain 5

EC Bronze working

IA Burial 9

IA Burial 10

IA Burial 11

IA Burial 13

IA Burial 18

IA Burial

IA Burial 17

IA Burial 2

Neolithic

IA Burial 15

Iron Age

IA Burial 16

IA Burial 14

Early Christian

Passage Tomb 3

Medieval

Passage Tomb 4

N

Passage Tomb 2

20m

mound was visible, currently visitors are guided around the tombs and other features revealed during the excavations. The tell-like accumulation of occupation at Knowth represents Irish history in microcosm.

Fig. 8 The excavations at Knowth revealed a tell-like accumulation of layers dating from the pre-tomb activity to the nineteenth century. The principal phase was the passage-tomb building period which saw the construction of eighteen small tombs and the main tomb which is the most ornamented in Western Europe. After the the Bronze Age – the long lonely years at Knowth – the mound once again became the focus of intense activity. Thirty-five Iron Age burials were placed around the mound which was subsequently fortified with a double ditch turning Knowth virtually into a hillfort. In the Early Christian period, the mound was terraced and houses with souterrains were constructed. This is the greatest concentration of souterrains and houses in the whole of Ireland. The extraorardinary level of settlement was due to the site's function as the royal centre for the kings of northern Brega. In the middle ages, Knowth was part of the Boyne Mellifont Cistercian holdings.

DÚCHAS/JIM BAMBURY

Fig. 9 Photograph taken at the time of the discovery of the eastern tomb in 1968.

DÚCHAS/CON BROGAN

DÚCHAS/CON BROGAN

Fig. 10 Decorated stone from the west recess of the eastern tomb chamber.

DÚCHAS/CON BROGAN

Fig. 11 The eastern tomb has a massive corbelled chamber. Small flattish stones were used for levelling between courses. The corbels decrease in size as the chamber ascends to a massive height of almost 6m.

Fig. 12 This is finest basin stone ever found in a passage tomb in Ireland. Because it is wider than the passage, it must have been placed in the chamber before the passage was built. The basin's interior is decorated with arcs and rays. Externally it is decorated with grouped horizontal bands and a circular motif above segmented arcs. The decoration is similar in form to that on the urn found at Knowth in the early eighteenth century (see figure 1, p. 48).

A

DÚCHAS/CON BROGAN

B

DÚCHAS/CON BROGAN

Fig. 13 A) Just beyond the bend in the passage of the western tomb, a sillstone obstructs access to the chamber area. This section of the passage contains dramatically decorated orthostats which appear almost life-like. B) This figure from the past guards the approach to the western chamber at Knowth very like megalithic art in Brittany. The visual impact is striking.

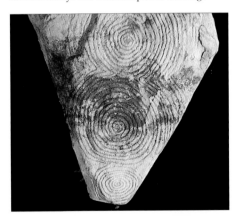

Fig. 14 A number of stones in the western passage have decoration on their bases, but hidden art is rare.

DÚCHAS/CON BROGAN

Fig. 15 The western tomb has a well-defined rectangular chamber with a sillstone cutting off the passage.

ART

More than three hundred decorated stones occur in the main tumulus at Knowth which represents the greatest concentration of megalithic art in Western Europe. The art makes a strong visual impact, particularly those stones at the approach to the chambers. Recurring motifs include circles, serpentine forms and spirals. Decoration was added to the natural smooth surface. Sometimes incised lines were used as a grid to guide the application of the designs. The art is found on the outer faces of the kerbstones and the inner faces of the stones in the passage and chamber. Hidden art is rarer at Knowth than at Newgrange. From the varying quality of work, it is clear that artists with a wide range of expertise worked on the stones. There is evidence for later modification. The art on the smaller tombs is far less accomplished.

Fig. 16 The pairing of horseshoe-shaped arcs on either side of a vertical line creates almost a mirror image.

Fig. 18 Many of the kerbstones at Knowth contain a single prominent motif. This kerbstone features a multiple concentric circle covering most of the stone's surface.

Fig. 19 Dolphin-like motif from the burial chamber of the undifferentiated western tomb.

Fig. 17 The decoration on this kerbstone at Knowth resembles a sundial.

Fig. 20 Simple incised dispersed circles on a kerbstone at Knowth.

DOWTH PASSAGE TOMB

DOWTH DISCOVERED[1]

The great passage tomb at Dowth was first described in 1769 by Thomas Pownall, as a large tumulus or barrow under which was a 'cave' like that at Newgrange.[2] Later eighteenth-century drawings by Gabriel Beranger indicated that the sides of Dowth mound rose steeply above its kerbstones to a rounded top, which contrasts with the flat top at Newgrange. Nineteenth-century accounts confirmed the presence of a burial chamber in the mound. In 1834 George Petrie said that the mound 'unquestionably contains a chamber within it, the entrance gallery to which is exposed but inaccessible, from the stones being, as it appears, violently displaced'.[3] In 1836 the Ordnance Survey mapped Dowth and their drawing of the mound shows an opening in the west side of the mound which is marked 'cave'. Samuel Lewis, in his *Topographical Dictionary*, (1837) reported the discovery of human bones in the passages of Dowth.[4] William Wilde visited the site and included a sketch by Wakeman in his *Beauties of the Boyne and Blackwater*. This sketch showed the monument prior to its 1847 'excavation' which greatly disfigured the site.

Fig. 1 Gabriel Beranger's drawing of Dowth in 1775 shows a round-topped mound with a pagoda-like structure on the top. Folklore has it that this is where Lord Netterville sat when Mass was being said in the old chapel below the mound. It seems to have had a distinctly different profile from either Newgrange or Knowth.

Fig. 2 Wakeman's sketch of Dowth prior to the excavations shows a level platform and berm near the top of the mound and a summer house in ruins.[5]

EXCAVATION

In 1847 explorations of Dowth were begun by R. H. Frith, an engineer, with the support of the Royal Irish Academy.[6] Frith excavated a large horizontal cutting into the west side of the mound, hoping to find a chamber. He succeeded in revealing the cruciform chamber of the larger passage tomb and explored the passage and chamber of the Early Medieval souterrain. His digging produced a number of finds, including rings, pins, a bronze knife, a glass bead and portion of a jet bracelet. All these objects were associated with the reuse of Dowth in the Early Christian period. Some human remains were found near the surface of the mound. When Dowth came into state care in the 1880s, extensive conservation works were undertaken, including the construction of the vertical shaft and iron ladder that is still a feature of the site today, the concrete roof in the southernmost passage tomb, and supports in the larger northernmost chamber.[7]

DOWTH PASSAGE TOMB TODAY

The great passage tomb at Dowth lies on the eastern edge of an elongated ridge. It compares in size and situation with Knowth and Newgrange, yet has remained relatively unexplored. Limited excavations

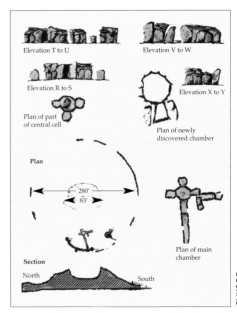

Fig. 3 Plan and sectional profiles by the architect T. N. Deane, 1885–86, drawn for the Board of Public Works prior to conservation.

which took place here in 1847 are indicated by the large crater in the fabric of the site. The line of the kerbstones can be traced for approximately half of the perimeter, with sixty-six stones visible. The remainder are buried beneath mound collapse and embedded in the field boundary to the west of Dowth. The large mound is made up of loose stones covering two burial chambers both in the west of the mound; the smaller southernmost tomb has a short passage and a circular chamber with a recess built into the south. At the end of the shortest day of the year, the rays of the setting sun illuminate this passage and circular chamber in a manner similar to the winter solstice event at Newgrange. The northern-most tomb is cruciform in plan, with a stone basin in the chamber large enough to accommodate two people lying down. The most unusual feature of the Dowth chamber is its annex, the addition of two segmented chambers reached from the south recess. The original entrance of the north tomb was disturbed by the construction of an underground chamber or souter-rain in the Early Christian period, which connects with the passage of the original tomb.

Fig. 5 Dowth today as viewed from the east.

Fig. 4 A kerbstone on the east side of the mound at Dowth is ornamented on the front with sun or wheel patterns. Hidden art, in the form of curvilinear shapes, has been exposed on the back.

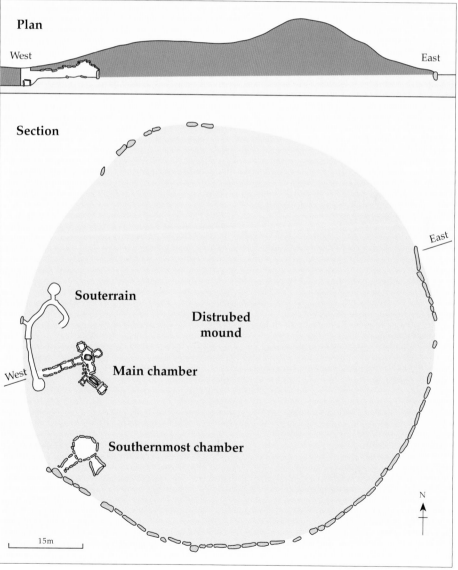

Plan

West

East

Section

Souterrain

Distrubed mound

East

West

Main chamber

Southernmost chamber

15m

N

Fig. 6   Ground plan and section of Dowth passage tomb.

DÚCHAS/CON BROGAN

Fig. 7 Approaching the inner burial chamber of the northernmost tomb one is struck by the sheer massiveness of the stone basin. This probably contained cremated human remains. The prehistoric art on the structural stones at Dowth is also highly dramatic.

Fig. 9 This is the finest ornamented stone in the chamber of the northernmost passage tomb at Dowth. A variety of motifs are continued around the corner of the stone in a dramatic fashion.

Fig. 10 Entrance to the southernmost tomb at Dowth. The entrance stone is decorated with cup marks and concentric circles.

Fig. 11 The setting sun on the winter solstice illuminates the inner chamber of the southernmost tomb at Dowth.

Fig. 8 The inner chamber of the southernmost tomb at Dowth from the sceptal stone at the tob of the passage. This chamber has an unusual circular plan with a single right-hand recess.

Dowth Art

At least thirty-eight of the stones at Dowth contain megalithic art, of which fifteen are in the kerb, eleven in Dowth 'North' and Dowth 'South' passages and chambers. Both the early geometric art and the later more dramatic art picked out in higher relief can be seen in the recess of the southernmost tomb. The circle is the most common motif used at Dowth. In general, less effort went into finishing the stones at Dowth and the quality of the art is naïve, mere doodling compared to Newgrange and Knowth.

NEWGRANGE PIT CIRCLE

Archaeological excavations in 1982 and 1983 under the direction of David Sweetman revealed a great circle of pits and post holes south of the main passage tomb at Newgrange.[1] O'Kelly had previously exposed some evidence for this impressive monument in the 1960s and 1970s without realising its full extent.[2] The enclosure was a ritual site where people gathered to offer animal sacrifices to their gods *c*.2000BC. It is comparable with such famous sites in Britain as the Aubrey Holes at Stonehenge.

Sweetman's excavation identified sub-surface evidence for six rows of pits and post holes. These formed a circle *c*.67m in diameter, incorporating an earlier passage tomb within the interior. Originally, the enclosure was defined by a row of large wooden posts. Inside the line of posts was an arc of large clay-lined pits. They showed evidence for intensive burning and some contained cremated animal remains. Inside the arc of great pits were a further three rows of holes. These also contained cremated remains and probably acted as receptacles for votive offerings. Two small habitation areas were found inside the circle where Grooved Ware and Beaker pottery was found.

DÚCHAS/DAVID SWEETMAN

Fig. 1 A rim fragment of Grooved Ware pottery, a body fragment with an applied knob decoration and a small ring made from lignite stone all found during the excavation at the pit circle.

DÚCHAS/DAVID SWEETMAN

Fig. 2 A flint blade found with cremated bone found in one of the burial holes and a stone adze.

DÚCHAS/BRIAN ROYNAYNE

Fig. 3 Artist's impression of Newgrange Pit Circle.

Fig. 4 Newgrange Pit Circle after conservation.

Fig. 5 Excavations showed that the Great Stone Circle was built on top of the remains of the pit circle after it went out of use. Both features, therefore, date from the Bronze Age and do not pre-date the tomb.

Fig. 6 Flint tools found at the pit circle include these triangular, round scraper and side scrapers and a barbed and tanged arrowhead; these are typical of Late Neolithic/Early Bronze Age sites in Ireland.

Fig. 7 Another pit circle was discovered by David Sweetman to the west of Newgrange passage tomb. It is similar in size to one discovered near the entrance to the eastern tomb at Knowth.

MONKNEWTOWN HENGE

A rescue excavation was undertaken at a prehistoric enclosure, or henge monument, in Monknewtown in the spring of 1971. This rescue excavation was necessitated when a building development threatened to destroy part of the site.[1] Monknewtown henge is the smallest of a group of thirteen prehistoric enclosures in county Meath. It is located south of the Mattock River and west of Rossin village. Like other ceremonial enclosures in the Bend of the Boyne, it lies close to a small passage tomb.

Prior to excavation the interior of this site was featureless. However archaeological investigations by David Sweetman revealed an extensive cemetery near the inner face of the bank and the remains of a wooden house within the interior. The house produced a large assemblage of

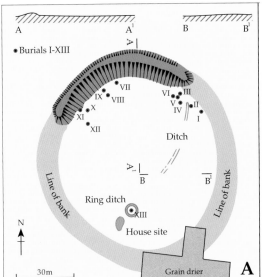

Fig. 2 A) Plan of Monknewtown. B) Embanked enclosures (henges) in the Boyne region.

Fig. 3 Remains of a burial found in the interior of the Monknewtown henge. At the centre of this ring ditch a small shallow pit was found which contained cremated bone and the remains of a flat bottomed pot. Some Beaker pottery was found at the bottom of the ditch.

DÚCHAS/DAVID SWEETMAN

DÚCHAS/DAVID SWEETMAN

DÚCHAS/DAVID SWEETMAN

Fig. 4 One of the burials found inside the henge was a cremation of a child between the ages of six and ten. It was contained in a Carrowkeel bowl. The ornament is of oblique stab and drag technique running right around the bowl. This style of pottery is normally found accompanying burials in passage graves and shows there was some cultural overlap between the communities who built tombs and the later henge builders.

Fig. 1 Only a section of the earthen bank defining the enclosure survived. The excavation revealed that this had been constructed from material gathered from the interior of the enclosure rather than by digging a deep ditch. This is the characteristic method of building these ritual enclosures, or henge monuments, in the Boyne Valley.

Late Neolithic/Early Bronze Age pottery and flint and stone tools. Radiocarbon dates derived from charcoal indicated a construction date *c.*1860BC.

Eleven pits were found near the bank. Six of these contained human cremations. Two contained cist-like structures. One of the pits yielded a Carrowkeel bowl containing a human cremation. A ring ditch was also found within the interior.

The monument was built from material scraped from the interior and not by digging a ditch. This is a diagnostic characteristic of the Boyne-type enclosures. This form of construction created an open ampitheatre where the community would have gathered for ritual activities. Although we cannot reconstruct the exact nature of the ceremonies which took place here, votive offerings were a key feature.

DÚCHAS/KEVIN O'BRIEN

Fig. 5 A reconstruction of the Monknewtown house. The area between the posts and the pit may have been used for sleeping while the area around the hearth would presumably have been used for cooking. The site of a house site comprised a sunken oval-shaped area with a central hearth defined by flagstones and surrounding post holes. A wide range of highly decorated and plain cooking ware was found at this site.

DÚCHAS/DAVID SWEETMAN

DÚCHAS/DAVID SWEETMAN

Fig. 6   Decorated Beaker pottery from the house at Monknewtown.

Fig. 7   Simple cist burial from Monknewtown.

HEROES AND SAINTS: THE EARLY HISTORIC LANDSCAPE

Brú na Bóinne, in addition to possessing the most imposing megalithic monuments in Ireland, has an equally imposing, if less obvious, concentration of place names associating some of the chief figures in early Irish mythology with a variety of natural and artificial features. The ancient name for this area is *Brug na Boinde*. A *brug* in ancient Irish tales is translated as a mansion or palace. As a place name in the Boyne Valley *brug* had a topographical identity by the tenth century. A poem by Ó hArtagain (d. AD975) refers to the cemetery at *Brug*. In a twelfth-century history of the royal cemeteries of Ireland known as *Senchus na Relec*, an origin tale is provided for the cemetery at *Brug*. This was the first historic survey of the *Brug* in which individual monuments were identified and interpreted in the light of traditional mythology. In 1837 John O'Donovan of the Ordnance Survey first identified the Boyne monuments as the royal cemetery of *Brugh na Boinne*. William Wilde popularised the term in 1849 when he described the area as 'an assemblage of mounds, caves, pillar-stones, and other sepulchral monuments forming the great necropolis which extends along the north bank of the Boyne from Slane to [Dowth]'. *Brug* as a place name still lingers, in a somewhat corrupted form, around Newgrange.[1]

The Boyne Valley is also where St Patrick began his Christian mission in Ireland. There is the exciting possibility that his first sermon was given at Knowth rather than atop the hill of Slane. Without question, however, is the central significance of Knowth as the seat of the kings of northern Brega, one of the most important dynasties in the kingdom of Mide.

Evidence for settlement from the Early Christian period is found in the numerous ringforts in the Bend of the Boyne and place names which indicated that numbers were originally even higher. Souterrains are found in large numbers in this area, most notably built into the mound at Knowth. Nine souterrains were found during excavations, a unique concentration within Ireland.

DÚCHAS/CON BROGAN

Fig. 1 The water-filled enclosure at Monknewtown may be a ritual pond dating from the later prehistoric period. Tom Condit has compared it with the King's Stables near Eamhain Mhacha (Navan Fort) in County Armagh which dates from the Late Bronze Age. Sword moulds, animal bones and human remains were recovered from the County Armagh site. Investigation at Monknewtown could yield similar results.

GERALDINE STOUT

Fig. 2   This lake at Ballyboy, beside Dowth passage tomb, may one day provide pollen cores which can be used to reconstruct the Early Historic environment of this area.

Pre-Christian Land Use

A description of the Boyne is contained in a pre-Christian entry from the *Annals of the Four Masters*:

> In the reign of Conaire, the sea annually cast its produce ashore at Inbhear-Colptha [Colpe, near Mornington on the Boyne estuary]. Great abundance of nuts were annually found upon the Boinn … during this time … and the cattle were without keepers.[2]

Unfortunately, there is no local pollen profile which covers this later prehistoric/early historic period in the Bend of the Boyne. The nearest pollen profiles which can be used to re-create the landscape are those taken from Redbog and Essexford Lough in county Louth, 35km to the north.[3] They present a general picture of a predominantly pastoralist Iron Age economy with a modest arable component.

The majority of sites sampled in Ireland show woodland regeneration and significantly reduced agriculture for the period 200BC to AD200, followed by dramatic clearances and a developed arable agriculture.[4] This is often referred to as the 'Late Iron Age Lull' (LIAL) and interpreted as a major fall in the nationwide population; some areas may even have been abandoned. The unprecedented burst of agriculture succeeding this lull has been associated with the influx of Celtic-speaking people from outside Ireland, possibly from north Britain entering through Ulster.[5]

Supporting archaeological evidence for this new population includes the appearance of the beehive quern in Ireland. This quern type was introduced from the Yorkshire–South Scotland area. They were utilised in Ireland over a six-century period, spanning the second century BC to the fourth century AD.[6] Given that these objects are associated with cereal processing, their introduction is associated with the expansion of arable agriculture. This underlines the significance of the discovery of such a quern at Newgrange, found on an exposed river bed near the north bank of the Boyne.[7]

In the study of pre-Christian landscapes, scholars have attempted to correlate early topographical descriptions of sites contained in *Dindshenchas Érenn* with field evidence. This is done to identify Early Historic sites and gain some insight into their original function. *Dindshenchas Érenn* also

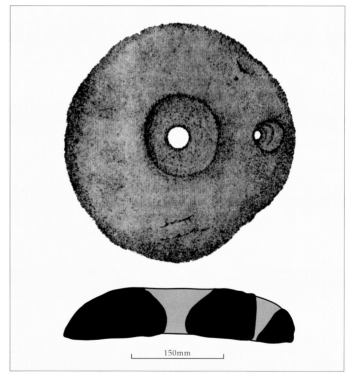

150mm

Fig. 3   This is an upper stone from a rotary quern with a funnel-shaped hopper (the diagnostic feature of beehive-type querns) made of local sandstone. Its discovery confirms, if such a confirmation were needed, the practice of tillage farming along the banks of the Boyne in the early centuries AD.

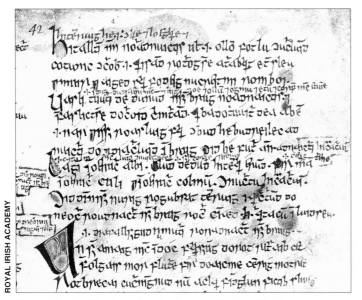

Fig. 4   The *dindshenchas* (place-lore) is contained in differing manuscripts and in various forms, including prose, poems and legends. These deal specifically with individual places, with the exception of the *dindshenchas* for *brug* which encompassed a complex of sites in the immediate environs of Newgrange. This extract from the twelfth–century *Book of Leinster* contains *dindshenchas* of the *brug*.

highlights sites which Early Christian society considered important. The *dindshenchas* incorporates a group of Middle Irish (AD900–1200) legends preserved in prose and poetry which purport to explain the origin and background of the names of the most prominent natural and man-made features in Ireland. The first element of the word – *dind* – literally means hillock, raised ground or landmark, and the second element – *senchas* – refers to the traditional lore of Irish places.[8] Many of these early stories contain topographical and geographical detail which allow one to locate the places described. The *dindshenchas* is contained in differing versions in the manuscripts of the *Book of Leinster* (dated to the twelfth century) and the *Book of Ballymote* (dating to the fourteenth/fifteenth century). The accuracy of the information contained in the *dindshenchas* has become apparent over recent years and has been used most successfully in the study of monuments on Tara Hill, county Meath. Here its accuracy demonstrates that it was based on an intimate knowledge of the monuments, to such an extent that it is considered by one scholar of early Ireland as 'tantamount to a medieval survey of the hill'.[9] Similarly, prehistoric and potential early historic sites in the Bend of the Boyne have been pinpointed using this source, notably the site of the House of Cleitech at Rossnaree and the Breasts of Morrigan at passage tombs K and L at Newgrange (see below).[10]

Ó hArtagan's poem 'Brug na Bóinde I' celebrates the pre-Christian warriors who are buried at the Brú, described by the poet as 'the centre of champions'.[11] This poem represents the first historic survey of the Brú in which individual monuments are interpreted in the light of traditional mythology. In the first part, the poem describes the graves of particular individuals still visible at the time of writing and then proceeds to list individuals known to have been buried there. The graves of the latter were not visible during his time. A further *dindshenchas* poem, 'Brug na Bóinde II' by Macnia Mac Oengusa, is preserved in the *Book of Leinster* (c.1160). In the first stanza, the author asks the nobles of Brega if they know the story of 'every lord that is here in the Brug of Mac ind Oc'.[12] The author, Ó hArtagan, is familiar with the area and the location of the individual graves. He begins his inventory from the top of a ridge ('above your stead') and works downhill to the riverside.[13] The poem describes sixteen sites in the *Brug* which lie in the immediate vicinity of Newgrange. Another 'inventory style' version of the *dindshenchas* for the *Brug* is in the *Book of Ballymote*.[14]

These sources describe the topography of Newgrange. The lush pastoral landscape of the Boyne Valley is introduced in an opening stanza:

> Every bright wonder hath adorned thee,
> O clear shining plain with scores of hosts,
> O lucent land of grass and waggons,
> O virgin mead of birds and islands![15]

The references to 'trág na Ros na rig' and 'a barc brainech' ('where the sea-tide visits your stead') suggest that there was a shoreline below Newgrange and that the Boyne was tidal as far as Rossnaree at this time.[16] This would place the ford (*áth*) at Rossnaree at the tidal limit, making it the most easterly crossing point on the Boyne.[17] The Slige Midluachra took advantage of this fact and it is also possible that the Vikings utilised this shore (see below).

'Brug na Bóinde I' describes another riverine feature, the location of which has a bearing on St Patrick's movements in the area. *Lind Féic na Fian* (the pool of Fiacc of the warriors) lies west of Newgrange.

Table 1 Frequently used topographical terms in *Dindshenchas Erenn*[18]			
Bárc	Ship, boat-shaped structure	*Lecht*	Grave, tomb
Carn	Mound, hillock	*Lia*	Pillar, standing stone
Comad	Grave		
Duma	Barrow, mound	*Lige*	Grave, flat burial place
Fán	Slope, depression, hollow	*Múr*	Wall, rampart
		Ráith	Earthen fort, rath
Fert	Mound	*Suide*	Seat
Forad	Mound, platform	*Tech*	House, dwelling

Table 2
Sites mentioned in *Dindshenchas* for *Brug*

'Brug na Bóinde I'	'Brug na Bóinde II'	Book of Ballymote Stanza 1	Book of Ballymote Stanza 2	SMR No.
Tech Mic ind Óc	Sid (i mBruig Míc ind Óc) (Lies on the valley floor)	Lecht in Dagda	Imdae in Dagda cetamur	Newgrange passage tomb 19:45
Ingen Foraind		Long ingine Foraind		Circular mound 19:58
Lind Féic na Fian (west of Newgrange)				Rossnaree
In ben mor, in Dagda donn	Imdai nDagdai deirg (on the slope)			
Lecht in Máthai	Matha's (cairn, duma ndur)	Lecht in Matae	Duma na Cnamh	Newgrange U passage tomb 19:51
Liac budi báin (Boadain)	Finn's Seat		Liag Buidi	
Fertai na Fáilenn				
Cellach's (grave)	Lecht Cellaig		Lecht Cellaigh	
Barc brainech	Sea tide visits your stead			
Crimthainn Nia's (grave)		Barc Crimthaind Nianair		
Niall's (grave)				
Fintan Feradach's (grave)				
Tuathal Techtmar's (grave)				
Fedelmed Rechtach's the lawgiver's (grave)	Fert Fedelmid Rechtmaid, the lawgiver			
Conn Cét-Chatach's (grave)	Carn ail (stone cairn) Cuinn Cet-Cathaig			
Cormac's (grave) tráig ic Ros na Rig				
Cairpre Lifechair's (grave)	Cumot (commensurate stone) Cairbre Lifeachair			
Fiachu Sraptine's (grave)		Fulacht Fiachach Sraiptine		
Muiredach Tírech's (grave)				
	Dá Cích rígnai (West of fairy mansion)	Mur na Morrigna	Dá Cíc na Morrigna	Newgrange K and L 19:46
	Mac ind Óc ónd áth			Ford of Rossnaree
	Duma Treisc		Duma Tresc	
	Ferta Escláim (path of grace)		Fert Escláim, britheman in Dagda (Fert-Patric-today)	Newgrange cursus and mound 19:45
	Derc mBuailc		Derc m-Buailc m-Oic	
	Lecht Gabra ind ríg	Lecht gabra Cinaoda		
	Currel na mná		Da cnoc-Cirr and Cuirrell, mna in Dagda	
	Aed Lurgneich's (grave) hillslope		Ferta Aedha Luirgneigh	
	Carcar ind Léith imbái in Líath		Carcar Léith Machae	
	Glend i mbíd Mátha		Glenn in Matae	
	Caiseal nOengussa		Caisel Aengusa	Newgrange henge 26:06
			Firt m-Bóinne mna Nechtain	
	Lecc Bend (Mátha killed)		Lecc Benn	Dowth standing stone D 19:53

I see the clear pool of Fiacc of the warriors
west of you [Newgrange] – not feeble the deed –
till the day of Doom – mighty boast –
shall he abide on the slope of the royal rath.[19]

This pool is named after Fiacc who is mentioned in the saga *Cath Ruis na Ríg* (see below). In *Agallamh na Seanórach*, *Linn Féic* is situated on 'the bright-streaming Boyne'.[20] If this is the same Fiacc commemorated in *Ferta fer Féic*, this would indeed suggest a location near the ford at Rossnaree, making it the same pool which is termed Linn Ross in the annals (AU 842).

There is some consistency between the three versions of the *dindshenchas* for the *brug*. The inventory of sites in 'Brug na Bóinde II' is almost identical to those listed in the second stanza of the later *Book of Ballymote*. Some sites, such as the primary monument (Newgrange passage tomb) and the grave of Matha (probably Newgrange U), are repeated in all versions. The association of Newgrange with Dagda is repeated in numerous early tales. According to a story in the eleventh-century *Book of Lecan*,

The Dagda built a great mound for himself and his three sons, Aengus, Aed and Cermaid. It was

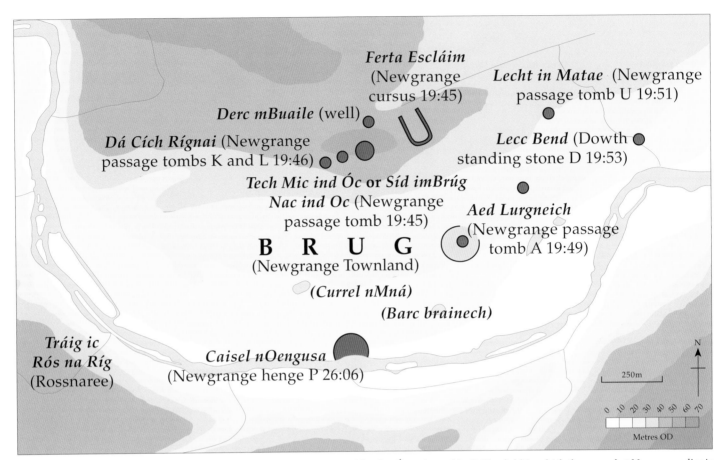

Ferta Escláim
(Newgrange
cursus 19:45)

Lecht in Matae (Newgrange
passage tomb U 19:51)

Derc mBuaile (well)

Dá Cích Rígnai (Newgrange
passage tombs K and L 19:46)

Lecc Bend (Dowth
standing stone D 19:53)

Tech Mic ind Óc or Síd imBrúg
Nac ind Oc (Newgrange
passage tomb 19:45)

Aed Lurgneich
(Newgrange passage
tomb A 19:49)

B R U G
(Newgrange Townland)

(Currel nMná)

(Barc brainech)

Tráig ic
Rós na Ríg
(Rossnaree)

Caisel nOengusa
(Newgrange henge P 26:06)

250m

Metres OD

0 10 20 30 40 50 60 70

Fig. 5   Conjectural map of places mentioned in the vicinity of Brug in *Dindshenchas Érenn* (see table 4). The field in which the mound at Newgrange lies is called Breo Park and in the immediate vicinity are Breo House, Breo Lock and the Ford of Brow. Indeed these place names all lie within the vicinity of the present townland of Newgrange suggesting that the pre-Norman name for this townland was in fact Brug.

Fig. 6   The denuded remains of a passage tomb south of Newgrange (Site U). This may be the 'grave of Matha' as described in *Dindshenchas*.

Fig. 7 Two standing stones are mentioned in 'Brug na Bóinde I' and 'Brug na Bóinde II' and there are two standing stones south of Newgrange. The linkage is likely but not certain. A) The standing stone in Newgrange townland overlooks the River Boyne (left) and a passage tomb (right). B) Standing stone in Dowth adjacent to the townland boundary with Newgrange.

upon these four men that the men of Erin made the Síd of the Brug.[21]

The two mounds associated with Morrigan are repeated in three versions and have been identified as the passage tombs Newgrange Sites K and L on the basis of locational detail given in the poems:

Behold the two breasts of the king's consort
here beyond the mound west of the fairy mansion:
the spot where Cermait the fair was born,
behold it on the way, not a far step.[22]

These *dindshenchas* texts describe morphologically different types of sites including cairns, mounds and standing stones. This range of sites is visible within the townland of Newgrange today but one cannot match existing monuments and *dindshenchas* references with precision. For example, the *Ferta Escláim* ('the path of grace') could refer to the cursus at Newgrange:

The trench of Esclam, pilgrimage revered,
where good men used to cast questions:
a sward with a brave portion, a deed without
   concealment,
for the son of Calpurn it was a path of grace.[23]

The *dindshenchas* also mentions monuments in the Newgrange area which have not been identified. A fulacht fiadh is associated in one poem with Fiacha Sraibhtine, an individual who also received an annalistic entry in AFM 276, and there are two references to boat-shaped burial mounds which could describe Viking burials.[24] None of these features are identifiable in today's landscape.

The topographical descriptions of *brug* contained in these poems refer to a limited area in the immediate environs of Newgrange. The *brug* as a place name still lingers, in somewhat corrupted forms, in that townland only. The field in which the mound at Newgrange lies is called Breo Park and in its immediate vicinity lie Breo House, Breo Lock (on the canal) and the Ford of Brow.[25] The Ford of Brow was still described as such in eighteenth-century estate maps (see chapter 7). The fact that all these place names lie within the townland boundary testifies to the antiquity of this territorial unit. It must also mean that the townland was called Brug before it came into the ownership of the monks at Mellifont in the twelfth century. However, since Wilde in 1849, this term has been falsely applied to the greater Bend of the Boyne area.[26] This inaccuracy has found its way into popular literature and common usage and cannot now be rectified.

There is a separate *dindshenchas* for Cnogba (Knowth), Cleitech (Rossnaree) and Dubad (Dowth). The *dindshenchas* poem for Cnogba associates the mound with Englec, the daughter of Elcmar, two individuals not associated with *Brug*.[27] The correct Irish name is Cnogba, interpreted as *Cnoc Bua* in *dindshenchas*. However, it has been argued that the true root is more likely to be *Cnoc Buí* (the yellow hill) but that the eleventh-century author consciously sought to associate the burial mound with the Celtic hag and local

Fig. 8   The *dindshenchas* for Dowth explains how it got its name, and suggests how the site was constructed and by whom.

mother-goddess Bua. She is associated with many megalithic tombs and presented as a builder of megaliths in Early Irish lore.[28] What is more significant about this *dindshenchas* is the wooded landscape in which Cnogba lies. Its environs provided *le cnód cró-deaga* (blood-red nuts) for Oengus and his band.[29] There is still deciduous woodland below Knowth at Crewbane, a designated Natural Heritage Area. Cnogba's position 'in the midst of Brega', an association not highlighted in the Newgrange poems, could be an oblique acknowledgement of Knowth's status as a royal site.[30] The poem for Cnogba also includes an origin tale for the passage tomb at Dowth.

Dubad (Dowth), or Cnoc Dubada (also termed Ferta Cuile) is described in the *Dindshenchas*, providing an explanation for its name:

> All the men of Erin were gathered from every quarter … to build a tower like the tower of Nimrod… His sister came to him, and told him that she would stay the sun's course in the sky, so that they might have an endless day to accomplish their task… Night came upon them, for the maiden's magic was spoiled … 'since darkness has fallen upon our work, and night has come on and the day is done, let each depart to his place. Dubad (darkness) shall be the name of this place for ever'.[31]

The text also describes Dowth's original flat-topped mound, like the mound at Newgrange, prior to its conversion to a motte in the twelfth century. Perhaps the Normans represent the 'doom' prophesised in the poem:[32]

> When it was no longer day for them thereafter
> (it is likely that it was night),
> the hill was not brought to the top,

the men of Erin depart homeward.
From that day forth the hill remains
without addition to its height:
it shall not grow greater from this time onward
till the Doom of destruction and judgement.[33]

The *dindshenchas* poem for Cleitech (Rossnaree) describes it as 'the top of all houses in Erin'. Although the poem does not associate this site directly with the Boyne, other sources allow Cleitech to be more precisely located. The poem recounts events recorded in the annals which, in turn, place the site on the river:[34]

> After Muircheartach (Mac Erca), son of Muirea-dhach, son of Eoghan, had been twenty-four years in the sovereignty of Ireland, he was burned in the house of Cleitech, over the Boyne, on the night of Samhain, after being drowned in wine. (AFM 527)

A late-fourteenth- early-fifteenth-century reference indicates that Cleitech lay near the *Síd in Broga* (Newgrange) and opposite Knowth. The 'Courting of Emer' from the Cuchulain cycle places Cleitech south of the river near Newgrange. Lastly, in a passage on the death of Muireadhach, Cleitech is near a glen close to Rossnaree.

Identifying the homes and settlements of Iron Age communities is notoriously difficult.[35] The meagre evidence from outside the Bend of the Boyne suggests that we should be looking for the remains of small, timber-built hut sites. The possibility that tent-like structures were used is raised by the discovery of wooden pegs in association with an Iron Age road at Corlea, county Longford.[36] Certainly there are frequent references to encampments of pitched tents in the early sagas associated with the Boyne. In the saga *Cath Ruis na Rig,* for instance, Conchobor Mac Nessa

Fig. 9   Topographical details from *dindshenchas* point to the present site of Rossnaree House as the location of Cleitech, a residence of the kings of Tara. The plateau overlooking Newgrange on which Rossnaree House now stands fulfils all the locational requirements as set out in the poems.[37]

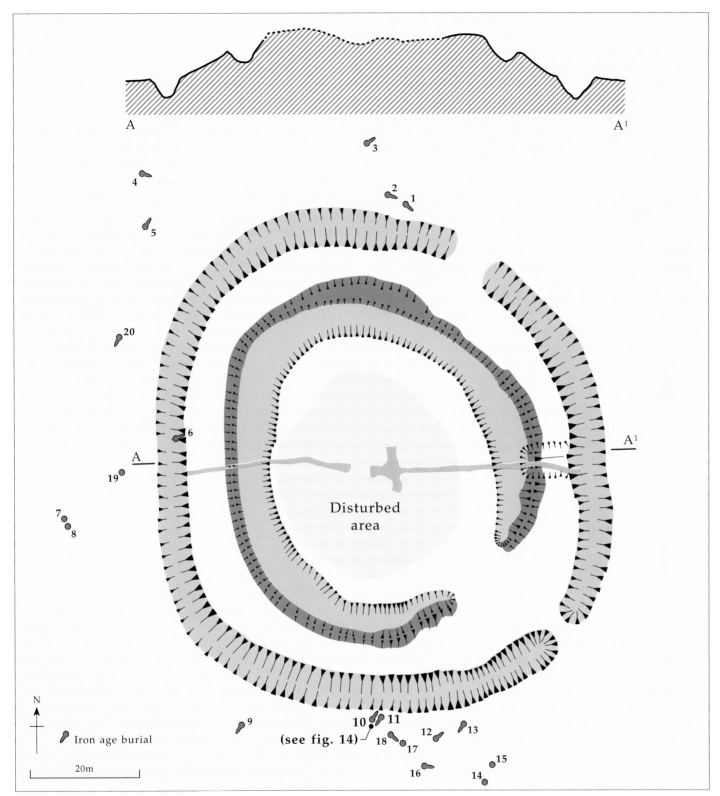

A   A¹

A   A¹

Disturbed
area

N

Iron age burial

20m

(see fig. 14)

Fig. 10 Ground plan of early fortifications at Knowth and position of Iron Age burials. At some stage in the first half of the first millennium AD, the main passage tomb mound at Knowth was enclosed by two concentric, pennanular ditches, centred on the summit of the mound, an area 40m in diameter.[38] There was an opening in the south-east. The lower ditch, which enclosed the base of the mound, had silted up by the late eighth/early ninth century when houses and souterrains were built on and inserted into the fill, evidence which offers a *terminus post quem* for its construction. The summit of the mound was damaged early in the last century by quarrying, which removed any structural remains associated with this fortification. Its substantial nature indicates the presence of a large community in the immediate environs of the site. A breakdown of the faunal remains from the ditch fill shows that cattle predominated, followed by pigs and sheep.[39] The range of faunal remains from the Knowth ditch compares broadly with those from the Late Iron Age inauguration site at Dún Ailinne in county Kildare, whose faunal remains have been interpreted as remnants of periodic feasting.[40] The function and dating of this structure at Knowth are by no means certain. It is as likely to represent the initial phase of the Early Christian horizon as it is to be a Late Iron Age fortification.

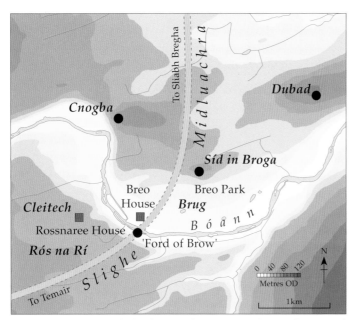

Fig. 11 Mythology in the landscape. Place name evidence substantiated by early documentary sources indicates that the fording point south of Newgrange known as the 'Ford of Brow' (below present day Breo House) was an important Boyne crossing in the Iron Age on a key route between Tara and Ulster. To the north is Síd Cnogba, or the other-world dwelling of Knowth; west is Rossnaree House, on the site of the House of Cleitech, an early residence of the kings of Tara; east is Fert Boadain, the grave of Boadan at Dubad (Dowth); and to the south is Bóann or the Boyne.

orders *'Gníter ár mbotha agus ar mbélscáláin'* ('the tents to be erected') at a *longport* (encampment) at Rossnaree overlooking the Boyne.[41]

Medieval scholars tell us that the kings of Tara were buried at Brú na Bóinne in the Late Iron Age period from the time of Conchubar Mac Nessa until the coming of St Patrick and Christianity. The excavations at Newgrange have not been able to substantiate the traditional claims of these medieval scholars, but a large number of extended burials of Iron Age date accompanied by dice and blue glass beads were revealed at the Knowth excavations. During the Iron Age the main passage tomb mound at Knowth became a fortified site with the digging of defensive ditches which enclosed the site. These were interrupted by a causeway in the south-east.

The *Annals of Ulster* (AU 4209) record the death of Cormac Mac Airt, grandson of Conn Cétchathach in Cleitech Brega, after a salmon bone stuck in his throat. His death is blamed on his turning against the druids and worshipping Christ despite them. This leads to the story (preserved in a twelfth-century text) of the final attempt to bury a king of Tara at the Brú. The tradition is also enshrined in the local place name of Rossnaree (the wood of the kings). According to this tradition, Cormac died at the house of Cleitech. After a careful examination of the topographical details in the story, Cleitech has been identified as the present site of Rossnaree House. Cormac told his people not to bury him at Brú, but his servants were determined to bring him to the place where the kings of Tara had always been buried. We are told that the Boyne river swelled up three times, preventing the bier from crossing. It was then carried down to *Ros na Rí*. This again suggests that the river was tidal up to Rossnaree in the Proto/Early Historic period.

There is a strong local tradition that Cormac's grave was a little mound which lay formerly on a river terrace northeast of Rossnaree House. When this mound was disturbed during the Emergency in the 1940s, the remains of a woman with an infant were found. She was wearing a silver finger ring which has been dated to the sixth century AD. The mode of burial with its accompanying jewellery and covering does not conform to Christian ritual. It may be a Viking burial. This burial is analogous to the inhumation discovered around the main mound at Knowth in cists, aligned east/west but without grave goods.[42]

Iron Age burials in the Bend of the Boyne are in simple unmarked graves, which nevertheless contain impressive grave goods. Excavations at Knowth have revealed thirty-five mostly female inhumations. Thirty-one of these are in pits, four in cists, with extended, crouched (the majority), and disturbed human remains.[43] These burials were found around the main mound and a number were actually placed in the passage tombs.[44] One undated burial was found in the bottom of the outer pennanular ditch. Carbon 14 dates between 190BC and AD250 have been established in four instances, but there are also later dates.[45] The most notable of these inhumations was a double burial of adult males, both decapitated, who were laid head to toe, accompanied by a number of gaming pieces and bronze

Fig. 12 An Emergency era pillbox (1939–45) was inserted into 'Cormac's grave' at Rossnaree. In the process, a burial was uncovered, dated to the sixth century on the basis of a silver ring found on the woman's hand.

Fig. 13   Die of polished bone found with the burials in figure 14.

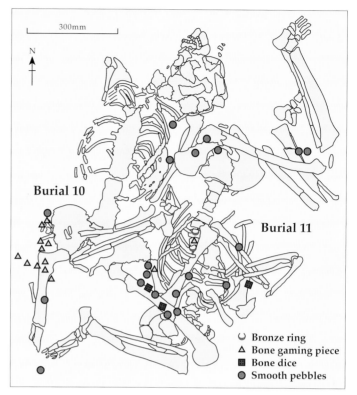

Fig. 14   The sagas contain many descriptions of gamblers and gambling. Iron Age burials at Knowth provide archaeological corroboration. These decapitated remains were accompanied by dice and gaming pieces. Were they beheaded for cheating?

rings, one with Irish engraving.[46] The gaming pieces were made from bone, in three cases horse bone. Small rectangular plaques, the remains of a pegged board game, were also found with this double burial.

Cath Ruis na Ríg for Bóinn, the battle of the Boyne, was the second of two battles of the 'seven years' war' which is said to have been waged before the end of the first century AD.[47] The battlefield is called Rossnaree on the Boyne. Seven different versions of the battle are identified, the earliest contained in the twelfth-century *Book of Leinster*, but the saga is considered pre-Christian in tone and texture.[48] It outlines the triumph of Conchobor mac Nessa and his Ulster warriors over the provinces of the south and west of Ireland. This conflict followed the battle of Táin Bó Cúailnge which resulted in Ulster's loss of the famous Cooley bull to Meadbh, queen of Connacht. After his humiliating defeat, Conchobor Mac Nessa vowed immediate vengeance and sought the assistance of foreign powers and Irish warriors who were warring away from Ireland. Conchobar chose '*cor Ross na Ríg as Bóind bán-solus*' ('above the clear bright Boyne') as the most strategic place to do battle. In one noteworthy incident, Conchobor asks Fiacc to estimate the army from a '*dúin na Bóinne bán-soilsi*' ('fortress of the clear bright Boyne'). This may be a reference to Cleitech. Fiacc crossed the Boyne at the ford of Rossnaree, was chased by the army and fell into a pool where he was drowned. This spot is subsequently identified as Fiacc's Pool.[49] This is the *lind Feic* which is also mentioned in *dindshenchas*. While the topographical detail contained in this saga is limited, Rossnaree was obviously considered a strategic position on the Boyne from which an Ulster army could best attack the southern provinces.[50]

Just prior to and during the early centuries AD, the period which coincides with the Roman occupation in Britain, communities living in the Bend of the Boyne would have had ready access to the Irish Sea, and were geographically well placed to exploit the developing trade with Britain. Contact between mercantile communities on

either side of the Irish Sea had begun towards the end of the Iron Age. The Roman historian Tacitus wrote of Ireland at the end of the first century AD:

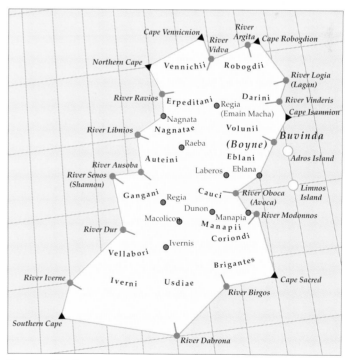

Fig. 15   Claudius Ptolemaius's mid-second-century 'map' showing the location of the river *Bouvinda* (Boyne).

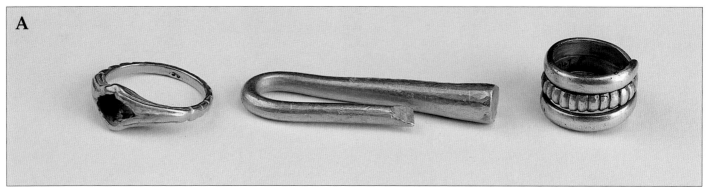

NATIONAL MUSEUM OF IRELAND

Fig. 16   Roman finds from Newgrange. A) Finger rings and the end of a torc. B) Portion of a side link of a bronze bridal bit through which a ring would have passed. C) Disc brooch of cast bronze with a gilded face. D) Assemblage of gold coins found at Newgrange. These were placed in front of the tomb as votive offerings by visitors from Roman Britain.

The interior parts are little known but through commercial intercourse and the merchants there is better knowledge of the harbours and approaches.[51]

Fig. 17   Locations where Roman material has been discovered. The area of the east coast between the Liffey and the Boyne has been identified as the key contact point with the Roman world.[52]

The Boyne valley or *Bouvinda* has been positively identified in Claudius Ptolemaius's mid-second-century survey of the known world. This document, based largely on information gleaned from Roman merchants, located rivers, lakes, capes, tribes and population centres by degrees of longitude and latitude. A map of Ireland has been reconstructed from coordinates given in his work.[53]

Boats used by merchants travelling the inland waters of the Boyne were presumably similar to the early Roman boat found in Lough Lene, county Westmeath. This was a slender, flat-bottomed boat with steep sides, built of planks held together with tenons, mortices and pegs.[54] On the basis of its unusual mode of construction, this vessel is considered to be either a Roman import or a boat built by someone from the Mediterranean ship-building tradition. Its construction suggests a date of not later than the fourth century AD.

Artefactual evidence for contact with Roman Britain has been identified from the two major excavations at Knowth and Newgrange. Roman finds from Knowth include a piece of Samian ware; a rim-sherd of Central Gaulish manufacture of Antonine age (*c.*AD138); a toilet implement of bronze which may be a ligula (a spoon used for extracting cosmetics out of a jar); and two tweezers of Romano-British style (one bronze, one iron).[55]

At this time the entrance to Newgrange passage tomb would not have been visible and the collapsed mound extended to surround the base of the outer stone circle. A traveller or pilgrim would have seen a high, flat-topped mound with sloping sides.[56] To judge from the prestigious offerings deposited there, Newgrange was venerated as a shrine by pilgrims of high social status over a prolonged period from the first to the late fourth century AD.[57] Roman coins of high value and personal ornaments of silver and gold, including finger rings, brooches, glass beads and earrings, were placed as votive offerings in front of the main tomb at Newgrange in the neighbourhood of the three tall stones of the stone circle.

The most likely explanation for these Newgrange deposits is that they were gifts from Romano-British traders, offering homage to the local (Irish) gods.[58] The objects also include specimens of recognisably native British workmanship such as disc brooches. There are a few native Irish objects, such as a bronze bridle bit and a strap loop with La Tène design.[59] Newgrange was a focus of devotion for both foreigners and natives, possibly members of a warrior caste.[60] Such practices were occurring at other temple sites and early burial mounds (such as West Kennet long barrow) in Roman Britain and Ireland. However, the high value of the offerings left at Newgrange is unprecedented.[61] Newgrange, unique for its passage grave elaboration as a solar observatory, retained a special sacred position into the Iron Age. It never became a focus of domestic settlement, unlike Dowth and Knowth.[62]

The Bend of the Boyne also lay astride a major overland route, a highway between Tara and Ulster known in early medieval 'place-lore' as the *Slighe Midluachra*.[63] This highway crossed the Boyne by the ford of Brow (Brú) just below Newgrange and near the old Rossnaree mill. Early texts trace its route from Tara to Ulster via the ford of Newgrange (Brug Meic an Oigh), Rossnaree (Dubhros), and on to Sliabh Bregha near Mellifont.[64] The discovery of a bronze bridle bit from Newgrange and horse bones at Knowth suggests that some of the traffic on this route was horse drawn.[65]

EARLY CHRISTIAN LAND USE

Controversy and uncertainty surround the accounts of St Patrick's early mission into this part of Ireland. A large body of vernacular prose and poetry highlights ideological conflict in the transitional period from paganism to Christianity. When the story of Patrick came to be written,

Fig. 18   Du Noyer's 1867 depiction of Erc's tomb in the graveyard on the Hill of Slane. Patrick is said to have ordained Erc as the first bishop of Slane. This house-shaped shrine is a typical tomb type for a prominent religious figure in the Early Christian period.

Table 3
Early Christian ecclesiastical sites
in the Bend of the Boyne

Location	Site type	SMR No.	Land use
Dowth	Church site	20:19	Pasture
Dowth	Holy well	—	Pasture
Knowth	Inhumations	19:30	Excavated
Rossnaree	Burial mound	19:59	Pasture
Rossnaree	Church site	NPL	
Stalleen	Holy well	—	Pasture
Stalleen	Inhumations	27:01	Pasture

DÚCHAS/CON BROGAN

Fig. 19 Slane Hill is traditionally associated with the beginning of Patrick's Christian mission in Ireland. According to the Annals, there was a major monastic centre on the hill with its own bell house (round tower?), high cross and wooden church. The remains on the hill today date from the later medieval period.

the Boyne Valley was chosen as the location for its symbolic if not actual beginning. According to the *Annals of Ulster*, Patrick arrived in 432:

> Patrick arrived in Ireland in the ninth year of the reign of Theodosius the Less and in the first year of the episcopate of Xistus, 42nd bishop of the Roman church. So Bede, Marcellinus and Isidore compute in their chronicles.

For the earliest descriptions of his arrival in Ireland, we are largely dependent on two texts from the second half of the seventh century, Muirchú's *Life of Patrick*, a saga text dealing with Patrick's initial activity in Ireland, and Tirechan's *Collectanea*, a collection of traditions and origin legends about churches which claimed to have been founded by Patrick.[66] According to Muirchú, Patrick and his followers landed at *Inbher Colpi,* at the mouth of the Boyne:

> They left their boat and went by foot to that great plain. In the evening they at last arrived at *Ferta fer Feic*, the burial place of the men of Fiacc ... There they pitched their tents, and then Patrick with his companions duly offered Easter to God.[67]

The location of *Fertae fer Feic* has usually been associated with the hill of Slane 3km west of the Bend of the Boyne. This identification first appears in the work of John Colgan in the seventeenth century which he based on an annalistic reference in AFM 512 recording the death of Erc of Slane, bishop of Lilcach and Ferta fer Feic.[68] However, this identification has been subsequently questioned.[69] Slane was never mentioned in the accounts of the early lives and there is no archaeological or historical evidence that Slane was then an important site.[70] The absence of evidence for the link with Slane draws attention to a fifteenth-century reference which places *Fertae fer Feic* south of the Boyne and west of a hill known as (the as yet unidentified) *Síd Truim*.[71]

Since *Ferta fer Fiacc* is most likely near Rossnaree in the Bend of the Boyne, it is possible that the Paschal fire could have been lit in the Bend of the Boyne.[72] There is an intriguing reference linking Patrick with Newgrange. *Fert-Patric* in the *dindshenchas* of *Brug* (Newgrange) contained in

the *Book of Ballymote* states: 'The grave of Esclam, the Dagda's brehon, which is called now *Fert-Patric'*.[73] The environs of Knowth and Newgrange were well established in the early centuries AD; this could make them a likely attraction for Patrick's mission, but could just as easily have kept him away from this pre-Christian centre of population. A factor against the association of these events with Slane is the surprising failure of the *dindshenchas* for *Slaine* to mention its association with Patrick or *Fertae fer Fiacc*.[74] Although Slane is the more prominent hill from which a fire could be seen from Tara, the Bend of the Boyne cannot be ruled out as the location of Patrick's first Easter in Ireland, on the basis of the written evidence.

Whether or not Slane Hill is the site of the enigmatic *Ferta fer Feic*, Slane indisputably developed very early as a major monastic centre. Because the Bend of the Boyne forms part of the original parish of Slane, and because Slane became its most important ecclesiastical site during the Early Christian period, it is appropriate to discuss the archaeology and history of this site and then examine the evidence for Early Christian ecclesiastical sites within the confines of the Bend of the Boyne. The oldest feature on Slane Hill today is the house-shaped shrine in the graveyard associated with St Erc (d. 512 or 514) whom Patrick made Bishop of Slane.[75] This shrine is comprised of two large opposing triangular-shaped standing stones. In Ireland and Britain, house-shaped shrines made of stone, wood or metal were common in the Early Christian period. In the seventh century, Bede described the shrine of St Chad in St Peter's Cathedral, Lichfield as a wooden

GERALDINE STOUT

Fig. 20 Annalistic evidence indicates an Early Christian foundation at Dowth. The holy well at Dowth – *Tobar Seannachain* – supports this contention. Remains of the early church may have been incorporated in the nearby Later Medieval church.

coffin in the shape of a 'little house'.[76] The record of Erc's death is an indication of the prominence of Slane. Patrick had reputedly made Erc the first bishop of Slane and his conversion is described in both the Muirchú and Tirechan *Lives*. Subsequently, the foundation at Slane blossomed and was adopted as the main religious centre for the local dynasty, the Síl nAedo Sláine (the seed – offspring – of Aed of Slane) with whom it was closely associated from the seventh century. There are frequent entries to the monastery at *Slaine* in both the *Annals of Ulster* and the *Annals of the Four Masters*. The taking on tour of the relics of St Erc of Slaine was recorded in AU 775, as is their arrival at the 'city' of Tailtiú in AU 784. The annals record the deaths of bishops, stewards and lectors from the monastery at Slane, and from the ninth to the eleventh centuries, they highlight a series of attacks on the monastery.[77] In one attack, Slane's bell house, high cross and wooden church were seriously damaged:

During the plundering of foreigners, the cross which was on the green at Slane was broken up in the air: it was broken and divided, so that part of its top reached Tailteann and Finn Abhair-Abha [Fennor].[78]

This entry has been corroborated by recent discoveries. A cross fragment embedded in the wall of St Patrick's church on the Hill of Slane and a cross head found at Fennor are possibly from the same cross.[79] Westropp (1901) states that 'fragments (of a cross) with interlacings, are set in another house in the village' of Slane.[80] The location of this fragment is currently unknown.

Slane was undoubtedly the main ecclesiastical centre in the area, but there were smaller ecclesiastical sites in the Bend of the Boyne, certainly at Dowth, and possibly at Stalleen, Rossnaree and Monknewtown. There is evidence for cemeteries of Early Christian date at Stalleen and Knowth. These provide some indication of the rapid spread of religious communities in the valley. The intriguing reference to the slaying of Oengus, *airchennach* (monastic manager) of Slane, by the *airchennach* of Dubad (Dowth) (AU 1012) indicates that there was a pre-Norman church at Dowth. The *Annals of the Four Masters* also list this church at Dowth amongst those burnt by Diarmait Mac Murchada in 1170. Further documentary evidence for an early foundation at Dowth is found in a twelfth-century missal. Known as the Dowth Missal, this book belonged to the Proudfoots of nearby Proudfootstown. It is also known as St Shengan's Book.[81] St Shengan is associated with a 'sheela na gig' (exhibitionist figure) on the exterior of the south wall of the present medieval church at Dowth. The holy well at Dowth was called Tobar Seannachain. St Shengan may be 'St Senchan', thought to have been the ecclesiastic responsible for recording the Táin Bó Cúailnge saga in the middle of the twelfth century.[82] The present medieval church at Dowth presumably replaced the Early Christian foundation. A number of recycled architectural fragments have been identified in the make-up of the church, including a Hiberno-Romanesque pilaster in the gatepost of the graveyard, and a worn arch stone used as a step.[83] A holy well near the medieval church at Dowth is known today as St Bernard's well. It was probably another element of this early foundation.[84]

The Ordnance Survey Letters for county Meath contain information relating to antiquities observed during the progress of the survey in 1836. The OS letters record:

A holy well called Tober san Mana which the people speaking English call St Anne's well. There was a pattern day in the 5th of July which is St Maine day.[85]

Fig. 21 The Bend of the Boyne formed part of the *mór tuath* (over-kingdom) of Brega. In the seventh century, the kings of northern Brega had their centre at Knowth.

This holy well in the townland of Stalleen might indicate the former existence of an early ecclesiastical site. Two slab-lined burials were discovered on the summit of a ridge south of the River Boyne in this same townland in the mid-1930s, during work for a new reservoir for Drogheda Corporation. One of these burials lay on a paved floor. They were both extended and oriented east/west in the form consistent with Early Christian practice.[86]

The OS Letters recount the tradition that St Columkille erected a church at Ros na Righ and prayed there for the soul of his great ancestor who opposed the religion of pagans. This tradition is perhaps based on Céitinn's account of the burial of Cormac Mac Airt at Rossnaree.[87] This site may be Cormac's grave where the remains of a woman and child were found in the 1940s (see above).[88]

Lastly, a holy well at Monknewtown, called *Tobar Sratha Baine*, is near the ruins of the medieval church. This is thought to be associated with the Early Christian saint

Baran or Barrind. The pattern day for this well was the first Sunday in August, establishing it as a Lughnasa site and suggesting pre-Christian devotion at the well. St Barrind has two feast days, 21 May and 8 November, neither of which is observed today.[89]

In the Early Christian period, the lower Boyne valley formed part of the over-kingdom or *mór tuath* of Brega, a territory which comprised much of the present county of Meath and north county Dublin. This was one of a number of petty kingdoms within the territory of the southern Uí Néill.[90] By this time, Irish society was divided into a series of petty kingdoms each ruled by a dominant dynasty. The territory of the southern Uí Néill was ruled by at least eight different dynasties claiming descent from Niall of the nine hostages, but the Síl nAed Sláine and the Clann Cholmáin became most dominant and great rivals.[91] The kingdom of Brega came to be ruled by the Aed Sláine dynasty, who rose to prominence in the late sixth and early seventh centuries as over-kings of Mide. In AD688 the kingdom was split into two kingdoms: northern Brega, centred at Knowth, and southern Brega, centred at Lagore Crannog. On several occasions, the kings of northern Brega are styled kings of Cnogba (Knowth). They had their royal centre at or near the passage tomb at Knowth and specifically gave themselves the title '*Rí Cnogba*'.[92]

The first annalistic reference to a king of Knowth is in AU 789: 'Gormgal, son of Eladach, rex Cnodhbai [king of Knowth] died'. Gormgal was of the Gailenga tribe who were widely spread through Meath and north county Dublin. They represented the main substratum of population of the Síl nAed Sláine under the Uí Néill

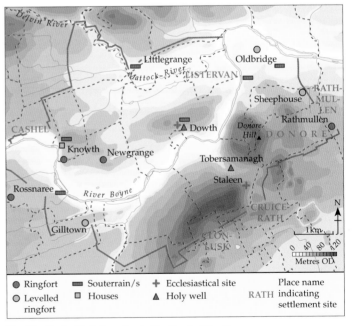

Fig. 22 Early Christian sites in the Bend of the Boyne.

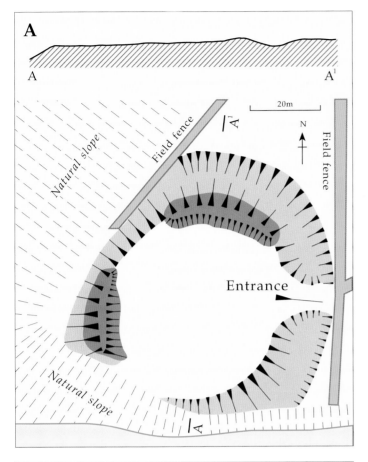

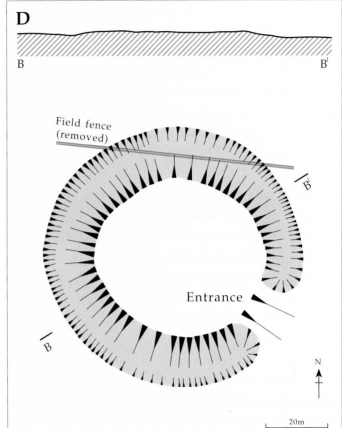

Fig. 23   The ringfort at Knowth (A) is located in a field below the passage tomb cemetery, at the edge of a ravine above the Boyne (B). It comprises a circular earthen fortification with a deep enclosing ditch outside and imposing inner earthen bank (C). It holds a commanding position over the countryside to the north-west and to the south, and must have helped to defend the river crossing into the ancient territory of Brega. The ringfort in the townland of Newgrange lies on the summit of a low ridge under pasture to the north of the main passage tomb (D, E). The ringforts at Knowth and Newgrange are the most impressive of the enclosed farmsteads in the Bend of the Boyne, and their relatively large dimensions suggest that the occupants had a high status within early Irish society.

Fig. 24 Vertical photographs taken in 1991 revealed traces of buried enclosures appearing as crop marks in tillage fields. This site, south of the Boyne in the townland of Gilltown, is a levelled ringfort with an annex adjoining its northern section.

Table 4
Ringforts in the Bend of the Boyne

Location	Site type	SMR No.	Land use
Gilltown	Enclosure (site)	26:22	Tillage
Gilltown	Enclosure (site)	26:23	Tillage
Knowth	Ringfort	19:38	Pasture
Newgrange	Ringfort	19:39	Pasture
Oldbridge	Enclosure (site)	20:03	Tillage
Rathmullan	Ringfort	20:21	Pasture
Sheephouse	Enclosure (site)	20:08	Tillage

dynasts of Brega. Up to AD818, when the death of Cernach Mac Congalaig, 'rex Cnodbai', is recorded, Cnogba was in the hands of the Gailenga. In the ninth century the Síl nAed Sláine made alliances with the Norse against the Clann Cholmáin. Maelmithig Mac Flannacáin became a powerful over-king in AD918, as did his son, Congalach Cnogba, in the mid-tenth century.[93] The period of their reign coincides with a major resettlement phase at the main mound at Knowth.

During this period, the settlement pattern was strictly rural and was dominated by the dispersed protected farmsteads known as ringforts, associated with a dairy farming economy.[94] Until at least the ninth century, the bulk of the population lived in ringforts, many of which are still traceable in the fields north and south of the Boyne. Townland names such as Cashel and Donore probably testify to the presence of further examples, now destroyed, as does the place name 'Listiveran' recorded in an eighteenth-century deed.[95] Within the Bend of the Boyne, there are three upstanding ringforts at Knowth, Newgrange and Rathmullan. In the tilled fields south of the Boyne, the ringforts have been mostly levelled and appear as cropmarks in aerial photographs taken at very dry times of the year. Four levelled examples appear as cropmarks in Gilltown, Oldbridge and Sheephouse. None of the upstanding or ploughed out ringforts have been excavated.

In general, ringforts in this area are on the summit of ridges, univallate, with artificially raised interiors. The latter feature is probably an adaptation to a low-lying landscape.[96] All ringforts here are of earthen construction, with entrances in the east. They vary in size from the largest at Knowth (63m in internal diameter), to New-grange (53m) and Rathmullan (40m). Their dimensions are

larger than the average for ringforts in Ireland, but low-lying areas like county Meath tend to have fewer but larger examples.[97]

The excavations of the main passage tomb at Knowth have provided extensive evidence for nucleated, unenclosed housing towards the end of the Early Christian period. The wide range of both artefactual and structural evidence recovered from this excavation facilitates a more holistic insight into one high-status early historic community in the Bend of the Boyne, albeit a very unusual one. This complex has been dated to the eighth century AD onwards, but the finds (including bone combs, pins, coins and querns) indicate a late-ninth- to twelfth-century date range. This coincides with its probable use as a royal residence (see above).[98]

Numerous houses and souterrains were built into the prehistoric mound. On the west side of the mound at Knowth, houses were constructed on top of the filled-in Iron Age ditch. Both entrances of the eastern and western tombs were remodelled and incorporated into a veritable labyrinth of souterrains. Their builders were literate and inscribed Irish lettering on the chamber stones of the eastern passage.[99]

Fig. 25 Approaching the upper beehive chamber at Dowth. Communities living at Dowth would have fled to these hidden chambers during Viking attacks or other lightning raids.

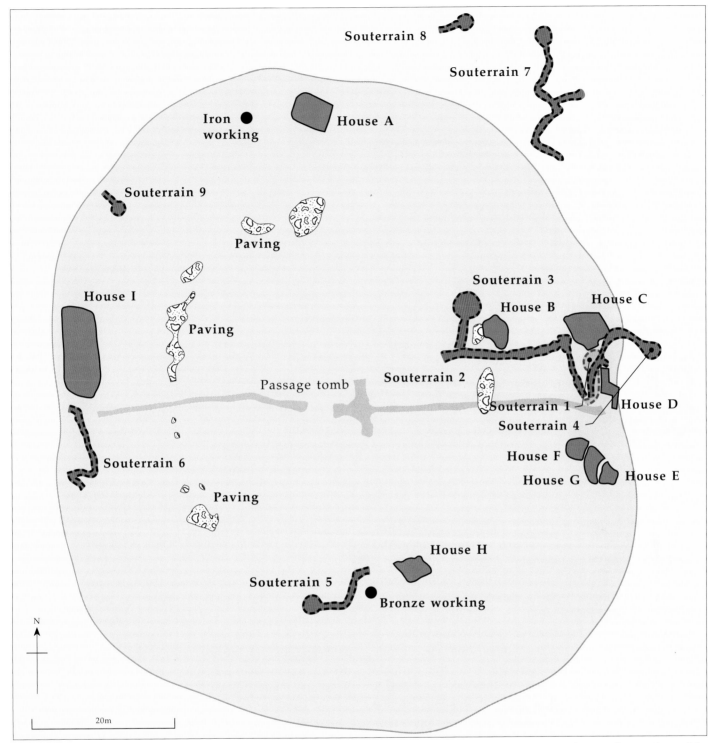

Souterrain 8

Souterrain 7

Iron ● working   House A

Souterrain 9

Paving

House I

Paving

Souterrain 3

House B   House C

Passage tomb   Souterrain 2

Souterrain 1   House D
Souterrain 4

House F   House E
House G

Souterrain 6

Paving

House H

Souterrain 5   ●
Bronze working

N

20m

Fig. 26   Thirteen timber houses, rectangular in plan, with paved floors, and nine souterrains were constructed on and in the immediate environs of the prehistoric mound. A souterrain is an underground passage constructed with drystone walling and capped with large stone lintels. These structures can consist of a variety of passages, chambers and constrictions. The unequalled density of these souterrains underlines the status and value of Knowth.

A range of industrial activities took place on the site, including the manufacture of combs, pins and fibulae from antler, ox and pig bone.[100] The discovery of part of a tuyère (or furnace) indicates that bronze was cast here. The presence of iron slag and furnace casts shows that iron was smelted as well.[101] Iron was used to make ringed pins, stick pins, pins and needles for sewing, horse-shoe nails and bridle bits. A rough-out for a grindstone and a reshaped quern show that a stone-cutter was present within this Early Christian community.[102]

Faunal remains of cattle, sheep and pigs were found, but animal bones on these rural sites cannot be

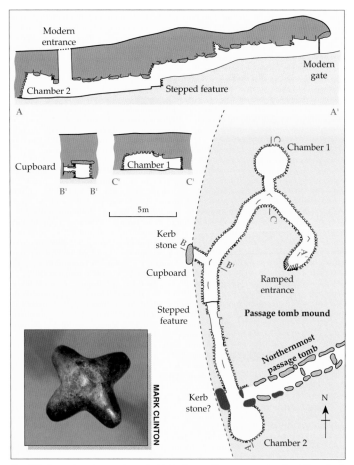

Fig. 27 A souterrain was inserted into the earlier passage tomb at Dowth. It has two beehive chambers, typical of souterrains within the kingdom of Brega. Inset shows a stone button found during the nineteenth-century 'excavations' at Dowth souterrain.

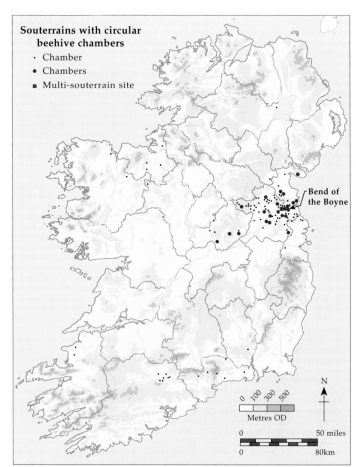

Fig. 28 The souterrains found in the Boyne valley are those with beehive chambers, a type of chamber that occurs in a tight cluster approximately corresponding to the kingdom of Brega. The Bend of the Boyne also lies in the midst of a marked concentration of souterrains (with a variety of chambers) in Meath, Westmeath, south Louth and north Dublin. The northern demarcation of the group is delimited by the rivers Dee and Inny while the Liffey and the northern borders of the ancient kingdom of Leinster mark its southern parameters.[107]

automatically assumed to represent produce of that farm, as agricultural produce was exchanged between nobles and commoners in order to maintain clientship.[103] Wheat and oats, ground on rotary querns, also featured in the Knowth diet. The presence of oyster, scallop and whelk shells shows that the local inhabitants also availed of the resources of the nearby coastline.[104] This concentration of underground artificial passages and houses in a prehistoric mound is unparalleled in Ireland, with the possible exception of Dowth and a site at Cabragh near Tara.[105] Certain similarities also exist between Knowth and the dense concentration of souterrains at Marshes Upper, near Dundalk, county Louth, where excavations produced a similar range of domestic and personal objects, faunal remains and querns.[106] That said, it is just as likely that Knowth is unique; it lay in a cultural zone where souterrains were preferred to ringforts, as well as being a wealthy and significant royal site.

A similar arrangement of souterrains on a passage tomb is evident at Dowth. A souterrain opening into the earlier passage tomb at Dowth North was discovered by a Board

of Works inspector in the early 1880s. Isolated souterrains are relatively numerous elsewhere in the Bend of the Boyne. There are two at Oldbridge and one at Rossnaree on the south side of the river, and the most recent discovery is at Sheepgrange on the north side of the river. An intriguing description by Reid concerns a discovery by workmen in Rossnaree House c.1800 of:

A souterrain building, consisting of several apartments constructed of stone without cement which had since been closed up.[108]

The remaining souterrains have been exposed by ploughing and reclamation of farmland. Two men ploughing on the Coddington estate (at Oldbridge) in 1983 came across flagstones. When they were raised, a passage leading to a circular chamber was exposed. Charcoal and ash were observed on the floor of the circular chamber. A further inspection of the site revealed a complex Z-shaped souterrain formed by a passage with two corbelled chambers off it.[109] Another site at Oldbridge was discovered in 1983 during land reclamation work; a bulldozer uncovered several 'tunnels'. This proved to be an impressive drystone built passage 6.5m long with two beehive chambers running off it.[110] In 1991 a local farmer uncovered another souterrain on his farm at Littlegrange, also during land reclamation works. This was a well-built structure with passage and corbelled chamber.[111] The townland name 'Clonlusk' (meadow of the cave) also suggests the presence of a souterrain in that townland.[112]

References to souterrains in the annals clearly show that these sites were refuges. The complex nature of many of these structures highlights their largely defensive nature.[113] They have been described as a 'defensive adjunct to settlements'.[114] Unenclosed settlements in this region far outnumber ringforts. This may reflect a change to more intensive arable farming in the later phases of the Early Christian period, with souterrains providing a modicum of protection for labourers (and/or slaves) in those farming communities that did not need a ringfort to secure safety for their herds during periods of cattle raiding. Many of the trap features in souterrains are designed to be sealed from the outside. From this it may be inferred that they were designed to prevent slaves being easily captured.[115]

This prosperous agricultural community in the Boyne Valley attracted the attention of raiding parties of Saxons and Norsemen. These repeated incursions were obviously profitable. Churches were the main focus of attack. Raids into the territory of Brega are first recorded in the *Annals of Ulster* AD685 when Saxons laid waste Mag Breg and many churches. This summer raid by Ecgfrith of Northumbria is the only known clash between the Anglo-Saxons and the Irish.[116] An attack from closer to home is recorded in the *Annals of Ulster* (AD720), which reports the wasting of Mag Breg by Cathal (son of Finnguine) and Murchad (son of Bran). Between AD837 and AD1032, there were several major Norse incursions into the Boyne Valley.

The Norsemen may have been encouraged to enter the Boyne Valley to support hostilities between the rival dynasties of Clann Cholmáin of Ulster and the Síl nAed Sláine of Bréga, or merely to plunder the wealthy churches in the area.[117] The scale of these incursions is highlighted in the annals, which record a naval force of sixty Norse ships on the Boyne and another sixty ships on the Liffey in AD837. These two forces plundered the plain of Brega, including 'churches, forts and dwellings'. This short entry clearly describes the main forms of settlement in the region; 'dwellings' is possibly a reference to unenclosed settlement associated with souterrains. A Norse naval force was on the Boyne at *Linn Rois* (Rossnaree) in AFM 842. That entry

Table 5		
Souterrains in the Bend of the Boyne		
Location	SMR No.	Land use
Clonlusk	NPL	
Dowth	20:17	Pasture
Knowth (9 sites)	19:30	Open to public
Oldbridge	20:04	Tillage
Oldbridge	20:07	Tillage
Rossnaree	19:48	Residential

also notes the plundering of Birr and Saighir by the foreigners of the Boyne. At this point, therefore, the Norse were actually using the Boyne as a base from which to attack monasteries in the Midlands.

The annals record the pillaging of the caves (souterrains) at Knowth, Dowth and Oldbridge in AD861:

> The cave of Cnoghbhai [Knowth], the cave of the grave of Bodan ... over Dubhath [Dowth], and the cave of the wife of Gobhann, at Drochat-atha [Oldbridge], were broken and plundered by the same foreigners [Norsemen].

and in AU 863:

> The caves of ... Cnodba, and of Boadan's Mound above Dubad and of Oengoba's wife, were searched by foreigners – something which had never been done before.

In AU 935 the cave of Cnogba was sacked by Amhlaib [Olaf, king of Dublin]. The kings of Knowth allied themselves with the Norse kingdom of Dublin.[118]

East Meath suffered terribly in the great dynastic wars of the eleventh and twefth centuries. It was divided between the kings of Breifne and Leinster and the power of the kings of Northern Brega at Knowth was eclipsed. In the Bend of the Boyne, the Early Christian period ended even before the arrival of the Normans. This occurred in 1142 with the imposition of European-style monasticism.

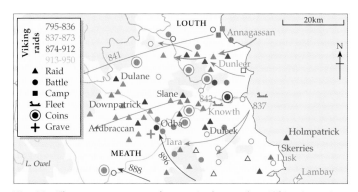

Fig. 29 There are numerous references in the annals to Viking incursions into the Boyne Valley, repeated attacks on localities within the Bend of the Boyne, especially Knowth, and the presence of a naval force of Norsemen on the Boyne at Rossnaree in AD842. A Norse base possibly existed for a lengthy period at Rossnaree. Underwater investigations there could also yield information on these raiders.

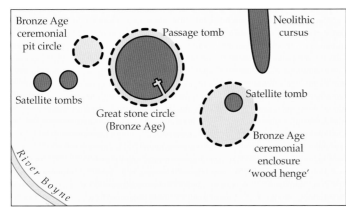

A) Prehistory

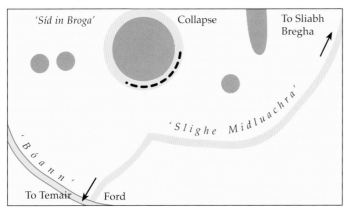

B) Iron Age / Early Christian

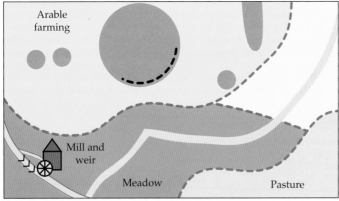

C) Medieval

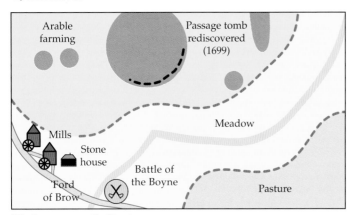

D) Seventeenth Century

CASE STUDY 1:
LANDSCAPE DEVELOPMENT AT NEWGRANGE

Seven thousand years ago, the wooded ridge above the north bank of the Boyne at Newgrange was intermittently settled by groups of hunter-gatherers who lived off the fish, salmon and eels of the river and its limited range of woodland mammals. Between 3900 and 3500BC, farming communities cleared this woodland and lived in timber houses. A large passage tomb was built on the summit of the ridge. Subsequently the periphery of the tombs became a focus for intense outdoor ritual activity. A free-standing stone circle encircled the main tomb, a ceremonial avenue was constructed across the ridge, a large timber circle enclosed one of the smaller tombs to the south-east of Newgrange and a smaller circle was built to the west. A mixed farming economy was practised (A). From the Middle Bronze Age to the Iron Age there is no evidence for activity on the ridge (B). Partly due to this lack of subsequent settlement, Newgrange retained a sacred position into the Iron Age and proto-historical sources portray its status as the royal cemetery of *Brug*. From the first to the fourth centuries AD, Newgrange became a place of pilgrimage for Romano-British and native populations. This was facilitated by its position on a major overland route that ran from Tara to Ulster. Unlike Knowth and Dowth, Newgrange was not the focus for domestic settlement in the Early Christian period. The *dindshenchas* suggests some association between one of the mounds on the ridge – *Fert Patric* – with St Patrick (B).

In 1348 the lands of Newgrange and the surrounding area became part of the farmlands of Mellifont Abbey. As

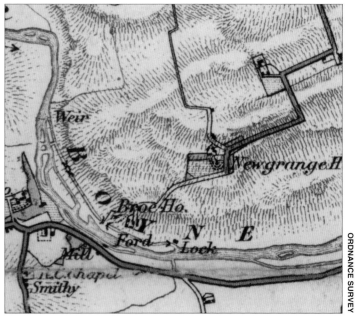

Newgrange *c.*1900

ORDNANCE SURVEY

ORDNANCE SURVEY

Newgrange c.2000.

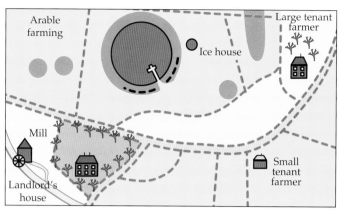

E) Eighteenth Century

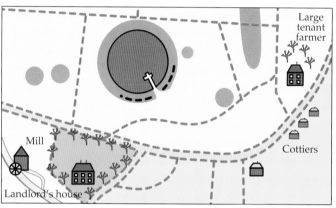

F) Nineteenth Century

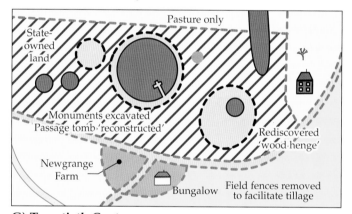

G) Twentieth Century

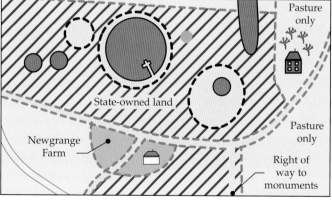

H) Future Trends

a result, the smaller burial mounds on the upper slope of the ridge were badly damaged by ploughing (C). The lands continued to be tilled into the seventeenth century. In 1654 there was just one stone house in the townland and mills by the river. During the Battle of the Boyne, Williamite troops passed down the lane to cross by the ford (D). From 1699 the lands of Newgrange were leased to Charles Campbell, who transformed them into a viable estate. By 1734 he had built a neo-classical mansion and outbuildings on landscaped grounds and enclosed the lands into tenant farms. An ice house was built to the rear of the main mound. The roads were improved using the stones from Newgrange which resulted in the re-discovery of the entrance to Newgrange (E). The fields were further subdivided as a result of sub-letting, and labourers working on the large tillage farms lived in cottages along the roadside (F).

Today, Newgrange passage tomb is state-owned, and has been 'restored' to become one of the most visited monuments in the country. The prehistoric timber circle has been revealed and partially reconstructed. Newgrange House has been demolished and a bungalow built nearby. The farmyard has been modernised with EU grant-aid and is now open to the public as 'Newgrange Farm'. Many of the field fences have been removed for more efficient, large-scale tillage farming (G). In the future it is intended that most of the land will be bought by the state and public paths are to be provided to allow access to the monuments. The land will no longer be tilled and will revert to permanent pasture (H).

MONKS AND KNIGHTS: THE MEDIEVAL LANDSCAPE

In the twelfth century, the Christian Church experienced a revolution in religious organisation and practice throughout Europe, resulting in the foundation of many new religious orders. The Cistercians were the first of these new Continental orders to come to Ireland, bringing with them new styles of monasticism, land management and architecture.[1] The ordered layout of their buildings, arranged around a square or quadrangle, contrasted sharply with the informal arrangement within the earlier Irish monasteries. Cistercian monks were firmly established in the Bend of the Boyne before the coming of the Normans. Their house at Mellifont, on the banks of the Mattock, a tributary of the Boyne, was the first in Ireland, founded in AD1142. The foundation was made by Saints Bernard and Malachy with the assistance of Donnchadh Ó Cearbhaill, king of Airghialla, who granted the monks the site and the land with which it was endowed.[2] The grant was at the recently conquered southern reaches of Airghialla territory, a frontier location which is typical of many Cistercian abbeys, as it was for many Early Christian foundations.[3] Putting so much land into the hands of this Continental order created an effective buffer zone on the southern frontier of Ó Cearbhaill's kingdom. Donnchadh's grant also had ecclesiastical implications because the 'mid-water of the Boyne' now became the southern frontier of the province of Armagh.[4] By the time the Normans arrived in Ireland in 1169, there were already twelve Cistercian houses in Ireland affiliated to it and their farms dominated the medieval countryside in the lower Boyne Valley.

Not all the land in the Bend of the Boyne was granted to the Cistercians, however. Augustinians held land on the southern shores of the Boyne, and Dowth remained under secular authority throughout the Middle Ages. Dowth provides a fine example of a nucleated medieval settlement. Sources from the period permit a tentative reconstruction of the Medieval landscape, whose ruins are some of the most picturesque in the area.

Fig. 1   Mellifont Abbey, founded in AD1142, was the first Cistercian monastery in Ireland. The Cistercian monks introduced a Continental style of architecture and a scientific approach to the management of their vast farms along the Boyne. Although this innovation occurred twenty-seven years before the coming of the Normans, they can be seen as part of the 'invasion' of European forces which was to transform the Irish countryside.

Fig. 2   This late-eighteenth-century drawing by Gabriel Beranger shows the nave of the abbey church at Mellifont and the lavabo (at left). The medieval pointed arches have since been removed and only the church foundations remain.

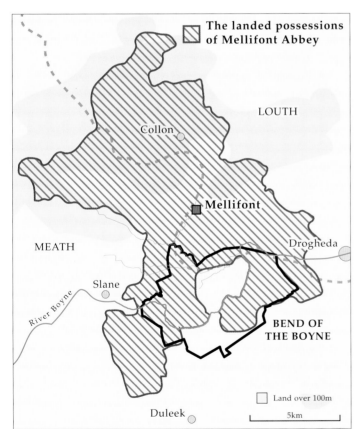

Fig. 3   The full extent of the Mellifont monastic estates in counties Meath and Louth has been estimated at 20,235ha (54,000 acres) and incorporated a large portion of the lands in the Bend of the Boyne. The legacy of the Cistercians in the Bend of the Boyne includes evidence for granges, mills, fisheries and monastic settlements.

Table 1
Places within the Bend of the Boyne
held by Mellifont Abbey

Place	Source 1 1178	Source 2 1185	Source 3 1203	Source 4 1539
Balfeddock				*Balyfadocke*
Cruicerath	*Croch*		*Croch*	*Croch*
Donore			*Dun Wabair*	*Donnore*
Gilltown				*Gyltone*
Knowth	*Cnogba*	*Cnogba*		*Knoythe*
Monknewtown				*Newtown of Monkland*
Newgrange				*Newgrange*
Oldbridge	*Grangia de vetere ponte*	*Drochetatha*		*Oldebryge*
Rathmullan		*Raithmolan*		*Ramolan*
Rossnaree	*Rossnaring*	*Rossnarigh*		*Rosinre*
Sheephouse				*Shephowse*
Stalleen		*Teachlenni*		*Staylyng*
Littlegrange				*Lytlegrange*

The year 1178 saw the first contact between the Normans and the monks.[5] In that year a charter and confirmation were issued by Henry II in relation to the Cistercian appurtenances of Mellifont as well as various lands and granges held by them prior to the invasion (source 1). In a charter of 1185 served by Prince John, two further places in the Bend of the Boyne are identified (source 2).[6] In a confirmation and grant by King John to the monks of the monastery of St Mary's, Drogheda in 1203, Donore is first mentioned (source 3).[7] An Inspeximus by Edward III in 1329 mentions six localities within the Bend of the Boyne, and records of 1348 mention seven places within the Bend of the Boyne.[8] Mellifont Abbey, with its vast lands, was dissolved on 23 July 1539.[9] In the extents of the Mellifont possessions following the dissolution, eleven places within the Bend of the Boyne were listed (source 4), and this extent was corroborated by a patent of 4 June 1612, which records a grant to Sir Garret Moore of the abbey and its precincts at Mellifont.[10]

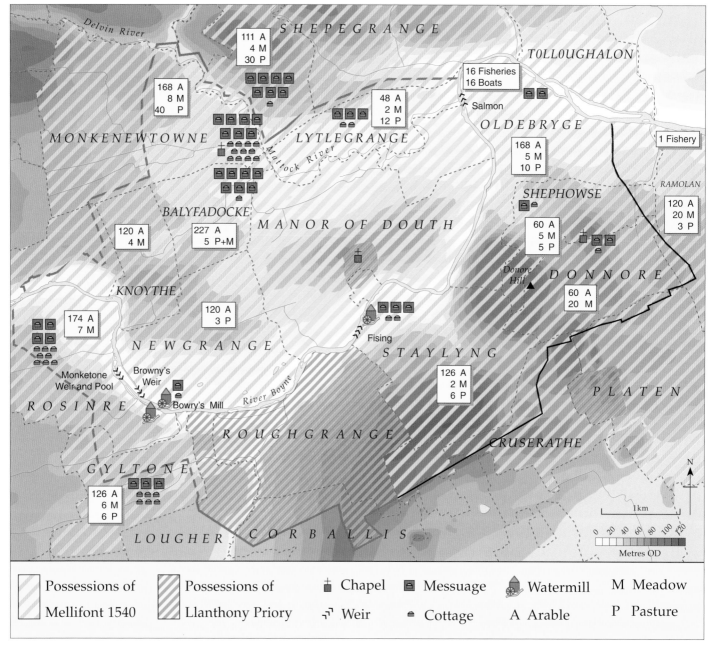

Fig. 4 Monastic possessions and settlement in the Bend of the Boyne c.1540.

THE CISTERCIANS 1142–1539

The Cistercians introduced into the Boyne Valley a revolutionary scheme of land management which had previously been pioneered on the Continent and in England.[11] Their rule demanded that each abbey be self-sufficient and their estates were accordingly divided into farms (granges) worked directly, using lay brothers for agricultural labour. The grange was the economic unit designed to provide a surplus for the use and enjoyment of the monastic order. Each grange had its own nucleus of farm buildings. Newgrange, Sheepgrange, Roughgrange and Littlegrange probably correspond with the location of these medieval monastic farms.

In Ireland, surviving buildings associated with these early granges are scarce; an insight into their arrangement survives in directions sent by Stephen of Lexington to the Cistercians in Jerpoint, county Kilkenny, in 1228.[12] He advised that buildings should not be erected in the centre of the granges, but rather along their margins in a defensive layout on account of thieves. Barns and animal sheds should be the only buildings within these granges. A grange existed at Knowth from at least AD1185 when it was mentioned in the charter granted by Prince John.[13] Excavations on top of the passage tomb mound at Knowth have revealed the grange buildings. They form a rectangular courtyard

Fig. 5 These earthworks are located in a natural marshy basin drained by a stream running eastwards into the Mattock River and located immediately northeast and downslope of the passage tomb cemetery at Knowth (A). The largest enclosure comprises a roughly circular area with an internal diameter of 80m surrounded by two banks and a ditch. None of the gaps in the banks appear to be original entrances, as there is no causeway evident across the ditch. In the field west of the large enclosure is a D-shaped enclosure, 18m long and 12m wide, which is defined by a bank and external ditch (C, D). To the north-east of the large enclosure is a ring ditch with a diameter of 10m. This archaeological complex is undoubtedly a multi-period site as earthworks overlay the probable ring barrow northeast of the large enclosure (C). It has been suggested that the large circular enclosure is a possibly a henge. Yet, morphologically, it differs radically from the English definition of that monument type and it differs from the type of henge monument found in the Boyne Valley. Superficially, the site has a profile associated with ringforts; however, it is unlikely to have been an Early Christian farmstead as the size of the enclosure is more than twice the size of a typical ringfort. Also, ringfort builders preferred well-drained sloping locations for their farmsteads, not waterlogged hollows. The earthworks comprising enclosures, a possible pond, field boundaries and strip lynchets could more probably be interpreted as the remains of a medieval farm. If this identification is correct, then this farm was probably associated with the Cistercian monks of nearby Mellifont Abbey and the grange buildings discovered on the top of the mound at Knowth. Excavations alone can provide a certain date for this earthwork complex.

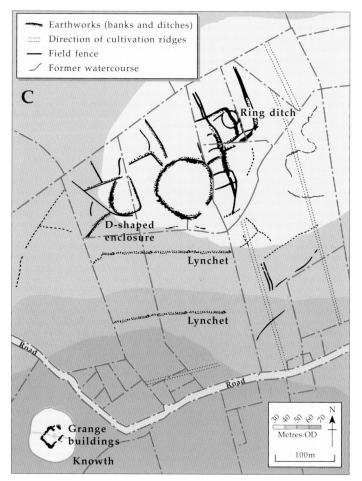

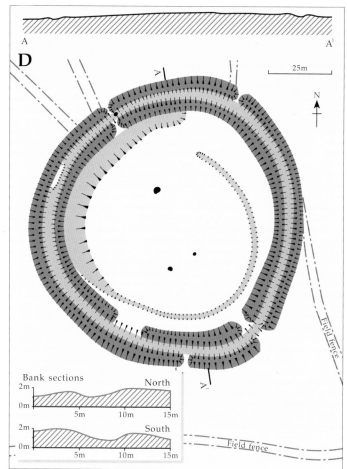

(36m long and 25m wide) enclosed by a masonry wall with lean-to buildings and an entrance in the southeast. One of the buildings had plastered walls, well finished with shaped sandstone blocks. A number of the structural stones were dressed, indicating a building of high status. The windows were divided into panels by a lattice of lead and were, therefore, presumably glazed. Amongst the finds were tiles bearing the name 'Maria' similar to those at Mellifont. A font was also found, conclusive proof of this building's religious function. The building might have been an oratory which served the lay brothers in the grange.[14] An entry in Bishop Dopping's *Visitation Book* of

DÚCHAS/CON BROGAN

Fig. 7 Under suitable conditions, evidence for cultivation in the form of ridge and furrow can be seen in the fields surrounding Newgrange. These run up and down across the contours: excavations southeast of Newgrange have dated these features to the medieval period.

DÚCHAS/CON BROGAN

Fig. 6 Excavations on the top of the main passage tomb mound at Knowth exposed the remains of farm buildings of the Cistercian grange. There was a walled-in courtyard (visible on the aerial photograph) with lean-to buildings which incorporated an oratory. In 1332 the 'vill' at Knowth was burned and the inhabitants murdered.[15]

1682–85 indicates there was still a church at Knowth in the late seventeenth century.[16] Finds from the site included domestic items like wheel-made pottery, a knife, personal ornaments, weaponry (including arrowheads and spearheads) and evidence for horses (horseshoe nails and iron spurs). Coins found here included some minted in the reign of King Henry III (1216–72). The configuration of this complex is similar to the grange buildings at Monkstown-Castlefarm in county Dublin, associated with the Cistercian abbey of St. Mary's, Dublin.[17] A series of low-lying enclosures north of the passage tomb cemetery at Knowth may be additional remnants of this medieval farm and fields. They are confined to three fields which border on a stream running into the Mattock. They are centred on a large oval enclosure c.80m in diameter with external and internal ditches and a counterscarp bank. Attached to this are a

series of small fields, one of which appears to overlie a circular ditched feature and a D-shaped enclosure.

These monastic granges were centres of intense agriculture, including grain cultivation and cattle and sheep rearing. Such medieval farming practices have left their impact in both the archaeological record and in place names. Wool was an important commodity linked to the thriving export industry which the Cistercians developed.[18] Sheepgrange and Sheephouse preserve the memory of these sheep farms (the latter name suggests the presence of a large barn in this townland). In England and

NATIONAL MUSEUM OF IRELAND

Fig. 8 At Newgrange, five plough pebbles were found in an extensive area from the vicinity of the main mound downslope to Site A. These plough pebbles were inserted into the mouldboard of a medieval wooden plough to prevent wear. They are worn stones, predominantly of quartz and flint, which show a flat facet on which fine striae can be seen.[19]

on the continent, magnificent barns survive on medieval monastic farms, the most impressive being that at Great Coxwell, Beaulieu, in England.[20] Whether there were buildings of comparable scale on the Cistercian estates in the Boyne valley remains to be seen. If they were built of timber and not stone, these barns would only be detected through excavation.

Entries in the Statute Rolls indicate that the rearing of cattle was also on a grand scale. In 1245 William Marshall received a mandate to make restitution to Mellifont for 600 cows which were taken by William Marshall, Earl of Pembroke, from the monastic lands to maintain the king's army in the war against Hugh De Lacy.[21] The archaeological evidence is represented by relatively high concentrations of sheep and cattle bones found during the excavation of buried field boundaries that ran east-west across the field just outside the stone circle at Newgrange. Glazed fifteenth- to sixteenth-century pottery was found in association with the animal bone deposits.[22]

The Cistercians contributed to improving the quality and increasing the volume of agricultural production. The huge quantities of grain exported from this area to England (including wheat, barley and oats) and the large arable area c.1540 indicate that tillage was the most important agricultural pursuit (table 2).[23] Ploughing was undertaken with a wooden mouldboard plough, whose sole was studded on the undersides and landward sides with pebbles (plough pebbles) set into holes to prevent undue wear where the timber made contact with the soil. The recovery of medieval plough pebbles in the fields at Balfeddock, Knowth, Townleyhall and Donore townlands provides further archaeological evidence that cultivation was extensive.[24] At Knowth, seventeen plough pebbles of quartz and mudstone were found with thirteenth-century potsherds. At Newgrange, ridge and furrow traversed the upper levels of Site Z, south-east of the main mound. Thirteenth-/fourteenth-century wares are the earliest dateable association with this ploughing activity. The tradition of mixed farming with an emphasis on tillage continued into the fifteenth century, as highlighted in a 1495 description of the area referring to 'fences', 'ditches', 'cornfields', 'grazing fields' and 'pastures' on the lands held by Mellifont.[25] This document demonstrates the intense exploitation of the abbey lands.

The preference for a tillage economy on this monastic land into the sixteenth century is highlighted by the large acreage listed as potentially arable (90%) in an *extent* of the monastic possessions at the dissolution of Mellifont Abbey in 1540. This high percentage indicates the use of the three-field system of agriculture (table 2).[27] The importance of

Townland	Arable	Pasture	Meadow
Balfeddock	227	5 (+ meadow)	-
Donore	60	-	20
Gilltown	126	6	6
Knowth	120	-	4
Littlegrange	48	12	2
Monknewtown	168	40	8
Newgrange	120	3	-
Oldbridge	168	10	5
Rathmullan	120	3	20
Rossnaree	174	-	7
Sheephouse	60	5	5
Stalleen (including Redmountain)	126	6	2
Total	1517 (90.0%)	90 (5.3%)	79 (4.7%)

Table 2
Agricultural statistics for the
Bend of the Boyne 1539[26]

tillage is further underlined by the unit of payment for local tithes which was in use, the *copule* of grain. Such expanses of corn and meadow were relieved by some wilderness at Monknewtown where there were 'furze and briars' and a local bog from which the residents of Rossnaree carted turf.[28] The presence of tillage and meadow suggests the need for fencing to keep stock from the crops and that the three-field system was in use. However, the fact that the extent mentions an 'enclosed pasture' at Oldbridge might indicate that fencing was uncommon.[29]

The Cistercians played a key role in developing a milling industry on the Boyne for the processing of corn and wool. Mills and millponds are specified in charters of 1185 and 1203 confirming lands to Mellifont. The extents of the abbey's possessions at its dissolution listed monastic mills at Rossnaree, Stalleen, and at Browe on the Boyne below Newgrange.[30] The Stalleen mill was considered unprofitable in 1539 for want of repairs.[31] These were vertical-wheeled mills, a type which may have actually been introduced by the Cistercians.[32] Vernacular-style water mills have replaced the medieval sites at Stalleen and Rossnaree but their location is presumably the same. Once mill races were established on these sites by the Cistercians, there was no need to relocate them for use by later mills. To harness the water, weirs were erected across the river to divert some of its flow along a head race to the waterwheels. These are mentioned in the medieval sources and still survive in the modern Boyne.

The Cistercian monks of Mellifont Abbey developed the resources of the Boyne for fishing.[33] The fish taken in the Boyne weirs supplied the markets of Dublin and Drogheda. The monks manipulated the water flow and installed devices to increase the harvest of fish. Amongst the possessions of the monks of Mellifont confirmed in a charter of 1203 were the fisheries above the Boyne tideway.

DÚCHAS/CON BROGAN

Fig. 9 This vernacular mill at Rossnaree, known locally as Johnson's Mill, occupies the site of an earlier mill which was run by the Cistercian monks at Mellifont from the twelfth century onwards.

The charter described a free and quiet fishery in the Boyne so far as their lands extend on each side of the river, and prohibited any private or common right of fishing on that river within the limits of their lands.[34] This grant was confirmed again in 1238.[35] The fisheries of the Boyne above the tideway included three valuable salmon weirs at Rossnaree, Knowth and Stalleen and these were confirmed in a charter of 1349 and in a legal adjudication of 1381.[36] At the dissolution of the monastery in 1539, there were weirs at Newgrange, Oldbridge, Stalleen and Rossnaree.[37] At that time, the income of Mellifont Abbey included the annual

ROYAL IRISH ACADEMY

Fig. 10 A Sheela-na-gig (Síle na gCíogh' = exhibitionist figure) from the south wall of the mill at Rossnaree. This carving of a naked female is of a type normally found on medieval castles and churches.

DÚCHAS/CON BROGAN

Fig. 11   The Boyne has always been an legendary salmon river. From the twelfth century, the Cistercians developed the river for fishing by building weirs and traps, such as this weir below Dowth.

PRIVATE COLLECTION

Fig. 12   Detail from a painting by Joseph Tudor, *c.*1746, showing fishermen dragnetting on the Boyne at Oldbridge. The man on the river bank (bottom right) is watching for salmon and directing the activities. This ancient manner of fishing would not have changed much from medieval times.

rent arising from sixteen fishing currachs or coracles at Oldbridge and a fishery at *Ramolan* (Rathmullan).[38]

The two methods of fishing given prominence in the sources are the use of weirs and nets.[39] A fishing weir is an obstruction wholly or partially across a river channel. It works on the basis of a constant flow of water in one direction. Salmon and other fish were caught on their way upstream in cribs or traps, and eels were taken while migrating downstream in the autumn. The weirs were formed of post and wattle barriers and/or stone walls. The fish were taken out from a pool within an enclosure or trapped in a 'coghill' net. The weirs at Oldbridge and Rossnaree are virtually the same as those erected by the monks in medieval times.[40] They are certainly very substantial structures. The fishing weirs at Newgrange and Stalleen have not been used recently for salmon but the weir at Stalleen has been deployed as an eel trap.[41]

Netting for salmon was another method of fishing practised on the Boyne in medieval times. The boat used in this form of fishing was the Boyne coracle. It was designed specifically for netting salmon, but was also used in haulage and carriage. Made from hide stretched over a

wickerwork frame, the Boyne coracle has a great antiquity substantiated by a number of early historical references. For instance, a judgement was registered against the abbot of Mellifont in 1366 for obstructing navigation on the river by erecting a weir at Oldbridge: 'where boats called *corraghs*, with timber for building and flotes had liberty to pass constantly free from Drogheda to the bridge at Trim'.[42] At the dissolution in 1539, the possessions of Mellifont included an annual rent arising from sixteen of these fishing *corraghs* at Oldbridge.[43]

From the thirteenth century onwards, the Cistercians changed from a regime of direct exploitation of their lands by monks to one of lessees. From as early as 1208, the renting of lands on certain conditions was permitted by the general chapter of the Cistercian order.[44] By the fifteenth century, the use of lay brothers on their farms had virtually vanished. The references to 'tenants and vassals' in correspondence of 1495 highlight the changes that had taken place. Cistercians had departed from their original observance which forbade tenants on monastic lands.[45] By this time the Cistercian monks had become great landlords, with the main source of income coming from rents, together with the tithes, altarages, and oblations from various churches.[46]

Settlements developed around the Cistercian churches at Monknewtown (or the Newtown of Monkland as it was known) and Donore, and these later developed as parish centres. The 1539 extents indicate that a basic settlement hierarchy had developed at these monastic settlements with *messuages* (a dwelling house with out-offices and land) and cottages being recorded. The presence of messuages

Fig. 13   The Boyne curragh is the only example of a basket-type boat in existence in Ireland.[47] The body, which is built bottom upwards, consists of an open-work of paired hazel wands arranged to form a steep-sided bowl, oval in plan. The mouth or *gunwale* is formed first, the bottom and sides put into position later. A closely wickered skirting of slender hazel rods holds the upturned ends of the frame rods in position and the whole is finished off by a marginal twist of stout hazels. The flexible natural willow growing on the river islands at Oldbridge provided the raw materials for this local industry. A tanned oxhide is then drawn over the wicker structure and laced to the gunwale at short intervals and at longer distances by an independent lacing which makes turns around both gunwale twist and gunwale rod. A wooden seat is slung at mid-length by paired cords at each end. A number of design features relate to its use a fishing vessel: a system of braces made of twisted hazel is attached to the framework which provides a platform where the net for fishing is piled and transported; the curragh is completed by lapping the gunwale in its median and stern sections with a strip of hide to prevent fraying of the net during paying-out and hauling-in operations. The boat is rowed with a short paddle of larch with a parallel-sided blade; on the whole, the paddle resembles a cricket bat. A) Early colour photograph (1913) of Boyne curraghs and their builder. B) Nineteenth-century illustration of Boyne fishermen and the Boyne-style currach at Stackallen.

suggests that individual property boundaries were in place. The greatest nucleation was at Monknewtown with its seven messuages and ten cottages associated with a church. There were nucleated settlements, unassociated with churches, at Balfeddock (seven messuages and one cottage) and Gilltown (three messuages and six cottages).

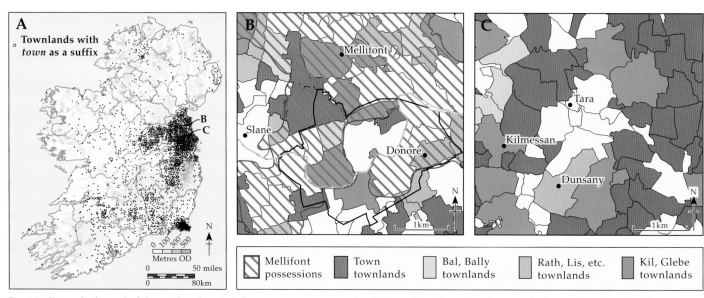

Fig. 14   Towards the end of the medieval period, former granges were replaced by small nucleated settlements similar to those found on lay manors. Nonetheless, these lands remained outside the process of secular sub-infeudation manifested in place name evidence by the townland suffix 'town' (A).[48] As a consequence, there is a lower frequency of 'town' place names in the Bend of the Boyne and on the Mellifont estate in general, despite its location within the Pale area, reflecting the impact of the Cistercians on place names (B). This is even more apparent when this part of east Meath is compared with a more 'Normanised' area like Dunsany where there is a contrastingly high frequency of 'town' names (C).

DÚCHAS/CON BROGAN

Fig. 15   The monastic church of Donore in the townland of Sheephouse is prominently located on a hilltop. It suffered greatly during the Battle of the Boyne. Foundations of the east end of the church and part of the north wall of the church are all that survives. A grave slab lying in the east end of the church comprises part of an altar tomb to John Genet (d. 1609).[49] According to *Dopping's Visitation* 1682–85, the church had been repaired by this John Genet. At this time, church furniture was needed and the churchyard was unfenced. There was no glebe associated with it.[50] The head of a disc-headed cross of seventeenth-century date lies in the graveyard.[51]

The extents provide a list of chaplains who were former monks of the monastery. By authority of king's letter patent, they were permitted to officiate in the chapels.[52] These churches continued to be used after the Reformation for Protestant services and were kept in reasonable repair. Many are described in 1622 by the newly established Bishop of Meath, James Ussher, who made a return on the state of the diocese when a Royal Commission was initiated for the visitation of the province of Armagh. This was Ussher's first episcopal act as bishop of Meath; his diocese was the best arranged in Ireland at the time.[53] Included in his report are two curacies in the Bend of the Boyne at *Donoure* (Donore) and *Munknewtowne* whose churches are described as being in reasonable repair. Nicholas Tedder (curate at Monknew-town) and Robert Burton (curate at Donore) were, nonetheless, both non-resident.

As recently as the early nineteenth century, communities on the earlier Mellifont estates still considered themselves to be distinctive. According to the Tithe Applotment Books, 'the tenants on these lands have taken them free from tithe [as they] originally belonged to the Lordship of Mellifont'.[54] Today, place names and the ruinous remains of these monastic chapels and churches survive as a testament to the extensive holdings of the Cistercians.

ROYAL IRISH ACADEMY

Fig. 16   Part of an east window evident at Donore church today, which was intact when illustrated by Du Noyer in the nineteenth century.[55]

NORMAN SETTLEMENT (1169–1539)

The kingdom of Meath, comprising the present-day counties of Meath and Westmeath, north-west Offaly and east Longford, was granted to the Norman Hugh De Lacy by King Henry II in 1172. This followed Henry II's declaration that he was Overlord of Ireland.[56] While this grant entitled De Lacy to the undivided kingdom of Meath, he in fact inherited the problems of a divided kingdom. Henry II had received only one submission in this divided kingdom from Ó Ruairc, who together with Ruaidhrí Ó Conchobhair, had partitioned the kingdom of

Fig. 17   A) The church at Monknewtown has an undivided nave and chancel; the west gable is nearly complete. The stone work is good, with courses of mainly large stones and rough ashlar used for the quoins. Its gable is surmounted by a double belfry with round-headed arches. The west wall has a round-headed window with a lintel arch and wide splay. The jambs are unbevelled with some bar holes. B) A corbel with a bearded face carved on it has been incorporated into the west wall.[57] C) A font from the church dated 1567 is now in the nearby Catholic church.[58] D) In the chancel of the church, in keeping with the long association between the Cistercians and fishing on the Boyne, a carved plaque depicts three salmon.

Midhe after the death of Diarmaid Ua Maelechlainn. As a result, De Lacy had to adopt a different approach to conquest in the west from that in the east of the kingdom of Meath.[59] The colonisation process in the east was facilitated by the submission of Ó Ruairc, then king of east Meath. Here, De Lacy was given access to the lands of a defeated Irish king. Gerald of Wales described how

De Lacy built strong castles throughout Meath and Leinster.[60] This military groundwork had been completed early in east Meath, allowing the lordship to extend and consolidate further westward.

De Lacy became active in Meath immediately upon receiving his grant. By 1174 Duleek had emerged as an early Norman base in the lordship. An extensive Norman presence elsewhere in Meath is suggested by a reference in the annals in the same year to castles built at Trim, Dunshaughlin, Skreen, Navan and, most importantly for this study, Knowth.[66] The castle at Slane near the northern boundary of the lordship was also established and well manned by 1174. Slane was the site of a town as well as a garrison, as some accounts note the presence of women and children. Richard Fleming conducted raids from there against Fir Midhe, Breifne and Airghialla.[67] The early sub-infeudation of the Liberty of Meath took place between 1172–73 with the initial land grants concentrated on its borders. These are described in *The Song of Dermot and the Earl*, a twelfth-century poem which lists the initial enfeoffments to barons by Hugh De Lacy.[68] In East Meath, De Lacy made at least ten major grants of land, each equivalent to a future barony in extent. In the Bend of the Boyne, these included the grant of Slane to Richard Fleming and smaller grants to Adam de Dullard around Dollardstown and Painestown in the barony of Duleek. Large areas of Duleek were retained as seigniorial manors, personally held by De Lacy.

The process of colonisation did not take place without setbacks. Gerald of Wales records that Ó Conchobair arrived in East Meath in 1174:

> And finding all the castles there empty and deserted, he burned them down and razed them to the ground up to the very borders of Dublin.[69]

In 1175 the Normans took part in a counter-campaign during which they laid waste to 'the whole of Meath from Athlone to Drogheda'.[70] Subsequently, the castle at Slane was destroyed in 1176 by Ó Cearbhaill.[71] Irish opposition was defeated, however, and by 1191 the conquest was completed and the lordship had assumed its final shape.

The Liberty of Meath was brought under military control through the construction of earthwork castles which housed garrisons. In the initial phase of the De Lacy conquest, large flat-topped earthen fortifications (*mottes*) were constructed in strategic positions within the major land grants. These were substantial earthen mounds, whose flat summits would have held wooden buildings and defences. *Primary mottes* had baileys and were built on the principal land grants, such as Slane; *secondary mottes* (without baileys) had a more limited role and were built to secure a manor. Further, mottes referred to in the sources usually have baileys, although this is not the case for Knowth.[72] The view that the presence or absence of a bailey can be used to classify mottes on functional grounds has yet to be satisfactorily established.

In the lower Boyne Valley, primary mottes were constructed on strategic heights above the river at

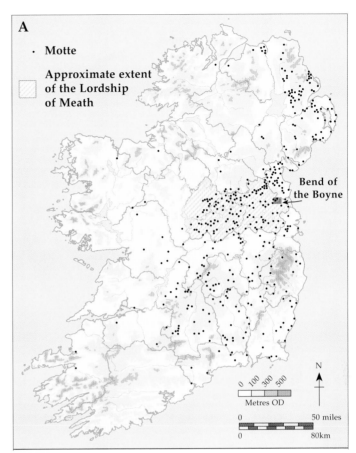

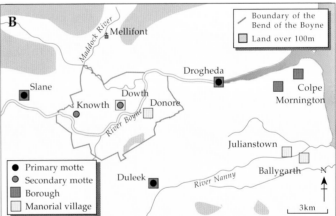

Fig. 18   A) East Meath (the present county Meath) became one of the most intensively settled Norman regions in Ireland. One hundred and ten mottes have been identified in the Liberty of Meath.[61] Thirty-three contain baileys (an enclosure at the base of the motte which would have protected the garrison).[62] They cluster along the major river valleys, particularly along the Boyne where they were sited to protect river crossings.[63]   B) In east Meath, ten boroughs developed around mottes on principal land grants or seigniorial manors including Drogheda, Duleek and Slane on the outskirts of the Bend of the Boyne. Below these in size and status was the manorial village, by far the most common rural settlement form in medieval Meath to have resulted from early sub-infeudation.[64] The manorial village is a settlement without borough status but containing a church and usually a castle and mill.[65] These are settlements with a primarily agricultural function. The manorial village focused on the church and motte, which was often subsequently replaced by a towerhouse. Towerhouses date from the period of renewed activity in ecclesiastical and military building which characterised the late fourteenth and early fifteenth centuries.

DÚCHAS/CON BROGAN

Fig. 19   An eighteenth-century drawing by Austin Cooper of the motte at Duleek. There are no longer any visible remains of this impressive monument.

Drogheda and on Slane Hill. To the south of these lay the primary motte at Duleek.[73] To secure the intervening territory, the prehistoric tombs at Knowth and Dowth were also fortified.[74] For a short time, Knowth was included in the land of the Norman knight Richard

NATIONAL MUSEUM OF IRELAND

Fig. 20   Iron axehead from Donore. It dates from the twefth century and is the type of weapon used during the Norman invasion. Gerald of Wales wrote in his *History and topography of Ireland*: 'From an old and evil custom they always carry an axe in their hands as if it were a staff. In this way, if they have a feeling for evil, they can the more quickly give it effect... Without further preparation, beyond being raised a little, it inflicts a mortal blow.'[75]

ROYAL IRISH ACADEMY

Fig. 21   The passage tomb at Dowth was reputedly used as the site of a De Lacy motte.[76] Drawings by Beranger (1775), shown above, and Wakeman (1848) show a barrow-like feature on the top of Dowth mound.[77] A section of this earthwork is still traceable on the summit of the mound. Its nineteenth-century excavator refers to a 'flattened space of nearly four yards wide forming the base of a capping'.[78] This could be the remains of a medieval motte built on the prehistoric mound. Reliable historical evidence is non-existent, but Dowth's use as a medieval fortification is corroborated by the fact that a medieval manor was established here and that these lands were not granted to Mellifont Abbey.

Fleming who fortified it in 1176 as an aid to holding his recently acquired lands around Slane. Knowth was only used for a short while by Fleming before its lands were incorporated into a Cistercian grange in 1185. Some believe that this fortification was in fact the re-fortification of the ringfort at Knowth, thereby converting it into a strategically sited ringwork.

Dowth Manor   The development of a manorial village around a motte is very common in Meath; at Dowth, a manor was established by the middle of the thirteenth century.[79] Dowth is the only manorial village in the Bend of the Boyne. Throughout the conquered areas, minute military tenancies were created to satisfy the desire of the settlers for knightly status.[80]

The process of sub-infeudation is seen at Dowth. The Fleming family had been enfeoffed of nearby Slane by Hugh De Lacy and Dowth was included in these holdings. The earliest English tenant of Dowth was Herbert De Rushbury, who received this holding from Richard Fleming in the 1170s. In about 1220, De Rushbury granted the tithes of the church of Dowth to the house of Llanthony.[81] The medieval manor at Dowth (with the exception of the church which now belonged to the Augustinians) passed into the hands of Ralph De Picheford.[82] The De Pichefords were a West Midland family who obtained lands at Dowth for part of a knight's service from Baldwin Fleming sometime after 1226, when he was sent on the king's service to Ireland, and before 1234, when he is found in the Boyne Valley as constable in Drogheda in custody of the castle there.[83] He

Enquiry into the lands of Ralph De Picheford 1253[84]

In Dunethe there are in demesne 132 acres of land and meadow; value of the acre, 12d.; the garden and dovecote, 6s; 2 mills, 5 marks; the fishery, 3 half marks… Free tenants, within and without the vill:- Alan Prutfot holds 2 carucates in fee farm, at 40s. a year; Gilbert *filius Presbiteri*, 21 acres in fee farm, at 9s. 2d. a year; Gillegmundi Mac Regan, 15 acres, at half a mark a year and six day's work in autumn, value of the days work 1d, Gillecrist Olnuthy, 19 half acres in fee farm, at 18s. 6d. a year, and 18d., for a house.; John le Sauvage, half a coruscate in fee farm, at 20s. and 10d. for work; David Fitz Walter, half a carucate in fee farm, at 24s. 4d. a year; Gelus son of Gelus, 25 acres in fee farm, at 5s., a year; the heir of William of Ardmilchan, who is in wardship, 30 acres whereof his mother holds one-third in dower at 4s. and 5d. and there remains 20 acres in the hand of the king, for 4 years, value of the acre, 12d. and when the heir is of age, he shall render 1 mark a year for the 30 acres; from the *coterelli* [cottiers?] for their gardens, and 85 acres of outward land held from year to year, and for their work, 6*l*, 15s. and 9d. Pleas and profits 20s. a year… Total extent of the manor, 31*l*. 14s. 8d, whereof Ralph's wife has one-third in dower, namely 10*l*.11s.6 half d. and there remains for the other two-thirds, 21*l*. 3s and 3 half pence.'

was also made sheriff of Louth in 1234.[85] In 1244 De Picheford was engaged on the king's service in fortifying a castle in the marches of Wales and could not be summoned to Ireland to answer a case against him brought by Baldwin Fleming. This case presumably involved his failure to provide knight service *in absentia*. In 1253 Ralph De Picheford died and in April of that year an inquiry was set up to establish how much land he held from the king. In the 'extent of the lands of Dunethe', the jury of twelve men recorded that 'Ralph held nothing of the king *in capite*' in Ireland but he held land from others:

> Of Baldwin [Fleming] of Dunethe, the manor of Dunethe, for 5 carucates of land, by service of one-eighth of one Knights fee.[86]

In August 1253 this case (an *inquisition post mortem*) was finally heard and a decision was made to return the manor of Dowth to the custody of Fleming to hold till the coming of age of De Picheford's heir:

> It appears by inquisition that Ralph De Picheford did not hold the manor of Duneth of the king *in capite* but of Baldwin le Fleming by knight service and that on Ralph's death Geoffrey of St. John, the King's escheator, in Ireland took it into the King's hand. The king, therefore gives to Baldwin the custody of the manor, to hold till the age of Ralph's heir, saving to his wife her dower. Mandate to the escheator aforesaid, to cause to Baldwin to have seisin of the manor and to take to him security for ten marks and two hogheads of wine.[87]

A charter of 1280 recorded in the cartularies of Llanthony *Prima* and *Secunda* refers to John de Picheford (Ralph's son) and Dowth, and indicates that the de Picheford family retained their hold on the Dowth property.[88]

DÚCHAS/CON BROGAN

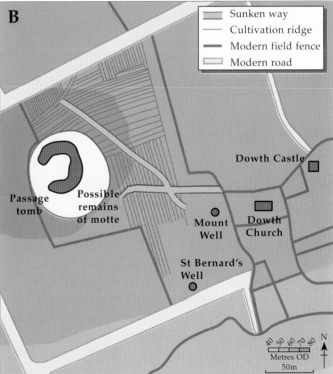

Fig. 22AB   Clear evidence survives of Dowth manor today. The parish church and towerhouse are upstanding. A sunken roadway leads up to these buildings from the modified mound. Traces of cultivation ridges run on a north/south axis across the present field system between Dowth passage tomb and the medieval church. At the northern end of the large field enclosing the manor today, there are remains of old spade-dug cultivation ridges in three irregularly shaped fields which are earlier than the modern field pattern and, as they are truncated by the road, appear to pre-date the present Dowth to Newgrange road constructed in the eighteenth century. These earthworks appear in a sequence of aerial photographs taken between 1963 and 1969.[89] The fields are defined by earthen banks *c*.2.5m wide and 0.3m to 0.5m high. They are not strip-type enclosures, which one would expect to find associated with a relic medieval three-field system. A field survey has tentatively identified house sites, paths and gardens.[90]

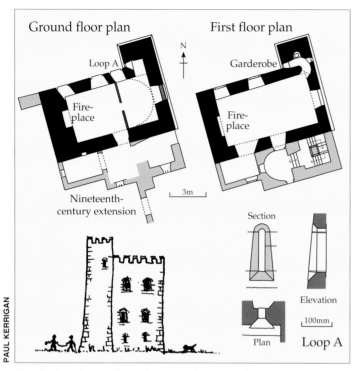

Fig. 23 Dowth towerhouse has a simple rectangular plan, rising to three storeys.[91] The turret contains a garderobe on the first and second floors with highly decorated airvents. Dowth has a vaulted ground floor with a fireplace in its west wall, the only towerhouse in county Meath with a ground-floor fireplace. It was extensively modernised in the nineteenth century with brick windows inserted into the walls and two extensions erected against the south side of the building.

Fig. 24 Dowth towerhouse stands in a characteristic location for a Meath example, on a good vantage point above the river. It is one of a line of defensive fortifications that run along the Boyne.[94]

Margaret, John De Picheford's widow, travelled to Ireland in 1301 and her son, another Ralph, travelled back and forth between Ireland and Wales during 1285–1302. With his death the connection between Dowth and the de Pichefords came to an end.[92]

The 1253 enquiry into the lands of Ralph De Picheford is of importance to this landscape study because it provides a detailed description of the tenant's land use and buildings in and around the disputed manor. It incorporated five ploughlands with 132 acres (the medieval acre was *c.*2.5 statute acres) set aside for De Picheford's demesne with its garden and dovecote and it was largely under meadow.[93] The manor contained two mills which suggests that grain was extensively cultivated on the manorial lands. The fishery was probably located on the Boyne, which lies south of Dowth manor. On this manor, there were nine fee farm tenants (six English and three Irish) of whom the English had holdings ranging from twenty-one acres to two ploughlands. The only other tenants on this small manor were a number of cottiers whose labour service had been commuted.

It is not known how the De Pichefords lost their title to Dowth after 1302. Neither is it known how the Netterville family came to be intimately associated with Dowth

manor. The Nettervilles were probably an immigrant family into Meath as feudatories of Hugh De Lacy. They are associated with Meath from an early date. Luke Netterville, for example, witnessed charters in Meath related to the Feypoe family of Skryne in 1220.[95] From the start, however, the Nettervilles of Dowth were in conflict with their neighbours, both lay and religious. They were first recorded in 1306 in a dispute over cattle stolen from Dowth manor.[96] In 1307, Nicolas Netterville sued the Prior of Llanthony for the rights to Dowth church.[97] In 1381, the Royal Escheator seized a salmon weir at Dowth which he was obliged to restore to Luke Netterville. The same individual had a confirmatory grant of all his possessions in Dowth in 1409: in 1430, John Netterville, proprietor of Dowth, had a release by letters patent of all crown debts affecting the rents and profits of this manor.[98] The Nettervilles kept a tenacious hold on Dowth into the nineteenth century.

There may have been another towerhouse within this manor on the lands of Proudfootstown. Alan Prutfot was the largest tenant described in the 1253 extent with two carucates, corresponding to the present townland of Proudfootstown. This family were still part of the manor of Dowth and still ensconced in Proudfootstown in the 1650s.[99]

Fig. 25A   Medieval church at Dowth.

Fig. 25B   The north doorway.

Fig. 25C   The medieval font from Dowth church is now outside the Catholic church at Monknewtown.[105]

Fig. 25D   Grave slab at Dowth church.

Dowth church   The church of St David at Dowth was established on an earlier monastic foundation soon after De Lacy's 1172 grant of the kingdom of Meath. It is mentioned in the cartularies as early as 1202–04, and again in 1220 and 1280.[106] In 1307 Nicolas Netterville of Dowth manor (adjoining this church) sued the Prior of Llanthony for the right to Dowth church.[107] This effort must have failed because Dowth remained associated with Llanthony Priory in Gloucestershire until the Reformation.[108] According to an entry in the cartularies for 1317, the Canons of Llanthony 'had … from time immemorial, obtained without distur-bance the parish church [at Douthe]'.[109] This particular entry describes 'a cottage and a courtyard', and at various other sites cottages and curtilages [courtyards] belonging to 'the glebe of the church … which were built long ago'.[110] These ancillary buildings must have been located south of the present church remains at Dowth in the present townland of Glebe. They also held '18 acres of arable and pasture', presum-ably located by the Boyne, beside a fishery: 'where there is … various nets designed for catching fish … and there is in the same place a number of weirs.'[111] It is referred to again in relation to financial matters in an entry for 1381 indicating that the church was still in use at that time.[112] The church of St David was situated at the site of the present medieval church remains at Dowth. This monument is more typical of a late-fourteenth-/early-fifteenth-century church with its divided nave and chancel, opposing round-headed doorways in the north and south walls, and a double belfry over the west gable. It also incorporates earlier features such as a pointed window in the nave which may be part of the earlier medieval church.[113]

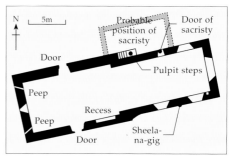

Fig. 25E   Plan of Dowth church as surveyed in the mid-nineteenth century.

Fig. 25F   The south doorway.

Fig. 25G   The sacristy door which has since collapsed.

Evidence for the towerhouse was mistaken for a round tower when what appears to have been a circular stair turret (a common attribute in examples from Meath and Louth) was blown down in the storm of 1839. Fragmentary remains of the towerhouse were still visible in the 1890s.[100] Towerhouses are largely absent from the Bend of the Boyne because in the Late Medieval period, when they were being built elsewhere in Ireland, the land here was still in the possession of Mellifont Abbey.

THE AUGUSTINIANS

Extensive areas of land were granted by Norman landowners to the various monastic houses established in Meath. Of these, Augustinian houses were most numerous. The twin Augustinian priories of Llanthony *prima* (in Monmouthshire) and Llanthony *secunda* (in Gloucestershire) were granted extensive lands around Colpe and Duleek (respectively) on the south side of the Boyne. Grants to these orders by the Normans brought about little change in the landholding patterns north of the river as grants here merely confirmed the Mellifont holdings. However, the exception is the parish of Dowth.[101]

The fourteenth-century cartularies of these two priories and their affiliated houses in Ireland contain documents of significant topographical interest including descriptions of the lands held and accounts of buildings in the farms or granges and of the tenants and their services.[102] The Llanthony cell at Duleek had lands in the townlands of Lougher, Donore, Platin and Gilltown, which lie south of the Boyne and Dowth on the north side. The descriptions of the individual properties contained in these cartularies reveal details of the landscape and land use in the medieval period.

Lougher   Llanthony Priory had a large holding at Lougher, corresponding to the present townland which runs down to the south bank of the Boyne. It is described in a number of entries in the cartularies. In 1287 the cartularies refers to the:

> Vill of Logher … with all its houses, gardens, curtilages, meadows, pastures, grazing, hedges, rents, gardens, curtilages, potatoes, fish, pastures … all its tenements and liberties.[103]

A central element in this village was the manor house, described in the cartularies for the year 1317 as a 'fortified manor-house'. There was a small hall with an attached chamber, both reserved for the use of the lord, occupied on one side of a single court; on the far side, an impressive gate house was adjoined by the lodgings of the tenant farmer. Within the court space was attached a barn, two pigsties, a dove cote and a house used for baking and brewing.[104] This layout of buildings is similar to that associated with the grange buildings and related structures identified at Knowth. Next to this manor house were unfree tenants such as:

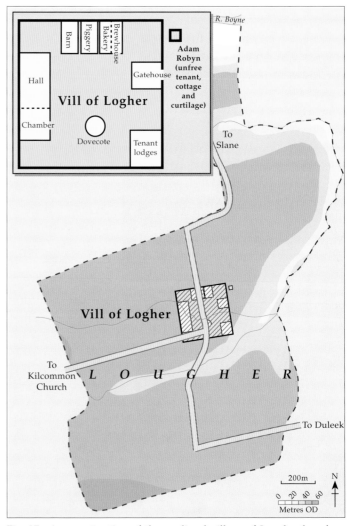

Fig. 26   Medieval silver and gilt spur found in a field adjoining the Boyne. The success of the Normans can be attributed to their superior horsemanship and weapons.

Fig. 27   A reconstruction of the medieval village of Lougher based on contemporary sources.

Fig. 28   No trace of the medieval village of Lougher has been identified. It was probably located at the present site of this extensive eighteenth/nineteenth-century farmhouse and yard in Lougher townland. A) Main avenue into Lougher farmhouse. B) Outbuildings at Lougher farm.

Adam Robyn, a *nativus* [unfree Irish tenant] … who held a cottage with a curtilage [courtyard] and croft and rendered yearly at Christmas and the nativity of St John the Baptist, 12d. by equal portions and a hen at Christmas and if he has more pigs or sows than seven, he shall give for each 2d. and pay from whatever saleable brew he brews two gallons of beer called 'tollbole' and he should reap with the lord, alongside the others, in the autumn when the lord should have anything to reap, receiving 13d. a day.[114]

This passage provides an insight into the life of a medieval tenant and the wide range of farming practices in the Bend of the Boyne during the Middle Ages.

In addition to Dowth and Lougher, the Augustinians also held land in Donore, Platin and Gilltown. The Llanthony cell at Colpe had land in Donore. A number of entries in the cartularies provide topographical detail. In 1260 Alice Jambe, the Lady of Colpe, gave the monks of Llanthony *Prima* 38 acres of land in Donore, and this 'lay between the great road to Drogheda and her domain'.[115] This entry establishes a thirteenth-century date for this section of roadway. A portion of the townland of *Platyn* (Platin) was included in the estates of Llanthony Priory and here the cartularies describe:

A certain chapel, now decayed … and to this chapel belongs a certain haggard annexed to it in some manner … not occupied because of lack of tenants.[116]

This entry refers to the site of the medieval church at Platin Hall.[117] It also probably refers to an earlier church building on the site as there is some evidence for the incorporation of earlier building material in the present remains.[118] Of particular interest here is the fact that churches such as

Platin had ancillary buildings attached which were rented to secular tenants. A portion of *Gyllyngeston* (Gilltown) was also attached to Llanthony Priory but no topographical information is provided.[119]

Table 3		
Settlement features in the Bend of the Boyne *c.*1540[120]		
Location	Site type	SMR No.
Balfeddock	Cottage	
Balfeddock	Messuages (7)	
Donore	Church	20:11
Donore	Cottage	
Donore	Messuages (2)	
Dowth	Church	20:19
Gilltown	Messuages (3)	
Gilltown	Cottages (6)	
Knowth	Messuages (4)	
Littlegrange	Cottages (2)	
Littlegrange	Messuages (3)	
Monknewtown	Church	19:19
Monknewtown	Cottages (10)	
Monknewtown	Messuages (7)	
Newgrange	Mill (Bowry's)	19:68 04
Newgrange	Weir (Brouny's)	26:20
Oldbridge	Messuages (2)	
Oldbridge	Weir (salmon)	
Rathmullan	Fishery	
Rathmullan	Mill	
Rossnaree	Mill	26:05 02
Rossnaree	Weir and pool (Monketone)	19:68 03
Sheepgrange	Cottage	
Sheepgrange	Messuages (7)	
Stalleen	Weir (fishing)	20:28 02/03
Stalleen	Mill	20:28 03

Table 4		
Medieval sites in the Bend of the Boyne		
Location	Site type	SMR No.
Dowth	Towerhouse	20:26
Dowth	Weir site	20:28
Proudfootstown	Towerhouse site	20:001

GERALDINE STOUT

GERALDINE STOUT

THE BOYNE WITHIN THE PALE

By the close of the fifteenth century, English control over Ireland had been reduced to such an extent that it became necessary to defend a reduced area of greater Dublin over which the English government exercised some control. Initially, this was implemented through a subsidy (in 1429) offered to Norman families to build castles as a defence against Gaelic attacks. This frontier area, incorporating the counties of Louth, Meath, Dublin and Kildare, came to be known as the Pale. The Pale was assigned a boundary by an act of parliament in 1488–89 and the Boyne Valley lay at the very heart of the Pale. In 1494 a further act of parliament at Drogheda declared that 'every inhabitant, earth tiller and occupant … do build and make a double ditch of six feet high above the ground at one side or part which mireth next unto Irishmen'.[121] The towerhouses at Dowth and Proudfootstown probably date from this turbulent period.

The Cistercian lands also suffered greatly from continuous incursions, and reports of 1495 describe total devastation of crops and farmland. The archbishop of Armagh received reports that:

> Certain nobles of the province had invaded … and laid waste, the lands, possessions, fields, farms, mills … crops, trees, plantations, woods, thickets, rabbit warrens, weirs, fisheries and meadows which … belong to the abbot and convent and their monastery and they have even presumed frequently and rashly with their horses … to destroy, waste … depopulate the fences, the ditches, the cornfields, the grazing fields and the pastures of the said abbot … wickedly committed and attempted against the said abbot and convent and their tenants and vassals.[122]

By 1539 the area under English control had contracted to such an extent that the lands at Mellifont formed the northern boundary of the Pale.

A radical change in colonial policy in Ireland in the sixteenth century resulted in the creation of an English-manned and military-based administration in Dublin Castle. From 1534 the English sought to regain control of crown land. This was achieved through confiscation of lands, such as the major monastic estate at Mellifont (facilitated by the break with the Roman Church), and the placement of regional officers in areas accompanied by a garrison, such as that at Drogheda.

Confiscation and subsequent secularisation of large areas of church property in the Boyne Valley was effected under the direction of King Henry VIII and the Reformation in the middle of the sixteenth century. The landed gentry of Meath and Louth passed through a period of religious

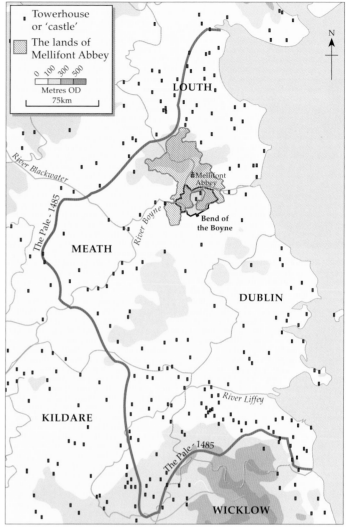

Fig. 29   In terms of settlement remains, the principal difference between the Bend of the Boyne and the rest of the Pale was that the construction of fortified residences did not occur on the nucleated settlements on Cistercian-held lands. Indeed, the general absence of towerhouses in south-west Louth and a portion of north Meath reflects this trend.

ambivalence, notably during the period when monastic properties were being distributed with many of the gentry supporting the state religion with consequential benefit to themselves. A predatory class arose from amongst the state officials and army officers dubbed the 'New English' and in 1566 the lands of Mellifont became the property of such an 'English soldier of fortune', Edward Moore.[123] Amongst the considerations for the grant of the lease was that:

> The said house was situate near the borders with Ulster and had been in all times of rebellion in those parts subject to the invasion of the enemy and could not be defended from burning or spoil.[124]

In the light of events that were to unravel in the subsequent century, it is worth noting the strategic importance of Mellifont and its Boyne Valley estate indicated by this remark.

Fig. 30 Repeated attacks on Mellifont in the fifteenth century resulted in the fortification of the abbey. Walls were built around the abbey and the entrance gateway was fortified. This illustration by Du Noyer dates from 1867.

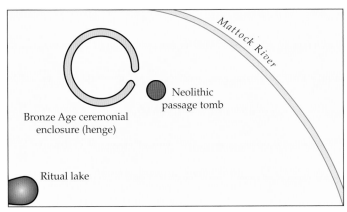

A) Prehistory

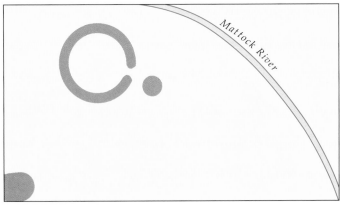

B) Iron Age / Early Christian

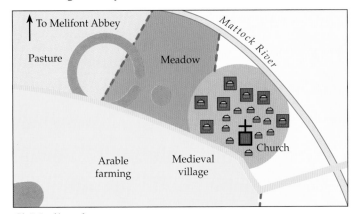

C) Medieval

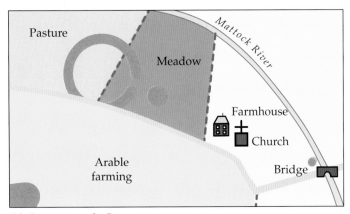

D) Seventeenth Century

CASE STUDY 2:
LANDSCAPE DEVELOPMENT AT MONKNEWTOWN

A Neolithic farming community erected a passage tomb in the Mattock Valley, albeit on the periphery of the main cemeteries on the north bank of the Boyne. Subsequently, this was replaced as a focus of communal worship by a large earthen enclosure or 'henge' (A). An artificial pond south-west of the henge and passage tomb at Monknewtown may have been of ritual significance and used for votive offerings from the Late Bronze Age/Iron Age. A well on the site was a focus for celebration at the pagan festival of Lughnasa (B).

In 1329 the lands of Monknewtown were granted to the nearby Cistercian monastery of Mellifont. East of the prehistoric remains, a village – the 'Newtown of Monk-land' – had grown around the monastic chapel, which would originally have served the lay monks working on the farm or grange at Monknewtown. This became the parish church for a largely secular community that inhabited seven messuages and ten cottages in the village by 1539 (C). Cistercian possession inhibited the development of a 'manorial centre' comparable to that at Dowth. For the same reason, no towerhouse was built in Monknewtown. In the post-Dissolution period, the population was depleted and by 1654 there was only one farmhouse, a church and a stone bridge across the Mattock. However, Monknewtown was still identifiable

ORDNANCE SURVEY

Monknewtown c.1900. The monks of Mellifont Abbey could reach Monknewtown along a disused lane via a ford over the Mattock River.

ORDNANCE SURVEY

Monknewtown c.2000

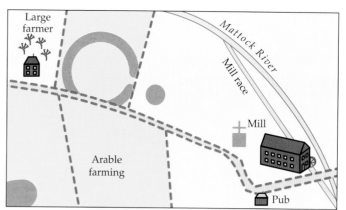

E) Eighteenth Century

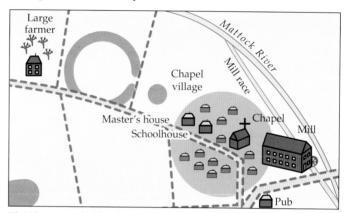

F) Nineteenth Century

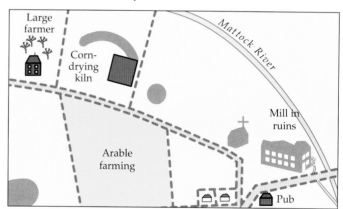

G) Twentieth Century

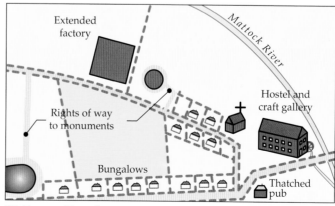

H) Future Trends

when General Schomberg passed by it during the Battle of the Boyne (D). In the eighteenth century, the lands were held by the Earl of Sheffield; he leased them to tenants who in turn built fine houses and enclosed their fields with thorn and furze hedges. Stone was robbed from the passage tomb to resurface the old lanes. In the later half of the eighteenth century, a large industrial mill using both steam and water was built at Monknewtown to process the corn grown in the surrounding fields. This revived the village's fortunes (E).

In the pre-Famine period, the village and surrounding area experienced population growth stimulated by the demand for labour in local tillage farming and the labour requirements of the mill. A settlement of labourers' cottages grew up at the junction of the Slane–Monknewtown road. A new chapel was built in 1837 and it became the focus for further institutional buildings, a schoolhouse and master's house. Structural stones removed from the passage tomb were reused as gateposts (F).

The population declined in the twentieth century and most of the nineteenth-century houses are now deserted and derelict; only the laneway survives. In the 1970s, an industrial corn-drying kiln was built on the site of the 'henge' which removed a large part of the monument. The mill is semi-derelict. The parish church remains unchanged and serves the population of the parish. The settlement at Rossin has largely disappeared and one of the larger vernacular houses is now a public house (G). In the future, housing pressure will probably result in building development around the church at Monknewtown and tourism needs could see the mill being converted into a hostel and craft gallery. The state will provide public paths to the passage tomb and ritual pond but a further extension to the kiln is likely to remove the remaining part of the 'henge' (H).

'BRISEADH NA BÓINNE': BATTLES ON THE BOYNE

From the time of dissolution of the monasteries to the final conquest of Ulster in 1609, the English government regained control over the island of Ireland. Plantation was part of this process, and throughout the seventeenth century, land was transferred into the hands of an immigrant and Protestant landlord class.[1] Within the Pale, however, confiscation was not as pronounced; a high percentage of Old English remained in the south Louth/east Meath region.[2] Where expropriation occurred, it was related to the seizure of monastic land rather than the expulsion of an indigenous landowning class. There was a remarkable degree of continuity, exemplified in the Boyne Valley by the survival of the Nettervilles of Dowth and other 'Irish Papists' who retained their lands throughout the turbulent seventeenth century.

The seventeenth century was a tumultuous one in the history of the valley. Major military conflicts of national and international significance took place here beginning with the Rebellion of 1641, continuing with Cromwell's campaign at Drogheda in 1649, and culminating in the Battle of the Boyne in 1690. These events highlight the strategic importance of the Boyne on the northern approaches to Dublin in the post-medieval period. Contemporary documentation of these military events allows intermittent glimpses of the valley, its landscape and its people. Though the evidence, by its very nature, is disjointed and the angle at times obtuse, it is possible to gain an impression of the countryside and to identify features and landmarks which are still in evidence. These features form a component of the Boyne landscape and provide a tangible record of a violent yet formative period.

DÚCHAS/CON BROGAN

Fig. 1 'This hallowed ground'. The grounds of Oldbridge House enclose the fields which played the major role in the Battle of the Boyne, 1690. Oldbridge estate is now in the ownership of the State and is now open as the visitor centre for this momentous episode in Irish history.

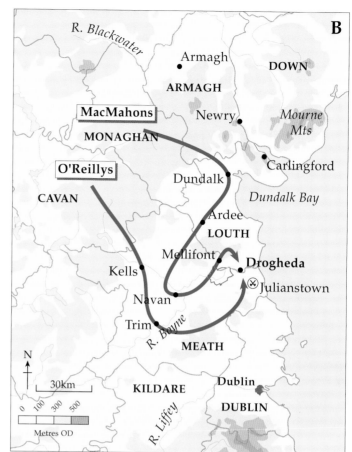

Fig. 2 A) The confederate wars, 1641–53. The Bend of the Boyne was disputed territory during this period. B) Confederate forces swept through the lower Boyne Valley in their advance on Drogheda.

THE CONFEDERACY WARS, 1641–49

In the post-Dissolution era, a large and influential landed group, Norman by descent and Catholic in religion still existed in Ireland, who are generally referred to as the 'Old English'. They retained one-third of the country's land and remained loyal to the English crown, but no longer controlled the government of Ireland. With growing fears of becoming marginalised, the Old English could not safely continue to enjoy their property and their freedom of worship unless they could establish firmly their right to use the Irish parliament to protect them against English government policies. This prompted some of the Irish, particularly in Ulster in 1641, to consider an armed rising. Their plan was to seize Dublin Castle, capture the principal members of the government, and take possession of the chief strongholds in Ulster in a series of local uprisings.[3] The Old English landowners of the Pale and their Ulster counterparts formed a loose alliance. The Pale nobility played a crucial role in the initial stages of the 1641 uprising and the subsequent development of confederate government structure.[4]

The lower Boyne Valley and Drogheda, a garrison town, provided the backdrop for a critical stage in the 1641

rebellion and again demonstrated the strategic significance of the Boyne river as a gateway to Dublin from Ulster. The securing of Drogheda and the Boyne by the loyalists in 1641 was important because it was essential to the protection of Dublin and the maintenance of communication with the north. Conversely, for the rebels the

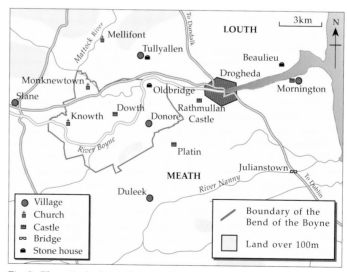

Fig. 3 Places in the lower Boyne Valley involved in the 1641 rebellion and subsequent events.

Fig. 4 The 1641 rebellion left scars on the landscape of the Bend of the Boyne. The medieval parish churches of Monknewtown (A) and Knockcommon (B) were two of many churches damaged during the rebellion. The window of Knockcommon, drawn by Du Noyer in the nineteenth century, no longer survives. Ireland is a land of ruins like these due to the vast majority of the Irish population becoming alienated from church property held by the Protestant Church.

control of Drogheda opened the approach to Dublin and provided the surest prospect of success.[5] In the early stages of the rebellion, the Ulster rebels met with only local resistance; it was not until they found themselves in control of most of Ulster and marched into Louth and Meath that they had their first engagement with government troops.[6] The rebel army was encouraged by a victory over the government troops at Julianstown Bridge in late November 1641 and the 'Old English' of the whole of the county of Louth annexed with the rebels.[7]

A major confrontation followed in Drogheda between the Ulster rebel army and the loyalist defenders, supported by disaffected Old English families in the area, including the Darcys and the Nettervilles. A 1641 deposition by Richard Streete refers to a garrison in Darcy's house in Platin and refers to a meeting with Lord Netterville of Dowth which took place in a 'room in the castle'.[8] The depositions detail the input of the local landowners in the

rebellion. Nicholas Darcy was appointed to the 'Council of War', while Lords Slane and Gormanstown were 'local captains' over the baronies of Slane and Duleek (respectively). Their job was to raise horsemen for the defence of the area.[9] Darcy was in constant touch with the leaders of the rebellion throughout the period of the siege.[10]

The sequence of events in the siege of Drogheda was as follows. After their victory at Julianstown, the rebels encircled the town. Sir Phelim O'Neill, leader of the rebels, established his headquarters at Plunket's castle in Beaulieu, and his detachments also occupied the castle of Rathmullan, Mornington, a stone house at Oldbridge, Tullyallen and Ballymakenny.[11] For four months rebel energies were concentrated on the siege and the creation of effective military units. Three attacks on the walls of Drogheda resulted in two breaches, but none succeeded in taking the town. Drogheda was effectively cut off until February when a small fleet of vessels containing supplies

Table 1
Topographical features in the Bend of the Boyne
associated with the 1641 rebellion

Location	Site type	SMR No.
Dowth	Castle	20:18
Dowth	Church	20:19
Knowth	Church	19:30
Monknewtown	Church	19:18
Oldbridge	Stone house	No precise location
Platin	Castle	Destroyed
Rathmullan	Castle	No precise location

entered the town. The degree to which local landowners supported the insurrection is highlighted in another 1641 deposition. Lady Netterville of Dowth refused to allow the grazing of cows belonging to those besieged in Drogheda on the lands of Netterville manor. The allegation was that Lord and Lady Netterville were associated with efforts to starve the defenders of Drogheda.[12]

Finally, in March 1642 the Boyne froze over, removing a barrier placed in the river by the rebels to block any supply boats getting to the townsfolk. Drogheda had survived the siege. The rebels retreated to fight a rearguard action at Ardee, aware of the approach of Crown troops with the Earl of Ormond. They fled northwards towards Dundalk, abandoning the local Old English landowners. Lord Moore had remained loyal to the crown and successfully defended his estate at Tullyallen.

In the aftermath of the siege (5 March 1642), Moore, Lord of Mellifont, led out 400 foot and 80 horse from his own estates and defeated the rebels in the area.[13] On 13 March, the Earl of Ormond was prohibited from passing the Boyne with loyal forces.[14] Confined, therefore, to the lower Boyne Valley, he marched to Slane, burning the town and many of the surrounding villages to strike terror into the Irish.[15] Ormond furnished Sir Henry Tichbourne, commander of the crown troops, with two pieces of cannon, two troops of horse and four companies of foot soldiers. Tichbourne then attacked Platin Castle, which ultimately surrendered on terms that the garrison might depart unharmed.[16] This stage of the campaign resulted in devastating damage to church property. Bishop Dopping's later visitations to the churches in county Meath in 1682–85 noted that the church and chancel in Slane were 'down' since 1641 and that Dowth church was also ruined. At Knockcommon the church and chancel walls were standing but out of repair since 1641. The church at Knowth was also ruined, and the chapel at Monknewtown out of repair.[17]

On 16 April 1642, the Old English supporting the 1641 uprising were identified as Nicholas Darcy of Platin, Lord Viscount Netterville of Dowth and Richard Porter of Oldbridge.[18] Nicholas Darcy's estate at Platin was confiscated but was later restored.[19] The tenacious Netterville family remained active against the crown and were involved in the Catholic Confederation which convened in Kilkenny in 1642 to establish a provisional government.[20] The Cromwellian Settlement would ultimately lead to the dispossession of the Nettervilles. However, under the Act of Explanation of 1665, the core of the estate at Dowth and Proudfootstown was returned and survived in Netterville hands into the nineteenth century. At Beaulieu, the Plunket castle used as a camp by Sir Phelim O'Neill was removed and a fine house built on the site by the family of Sir Henry Tichburne who commanded the troops that captured the estate in 1642.[21]

War continued unabated for another seven years until the arrival of Oliver Cromwell in 1649 and his decisive conquest of Ireland. Cromwell's campaign in Ireland was an extension of the English civil war between parliament and the royalists who supported Charles II. In Ireland, this support was organised by the Earl of Ormond who, in 1649, succeeded in making terms with the Confederate Catholics. Again Cromwell identified the Boyne and Drogheda town as his passport to the northern portion of Ireland and the securing of Dublin's northern approaches.[22] For operations against Drogheda, Cromwell used eight infantry regiments and six cavalry regiments, plus some troops and dragoons (infantry on horseback) totalling c.10,000–12,000 men and eight field guns. Drogheda was treated with particular severity and the atrocities suffered by the townspeople are well documented.[23]

Cromwell's campaign was concentrated in the immediate environs of Drogheda and had little impact on the settlements further up river in the Bend of the Boyne area. There had been some attempts at crossing the Boyne further west of the town at Oldbridge and Drybridge. On 3 September, news reached Sir Arthur Aston, governor of Drogheda, that 500 of the enemy's horse was drawing towards the ford of Oldbridge.[24] Two days later Aston reported to Ormond that a party of Cromwell's men had crossed the Boyne at a ford near the town at low tide on the previous day but had been driven back down Drybridge Hill to the river. They had little success up to the time the town was stormed.[25] Prior to Cromwell's arrival in Drogheda, some effort was made to destroy strongholds in the vicinity which could be used against them. Aston reported to Ormond that he had been demolishing or burning castles in the area including Gormanstown (on the Delvin River), Ballygarth, Dardistown and Athcarne (along the Nanny River). He also described Platin Castle as 'a strong place which had no water in it', meaning that it

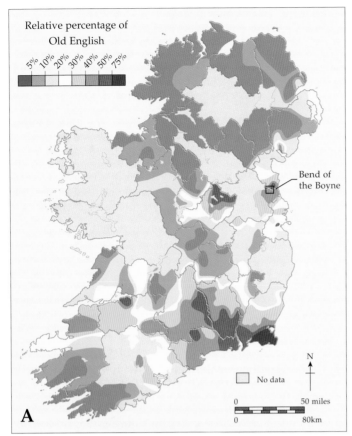

Relative percentage of
Old English

5% 10% 20% 30% 40% 50% 75%

Bend of
the Boyne

No data

N

0   50 miles

0   80km

A

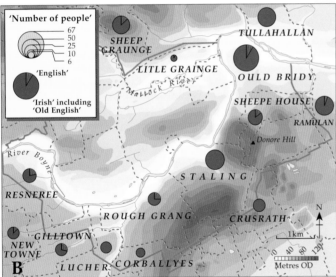

'Number of people'

67
50
25
10
6

'English'

'Irish' including
'Old English'

SHEEP GRAUNGE

TULLAHALLAN

LITTLE GRAINGE

OULD BRIDY

Mattock River

SHEEPE HOUSE

RAMULAN

Donore Hill

River Boyne

STALING

RESNEREE

ROUGH GRANG

CRUSRATH

N

1km

GILLTOWN

NEW TOWNE

LUCHER CORBALLYES

0 40 80 120
Metres OD

B

Fig. 5 A) Old English names predominate (over 40%) among those recorded as being Irish in Census returns of 1659. B) Irish (which include Old English) comprise 90% of the area's population. The 'Census' of 1660 is an abstract of the poll-tax returns of 1660. It provides details of the population within each townland; the number of families, the principal person of standing in the locality and whether those enumerated were 'English' or 'Irish'.[26] The distribution of Old English as a percentage of the principal Irish names listed in the Census shows a high concentration within the Bend of the Boyne.[27] This is testimony to the continuity of population from the medieval period. The picture is incomplete, however, because the records for the barony of Slane – most of the core area of the Bend of the Boyne – do not survive. Of those places listed, 90% are described as being Irish. Oldbridge was the most populous townland at this time.[28] The first known reference to Roughgrange is included in this source and on the Down Survey maps.

either had no moat surrounding it or that the castle lacked a source of water for withstanding a siege.[29] On 5 September, Aston reported that Cromwell's men had in fact repossessed these castles.[30]

MID-SEVENTEENTH-CENTURY SURVEYS

The Civil Survey   Following the success of the Cromwellian campaign, the Civil Survey was undertaken to obtain accurate information on the location and contents of the confiscated lands. In 1642 the English parliament had passed the 'Adventurers Act', inviting Englishmen to contribute money towards the cost of conquering Ireland. In return, they were guaranteed land in Ireland at the end of the war. The intention was to provide allotments of Irish land to pay officers, soldiers and those who invested in the war of the Commonwealth government. The survey was by inquisition, and was termed the Civil Survey because it

Table 2
Population from the Census of Ireland 1660

Townland		English	Irish	Total
Corballis	Corballyes	0	12	12
Cruicerath	Crusrath	0	23	23
Gilltown	Gilltown	6	15	21
Lougher	Lucher	0	18	18
Littlegrange	Litle Grainge	2	24	6
Newgrange	Ould Bridy	6	61	67
Rathmullan	Ramulan	3	48	51
Rossnaree	Resneree	6	21	27
Roughgrange	Rough Grang	6	18	24
Sheephouse	Sheepe house	5	28	33
Stalleen	Staling	0	54	54
Total	**11 Townlands**	**34 (10.1%)**	**302 (89.9%)**	**336**

Table 3
Agricultural statistics for the Bend of the Boyne 1654[31]

Townland	Arable	Pasture	Meadow	Other
Balfeddock	227	5 (+ meadow)	-	10 (bog)
Clonlusk	-	2	30	-
Corballis (part)	40	17	3	-
Cruicerath	200	100	4	-
Donore	80	70	10	-
Dowth	340	60	30	12 (bog)
Gilltown	125	101	4	-
Glebe	-	5	-	-
Knowth	240	0	8	5 (bog)
Lougher	160	38	2	-
Littlegrange	48	12	2	-
Monknewtown	500	40 (+ meadow)	-	50 (wood)
Newgrange	300	3	-	-
Oldbridge	250	40	12	-
Platin	400	200	2	2 (wood)
Proudfootstown	100	20	12	-
Rathmullan	250	180	40	-
Rossnaree	300	46	4	-
Roughgrange	200	45	-	-
Sheephouse	60	54	8	-
Stalleen (inc. Redmountain)	200	100	2	48 (mtn)
Total	**3685 (73%)**	**1148 (22%)**	**171 (3%)**	**127 (2%)**

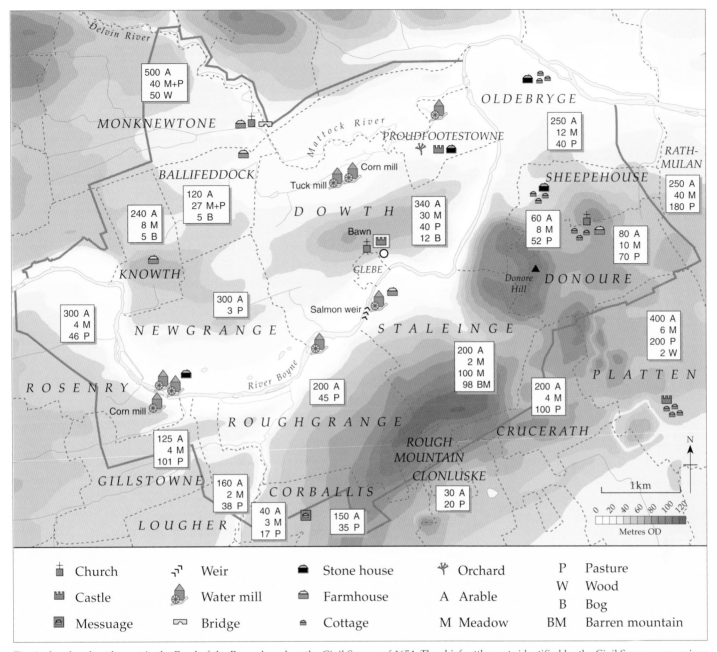

Fig. 6   Land and settlement in the Bend of the Boyne based on the Civil Survey of 1654. The chief settlements identified by the Civil Survey were minor nucleations around the large stone houses of Oldbridge and Sheephouse, adjacent to Donore church and Platin Castle. This is a radically different picture from the one recorded just a century earlier. The change of ownership from Cistercian to secular entrepreneurs initiated a centrifugal process which resulted in the virtual disappearance of Monknewtown, Sheephouse and Balfeddock villages. The minor settlements of Rossnaree and Gilltown disappeared between 1540 and 1645. The dispersed settlement form clearly has its origins in the seventeenth century.

was made under the jurisdiction of special courts called Courts of Survey and concerned the civil authorities. These courts were to establish and record the possessions of landowners and the tenure and titles of their estates. A survey founded on authentic information of the old inhabitants was directed to be made.[32]

The Civil Survey for county Meath opens with a description of barony boundaries based on actual perambulation by the jurors. It provides information on proprietorial geography, settlement, land quality and valuation.[33] The subdivision of the barony into parishes and the division of the parishes into townships or villages localised the data which is so important for historical geographical research. From an administrative viewpoint, the lands on the north side of the river lay in the barony of Slane and civil parishes of Monknewtown and Dowth; south of the river the lands lay within the barony of Duleek and parishes of Donore, Duleek, Duleek Abbey and Knockcommon. The largest owners were Lord Moore, who held the lands formerly belonging to Mellifont; Lord

Table 4
Topographical features in the Bend of the Boyne
mentioned in the Civil Survey of 1654

Location	Site type	SMR No.
Balfeddock	Farmhouse	No precise location
Corballis	Messuage	No precise location
Donore	Cabins	No precise location
Donore	Church	20:11
Donore	Farmhouse	No precise location
Dowth	Castle and bawn	20:18
Dowth	Church	20:19
Dowth	Corn mill	No precise location
Dowth	Orchard	Destroyed
Dowth	Pigeon house	Destroyed
Dowth	Salmon weir	20:28
Dowth	Stone house	20:18
Dowth	Tuck mill	No precise location
Knowth	Farmhouse	No precise location
Monknewtown	Church	19:19
Monknewtown	Farmhouse	No precise location
Monknewtown	Stone bridge	No precise location
Newgrange	Mill	19:6804
Newgrange	Mill	Destroyed
Newgrange	Stone house	No precise location
Newgrange	Weir	Destroyed
Oldbridge	Cabins	No precise location
Oldbridge	Stone house	No precise location
Platin	Cabins	No precise location
Platin	Castle	Destroyed
Proudfootstown	Castle	20:01
Proudfootstown	Mill	No precise location
Proudfootstown	Orchard	No precise location
Proudfootstown	Stone house	No precise location
Rossnaree	Corn mill	26:0502
Roughgrange	Mill	Destroyed
Sheephouse	Cabins	No precise location
Sheephouse	Stone house	No precise location
Stalleen	Farmhouse	No precise location
Stalleen	Farmhouse	No precise location
Stalleen	Mill	20:2803

Netterville who held most of the parish of Dowth; Stephen Cormacke of Cruicerath; Nicholas Darcy of Platin; Peter Hussey who partly held Corballis and Clonlusk; John Draycott of Mornington and Roughgrange; and at Lougher, Robert Allen 'of St Wolstans' in county Dublin. Thus the land in our study area in the middle of the seventeenth century was held by just eight landowners; all, with the exception of Lord Moore, were termed 'Irish papists'.

The lands in the barony of Duleek were described as 'generally good and profitable being arable, meadow and pasture'.[34] The barony of Slane was said to be 'in general arable, having meadow and pasture, being good and profitable land'.[35] In the middle of the seventeenth century, the Bend of the Boyne community practised a largely tillage economy with 73% arable (land capable of producing good tillage crops rather than actual land in tillage at that time), 22% pasture, 3% meadow, and 2% under bog, mountain or woodland (table 1). In the seventeenth century, the Boyne Valley was part of a great corn-growing area that stretched from north county Dublin

to south Louth.[36] It was also an important corn-milling region as indicated by the concentration of mills in the valley recorded in the Civil Survey. There were eight mills in the study area in 1654 compared to just three mills in 1540. There were also many tuck mills in the valley (one within the study area), which shows that the sheep and wool trade, initiated by the Cistercians, continued to make a significant contribution to the local economy.

Although the settlement hierarchy indicated in the earlier sixteenth-century documents is still in evidence – with castles and their outhouses, stone houses, farm houses and cabins – the number of dwellings mentioned in the Civil Survey is much lower than that in the earlier medieval extents. They fell from 61 to 14 dwellings, a reduction of 77%. This may suggest that Lord Moore deliberately removed a large number of tenants on taking over the Mellifont estate. In the mid-seventeenth century, the Boyne Valley had a more dispersed character of settlement which is in stark contrast to the numerous small villages described in the Medieval extents. However, the mills and weirs, formerly developed by the Cistercian monks, continued to be used.

The Civil Survey contains the first detailed description of the parish of Dowth since the fourteenth century, which incorporates the townlands of Dowth and Proudfootstown; these had been outside the Mellifont estates.[37] The manor of Dowth contained one ploughland and a half, calculated at 442 acres incorporating 340 arable, 30 meadow, 60 pasture and 12 bog. At Dowth a manorial village still focused around a castle with a bawn and a church. Within the village centre was a stone house, a stable and outhouses. There was also a farmhouse, malt house, corn mill, tuck mill, pigeon house and one salmon weir on the Boyne.

The Down Survey maps   The mapping project which came to be known as the Down Survey was the most complete survey of Ireland prior to that of the Ordnance Survey in the mid-nineteenth century. It was established at the end of 1654 when William Petty undertook to 'admeasure all the forfeited lands' of Ireland.[38] Because this enterprise was an aspect of plantation and confiscation, less attention was paid to lands which were not to be transferred. Consequently, areas within the Pale were not so thoroughly mapped and much of the Bend of the Boyne was not mapped in detail.

Some landscape detail is included on the Down Survey map of the barony of Slane. The sketch of the towerhouse at Dowth depicts a substantial building with a surrounding bawn. It also shows the two mills on the Mattock River at Dowth and two houses are indicated at

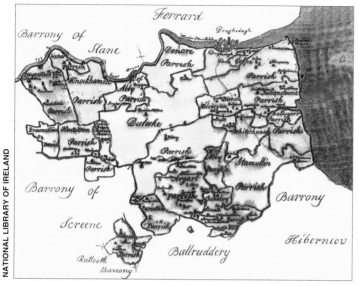

NATIONAL LIBRARY OF IRELAND

Fig. 7 Detail from the Down Survey map of Duleek barony, 1654. Although ownership of land remained remarkably unchanged within the Bend of the Boyne, changes in land ownership elsewhere in Ireland gave rise to an unprecedented upsurge in mapping enterprises and accompanying surveys. The Boyne Valley was included in this recording process and the seventeenth-century surveys provide a baseline for studies of the modern landscape within the area: the Civil Survey, Down Survey maps of 1654, and the Census of 1659.

Proudfootstown which, according to the Civil Survey, contained a castle, stone house, orchard and corn mill.[39] For the area south of the Boyne, the Duleek parish map shows a building by the river at Roughgrange, and turretted buildings at Lougher and Platin. The Duleek barony map shows a river crossing between Slane and Rossnaree. This corresponds with the location of the crossing chosen by Schomberg in the Battle of the Boyne as depicted in Story's drawing of the battle.

LANDSCAPE AND THE BATTLE OF THE BOYNE 1690

The 'Glorious Revolution' of 1688 in England deposed James II, the last Catholic English King, and replaced him with his daughter Mary and her Dutch husband William III, the Protestant Prince of Orange and ruler of the Dutch Republic.[40] In February 1689, William and Mary were crowned joint monarchs of the three kingdoms. Although William controlled England, he had not brought Ireland and Scotland under his sway. As a ploy to distract William, who had been involved in a war with France, Louis XIV decided to back James II in a war against William in Ireland and thus keep him out of Europe. This war was to decide both international and Irish issues and had been prosecuted for a year before the Battle of the Boyne. By the spring of 1690, William was determined to break the deadlock in Ireland and redirect his resources to the European campaign against Louis XIV. By that time James had secured his position in the three southern provinces

but had failed to take Ulster. If James wished to hold Dublin, he had to make the Boyne his line of defence, described in contemporary terms as the 'old Rubicon of the Pale'.[41] The Boyne offered the last significant natural barrier before Dublin and a formidable line of defence.

In the summer of 1690, this major conflict decided the destiny of the crowns of England, Ireland and Scotland. Around 60,000 men, in two multinational armies, met at the Boyne. James's army of 25,000 included mainly Irish and French, but also Germans, Walloons and British Jacobite exiles. William's 35,000 troops included principally British and Dutch, but also Danes, French Huguenots, Germans, Irish Protestants, Latvians, Poles, Swedes and Swiss. With an outflanking movement led by the Duke of Schomberg upstream at Rossnaree and a frontal attack at Oldbridge on 1 July 1690, King William of Orange defeated James II, and strengthened his hold on the English throne.

For the purposes of this study, the most relevant aspect of accounts and illustrations of the Battle of the Boyne is their insight into the terrain over which it was fought.[42] The core area of operations extended from Drogheda to Slane and south to Duleek; the position of bridges across the Boyne at Drogheda and Slane and fords at Oldbridge, Stalleen and Rossnaree largely determined its extent. By following the stages of the battle on the ground, we can look at the local terrain with the eye of a military strategist, identifying the high ground, fords and passes which provided natural defence and military advantage.

The area of operations of the battlefield largely coincides with the Bend of the Boyne. The historical sources provide considerable topographical information facilitating a reconstruction of the seventeenth-century landscape in the Bend of the Boyne. The sources also allow for the identification of present landmarks associated with this famous battle. By extracting topographical detail from eyewitness accounts of the battle contained in letters, diaries, secondary sources and local traditions, combined with contemporary prints and maps of the battle and excavation evidence, an attempt can be made to reconstruct the entire landscape at the time of the battle. Contemporary prints of the Boyne battle are few and unreliable, largely products of the Dutch market for domestic sale in the Netherlands.[43] Illustrations of the Boyne battlefield were drawn or painted well into the eighteenth century, but we cannot depend on these for accurate depictions of the seventeenth-century landscape. However, amongst the many accounts of the Battle of the Boyne, George Story's *Impartial History* (1693) is particularly enlightening, with its accompanying topographical maps of the battlefield and the surrounding countryside.[44]

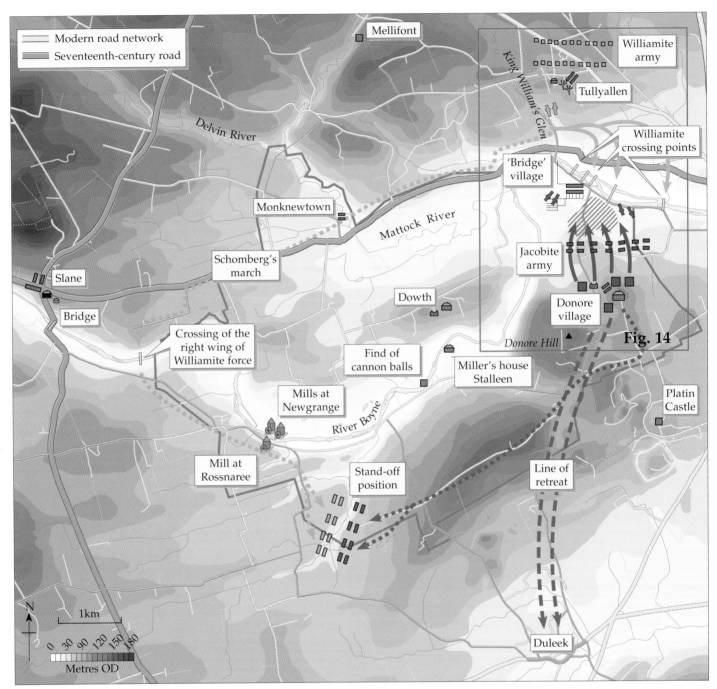

Fig. 8   The fighting was largely confined to the area of Oldbridge, the first fordable point of the Boyne above Drogheda, where the deep river banks made the task of defence easy. The defending Jacobite army had local cover to the river's edge with good defensive terrain back to Donore Hill. The buildings at Oldbridge and the fences and ridges on the hillside provided excellent cover; the gradual slopes of the valley were ideal for cavalry charges. The Roughgrange/Donore Hill area screened observations from the north for the full extent of its length. Yet the position was vulnerable: the bend in the Boyne meant that troops at Oldbridge were positioned in a loop of the river and were in danger of being outflanked, which is in fact what happened. In contrast, King William's Glen in the north was the only place where there could be concealment for the Williamite forces.[45] The high ground of Tullyallen could be seen from the south bank of the river and from Drogheda town.

What follows is a discussion of the seventeenth-century landscape as it was seen by the participants of the Battle of the Boyne, under the headings of topography and land use, roads, settlements and battle landmarks based on paintings and written sources concerned with the conflict. The objective is to identify and map all the features associated with the battle site.

Battle landmarks   From the battle accounts, it is possible to locate the position of the encampments, the placement of field pieces, the areas over which combat took place and the terrain through which troop movements occurred. These are the areas likely to contain archaeological deposits and to be identified for public interpretation. Despite the international importance of this battle, they remain unmarked!

On the day before battle, the Williamite army camped on the north side of Tullyallen, described by Story as 'a small village'. The exact position of 'the English Camp' is indicated as two broken lines (G), a good distance apart, running for 3km east–west. The position of the 'Irish Army or Jacobite encampment' is shown by two closely spaced broken lines (B) on the north-facing slope below the old church at Donore and to the rear of Oldbridge village. The Jacobites also camped nearer to Drogheda, in two lines from the hills of Rathmullan to Oldbridge (see fig. 11, p. 117).[46]

The Williamite battery was located on an upper south-facing slope on the east side of King William's Glen roughly where there is a viewing platform located today. This position overlooked the ford at Oldbridge. It comprised thirty-six heavy field guns, not including siege pieces and mortars.[47] Some of these are shown in Theodore Maas's engraving and Jan Wyck's painting of the battle scene. Maas also shows a battery at the river's edge on the south side of the road. The Jacobites had eighteen field guns, mainly six and twelve pounders, in three batteries which were planted on two eminences commanding the ford at Yellow Island. A third small battery was placed opposite the ford, at the confluence of the Mattock River, and west of Oldbridge village.[48] Story's map (1693) shows five fording points between Drybridge and Oldbridge.[49]

The fording points across Grove and Yellow Island are shown by Story. The river could also be crossed at Drybridge at the point identified on the OS map as 'Pass If You Can'.[50] One of the last battles of the day took place when William crossed the river at 'Pass If You Can' and attacked Donore.

William's strategy for the battle involved a major diversion near Slane, commanded by Schomberg's son Meinhard, with the main attack directed across the ford at Oldbridge. Whilst the right wing of the Irish army was well defended at Drogheda bridge, on an important north-south route, its left wing was left unprotected at Slane. In the early hours of 1 July, Schomberg, with an infantry of 3,000 men, 4,000 troops on horseback and two dragoon regiments, crossed the Boyne below Knowth.

Between Oldbridge and Slane, the only ford capable of being used by the infantry was at Rossnaree. Story's map shows only one ford at Rossnaree on the Slane side of the bend in the river, to the west of the present Rossnaree House. This section of the river provides easy access to and from the river. This may have been the ford used by Schomberg.[51] An eyewitness account of a trooper in Schomberg's force describes the crossing of the Boyne thus: 'the passage was a very steep hill, and a shallow river at the bottom, that led into a very fine plain.'[52] This account

Fig. 9   This drawing by Theodor Maas represents infantry crossing the river below Oldbridge with Donore Hill in the distance; a corn field can be seen in the middle distance. This is one of the few contemporary engravings of the battle to appear in England. Dutch military artist Theodor Maas (or Maes) was invited by William to Ireland to cover the campaign. One other sketch survives from his time in Ireland.[53]

PRIVATE COLLECTION

Fig. 10 This depiction of the Battle of the Boyne, by Jan Wyck, was based on a drawing by his fellow Dutch artist Theodore Maas executed during the battle. The painting accurately portrays the countryside of the day: the village of Oldbridge, the church on Donore Hill, the placement of batteries in King William's Glen, roads and trackways, and the generally unenclosed landscape. A large number of canvases survive purporting to depict the Boyne, the majority by Jan Wyck. Born in Haarlem, he followed the exploits of the Prince of Orange. When William went to Ireland, it is unlikely that Wyck accompanied him; he probably copied details from Maas.[54]

describes the area aptly. Story's map places Schomberg's crossing much further west than the ford of Rossnaree, at Fennor in fact, where a river crossing is marked on the Down Survey map. After fording the Boyne, Schomberg marched his forces further south until they reached low boggy terrain which effectively blocked their advance.

James, convinced that the movement at Rossnaree was the beginning of the main attack, dispatched Lauzun and the French brigade with Maxwell's dragoons and Patrick Sarsfield's cavalry regiment. The six regiments of Lauzun's French brigade stumbled across an impregnable defensive position on rising ground fronted by a bog and steep ravine protected to the south by the bog of Gilltown. Sarsfield and Maxwell, who had gone over the ground thoroughly, explained to James that counter-attack was impossible because the ravine blocked their entire front.[55] The only counter-attack came from Neale O'Neill with a small force of his dragoons, but this attack foundered. The Jacobite dragoons had to fall back in the direction of Duleek. This engagement was virtually over by nine o'clock when William dispatched Douglas to reinforce Schomberg with the remaining cavalry. Physical conditions dictated a stand-off at Roughgrange.

Two regiments of foot, Antrim and the Earl of Clanricarde, had been delegated to defend Oldbridge for the Jacobites. The other five infantry regiments, under overall command of Hamilton, were spread out on a wide front to the south and east of Oldbridge. The Jacobite cavalry, led by Sheldon, was stationed in reserve behind the church at Donore. Two dragoon regiments screened the far right at Rathmullan. The fighting was largely confined to the area of Oldbridge where the Boyne was fordable and extended as far south as Donore old church where James took up his position. Story's map shows five crossings from west to east. The Blue Dutch Guards, who relied on pistol fire, gathered at King William's Glen, crossed first and were attacked by the Jacobite foot guards (L). The Jacobite guards soon fell back and the Dutch advance guard re-grouped south of Oldbridge. The first line of William's centre then moved down to the fords of Oldbridge and Yellow Island. Colonels John Mitchelbourn and Gustavus Hamilton's regiments of Derry and Enniskillen infantry crossed the river. On their left, facing the Irish infantry, the two Huguenot regiments of Comte de la Caillemote and Cambon also forded the river. The next Williamite units to cross were Colonel St John's Derrymen and Sir John

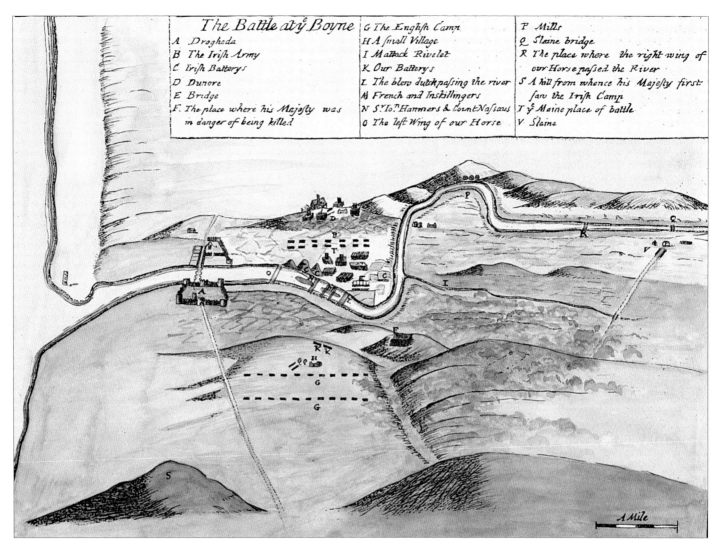

The Battle at ÿ Boyne

A Drogheda
B The Irish Army
C Irish Batterys
D Dunore
E Bridge
F The place where his Majesty was in danger of being killed

G The English Camp
H A small Village
I Mattock Rivelet
K Our Batterys
L The blew dutch passing the river
M French and Inskillingers
N Sr Tos Hanmers & Count Nassaus
O The left Wing of our Horse

P Mills
Q Slaine bridge
R The place where the right wing of our Horse passed the River
S A hill from whence his Majesty first saw the Irish Camp
T ÿ Maine place of battle
V Slaine

Fig. 11   This reconstruction of the Battle of the Boyne is primarily based on Story's map of 1693, with some additional detail recounted in other eyewitness accounts. The reconstruction is drawn from the 'Protestant' perspective, looking south with north at the bottom of the map.

Hanmer's English, supported by the Dutch regiment of Hendrik van Nassau, a cousin of William's. On the Jacobite side Richard Hamilton moved his infantry down the hill to contest the new crossings whilst Sheldon and Berwick advanced on the Dutch Guards with the cavalry. The Danish division forded the Boyne at Yellow Island around eleven o'clock with nine regiments of infantry spearheaded by the grenadier company of the Danish Royal Guards. The first Williamite horsemen crossed the Boyne about noon, led by Ginkel, managing to haul two small cannons over with them. They were attacked by James's dragoons who had been protecting their right flank. The Jacobite army under Hamilton retreated to Donore churchyard. The Irish horse wheeled and charged for the last time at Platin.

A number of finds have been collected from the battlefields of Oldbridge. These include coins and weaponry, now held in the National Museum of Ireland (table 2). Most recently, two seventeenth-century cannon

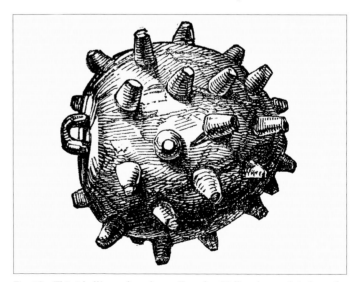

Fig. 12   This 'shell' was found near Townley Hall and may date from the Battle of the Boyne. It is supposed to have been used in a weapon known as the 'Morning Star'. The public house of the same name in the village of Tullyallen could have taken its name from this weapon.

DÚCHAS/CON BROGAN

Fig. 13 View of Oldbridge from the site of the Williamite battery at King William's Glen.

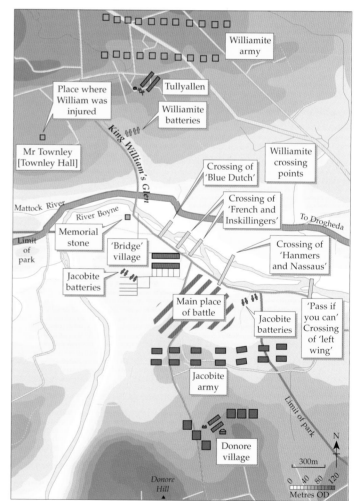

balls were recovered from the Boyne at Stalleen during an underwater excavation on the bed of the river where a footbridge for the Brú na Bóinne Visitor Centre was to be constructed.[56] More recently, a pilot archaeological survey of the estate discovered battle-related material such as musket balls and a coin from 1659. A metal-detecting survey of the battlefield site identified zones with high densities of metal artefacts. Conflicts may have taken place in these areas.[57]

Topography and land use The Williamite forces were impressed by the fertility of the plain watered by the Boyne.[58] One trooper described the area as 'a very fine plain'.[59] The Danish ambassador Foulerasse was to record:

> As we descended the small hills [drumlins] with which the northern part of the kingdom is studded, we discovered a very fine fertile plain watered by the Boyne.

According to Story's account, William 'rode along and said it was [land] worth fighting for'.[60] The account describes cornfields fronting the north side of the river, and fences and stone walls bordering the fields.[61] Story's map has sketchy indications of these enclosures. He also records that 'a party of about 40 horse ... stood upon a ploughed

Fig. 14 The main area of conflict during the Battle of the Boyne based on Story's 1693 map.

NATIONAL GALLERY OF IRELAND

Fig. 15   Detail from The Battle of the Boyne by Jan Wyck. It shows the village at Oldbridge on the south bank of the river. The buildings were removed during the construction of a canal a century later and the subsequent creation of a demesne at Oldbridge.

GERALDINE STOUT

Fig. 17   'A damned deep bog' at Roughgrange separated the two armies on the south side of the Boyne. Sarsfield and Schomberg were forced to a stand-off at this point due to the impassable terrain. James wrongly believed that Schomberg's movement marked the beginning of the main attack.

field' on Donore Hill.[62] The south side of the Boyne is shown as hilly and inhospitable on Story's map and depicts the difficult terrain which both armies experienced at Roughgrange. As noted above, the boggy valley west of Roughgrange was of crucial importance well into the battle. Sarsfield and Maxwell reported that a cavalry charge was impossible as there were two double ditches with high banks and a little brook between them in the valley that separated the two forces:[63]

> We drew up to enclose the enemy's whole army but a damned deep bog lay between us, we could not soon pass.

This terrain is still evident today, but it is not as boggy due to eighteenth- and nineteenth-century field drainage. It is impossible to quantify the extent of field enclosure from these seventeenth-century records. It is certain, however, that extensive areas had been enclosed before the beginning of the century.

Roads   These accounts provide the earliest detailed description of the routes between local communications in the Bend of the Boyne. By the late seventeenth century, a well-developed infrastructure of roads and surfaced lanes was bordered by banks and high hedges. This network of

GERALDINE STOUT

Fig. 16   A) Du Noyer's 1842 drawing of Colonel Caillemote's grave at Oldbridge. It was then marked by an elm tree. He was leader of the Protestant French during the battle and died alongside Duke Schomberg and Dr Walker of Derry. B) This commemorative stone now marks Colonel Caillemote's grave. It can be found just behind the gate lodge at the entrance to Oldbridge House.

Table 5
Archaeological finds from the Boyne battlefield site
at Oldbridge in the National Museum of Ireland

1860:368	Iron cannon ball found near obelisk

1A/284/89 (finds from metal-detecting activities at Oldbridge 1989)

No. 6	Coin of William III, sixpence, silver
No. 10	Coin of William III, sixpence, silver
No. 15	Flintlock hammer, found in ploughed field
No. 25	Lead ball, possibly miniature cannon shot
No. 33	Coin of Charles II, Hibernia farthing
No. 34	Coin of Charles II, farthing 1674, St Patrick's coinage
No. 35	Coin of Charles II, farthing 1674, St Patrick's coinage, found at Oldbridge
No. 36	Coin of Charles II, Hibernia farthing
No. 37	Coin of James II, half penny, regular coinage 1686
No. 38	Musket balls, 100 fired and unfired; coin of James II, half penny 1685–91, found in ploughed land
No. 59	Powder measure

Table 6
Topographical features in the Bend of the Boyne
associated with the Battle of the Boyne

Location	Site type	SMR No.
Dowth	Dwelling	20:18
Drogheda	Bridge	19:24
Drogheda–Slane	17th-century road	
Drogheda–Oldbridge	17th-century lane	Site
Drybridge	Ford	
Duleek–Oldbridge	17th-century road	Part of
King William's Glen	Mill house	
Mellifont/		
Monknewtown	17th-century road	
Monknewtown	17th-century village	Site
Newgrange	Ford	
Newgrange	Mill	Site 19:68904
Newgrange	Pass	
Oldbridge	Battlefield	Site 20:25
Oldbridge	Caillemote stone	
Oldbridge	Find spot	
Oldbridge	Fords	
Oldbridge	Jacobite battery	Site
Oldbridge	Jacobite encampment	
Oldbridge	17th-century road	Part of
Oldbridge	Village	Site
Oldbridge–Tullyallen	17th-century road	
Platin	Castle	Site
Rathmullan	Jacobite encampment	
Rossnaree	Ford	
Rossnaree	Mill	Site 26:05
Rossnaree	Pass	
Roughgrange	Battlefield	
Sheephouse	Donore church	20:11
Sheephouse	Donore 17th-century vill.	Site
Sheephouse	Jacobite battery	Site
Sheephouse	Jacobite battery	Site
Sheephouse	Jacobite encampment	
Slane	Bridge	
Stalleen	Find spot	
Stalleen	Houses (Loughwanny)	Site
Stalleen	Mill house	20:27
Townleyhall	Dwelling	Site
Tullyallen	Williamite encampment	
Tullyallen	17th-century village	Site
Tullyallen	Williamite battery	Site
Tullyallen	Williamite battery	Site

roads would have aided, to some extent, the movement of the large bodies of troops involved in the battle to their desirable positions. On the north side of the river, the main highway between Drogheda and Slane was in place with access off this to the village of Monknewtown and to Tullyallen via King William's Glen. Both Maas's drawing and Jan Van Wyck's painting show some of these roads. It is presumed that Schomberg took the back roads from King William's Glen in the direction of Slane, passing north of Townley Hall before joining the main road from Drogheda to Slane by Monknewtown. Sections of this old road run northeast from Monknewtown, cross the Mattock at a ford, and continue to Mellifont.

On the south side of the river, a little lane, also described as 'a stony path bordered by a hedge', ran close to the river's edge from Drogheda to the village of Oldbridge. Ginkel's Williamite regiment was led in a charge along this lane.[64] The exact route from Oldbridge to Duleek taken by the retreating Jacobite army is difficult to determine. A section of disused roadway on the grounds of Oldbridge House may have been part of this seventeenth-century network. It comprises a roughly levelled area defined on each side by a bank and ditch, 10m wide traceable for 400m.[65] A commemorative stone, marked 1690, lies beside the southern terminal of this road. This is thought to commemorate Caillemote, one of the Williamite commanders, who died in the battle.[66] From this old road on the Oldbridge estate, the road to Duleek took a different line from the current road. An older route has been traced on the ground by a local historian in Donore. It ran by Reid's lane and by the Castle Hill to come out at Tobersamanagh at Stalleen. From Tobersamanagh, the road went by Everard's lane and over the hills to Duleek. This road, running over Donore Hill, is visible on Jan Van Wyck's painting.[67] The Jacobites joined the existing main

road to Duleek. We know that there was a road from Oldbridge to Platin because during the battle Hamilton withdrew his Jacobite cavalry back to Platin Castle.[68] The approximate course of this road is indicated on fig. 13.

The road system on the south side of the river between Rossnaree and Stalleen is difficult to determine. One would at least expect that there were roads running north–south either side of the fording points at Rossnaree and Stalleen. The course of east/west routes at this point is uncertain. Story describes a lane by the pass of Rossnaree where there was an encounter between Jacobite Dragoons and Williamite forces.[69] This probably refers to the Slane–Rossnaree road. There is no evidence that a road ran east/west along the river between the two fording points. The absence of roads across the wetlands between Stalleen and Rossnaree hampered the Williamite advance in the south-western field of action.

Settlements   Many settlements and dwellings referred to in earlier documents (some of which have since been removed) are illustrated in some detail in accounts of the battle and contemporary illustrations. The village of Tullyallen is termed 'a small village' on Story's map. A Williamite Colonel Bellingham called on 'Mr. Townly's place', on the present site of the eighteenth-century mansion Townley Hall.[70] The village of Monknewtown, through which Schomberg and his troops passed, is shown in De Hooge's painting off the Drogheda–Slane highway. The village of Slane is depicted as an insignificant street of houses on either side of the main road, its form prior to extensive eighteenth-century remodelling. Buildings are shown at Dowth.

Because the Jacobite position was near Oldbridge, detailed descriptions and drawings of the village exist. This is of particular importance because the village is no longer extant. The village was located close to the river, amidst cornfields and meadows approximately east of the outbuildings beside Oldbridge House near the present canal. Field walking, the analysis of phosphate, and geophysical surveys have identified features which are believed to be the remains of the village.[71] The accounts describe: 'Several hedges and little Irish houses close to the river. There was one house of stone that had a court and some little works about it.'[72] This precisely locates a stone house mentioned in the *Civil Survey* of 1654. A Danish envoy, Foulerasse, wrote of a 'street of the village' suggesting that these houses were arranged on either side of a street.[73] William's Secretary of War, George Clarke, observed that

> About eight or nine of our cannon began to fire upon two houses with yards walled about, that stood on each side of the road on the other side of the Boyne, just over against the ford where the guards were to pass.[74]

This is how the village is shown on Story's map. The French General Hoguette had batteries set up at Oldbridge, and earthworks were dug along the river bank on the day before the battle.[75] De Hooge's painting shows that large holes were blown in the houses and part of what appears to be a church tower had been smashed. This tower is identified as 'a squat church' on the terrier which accompanies the painting. This turret also appears on the Maas engraving. No previous record puts a church at this location, nor is there any mention of a church here in subsequent records. If it was indeed a church, it was constructed after 1654 and destroyed prior to the construction of the Boyne Canal *c*.1750. The vernacular buildings that made up the village of Oldbridge are shown

Fig. 18   Detail from *The Battle of the Boyne, 1 July 1690* by Maas showing Oldbridge village.

in convincing detail on Maas's engraving. They were rectangular in plan, one storey high with thatched roofs and entrances opening onto the Boyne. The houses look more elaborate on De Hooge's painting where there looks to have been some artistic licence taken.

The village of 'Donore' is shown in these contemporary sources on a hill above Oldbridge where the medieval church of Sheephouse is located today. Story's drawing shows that the church (a turreted building) was then in ruins and its walls had been pierced with firelocks. This building is also shown on Maas's engraving. Another roofless building is depicted beside the church on Story's map. The place was said to have been 'full of dungpits and the passage narrow'.[77]

Fig. 19   Detail from *The Battle of the Boyne* (1690) by De Hooge showing the villages of Slane, Monknewtown and Oldbridge at the end of 1690. Romeyn De Hooge, an artist and engraver born in Amsterdam in 1645, produced a view of the fighting at Oldbridge showing the mortal wounding of Dr George Walker.[76]

Fig. 20 The meagre remains of the medieval church on Donore Hill. This building was fortified by the Jacobites during the Battle of the Boyne.

Fig. 21 Many traditions relate to the Battle of the Boyne. During the battle, bread was baked for the men in the oven of this miller's house at Stalleen.

Fig. 22 There is a tradition that an old farmhouse at Sheephouse was a rallying point for the Jacobite army during the battle. It is said to have withstood prolonged attack after the defeat at the ford of Oldbridge. A) The approach to Sheephouse via the line of the old bridle road from the original medieval church at Donore. B) The derelict remains of Sheephouse. C) Sheephouse as depicted in an illustration by George Du Noyer in 1842.

Subsequently, a chapel village developed further south at the base of Donore Hill which was also called Donore. This has led to some confusion about the precise location of one the key encounters during the Battle of the Boyne.

Significant events which took during the battle at Platin Castle provide no details about the settlement there; nevertheless, the site of this castle provides a tangible link with the past. Following the Battle of the Boyne, the castle was looted by the Williamites and the Darcys were outlawed. Later, their estate was confiscated and eventually sold to John Graham of Drogheda. A house was built at Platin *c*.1700 by Graham, replacing the earlier castle which had been involved in the 1641 rebellion. In other troop movements, the Jacobites skirted a small cluster of 'deserted crofts' on the retreat towards Duleek.[78] Local tradition recalls a village called Loughawanny that once stood in the townland of Stalleen. This could be the site of the deserted crofts mentioned in the sources.

Mills are shown on south side of the river on the map accompanying Story's *Impartial history*. These are probably the mills at Newgrange and Rossnaree which are recorded in the Civil Survey of 1654. Local tradition records two associations of millers' houses with events in the battle. Patrick Sarsfield was said to have been brought to a house in King William's Glen. This is probably the mill of Alt mentioned in eighteenth-century deeds. In King William's Glen, there is an area known as the mill rock where this mill presumably stood. Tradition points to a house in Stalleen where bread was baked for the Jacobites. If this tradition was true, this could only have been a small group of Jacobite dragoons on reconnaissance prior to the battle.[79] In seeming confirmation of this tradition, excavations immediately west of the mill produced remains of cannon from the Battle of the Boyne in a place with no other recorded history of involvement in the battle.[80]

EIGHTEENTH-CENTURY ECONOMIC BOOM

If it is claimed that the Irish landscape essentially derives from the eighteenth century,[1] the observation highlights the dramatic changes which occurred at this time. The post-Williamite period in Ireland witnessed the creation of a system of estates leading to a rural landscape of demesnes, farms and fields. Whether these estates were of long standing, recently gained due to seventeenth-century expropriations, or acquired purely as a business speculation, agriculture was reorganised on a fully commercial basis within all of them.[2] With the market economy came improvements in trade and communications. Running through this period of economic boom was the diminution of Catholic rights under the penal laws in favour of a now firmly established Protestant ascendancy.

The eighteenth century was a time of stability in the Boyne Valley. The embattled profile of defensive towerhouses was replaced by grand houses with a domestic spirit.[3] The resident owner maintained a home farm and created an ornamental park, or demesne, as a setting for his mansion. From the Middle Ages, demesnes were the lands held by the manor for its own use and occupation. While retaining their primary function as home farms, they went through a process of landscape ornamentation in the eighteenth century. This transformation was inspired by ideas from abroad, and land-owners grew increasingly aware that the countryside around their house could be designed on a large scale. Demesne components included: tree-lined approaches with complex avenues radiating across the landscape; field boundaries lined with trees; woodland planted in blocks; kitchen gardens in walled enclosures isolated from the house; and lodges at the demesne gates.[4] The impetus to improve the landscape arose, in part, from concern about the precipitate loss of trees in the turbulent seventeenth century. Acts were passed to promote tree planting by landlords and to enforce the planting of trees by their tenants.[5]

Estate records and the first detailed maps of the Bend of the Boyne make it possible to chart the overall process of change. In many cases deeds provide precise dates for new landscape features. Today we come to the Boyne Valley to see its megalithic tombs, but the landscape we travel through was largely shaped in the eighteenth century.

Fig. 1   The most conspicuous development on the north side of the Boyne was the development of Dowth demesne and the enclosure of its adjacent farms in the first half of the eighteenth century. The small amount of woodland which survives in the Boyne Valley is largely a legacy of the eighteenth century.

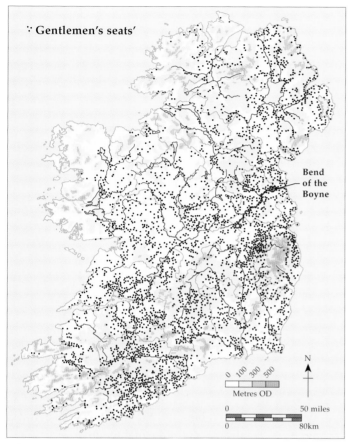

Fig. 2 'Gentlemen's seats', 1785, from Charles Vallancey's 'The royal map of Ireland'. The Liffey, Lee and Blackwater valleys are most densely settled. 'Gentlemen's seats' in the Bend of the Boyne are part of an even distribution in counties Meath and Louth (after Andrews, 1986).

The Landscape of Estates

In the Bend of the Boyne the century of peace which followed the Williamite wars saw the creation of the current enclosed landscape of farm, field and demesne. The main medieval estate blocks survived into the early eighteenth century. In the early 1700s much of the land in the Bend of the Boyne constituted an outlying part of the Moore estate (the major exception was the parish of Dowth which continued to be held by the Netterville family). During the eighteenth century, the Moore estate was leased to a number of speculative middleman interests, largely based in the city of Dublin. The first edition Ordnance Survey 1:10,560 maps of 1837 provide a view of the Boyne Valley landscape as it had evolved in the eighteenth century under these substantial middlemen and landowners. Demesnes at Dowth and Oldbridge were complemented, on a less elaborate scale, by landscaped grounds at Newgrange, Rossnaree, Staleen and Knowth. Mansions were the centrepieces in these landscaped demesnes surrounded by enclosed farms and connected to their markets by new roads and the Boyne navigation canal.

These dramatic landscape changes are exemplified by three estates in the Bend of the Boyne: the Netterville estate at Dowth; the Campbell/Caldwell estate at Newgrange; and the Coddington estate at Oldbridge. Estate records are a key source in chronicling the transformation of the landscape during this period.[6] The shaping of these estates and their constituent farms involved leases from landlords to tenants and strategic marriage arrangements. A useful by-product of the penal laws affecting property was the creation of the Registry of Deeds, established in 1704 to allow all land transactions and conveyances to be registered.[7] A key source material for this period in the Bend of the Boyne are the resulting deeds, the memorials of which are held in the Registry of Deeds, Dublin. The Caldwell and Coddington estate papers in the National Archives also provide valuable insights into the formation of the eighteenth-century landscape.

The Netterville estate   The medieval manor of Dowth had been held by the Netterville family since the thirteenth century. The transformation of the manor lands in the first half of the eighteenth century was principally the work of Viscount Nicholas Netterville, who succeeded to the property in 1727 following the death of his Catholic father. Nicholas had spent two years at the University of Utrecht, returning to Ireland to take over his father's property in August 1728. After conforming to the established church, he took his seat in the House of Lords in the following year.[8] He married Catherine, only daughter of Samuel Burton of Burton Hall, county Carlow, in 1731.[9] Their marriage settlement contains the earliest reference to the 'mansion house' and 'demesne' of Dowth.[10] A series of

Fig. 3   Dowth Hall is a plain rectangular block with one 'show front' set on a ridge above the Boyne river. The main facade is two storeys with five bays. It is probably the work of George Darley, a mason architect who, in 1767, built the Nettervilles' town house in Dublin.[11]

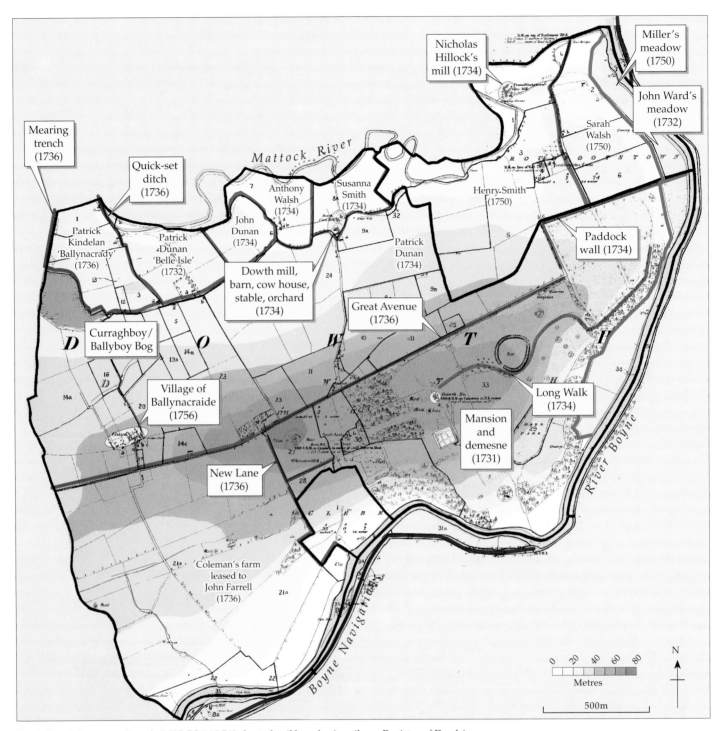

Fig. 4 Dated features at Dowth (1837 OS 1:10,560 sheet, detail based primarily on Registry of Deeds).

subsequent deeds chronicle the creation of a landscaped parkland around this mansion called Dowth Hall, which would not be definitively mapped for another hundred years. A 1734 marriage settlement describes the 'paddock wall' and 'the long walk' which formed a boundary to the 'meadow at the Boyne'.[12] In 1736 the limits of a particular farm are described as being bounded on the east by Lord Netterville's 'new lane', 'grove' and 'the land called glebeland' and on the north by the 'great lane or avenue leading through Dowth to the lands of Newgrange'.[13] A deed of 1750 refers to land in Proudfootstown that bounds in the south with the 'paddock wall' of Dowth (providing a location for this feature) and the 'new walk ditch leading to the Boyne'.[14] The mansion was obviously built before 1731: over the next twenty years, its demesne was created.

The new mansion of Dowth Hall and its demesne turned its back, metaphorically speaking, on the medieval castle. The new residence faced east towards Drogheda and was

Fig. 5 A) In the eighteenth century, a Neolithic passage tomb was incorporated into the pleasure grounds at Dowth. B) The interior of the passage tomb.

separated from the old manorial centre by a plantation of trees. An axial vista to the rear with pleasure grounds incorporated two small Neolithic passage tombs. An orchard was planted behind the Medieval towerhouse and church. Eight acres (3ha) of parkland were delimited in an elongated oval shape and bounded by a row of trees to form the deerpark between Dowth Hall and the Boyne. The only true ornamental feature was the old race-course. This was a parkland of over 57 acres (23ha) in area divided into four rectangles by parallel lines of trees. The road from Dowth to Proudfootstown has three right-angle turns to allow for this race-course. A lodge marks the north-west entrance – probably a nineteenth-century addition.

Once the area for the development of Dowth demesne was decided upon and the work well in progress, the creation and enclosure of estate farms proceeded between the demesne boundaries and the Mattock River. Probably owing to these building projects, the Dowth estate was £11,000 in debt by the 1730s. This led to the sale of Netterville's Westmeath property in Ballymore in 1739 and

Fig. 6 Detail from Beranger's drawing of Dowth passage tomb in 1775. It shows a pagoda-like structure on the top. The 'modern temple' is a summer house where Lord Netterville is said to have attended Mass while it was being said in the old chapel below.

the subsequent vesting of part of the Dowth estate in the hands of trustees. Leasing of the manor was an immediate source of funding for the estate. At least eight leases, ranging from eight to thirty-one years' duration, were issued to Catholic tenantry in the 1730s. There is no cartographic record for the Netterville estate until the 1830s, so we are dependent on the eighteenth-century deeds for descriptions of the leased property.

Deeds from Lord Netterville concerning property at Dowth

Lord Netterville and Patrick Dunan in 1732 for that part of the lands lately called Bell Isle … mearing on the east with John Dunan's farm on the south with the drain leading from the bog of Balliboy to the manor mill of Dowth on the west with the quickset ditch that lies on the east side of Patrick Kindelan's farm in Ballyboy and on the north with the river Mattock and part of the lands of Littlegrange … containing 40 acres of arable land together with one acre of the bog of Balliboy then lately likewise in his possession … to hold for thirty-one years … and also the meadow at the Boyne commonly called John Wear's meadow from the Boyne up to the paddock wall and also the path of the long walk which lay between the said paddock wall and Boyne containing in all about three acres and half and … for yearly rent of twenty shillings per acre for the above mentioned twenty acres and two pounds for the acre of bog also for the above meadow fifteen shillings.[15]

Lord Netterville to Kindelan 1736, … All that and there part of Ballynacrady by then formerly in tenure and occupation of Richard Heany and John McNally containing 23 acres … one part of the lands of Balliboy mearing on the east with a quick set ditch, that leads from the drain of Ballyboy aforesaid northerly on the south to part of the said drain on west to a new ditch made between the said premises and the said bog of Ballyboy and on the north with a ditch leading from the quickset ditch down the mearing trench between Dowth lands and the lands of Ballfaddock and also one park of land that lies on the south side of the drain and the boundary on the east to the houses and gardens near the said drain on the south to a ditch separating the said park from an enclosed piece of ground on the west to a part of the said lands formerly set to Peter Dungan and William Reilly and on the north with part of a said drain … containing by a late survey 19 acres … to hold for 31 years at 9 shillings per acre.[16]

The holdings vary in size from 74 acres (30ha) on Sarah Walsh's farm to Luke Hall's 12 acre holding (5ha).[17] These were enclosed with 'drains' and 'quick set ditch[es]'.[18] A wide variety of agricultural practices are attested to by references in the deeds to 'arable', 'meadow', 'paddock' and 'orchard'.[19] Every lease specified the right of the tenant to exploit an acre of bog at Ballyboy. The holdings are often identified by names that are no longer in use such as 'Belle Isle', 'Dremsale', 'Strevade' and 'Listiveran'.[20] There is a range of buildings on these holdings. 'Cabbins and gardens' are described at Ballynacrade, a place name denoting a clachan or farm village.[21] An impressive cluster of buildings is recorded beside Dowth mill, including a 'dwelling house', 'barn', 'cow house', 'stable' and two other houses or 'tenements'.[22] There are corn mills at Dowth and Proudfootstown; at the latter there is also 'the old tuck mill in the parcel of land called Listiveran'.[23] At least five surnames mentioned in these deeds were still present on the same holdings in the 1830s as recorded in the Tithe Applotment Books: Heeny, Cunningham, Kelly, Farrel and Smith.[24]

The Campbell/Caldwell estate, Newgrange On 14 August 1699, Alice Moore, Countess Dowager of Drogheda, leased the lands of Newgrange for ninety-nine years to Charles Campbell, a Williamite settler.[25] Campbell also shared a lease for the term of seventy-five years with Henry Hall for the lands of Balfeddock that same year.[26] Campbell was described by Edward Lhywd as the 'gentleman of the village who had employed his servants to rob stone from the tomb at Newgrange'.[27] Campbell was able to aquire so much land because he undertook numerous services for the Moore family.[28] Having acquired the lands of Newgrange and Balfeddock, Charles Campbell built a 'mansion' on the property with 'outhouses, coach houses, stables, orchards and gardens'.[29] This settlement is identified on a map of the Caldwell estate in 1766. Caldwell commissioned the noted cartographer Bernard Scalé to map his lands and on this map the Campbell property corresponds with the location of Newgrange House. The origins of this map are discussed below.[30] The 1837 OS 1:10,650 sheet shows blocks of planting to the north of Newgrange House and limited roadside planting. These probably date from the eighteenth century. In 1744 Isaac Butler saw Newgrange House 'buried among trees'.[31]

The middleman Charles Campbell issued leases in the early 1720s in the townlands of Balfeddock, Newgrange and Monknewtown. These farms varied in size from 215 acres (87ha) held by Francis Berrill at Newgrange, to a 152 acre (62ha) holding at Peter Ever's farm at Belfeddock, and a 20 acre (8ha) holding leased to Edward Hall at Rossin in

NATIONAL ARCHIVES

Fig. 7 A Caldwell estate map in 1781 contains a sketch of the mansion at Newgrange.[32] This shows a two-storey building with three bays, two chimneys and a semicircular forecourt. It also shows three cottages north of this, two with chimneys, one without, and another two-storey, three-bay building which is probably Broe House.

1724.[33] Rossin is a settlement off the main Slane road on the borders of Balfeddock and Monknewtown. These lands had only recently been enclosed. The deeds refer to 'a ditch lately made' and 'a new ditch adjoining to the ditch on the highway' at Balfeddock.[34] Reference to 'a little bridge lately made' suggests improvements to the road network.[35] Two memorials indicate that mixed farming was being practised at an intensive level. Mention is made of 'a winter crop' and a 'spring crop', 'cattle' and the use of a 'plough harness' and 'harrow'.[36] There are several references to houses for both tenants and sub-tenants which had 'out houses' and 'gardens' and one had a 'little grove'. There is evidence for another clachan alongside a 'street' in the town of Balfeddock.[37]

DÚCHAS/CON BROGAN

Fig. 8 The ice house, which belonged to Newgrange House, lies to the east of Newgrange tumulus. It is first shown on the 1837 OS map but probably dates from the eighteenth century.

In 1725 the ownership of Newgrange and Balfeddock changed. In his last will and testament, Campbell left them to his grandson, Benjamin Burton of Burton Hall in county Carlow.[38] In 1734 Burton leased this property and the surrounding 191 acres (77ha) to Nicholas Netterville of Dowth who was an in-law through marriage to Catherine Burton.[39] Meanwhile, Andrew Caldwell, brother-in-law of Campbell, had purchased Knowth in 1729.[40] In 1766 Benjamin Burton sold the lands of Newgrange and Balfeddock to Andrew's son, Charles Caldwell, for £8,000. The Caldwell estate now embraced the townland of Knowth which at that time included the present townlands of Crewbane, Newgrange and Balfeddock, with parts of Monknewtown and Littlegrange on the north side of the Boyne and Gilltown on the south side.

The subdivision and additions to the estate started by Charles Campbell were further encouraged by the Caldwell family. As part of this programme of landscape management, Charles Caldwell commissioned Bernard Scalé to undertake a survey of part of his estates in counties Meath and Louth at a scale of forty perches to an inch (1:10,080, the Irish perch measured 21 feet or 6.40m). Antiquities were included on the map making this the first cartographic record of the passage tombs of Knowth and Newgrange. The main function of this map was to identify the tenants and the boundaries of their farms on the estate. Their settlements are identified but there is little indication of fields or land use. Mills are present at Rossnaree and Newgrange. The contemporary network of roads was essentially in place by this time. This important map allows

DÚCHAS/CON BROGAN

Fig. 9   The stone buildings at Newgrange are the outhouses and stables constructed by Charles Campbell in 1734.

Fig. 10   Bernard Scalé's Map
of the Caldwell Estate, 1766

This map allows us to see the transformation that had taken place on the lands along the Boyne since they were leased by the Moores at the turn of the eighteenth century. It also sheds light on the evolution of the townland system. A general trend which becomes apparent from an analysis of both the deeds and cartographic sources is the gradual subdivision of the landscape that takes place as communities develop, rear families and divide resources. The present townland of Crewbane is identified in 1766 as being part of a greater Knowth townland. The boundaries of the farm of Robert Berrell on 297 acres (120ha) coincide with the present townland of Crewbane, except for a portion of land in the north-east corner of the townland which is bisected by the road from Knowth to the main Slane road and shown in 1766 as part of Monknewtown. In 1806 these lands were incorporated into the present townland of Knowth when they were leased to John Cooper of Beamore.[41] A pocket of bog is shown along the northern boundary of the farm and is apparent today. Four buildings are shown on the map in the centre of Robert Berrell's farm, two of which coincide with buildings on the first edition OS map. The most southern building on the 1766 map, Crewbane House, is still occupied.

The eastern townland boundary of Knowth differs from that depicted on the first edition OS map. The irregularity of the eastern boundary coincides with the presence of low earthworks in these fields. Scalé's map shows that the farm of 142 acres (58ha) at Knowth was held by Andrew Maguire. This is the same individual who received a premium of £12 from the Dublin Society for ditching 346 perches (2.2km) in 1768.[42] A group of buildings on the farm corresponds to the present Knowth House and outbuildings, although Knowth House had not been built at this time. Some further structures are depicted on the west side of the road opposite the group of buildings. Maguire's farm incorporated the main passage tomb. On Scalé's map, it is shown with a line in the south-west which appears to indicate an opening. If this is correct, then George Eogan may not have been the first to discover the western tomb.

The townland boundaries of present-day Newgrange correspond with those on Scalé's map. Two tumuli are marked at Newgrange, the main monument and the satellite mound south of this on the bank of the river. Newgrange is divided into five farms: Robert Berrell, Richard Berrell, Andrew Berrell, Edward Ellis and Nicholas Magrain. The Berrill family were leasing land at Newgrange at least as early as 1724 and re-leased land in 1737 from Benjamin Burton.[43] A group of buildings clustered around the mansion house of Newgrange with outhouses, coach houses, stables, orchards and gardens were willed by Charles Campbell to his grandson.[44] There is another building and a pond or canal-like feature north-east of Newgrange passage tomb. A third group of buildings on Andrew Berrell's farm lies along the eastern townland boundary where there is a water feature. A corn mill (Brow mill) existed on the bank of the river on Robert Berrell's land and a section of canal.

The townland of Balfeddock is larger on Scalé's map than is the current townland as it includes part of present-day Knowth, and some of the present townland of Balfeddock was part of Monknewtown. Four tenants are shown in this townland on Scalé's map: Luke Hall, Richard Smith, Edward Ellis, and Robert and Richard Berrell. Luke Hall's holding of 20 acres (8ha) is identified as Rossen.[45] Settlements are associated with only one of these farms, Richard Smith's holding at a T-junction in the south of Balfeddock townland. Shown for the first time on Scalé's map, these are the buildings mentioned in the Smith deeds of 1723.[46] They do not appear on the first edition OS map although some of the enclosed yards correspond to those marked on the earlier map. The 'street' was not a through road in 1766. There is a new road on the OS map and a new 'village' at Rossin. All the buildings in this cluster post-date 1766.

In 1766 the Caldwell estate extended onto the south side of the Boyne into the townlands of Gilltown whose boundaries coincide with the present townland. It was divided into three farms: John Connolly, Matthew Connolly and Richard Smith. There are groups of buildings in each farm. These coincide with those on the first edition OS map. The corn mill site at Rossnaree is also indicated on Scalé's map.

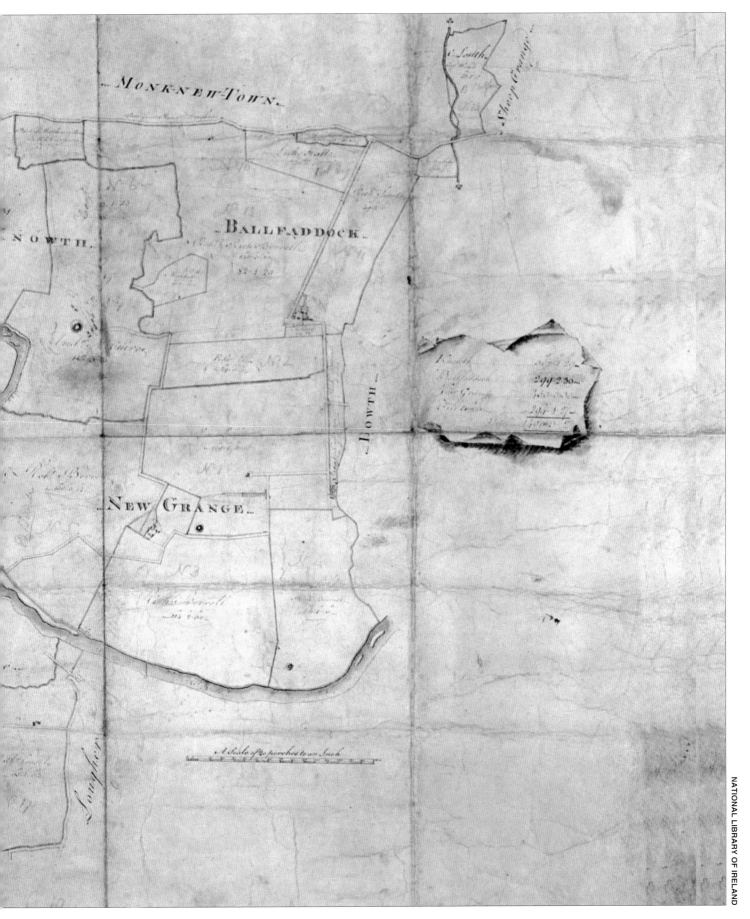

Fig. 11 Andrew Caldwell of Newgrange painted by Gilbert Stuart in 1776 and completed by Robert Woodburn in 1795. Stuart was an American artist famous for his portraits of George Washington. The patronage of such an established painter is evidence of both the wealth and aesthetic awareness of at least one local landlord.

us to date the buildings extant today that are on Scalé's map and provides an approximate date for constructions on the 1837 OS map but not on the earlier map.

Fig. 12 'Maguire's seat' at Newgrange, overlooking the Boyne. The Maguires have held land in this area since the eighteenth century. At some stage, this seat was erected so people passing along the road could rest and enjoy the view.

Fig. 13 Bookplate of Charles Caldwell. Son of Andrew, he commissioned the famous cartographer Bernard Scalé to survey his estates in Meath and Louth. Patronage of printers and cartographers was part of the improving ideology of the eighteenth-century Anglo-Irish landlordry.

Oldbridge estate   The Coddington family of Holmpatrick near Skerries in county Dublin acquired the land of Oldbridge and Sheephouse in the 1720s and were certainly in residence by 1724 on land formerly held by Henry Moore, Earl of Drogheda. The Coddington papers refer to a Declaration of Trust by 'John Coddington, Oldbridge,' in 1724.[47] Further, the Drogheda Papers (relating to the Moore estate) refer to a 'conveyance of lands of Oldbridge to John Coddington on 18 February 1729'.[48]

The Oldbridge estate is enclosed on three sides by the Boyne. This self-contained area was developed according to the principles of eighteenth-century parkland design. These principles strove to set a formal building of some architectural merit – Oldbridge House – in an apparently

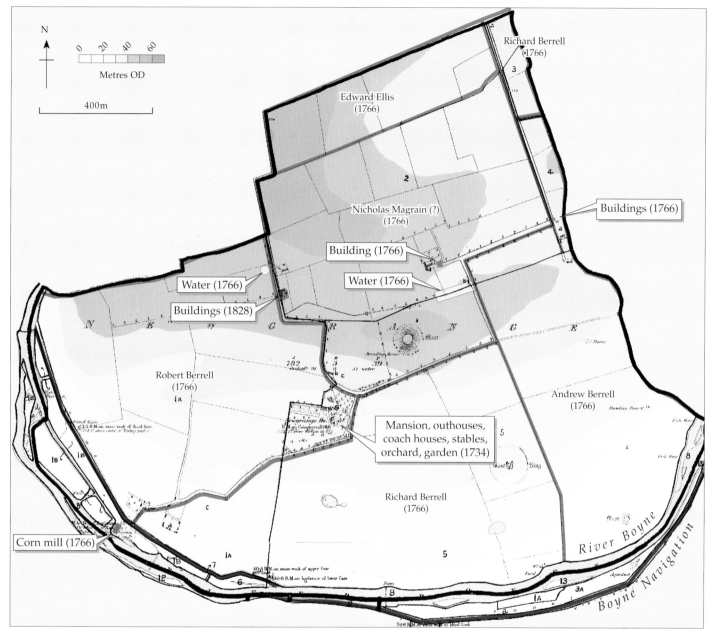

N

0 20 40 60

Metres OD

400m

Richard Berrell
(1766)

3

Edward Ellis
(1766)

2

4

Nicholas Magrain (?)
(1766)

Buildings (1766)

Building (1766)

Water (1766)

Water (1766)

Buildings (1828)

Robert Berrell
(1766)

Andrew Berrell
(1766)

Mansion, outhouses,
coach houses, stables,
orchard, garden (1734)

5

Richard Berrell
(1766)

River Boyne

Corn mill (1766)

5

Boyne Navigation

Fig. 14 Dated features within Newgrange estate (1837 OS 1:10,560 sheet, detail based primarily on estate maps and Registry of Deeds).

natural landscape of broad valley parkland and clumps of deciduous trees. The house was placed in a position to afford views of the skyline of Drogheda and the natural plain whenever possible. Dixey Coddington built the present house in 1750.[49] A painting by Joseph Tudor dated 1746 shows part of the Coddington estate.[50] It was well established at this time, with tree-lined avenues, mature groves enclosing a courtyard of outbuildings, and another group of buildings on the road to Sheephouse. This indicates that the elaborate landscape design was put in place before the mansion was built.

Running south-west of Donore is a low ridge of shales which appears in the river gorge at Glenmore and Glen

Articles of marriage concerning property at Newgrange and its environs

Peter Evers to Frances Farrell 1733. Articles of intermarriage between Peter Evers and Frances Berrill of Newgrange re-marriage between John Evers 1733 and Jane Berrill one half of farm together with one half of winter crop ... spring crop ... one half of the cattle ... one half of his plough, harness and harrow ... John and Jane will live with them as long as they please ... should they separate provide convenient house and offices for his son John Evers.

Edward Hall to Edward Norris 1727. Articles of marriage between Edward Hall, Rossen, farmer and Edward Norris of Rootstown ... 1727 ... marriage between Luke Hall and Mary Norris ... half of crop and half of cattle ... etc. give half of the lands of Balfaddock incl. 4 acres of meadow in Monknewtown with the white house and croft thereto annexed until the expiration of the leases ... the said Edward Hall obliges himself to extend to Luke, his wife and children with meat, drink, washing and lodging and other necessities during the lease if they are content to share with them.[51]

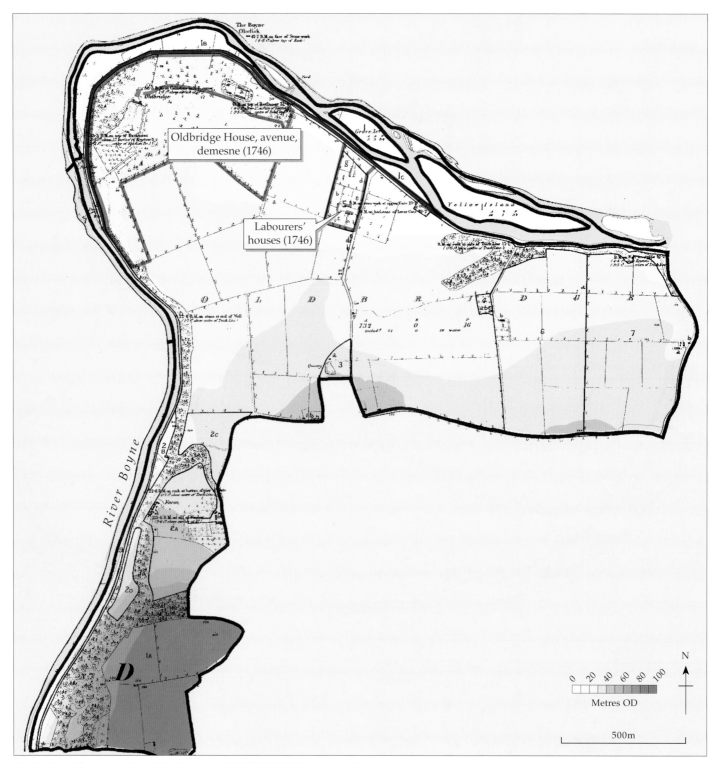

Fig. 15 Dated features within Oldbridge estate (1837 OS 1:10,560 sheet, detail based primarily on contemporary paintings).

cottage, a rare rock exposure in the drift-covered valley. Glenmore House, belonging to Oldbridge estate, is located on this outcrop above a steep wooded gorge. This house once had a small parkland, with outbuildings and garden. The ruins of the house and outbuildings remain today but none of the trees have been spared, except for those on the steep slope which leads down to the river.

AGRICULTURAL AND INDUSTRIAL DEVELOPMENT

The Cattle Acts of 1663–66 prohibited the export of fat stock into Britain and Irish woollen goods were similarly excluded by high tariffs in place from 1660. But when trading prohibitions were relaxed in the eighteenth century, Ireland's key location between English and American markets gave rise to a thriving provisions trade.

Fig. 16 A) Oldbridge House is set within a natural parkland of late eighteenth-century design, although there are remnants of an earlier formal landscape. Note the impressive walled garden and octagonal plantation. B) The house, built c.1750, is a long three-storey house with a plain ashlar (dressed stone) frontage of seven bays (windows). It was originally a classical Georgian three-bay, three-storey block with low single-storey wings until it was altered by architect Frederick Darley c.1832. C) These fine outbuildings are part of an extensive range of agricultural buildings which form part of the estate.

Beef production was facilitated by a network of fairs instituted by improving landlords.[52]

Abundant Irish grain harvests in the 1690s created large surpluses for export and the prices were good for Irish farmers in a decade in which harvest failure was general throughout many parts of Europe.[53] After a period of modest growth – there was an increasing shortage of home-grown grain for the domestic market in the early 1800s – the commercial tillage sector increased rapidly in the second half of the eighteenth century. The Irish

Fig. 17 Detail of painting *The Battle of the Boyne* by Joseph Tudor (*c.*1746), showing the early stages of the development of Oldbridge demesne.

Table 1
Surviving eighteenth-century buildings on the Netterville, Campbell/Caldwell and Oldbridge estates

Location	Site type	Historical note and status
Campbell/Caldwell estate		
Crewbane	House	Robert Berrill's farmhouse (1766)
Gilltown	House	John Connolly's farmhouse (1766)
Gilltown	House	Richard Smith's farmhouse (1766)
Knowth	Outbuilds.	Andrew Maguire's farm (1766)
Newgrange	Outbuilds.	Robert Berrill's farm (1786)
Newgrange	Ice house	First shown on 1837 OS 1:10,560 map. In state ownership.
Netterville estate		
Dowth	House	'Belle Isle', Patrick Duran's farmhouse (1732)
Dowth	Mansion	Dowth Hall, Netterville's seat (1731) Meath County Council (C.C.) listing
Proudfootstown	Millhouse	Kelly's residence (1750)
Oldbridge estate		
Oldbridge	Mansion	Oldbridge House, Coddington's seat (1740–50) Meath C.C. listing
Oldbridge	Courtyard/ Outbuilds.	Oldbridge House (*c.*1740) (2 sets of outbuildings)

parliament provided a subsidy on domestic grain transported to Dublin in 1761 and in 1784 Parliament passed another act subsidising grain exports and placing tariffs on imports. About three-quarters of the total payments went to the corn counties of the east. Under the stimulus of rising rents, smaller farmers found that tillage was more profitable.[54] Arable farming became a major source of employment both on the land itself and in subsidiary corn-based industries such as milling. The bounties on corn and flour carried by inland routes to Dublin helped to channel investment into flour mills at inland situations.[55]

Another element of this agricultural 'renaissance' was the potato, which assumed an ever-greater importance in the eighteenth century. The potato made possible the growing cottier community who could provide for a family by leasing a small field, already dunged, for a one-year term.[56] This nutritious, land-efficient crop also permitted the upsurge of flax growing and linen manufacturing in north-eastern Ireland. The Bend of the Boyne lay at the southern margin of the linen-weaving zone (see below).[57]

Agricultural improvements The impact of eighteenth-century agricultural improvements in the Bend of the Boyne is well documented in Arthur Young's *Tour of Ireland* (1780). Young's account represents the most comprehensive guide to late-eighteenth-century Irish agriculture. He visited the Slane area in the summer of 1776. The farms were relatively large by eighteenth-century standards, rising from 100 to 300 acres (40–120ha) in the Slane area. Young visited John Baker Holroyd of Monknewtown. Holroyd, the first Earl of Sheffield, wrote widely on Irish matters in the late eighteenth and early nineteenth centuries, including accounts on the manufacturing trade, woollen trade and corn laws.[58] Holroyd's Monknewtown estate had very fine corn land which had been divided into farms from 70 to 150 acres (28–61ha) in size and let in general for thirty-one years. He had made large ditches, planting them with 'quicks', round each farm. He had allowed his tenants half the expenses of building inner fences and had also provided a quarry in the neighbourhood and built a large double lime kiln at the centre of the estate. Generally, 'hollow draining' was used in the area:

> The fences about new inclosed pieces and those made in general by gentlemen, are ditches six feet deep, seven feet wide and fourteen inches at bottom, with two rows of quick in the bank, and furze sown on the top, or a dead hedge of brush.

A

B

GERALDINE STOUT

GERALDINE STOUT

Fig. 18A,B   Glenmore House belonged to Oldbridge estate. It has a dramatic location overlooking a steep wooded gorge.

This enthusiasm for enclosure on the part of both landowners and tenants was encouraged by the influential Dublin Society. They paid premiums to construct hawthorn hedges with trees planted at regular intervals. The Dublin Society provided substantial premiums for trees planted between 1766 and 1806.[59] The planting of newly introduced hardwood species was also encouraged.

All the ploughing was done with six horses to a plough. The main seed crops were wheat, barley and oats and the yields were relatively high. Crop rotation was practised and the land limed. Although Young was impressed with the improved state of agriculture in the Bend of the Boyne, he was angered by the farmers in the area who burnt their straw, 'for which they deserve to be hanged'.[60] Young also observed that poultry, pigs and cows were plentiful. The cottagers grew potatoes in six-foot-wide ridges with furrows two-and-a-half feet wide (a description of the efficient lazy-bed). Pigs were fed on potatoes alone which was considered more successful than pollard (young shoots of trees). Dairies of fifty to sixty cows were kept for butter. The Kelly farm at Oldbridge had 200 cows, half English, and half Irish breeds.

Milling   Milling was one of the most intensive industrial activities in the eighteenth century.[61] Mills had been a common feature of the manorial economy of the Medieval Period, and the Civil Survey furnishes a count of one hundred mills in an incomplete survey of county Meath in 1654, but these early mills were very small

structures grinding for a local market.[62] Early mills ground the grain while it was still uncleaned; the bolting or sifting of the ground flour was left to the baker. In the second half of the eighteenth century, larger industrial-style mills were constructed to cope with the escalating demands of the Dublin market. Bounties were granted from 1758 for the transport of grain and flour to Dublin. Meath was the first of the counties to respond to these new bounties with the construction of large industrial mills. The secret of these new mills lay in the addition of processes preparatory, and subsequent to, the actual grinding of the wheat. In the new mills bolting or sifting was done mechanically. The bolting mills were large

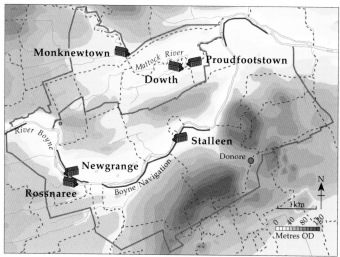

Fig. 19   Mills in the Bend of the Boyne.

structures, while the first were three-storey structures; the later larger mills were at least five storeys high. The wave of mill construction reached its peak during the years of high prosperity associated with the American Revolution and Napoleonic wars.[63]

The capital to establish mills seems to have come from the landed classes themselves. The interest of landlords in milling was part of a wider interest shown by their class in improvement and in the promotion of economic activity in their area. Landlords often had some inherited interest in milling in the form of manorial milling rights. For instance, in a covenant of 1775 between John Chamney of Platin and William Sharman Crawford of Stalleen there is a condition that the grantee grind 'all kinds of grain at the mill or mills at Stalleen and pay the accustomed toll for grinding the corn'.[64] There is still a small vernacular mill on the site. The first really big mill in east Meath was at Slane. It began production in 1766. Viscount Conygham leased a pre-existing mill at the bridge of Slane and 14 acres (6ha) of adjoining land as well as the weir on the river to the promoters of the new mill: Blaney Townley Balfour (of Townley Hall), William Burton and David Jebb. Each

Table 2
Eighteenth-century mills in the Bend of the Boyne

Location	Description	SMR No.
Dowth	Mill (site)	
Newgrange (Broe)	Mill (site)	
Newgrange	Tuck mill (site)	No precise location
Proudfootstown	Mill (associated buildings)	
Proudfootstown	Lessiteveran mill (site)	
Rossnaree	Mill	26:0502
Stalleen	Mill	20:2803

invested c.£1,500. The lands within a ten-mile radius supplied the mill with grain. By 1838 lands actually in the possession of the mill company had stretched as far east as Crewbane when, in a deed of lease, David Jebb was advised 'not to dig up or plant any part of the land ... bounded in the west by lands in the possession of Slane Mill Company'.[65]

The Caldwell papers and eighteenth-century deeds identify corn and tuck mills on properties in the Bend of the Boyne, as well as the names of the different millers and lands associated with the mills. The mills were mainly the older vernacular-style, two-storey buildings which served

DÚCHAS/CON BROGAN

Fig. 20   In 1780 the operations of the modern mill at Slane were described in detail by Arthur Young. He considered this mill to be one of the finest in the 'British Isles'. The construction of Slane mill was well timed to take advantage of the law to encourage the milling of corn and its transport to Dublin.

Fig. 21   This vernacular mill at Stalleen was in use in the eighteenth century and occupies the site of a medieval mill founded by the monks at Mellifont.

Fig. 22   Substantial grain storehouse at Proudfootstown, part of a larger eighteenth-century mill complex.

the local community. The massive mills at Monknewtown and Proudfootstown were redeveloped in the second half of the century to serve a larger market. The 'mill of Dowth' is recorded in a deed of 1734 when it was in the hands of Susanna Smith. This mill had been in the Smith family prior to that date. Accompanying the mill were 25 acres (10ha), a dwelling house, barn, cow-house, stable, orchard and two other dwellings.[66] Subsequently, Susanna Smith married Patrick Evers of Platin.[67] The 'mill of Dowth' was in the possession of Luke Elcock in 1775.[68] Today only a millstone and traces of a mill race survive at this site.

In 1734 the lands attached to Smith's mill bounded with another mill, that of Nicholas Hillock in Proudfootstown.[69] Hillock is also mentioned as 'Dowth miller' in 1736.[70] A lease of 1750 suggests that improvements were taking place at the Proudfootstown corn mill.[71] This memorial also mentions an old tuck mill in the adjoining lands called 'Lestiveran'. Belonging to the corn mill in 1750 was 'the miller's meadow', 2 acres (0.8ha) adjoining the Boyne.[72] Today a large storehouse exists on the site of the mill, but no surviving mill works are discernible.

The Caldwell papers describe at least three mills on the estate between 1721 and 1766. The mill at Rossnaree is the subject of an indenture dated 1721.[73] This mill is shown on the south side of the river on the estate map of 1766 where the present mill, locally referred to as Johnson's Mill, is located today.[74] This is probably the site of a mill mentioned in the Civil Survey in 1654 and shown on the Down Survey barony map.[75] A 1732 deed records the 'water cornmill of Broe'.[76] The location of the corn mill is indicated on an estate map of 1766 and the mill race, described as such in the terrier of a map from 1781, lies south-west of the lane that runs from Broe House where it terminates before the river.[77]

In 1752 the mill of Broe and a tuck mill at Newgrange were leased for one year.[78] Again in 1766 these mills were leased to Charles Campbell for one year.[79]

Flax cultivation   The Irish linen industry exhibited a strong regional concentration in the eighteenth century. The main areas of flax cultivation and the main linen-producing areas were north of a line from Drogheda to Sligo.[80] The trade was flourishing because of the privilege of free access to the British market at a time when imports from Continental Europe faced a tariff barrier.[81] A further boost to the economy in the Boyne Valley occurred with the establishment of the Linen Board in 1711. This body took positive steps to develop the linen trade outside Ulster. Flax was the agricultural basis for this textile industry, a crop that required considerable processing before it left the agricultural sector.[82] Those living in the Bend of the Boyne in the mid-eighteenth century were ideally placed between Drogheda, where there was an expansion in the linen industry, and Slane where, according to Young, a cottage industry had emerged for the manufacture of coarse cloth which was exported to Liverpool. To meet the needs of this proto-industry, Young tells us, 'every farmer' grew a 'little flax' between Slane and Drogheda.[83] Premiums for growing flax in 1796 were collected by many in the Bend of the Boyne and grants were awarded by the trustees of the Linen Board.

Young's observation that 'a little flax was grown' is an accurate indication of the lower status of this industry in the Bend of the Boyne. A flax school was established at Newgrange. Three families from Dowth parish applied for 'one spinning wheel's worth of flax each i.e. one rood'. Twelve families from Monknewtown parish were awarded

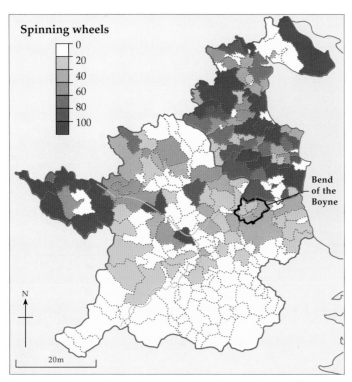

Spinning wheels

Bend of the Boyne

N

20m

Fig. 23 Spinning wheels in counties Louth and Meath 1796 (Linen premiums). The distribution shows that the Boyne and Mattock formed the boundary of intensive linen manufacturing. Only in the extreme west of county Meath was there a level of spinning on a par with Louth.

a total of seventeen wheels. In 1795 the Linen Board specified a premium of £300 to encourage the development of mills and by 1802 scutch mills were found in every parish in the Bend of the Boyne.[84] This was the period of handweaving workshops whose artisans would buy the linen yarn in the town market. This market was so active that a linen hall was erected in Drogheda in 1774. This was a large two-storey, quadrangular building where the linen yarn was displayed on raised wooden benches.

COMMUNICATIONS

Roads With an interest in the promotion of industry and trade displayed both in parliament and their own estates, Irish landowners were inevitably drawn towards improving the existing communications network. Initially roads were financed by tolls but in 1765 authority was granted to the grand juries to levy a county cess for road building.[85] In 1776 the assessments for making and repairing the roads in the Slane area amounted to 10d per acre for each tenant.[86] Irish roads were cheaply made with layers of earth, gravel and broken stones, flanked by drainage ditches.[87] Scalé's map shows that the contemporary road network was largely in place by this time. The Grand Jury Query Book of the 1760s records that in 1761 a total of £25 was to be raised on Slane barony and paid to Edward Ellis and Richard Smith for:

> gravelling 142 perches [909m] of the great road leading from Drogheda to Trim beginning at the lands of Balfaddock and ending at the lands of Newgrange. This was 14 feet wide at 3s a perch, the said road now being of the breadth of 25 feet between inclosure and inclosure.[88]

In 1764 a sum of £167 was paid to David Jebb, William Burton and Benjamin Burton for building a bridge over the Mattock River on the Drogheda–Slane road which required '669 perches (400m) of mason works at 5s a perch to build the Meath side of the bridge'.[89] Road development continued into the nineteenth century. A Grand Jury Presentment Book for the period 1809–14 refers to numerous road improvements such as the repair and underpinning of a bridge at Roughgrange in 1810, making a shore on the lands of Rosnaree in 1811 and the building of a wall at Stalleen in 1813. The

ULSTER FOLK AND TRANSPORT MUSEUM

Fig. 24 William Hinck's 1783 engraving of women and children involved in linen spinning (either side of the fire) and reeling (right).

DÚCHAS/CON BROGAN

Fig. 25 Bridge of the Mattock River on the Drogheda–Slane road. It was financed by the Grand Jury in 1764.

Fig. 26 Boyne Navigation canal features. A) A lock-keeper's house at Staleen. B) A bridge over the lock at Oldbridge. C) Lock at Oldbridge.

effects of road building were also beneficial for roadside dwellers. Arthur Young describes the practice of grazing the 'long acre' in the area between Slane and Drogheda: 'the cattle in the road have their forelegs all tied together with straw [súgan], to keep them from breaking into the fields.'[90]

The Boyne Navigation   Ireland's waterways, unlike its roads, were in part financed by central government during the eighteenth century: schemes were proposed for improvements in navigation on many of the country's rivers, including the Shannon, Nore and Barrow. Works such as dredging and the making of locks and lateral canals were carried out on a number of rivers. There were also schemes for the construction of stillwater canals linking river basins across their watershed, such as the Newry Canal.[91] A passionate plea to construct a navigation on the Boyne was first made in 1710 by Markes Plunkett for the attention of the parliament and those who lived along the river. In the Bend of the Boyne these were Netterville at Dowth, Osborne at Knowth and Hamill at Newgrange. According to Markes Plunkett:

Meath could become by means of this navigation traffic as rich and prosperous as the Indies with trade and employment booming.[92]

The Boyne, one of the earliest navigation schemes in Ireland, was canalised between 1748 and 1790 in order to encourage trade with the Dublin market and to transport corn to the port at Drogheda from inland markets.[93] The Lower Boyne Navigation was heavily subsidised because of the benefit it would bring to the Slane mills. In 1756 the Inland Navigation Corporation set up a body of local noblemen and gentry to oversee the ongoing work of making the Boyne navigable. In 1765 Dixie Coddington of Oldbridge was a Boyne Navigation Commissioner.[94] Under a new act passed in 1787, the Boyne Commissioners became a corporate body. Andrew Caldwell and Henry Coddington were Boyne Navigation Commissioners in 1779.

The original engineer for the Boyne Navigation was Thomas Steers. Of Dutch origin, he had actually held a commission in the 4th regiment of foot (the King's Own) which took part in the Battle of the Boyne in 1690. Ironically, he died in 1750 just after the completion of Oldbridge Lock near the site of the battle. Eight locks were

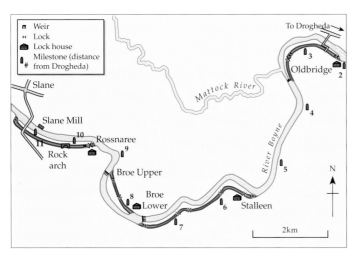

Fig. 27   The Lower Boyne Navigation.

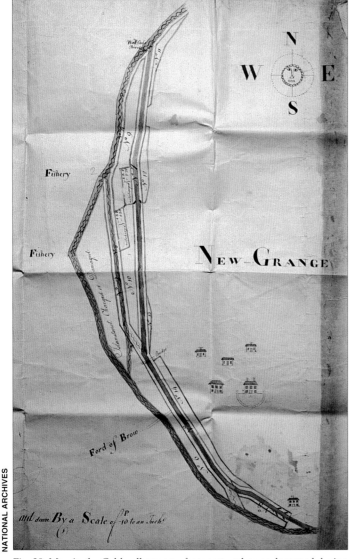

Fig. 28 Map in the Caldwell papers of property taken or damaged during the construction of the canal.[95] This document was forwarded to the navigation authorities as a plea for compensation or additional drainage works. The map itself is an amateurish production, especially when compared to the work of Scalé. The north point is incorrect.

built between Drogheda and Slane: Oldbridge, Staleen, Roughgrange, Newcomen's Lock, Broe, Knowth, Fennor and Slane. The locks built along the canal were to be made of the largest 'rude stones' available and the 'walls of lime and stone [made] in the best manner'.[96] The masons employed were mostly locals such as William Norris of Oldbridge, and Patrick Begg and John Elliott of Dowth.

The earliest mapping of the Lower Boyne canal is in Scalé's map of 1766, which shows two cuts on the north bank at Broe in Newgrange townland, one a mill race to serve the mill of Brow and the other for the canal. A navigation towpath is located on the banks of Robert Berrill's farm at Knowth and the position of the lock house at Broe is shown. A later map describes, on an accompanying terrier, the impact of the canal works on the former meadows at Newgrange since the commencement of the construction of the Boyne Navigation.[97] Soil stripping to raise a rampart had turned an area into a 'shaking bog'. Eleven acres (5ha) of land were allegedly 'lost' while others fields were 'rendered into a bed of flaggers ... with not a bit of grass ... ruined partly by the overflow and partly for want of back drains'. This document, an appeal to the navigation authorities for compensation or additional drainage works, seems to have been successful. A back drain was constructed and a rent of 12s paid for the land between Broe ford and the 'new lock'. In 1782 the local navigation commissioners found 'the navigation from Drogheda to Slane bridge ... to be perfectly useful'.[98]

THE PENAL LANDSCAPE

The Williamite victories of the 1690s ushered in government legislation at the end of the seventeenth century aimed at keeping the Catholic community of Ireland in a state of permanent subjection. When George I came to the throne, the Anglican Church of Ireland was 'established' by law. Thus it was entitled to be supported through the tithes of the whole population. However, no organisational change took place and there was little physical infrastructure set in place for mass conversion to Protestantism apart from ineffective charter schools. No new churches were built and the general state of the church stock remained ruinous. By 1718 in the diocese of Meath churches were dilapidated in many parishes.[99] In the Bend of the Boyne there is no indication that the church stock – inherited from the medieval period and in the hands of the Church of Ireland – was ever in use in the eighteenth century.

The Catholic Church in the course of the eighteenth century gradually recovered lost ground, renewed its organisation and consolidated its position. This recovery had a physical dimension in the landscape. Mass houses

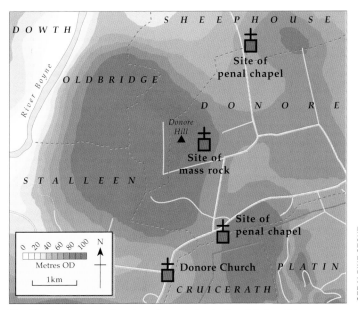

Fig. 29   Approximate location of penal sites in the vicinity of Donore.

Fig. 30   A) A stone pedestal outside the door of the present church at Donore village, dating to 1727, is testimony to the presence of a Mass house here in the eighteenth century. B) Wooden penal crosses from county Louth.

were discreetly placed in out of the way places and Mass rocks erected. Patterns at holy wells were revived. The use of traditional burial places continued in spite of the act of 1697 which declared that 'none shall bury in suppressed monastery, abbey or convent, not used for divine service, or within the precincts of monuments'.[100] The earliest and healthiest Catholic communities were in areas with Catholic or 'crypto-Catholic' landlords, precisely the conditions found in Meath, and more specifically, in the lower Boyne Valley.[101] In the Bend of the Boyne, the Catholic Nettervilles fostered a sub-gentry of middlemen and leaseholders who became patrons of the Catholic Church. In Meath, despite efforts to close Mass houses by proclamation in 1714, 1715, 1719 and 1723, there were 103 Mass houses and 108 priests in 1731.[102]

A record of this period of Catholic suppression within the Bend of the Boyne is found in oral traditions and place names, diocesan records, local history and monuments. In the eighteenth century, the diocesan archives record a Mass house or thatched chapel on the site of the present Donore village church and a thatched school nearby.[103] The thatched chapel at Donore was visited in 1797 by the reforming Bishop of Meath, Dr Patrick Plunkett, who found it to be in very bad condition. The parish priest at the time was Fr Walter Johnston, who was born in Rossnaree.[104] There is a locally held tradition that Lord Netterville of Cruicerath participated at Mass in this church while sitting in his 'castle' to the south of the village. The tradition records that a flag was raised at the gable end of the chapel to signal the important parts of Mass.[105] This tradition is also associated with another member of the Netterville family. A house was erected on

top of the passage tomb at Dowth for the purpose of praying, and Netterville 'usually knelt at the window of this house while the Holy Sacrifice was being offered, on Sunday mornings, in the old chapel of Dowth'.[106] These traditions suggest that the Netterville conversion to the Established Church in 1728 was made for legal reasons only and that they remained, at heart, Catholics.

Mass was often said in a corner of a field where there was a Mass rock in Sheephouse. Local tradition holds that on one occasion Fr James Plunkett (d. 1731) was so closely pursued by priest hunters that the Doggets (farmers in the townland of Sheephouse) hid him in a straw rick. Fr Plunkett is buried in Donore graveyard.[107]

There was another chapel in the penal days at the top of a steep hill between Sheephouse and Tubberfinn. Later on there was a chapel on the Donore road.[108] The assertion of Catholicism is confirmed by Mrs Delany who, while travelling through the Boyne Valley in the summer of 1752, observed that on the 'Eve of St. John, a great Roman Catholic holiday … [we] were forced to pass by several monstrous fires (actually made of bones) and firing guns and squibs'.[109]

Table 3
Penal monuments in the Bend of the Boyne

Location	Site type
Donore	Mass house (site)
Donore	Font (1727)
Donore road	Chapel (site)
Sheephouse	Tubberfinn Mass rock
Sheephouse	Tubberfinn chapel (site)

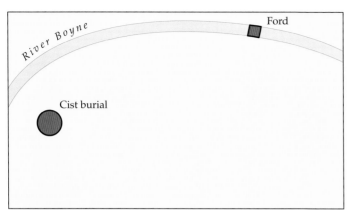

A) Prehistory

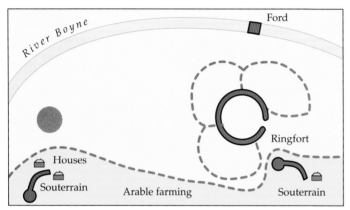

B) Iron Age / Early Christian

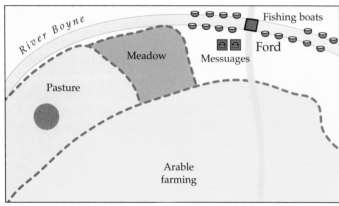

C) Medieval

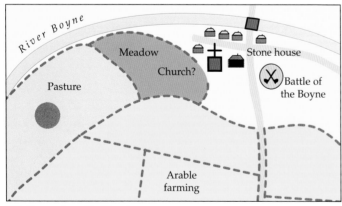

D) Seventeenth Century

CASE STUDY 3:
LANDSCAPE DEVELOPMENT AT OLDBRIDGE

A small community settled on the south bank of the Boyne near a fording point in the Middle Bronze Age and buried their dead in stone cists covered by a round mound (A). Some two thousand years later, a Christian family practising dairy farming built a ringfort and enclosed some land for pasture. The more progressive tillage farmers in the area dwelling in unenclosed settlements with timber houses built souterrains to protect themselves against attacks from foreigners which had been taking place in the valley. One of their homes was pillaged in AD861 (B). The lands of Oldbridge became part of the farmlands of the Cistercian abbey of Mellifont and were held by them until 1539. The land was extensively tilled, destroying the surface remains of earlier settlements. A fishing village developed along the river's edge. Willows were taken from the river islands to build fishing vessels or coracles (C).

In the summer of 1690 Oldbridge found itself at the heart of the Battle of the Boyne. By this time the village had grown and lay amidst cornfields and meadows. The houses were located either side of a street and there was a

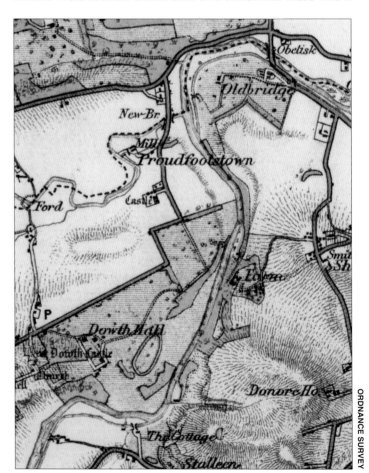

The Oldbridge and Dowth estates *c*.1900.

ORDNANCE SURVEY

ORDNANCE SURVEY

Oldbridge *c*.2000

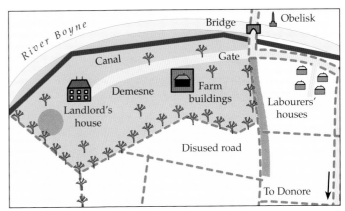

E) Eighteenth Century

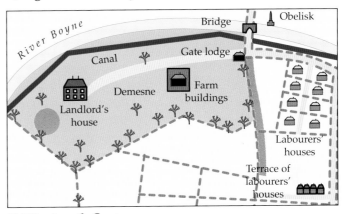

F) Nineteenth Century

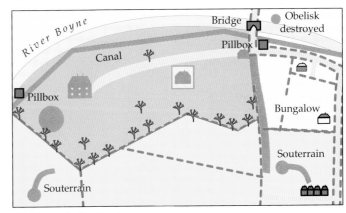

G) Twentieth Century

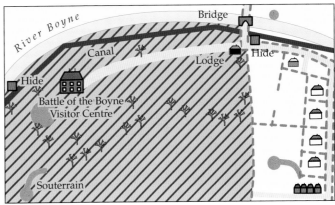

H) Future Trends

house of stone with a courtyard and thatched cottages either side of it (D). In the eighteenth century the Coddington family took over the lands of Oldbridge and built a mansion with landscaped parklands on the site of the earlier village. A new canal cut through the riverine section of the earlier settlement. In 1736 an obelisk was erected opposite the scene of the fiercest fighting in the Battle of the Boyne by the 'Protestants of Great Britain and Ireland' (E). The Coddington estate continued to grow in the nineteenth century. The lands were enclosed and a terrace of labourers' cottages was built at Sheephouse (F).

In 1923 a party from the Irish army garrison in Drogheda destroyed the obelisk at Oldbridge with landmines. This was intended as a gesture against Protestant attacks on Catholic ghettos in Northern Ireland. During the Emergency years the lands bordering the Boyne at Oldbridge were fortified with pillboxes, becoming part of a major defence line in preparation for a putative British invasion. As occurred elsewhere in Ireland, the Coddington estate declined in the post-war period (G). Oldbridge Demesne is now in state ownership and plans are well advanced to turn part of the estate into a Visitor Centre for the Battle of the Boyne. Dúchas will probably restore the many features of the eighteenth-century demesne (H).

BUILDINGS IN THE NINETEENTH-CENTURY LANDSCAPE

The Bend of the Boyne is a rural area where the farming community determines the general appearance of the built environment. Given the dispersed nature of the rural population, buildings are scattered but are, nonetheless, a pervasive element of the Boyne landscape. Nineteenth-century land ownership patterns and farming practices greatly influenced the character of buildings along the Boyne. The eighteenth-century legacy was the elaboration of large demesnes along the river held by a handful of landlords, each with their individual mansions; the basic territorial entity was the estate maintained by rents with a system of middlemen and sub-lessees.[1] Nineteenth-century rural society in the Boyne Valley had a tiered social structure comprising three main groups defined by their relationship to the ownership and occupation of land: landlords who owned the land, tenants who occupied it, and labourers who worked on the larger farms.[2] This hierarchical society was clearly reflected in the diversity of house types in the period and the range of holdings associated with them.

This chapter initially examines the economic pursuits which largely determined the type of housing and holdings associated with each social class. The detailed information contained in the rateable valuation of properties in 1854 (known as *Griffith's Valuation*) provides the broad statistical and geographical information which forms the basis of a housing classification.[3] This is supplemented by archival material relating to the valuation process and by census data. Extensive fieldwork has enabled the identification of those houses listed in the valuation record and the association of house typology with social class. The variation in housing quality has resulted in differential rates of preservation in the current countryside. In addition to domestic housing, this chapter also examines a wide range of other types of buildings listed in *Griffith's Valuation* illustrative of nineteenth-century society. Throughout the century, the conditions of land tenure influenced the type and location of houses and the likelihood of their survival in the landscape. This chapter also considers the effects of the Famine on both population and housing stock. On the basis of this analysis of documentary and field evidence, an informed conservation strategy should be developed which will guarantee the survival of a representative sample of nineteenth-century housing.

Fig. 1   In the nineteenth century this was a small farmer's cottage on a holding leased from the Crawford estate at Stalleen. It is one of the very few vernacular buildings in the Bend of the Boyne that is still lived in.

HOUSING, LANDHOLDING AND SOCIETY

Economic background   Thompson's *Statistical survey of county Meath* (1802) provides a valuable insight into the life of the farming community in the Boyne Valley at the turn of the century, especially farming practices and land ownership.[4] The Boyne farmers were in a favourable position, with easy access to the best grain market in the country at Drogheda, and the immense growth in trade stimulated by the Boyne Navigation. Rapid improvement in roads also encouraged trade with the nearby markets in Dublin. Thompson observed that the Slane area was under both tillage and grazing,[5] and that the area around Drogheda was particularly good for red wheat, producing large quantities of rye for boiling and seed, with a good deal of oats and barley.[6] Lewis (1837) describes the land in the parish of Monknewtown as divided equally between tillage and pasture; in the parish of Duleek, two-thirds of the land was under tillage.[7] Beans and white peas were grown in quantity. Lewis also noted that the Boyne Navigation generally encouraged corn growing in the area.

These observations are substantiated by more localised data in the Field Books (1837–39) held in the Valuation Office archive. While mixed farming predominated, the land was used exclusively for tillage in some townlands, such as Monknewtown. In contrast, all of Knowth was in meadow. At Newgrange there was both pasture and arable.[8] These mixed farming practices of the nineteenth century are reflected in the survival to the present day of ploughmen's and herds' houses. The number of herds' houses listed in *Griffith's Valuation* for the area indicates a greater dependence on stock rearing. This is consistent

Fig. 3   A herd's house at Rossnaree. This is one of a number of herds' houses in the area, reflecting the importance of stock rearing in the nineteenth century.

with Tom Jones Hughes's study of the entire county; in the 1850s, over one-quarter of the holdings was in the care of herds, suggesting extensive pastoralism in Meath.[9] This in turn reflects the heavy clay soils of the county, which were more suited to grass than tillage under pre-mechanised agricultural production methods.

Despite the dominance of cattle, the mid-nineteenth century saw the high tide of arable farming in county Meath.[10] This was a labour-intensive activity and a large proportion of the labourers in Drogheda was employed as field labourers.[11] The Boyne Navigation (built at the end of eighteenth century) had greatly facilitated corn growing and milling in the lower Boyne Valley. Grain and flour accounted for a high proportion of the total tonnage carried eastwards.[12] Timber, slates, stone and coal came up the canal to the village of Donore.[13] There were small vernacular mills in close proximity on the Boyne at Dowth, Rossnaree, Stalleen and Roughgrange, with more modern ones using steam power at Monknewtown and Proudfootstown. These mills all processed locally grown corn.

Grazing, corn growing and milling were not the only economic pursuits. There were fisheries on the Boyne at Stalleen, Roughgrange and Rossnaree. Coarse linen was woven in the village of Tullyallen for the Drogheda market.[14] D'Alton refers to the steeping of flax in the Boyne.[15] The mill at Dowth was a tuck mill in 1820,[16] and the processing of wool testifies to the presence of sheep in the area, continuing a tradition established by the Cistercians of Mellifont in the Middle Ages. There was a quarry at Sheephouse; according to Lewis (1837), it was well worked and contained an abundance of limestone of a handsome light colour used in the construction of churches in the Drogheda area.[17]

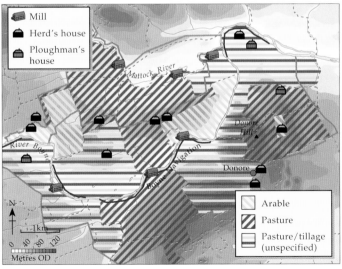

Mill
Herd's house
Ploughman's house

Arable
Pasture
Pasture/tillage (unspecified)

Mattock River
River Boyne
Boyne Navigation
Donore Hill
Donore

N
1km
0 40 80 120
Metres OD

Fig. 2   Land use, mills, and ploughmen's and herds' houses in the Bend of the Boyne in the mid-nineteenth century (based on OS field books [1838–39] and *Griffith's Valuation* [1854]).

GERALDINE STOUT

Table 1
Thompson's classification of Meath rural society 1802

Social class	Dwelling type	Farming type
Nobleman's seat	Elegant mansion houses belonging to resident gentlemen of large property.	Mixed
Common farmer		
Occupants of 100–200 acres	Mud wall cottage with stable and cow house, foddering yard in front. 'Worst lodged than any part of the community.'	Grazier
Occupants of 50–100 acres	Mud wall cottage. 'Hardly any better off than the common labourer.'	Tillage
Occupants of 2–10 acres	Mud wall cottage. 'At rack-rent … a real disaster.'	Potato ground
Labourers		
Cottiers	Cottage	Potato ground
Bound labourers	No house	
Out labourers	No house. 'Works when he can get it.'	Conacre

BUILDING TYPOLOGY

Classification   In his 1802 breakdown of the main rural classes in the county, Thompson identified a close link between house type and holding size, ranging from the 'elegant mansion' of the 'nobleman's seat', to 'common farmers', and to the cottier with a mud-walled house on 'a half acre and potato ground' (table 1).[18] Thompson observed that the typical 'nobleman's seat' in Meath was 'an elegant mansion house belonging to the resident gentlemen of a large property' and that the 'offices [are] compact and convenient'. Below this in social status were the common farmers, whom he further subdivided into three categories; first were those occupying 100–200 acres (41–81ha) who were, in his view, 'worst lodged than any part of the community'. According to Thompson, he 'builds the same kind of low mud wall as his tenant and to this he adds a stable and cow house'. The farmers occupying 50–100 acres (20–41ha) were 'hardly any better off than the common labourer' and those occupying 2–10 acres (0.8–4ha) were a 'real disaster'. The third class identified by Thompson was

Fig. 4   Rateable valuations for the 290 houses ranged from 65 pounds to 5 shillings (appendix 1). When these figures are presented as a horizontal bar chart, a pyramidal structure appears with a broad base and a narrow top which mirrors the highly stratified nature of nineteenth-century society. Four distinct valuation groups emerge. Fieldwork and an examination of House Books make it possible to link this statistical classification with building types. Noblemen's seats and the large houses of entrepreneurs – houses valued at 150 shillings and over – comprised 6% of the buildings in 1854. Landholdings associated with the mansions of the major landlords range from 70 to 700 acres (28–283ha). The lower figure of seventy acres could not have supported a house of this high valuation and presumably the house had other holdings in neighbouring townlands outside the Bend of the Boyne. Four of these houses are occupied by a small group of entrepreneurs and do not have significant landholdings. The houses of strong farmers comprise 6% of the building stock. These houses had a rateable valuation between 75 and 150 shillings, and are associated with 100 to 250 acre (41–101ha) holdings. Small to medium farmers are housed in buildings valued between 15 and 75 shillings, comprising 26% of the housing stock. Holdings associated with these buildings are usually under 100 acres (41ha). At the bottom of the scale, the wide base of the social pyramid, are the homes of the cottiers and landless labourers. Almost two-thirds of these houses had a rateable valuation of 15 shillings and under (63%). Most of these houses had no land associated with them.

the labourer. This class he also subdivides into three categories: cottiers who were given 'a house (built with mud) and a half acre and potato ground … few have chimneys'; 'bound labourers without a house', (presumably those in service and accommodated in the farmers' outhouses); and finally out labourers who were given no house and worked whenever they could. They were casual labourers, like those D'Alton described as coming out from Drogheda to work on the adjacent tillage farms.

Thompson's classification of rural society at the beginning of the century is still applicable to mid-

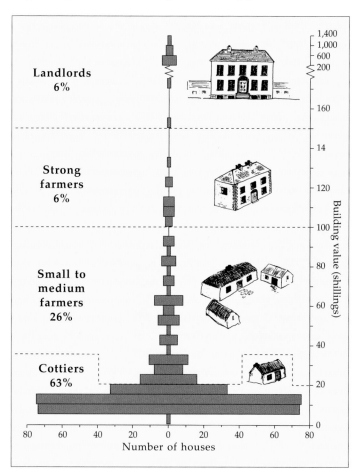

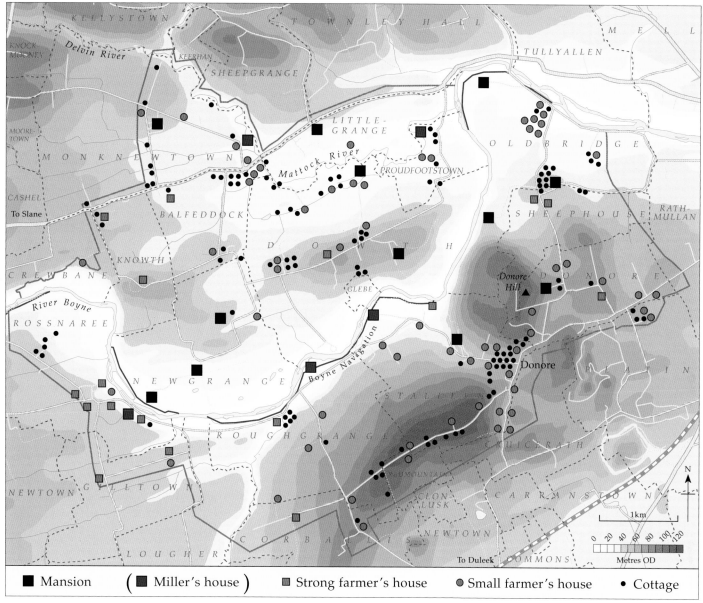

■ Mansion (■ Miller's house) ■ Strong farmer's house ● Small farmer's house • Cottage

Fig. 5 Housing in the Bend of the Boyne in the mid-nineteenth century showing the four distinct classes of buildings identified (based on *Griffith's Valuation*, 1954). Mansions are centrally located within virtually empty demesne townlands. Tillage areas are particularly devoid of settlement. An unusual cluster of small farmers' houses was built on the Coddington estate in Oldbridge. Most cottages are spread evenly along laneways but large clusters occur in a few places, such as Monknewtown and Donore.

nineteenth-century society in the Bend of the Boyne. This is confirmed by the rateable valuations for 1854 followed by field inspection of surviving houses.[19] *Griffith's Valuation* presents rateable valuation figures for the houses, buildings and landholding of 290 households in the Bend of the Boyne, the vast majority being leaseholders to the large estates in the area. Because there is also a strong correlation (r = 0.841) between house type and holding size, it is possible to devise a classification which encompasses both farmhouse and farm.

Houses that have been demolished since 1854 are described in the 'House Books'.[20] They were compiled for the Boyne Valley from September to November 1838.

They contain details on dwellings and outbuildings which are classified according to function. Dimensions of both dwellings and out-offices are given in tabulated form, accompanied by an assessment of their quality; houses with more than nine rooms are first class; those with five to nine rooms are second class; those with two to four rooms are third class; those having a single room are fourth class. These descriptions are often accompanied by remarks which explain the basis of the valuation; the condition of the building, proximity to the road, deductions for repairs, etc. The compilers of the House Books did not concern themselves with lower class (class 4) housing.[21]

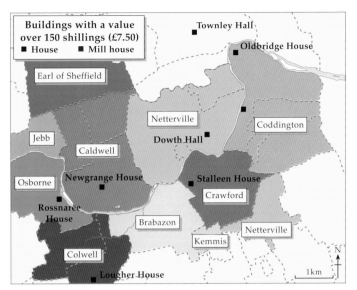

Fig. 6 The main landowners in the Bend of the Boyne in the mid-nineteenth century, the principal estate cores (named) and houses over 150 shillings in value.

Mansions Fourteen properties in the Bend of the Boyne had a valuation over 150 shillings. Ten of these were houses of landlords or the homes of sizeable middleman tenants. Four of these highly valued houses belonged to local entrepreneurs (appendix 1). They are an easily recognisable class of housing, the country mansions with their demesnes which are largely a legacy from the eighteenth century. They are the properties of the resident landlords who held the land in fee. There are portions of ten estates in the Bend of the Boyne; only six of these have their demesne in the area. The largest demesne houses were Oldbridge House (on the Coddington estate of 3,737

Fig. 7 The main feature of Oldbridge House is the entrance front made from Ardbraccan stone (from a quarry near Navan). The entrance doorcase is in the style of those executed by the famous architect Richard Castle (1690–1751) who worked in Ireland from 1727. Oldbridge House was redesigned in c.1832. Originally it was a three-bay, three-storey block, with low, single-storey wings. The architect involved may have been George Darley.[22]

Fig. 8 The terrace of labourers' cottages at Sheephouse is a nineteenth-century improvement on the Oldbridge estate.

acres/1,512ha) and Dowth Hall (on the Netterville estate of 3,332 acres/1,349ha).[23] Oldbridge House had the highest rateable valuation (£65) in the Bend of the Boyne; it was followed by Dowth Hall (£35), residence of Richard Gradwell, owner of the former Netterville estate.

These mansions were located with great care and usually placed in a prominent position above the Boyne. Typical of this is Oldbridge House. The house is approached by a sweeping driveway, flanked by attractive cut-stone gate pillars and a nineteenth-century gate lodge. It is flanked by two courtyards containing former stables, servant quarters and greenhouses. A separate courtyard of outhouses lies to the north of this avenue, isolated from the main house. On the south side of the demesne is an eight acre (3 ha) walled garden and estate wall.

Oldbridge also has a planned range of estate buildings which forms a self-contained territory in itself. Housing on this large estate was provided by the landlord using durable stone walls and slate roofs. The farm layout with its buildings and the descriptions of these houses in *Griffith's Valuation* indicate the type of farming practised on the estate. Two villages were built for workers at Sheephouse and Oldbridge. Cul-de-sacs off the roads on the boundaries of the estate contain these houses of the more specialised estate workmen such as the ploughman and woodranger. The farmyards on the Oldbridge estate achieved high standards in layout and each type of building was carefully designed around a courtyard. All were built with the same materials.

The present Broe House in Newgrange townland, valued at 200 shillings, is a fine example of the residence of a long-established large tenant/middleman with a leasehold of 193 acres (78ha) dating back to the eighteenth century. The house probably dates from that period as well. Broe House is a classical-style, two-storey, three-bay

GERALDINE STOUT

Fig. 9 This finely laid-out courtyard is all that remains of nineteenth-century mansion Donore House.

house. The present central offset porch is not mentioned in the House Books, indicating that it is a later addition. Associated with this house is a courtyard of nine outbuildings of the finest quality.[24] Another example of this class is found at Monknewtown where James Drew held 181 acres (73ha) and lived in a fine two-storey house valued at 300 shillings. A complex of outbuildings is attached to the house.[25]

Thompson's classification of housing excluded the well-housed entrepreneur class. Four of the fourteen properties with the highest valuation in the study area are houses associated with industry: three associated with mills and one with a quarry at Sheephouse. These are impressive, well-designed houses but, unlike houses on demesnes, have only small holdings.

Because of their solid and impressive nature, the mansions have a very high survival rate and are still a prominent feature of the countryside; only two of the fourteen mansions (14%) have been destroyed since the

1850s. Newgrange House, valued at 400 shillings, is listed in 1854 as Richard Maguire's property at Newgrange and in the House Books as a large two-storey property with a basement and porch. All that remains of this house are the impressive stone buildings that form part of the present farmyard open to the public at Newgrange Animal Farm.[26] Donore House was valued at 300 shillings; although it is now destroyed, its finely laid-out courtyard is still in use. A number of these large houses are in extremely delapidated condition. Glenmore House located on the Oldbridge estate, valued at 700 shillings, lies in ruins. Oldbridge House has been vacant since the late 1970s but it is now being restored by the State.

Strong farmers' houses The homes of the predominantly Catholic strong farmers in the Bend of the Boyne have values ranging between 75 and 150 shillings. There are sixteen of these houses, comprising 6% of the housing stock (appendix 1). Strong farmers are the larger tenants in the Bend of the Boyne and in some cases acted as middlemen. They tended to have 100 to 200 acre (41–81ha) holdings and resided in solid, modest-sized, architecturally designed houses of a classical, 'pattern-book' style.[27] These are detached properties on private, planted grounds. They are not present in every townland in the Bend of the Boyne but are the houses referred to as 'townland houses'.

Anne Maguire's farm at Knowth epitomises the strong farmer's house. Known as Knowth House, this two-storey farmhouse was valued at 120 shillings, with a well-planned yard and some planting to the rear.[28] The yard is shown on an eighteenth-century map and is, therefore, earlier than the house. A large 191 acre (77ha) farm was associated with this house.

GERALDINE STOUT

Fig. 10 Knowth House epitomises the strong farmer's house of the nineteenth century. It is now in state ownership.

Fig. 11 A strong farmer's house at Roughgrange. Its style owes more to the vernacular tradition than to classically inspired architecture.

Fig. 12 Strong farmer's house at Balfeddock. It is two storeys high and slated with a centrally located entrance and chimneys at the gable ends.

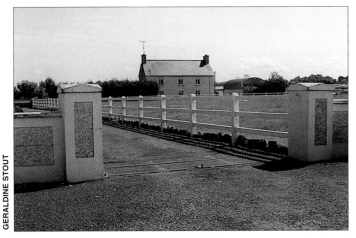

Fig. 13 This strong farmer's house at Donore is unique in the area because of its thatched roof. This was the home of Patrick Fulham, MP for South Meath in the 1890s. He was the first chairman of the initial Meath County GAA Board.

There are some variations in the house style associated with these large farms. The second-class farm at Roughgrange on the south side of the Boyne differs from Knowth in that its design owes more to the vernacular tradition. The House Books refer to potato houses and a piggery at this property, indicating a mixed farm economy.[29] The house was valued at 105 shillings and 176 acres (71ha) were farmed by the occupants. Today this house shows evidence of rebuilding. Laurence Gogarty's house in Corballis was classified by the valuers as a first-class house, showing how impressive some of the buildings associated with the strong farmer were.[30] In the House Books, it is described as a two-storey building with a west wing. It was valued at only 100 shillings despite receiving a 'high rating'. A 193 acre (78ha) farm was associated with the house.

At the lower end of the strong farmers' houses are single or two-storey, developed or transitional vernacular farmhouses with outbuildings often organised to form a front yard.[31] These modest farmhouses have adopted features from formal houses but still tend to conform to the old vernacular pattern of being one room in width. The house at Balfeddock, where Patrick Drew farmed 84 acres (34ha), is typical of this transitional architecture. The house was valued at 75 shillings. These houses can be elementary in plan with ground floor rooms arranged either side of a central hallway and two to three bedrooms on the first floor. Catherine Fulham's property at Donore, on 95 acres (39ha) and valued at 110 shillings, is unique in being thatched. Peter Roche's farmhouse at Littlegrange on 90 acres (36ha) is two storeys with a central chimney stack. This house, valued at 100 shillings in 1854, is a good example of a townland house and it is still referred to as 'The Grange'.

Like the houses of the landlords, these substantial farmhouses have a high survival rate. Only one of the sixteen houses (6%) has been destroyed since 1854. This was a house in Stalleen townland valued at 80 shillings but with only 30 acres (12ha).

Small farms The houses of the small farmers were valued between 15 and 75 shillings. There were seventy-six of this class of houses in 1854 (appendix 1). According to Thompson (1802), the small farmers in county Meath (those with holdings of 1–10 acres/0.4–4ha) in his classification) were a 'real disaster' because the tenants were finding survival difficult due to high rents. On the basis of the properties which have survived, the typical house of the small farmer in the Boyne was vernacular in style, and rectangular in plan, with a central hearth and lobby entrance, a house type typical of eastern Ireland.[32] Rooms extend the full width of the house with one room opening off another. A porched entrance is typical. Stone is widely used but clay is often used in the gables. Oaten straw was used for thatching because in county Meath wheaten straw apparently grew too strong. In the thatched examples, the roofs are generally hipped. This house type is best exemplified by two adjoining properties at Stalleen. The slated house was valued at 15 shillings and had seven acres (3ha). The other house was thatched and valued at 25 shillings; it had nine acres (4ha).

In some cases the buildings in this range of valuation have two storeys; the second storey was probably a later addition. This remodelling seems to have taken place at Monknewtown on Thomas Ward's farm of 59 acres (24ha) with a house valued at 50 shillings. The smaller windows of the first floor are evidence of the second building phase. This house has farm buildings to the front creating a yard in rudimentary imitation of the formal courtyards of farm buildings associated with strong farms.

Today, one-third (33%) of these residences have disappeared from the Bend of the Boyne, and many that do survive are in poor condition.

GERALDINE STOUT

Fig. 15 Small farmer's house at Stalleen. This is the building depicted by Du Noyer in 1866 – only the children have changed.

Cottiers/labourers The pyramidal structure of rural society in the nineteenth century had a very narrow top and a very broad base. Indicative of this is the large number of houses with values of 15 shillings and less (appendix 1). There were 184 of these 'fourth-class' houses in 1854, comprising almost two-thirds (64%) of the housing stock. These were the homes of labourers but more often

ROYAL SOCIETY OF ANTIQUARIES OF IRELAND

Fig. 14 'In village of Donore in Meath, May 1866' by Du Noyer, May 1866. The typical house of the small farmer in the Boyne is vernacular in style and rectangular in plan, with a central hearth and lobby entrance. A remarkable feature of this house below Donore Hill (upper left) is the cone-shaped thatched piggery. The house is in ruinous condition and the piggery depicted in the drawing is gone. Pigs served as a form of savings account. In times of surplus food they were fed on potatoes, in times of hardship they could be sold or slaughtered

Fig. 16 On the right of this photo are the remains of the one-roomed cabin at Red Mountain drawn by Du Noyer in 1866.

Fig. 18 The Ordnance Survey Letters of the first half of the nineteenth century describe a 'hamlet' of thatched houses at Craud.[33] The only indication of their existence today is a lane with low earthworks adjoining the remains of house foundations. In many places, the sole trace of these houses is a weed-entangled gateway with everlasting sweet pea pushing up through the undergrowth.

housed the marginalised of society whose survival was only possible because of the nutritious potato. Usually, only a garden was associated with these houses, or an acre of potato ground.

This housing was dispersed throughout the area, with distinct clusters of houses at the now deserted nineteenth-century hamlets of Craud in Dowth townland, 'Rossin' in Balfeddock townland, and in the settlement which grew up around Donore chapel in the townland of Stalleen. Many of the roadside dwellings were replaced by public housing in the late nineteenth century. Of the few remaining examples, a pair of houses at Stalleen townland epitomise this house type. Both 'halves' had a value of 10 shillings.

Peter Quinn had 4 acres (2ha) and Mary Hamill had no land with her cottage. These houses were single-storey, stone and mud-walled thatched dwellings.

Allied to this impoverished class of houses were better-built (albeit similarly valued) labourers' cottages on the margins of the demesnes. These were built by improving landlords for their labourers. The grouping of dwellings together on an estate was a mid-nineteenth-century development and considered to be an improving measure.[34] At Platin, seven labourers' cottages were laid

Fig. 17 'Townland of Red Mountain near Donore in Meath' by Du Noyer, May 1866. Labourers' cabins were one of the most common building types in the Bend of the Boyne and throughout Ireland. Today they are very rare. Du Noyer's drawing paints an idyllic portrait of the self-sufficient poor; children play outside the house, chickens roost in the thatch, a slán resting against the gable wall testifies to the availability of turf, a 'pillock' (a locally made woven basket) holds spuds from the garden plot that was part of this small holding.

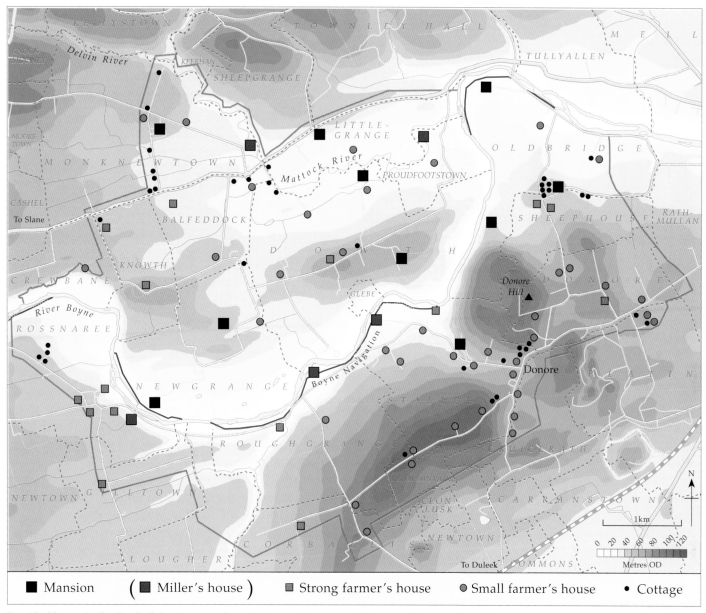

Mansion (**Miller's house**) **Strong farmer's house** ● **Small farmer's house** • **Cottage**

Fig. 19 Houses in the Bend of the Boyne in the mid-nineteenth century which are still upstanding. The main casualties to the housing stock in the intervening 150 years have been the homes of the small farmers and the 'fourth-class houses' of the cottiers and labourers. Compare this with figure 5.

out on both sides of a lane. These houses were valued between 8 and 12 shillings.

Although these fourth-class houses were once the most numerous, they are now a rarity in the Boyne Valley. Of 181, only thirty-seven still stand, a survival rate of just 20%. Many of those that do survive are in a ruinous condition. D'Alton (1844) described fifteen 'cleanly washed cottages' in the village which grew up around the Catholic chapel of Donore.[35] Only one of these survives (for now), a typical central-hearth, lobby-entrance house with a galvanised roof replacing an earlier thatch. It was valued at 12 shillings and there was no land associated with the house. During the course of this fieldwork, the second last of these cottages was demolished. Many of the

Fig. 20 Two labourers' cottages at Stalleen, adjoining single-storey, stone and mud-walled dwellings.

GERALDINE STOUT

GERALDINE STOUT

GERALDINE STOUT

Fig. 21   Labourers' cottages.   A) This is the only surviving cottage of fifteen described in 1844 by D'Alton as 'cleanly washed cottages' in the village of Donore.   B) Nineteenth-century labourers' cottages on the Platin estate.

houses that were spared are the better built houses on the improving estates.

If, following this analysis, we review Thompson's classification of rural society, it is clear that his observations regarding the labourers and noblemen still stand. However, he gives an inaccurate picture of what he refers to as the 'common farmer'. Those tenants with a 100–200 acreage (41–81ha) were certainly not 'worst lodged' in the Boyne Valley. They lived in formal, classical-style houses. Those with 50–100 acres (20–41ha) were also reasonably well housed. This criticism of the farmhouses could reflect a begrudging attitude on the part of the observer, and possibly the untidiness of the grazier holdings.[36]

INSTITUTIONAL AND INDUSTRIAL BUILDINGS

Ecclesiastical architecture   The first half of the nineteenth century saw an outburst of church building in eastern Meath, a phenomenon which accelerated throughout Ireland after Catholic Emancipation. The earliest and strongest Catholic communities emerged in areas with Catholic landlords. Their presence fostered the existence of a sub-gentry of Catholic middlemen and strong farmers who encouraged the construction of ecclesiastical and institutional buildings in their locality. Many of these churches replaced vernacular buildings and became a focus for the development of villages in the mid-nineteenth century.[37]

Griffith's Valuation lists three Catholic chapels within the Bend of the Boyne: Cruicerath, Monknewtown and Rossnaree. All three churches had a rateable valuation of 200 shillings. Fr Walter Johnston, who was born in Rossnaree, built the present Rossnaree church in 1819 on a

site given to the community by the Osborne family of nearby Rossnaree House. The site for the new church lay close to the old church which it replaced. The entrance to the site of the previous church was known as 'Priest's lane' and a stone font from the earlier church was apparently removed to the Osborne estate at Rossnaree.[38] Fr Denis Walsh, who replaced Fr Johnston, built the present stone church in Donore which replaced a thatched chapel, on ground granted to the church by the Nettervilles of Cruicerath. Donore church opened in 1838.[39] Thomas Hammond of neighbouring Sheephouse Quarry volunteered to supply all the cut stone for the front of the church.[40] At Monknewtown the Church of the Assumption of the Virgin Mary was built *c.*1837. In that year Rev Duff invited tenders for raising walls and re-roofing the chapel of Monknewtown, indicating that the church here is a re-modelled version of an earlier church on the same site.[41]

Fortunately all three churches survive in their original form and retain unchanged interiors. This is remarkable in

DROGHEDA INDEPENDANT

TO
BUILDERS
OR
STUCCO PLAISTERERS.
—o—

PROPOSALS will be received from competent persons for executing the Stucco Work of the ROMAN CA-THOLIC CHAPEL OF ROSNAREE.

Plans and Specifications of the work contemplated can be seen at the Office of Mr. HAMMOND, James's street, who will give any additional information required.

Drogheda, 18th July, 1849.

Fig. 22   An advertisement from the *Drogheda Independent* provides a precise date for building works on the 'chapel' at Rossnaree.

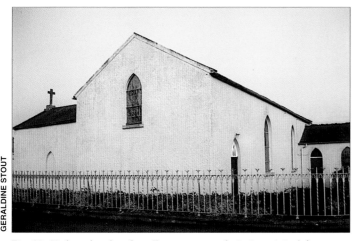

Fig. 23 Today, the church at Rossnaree stands in its original form as a simple T-plan structure with panelled timber galleries in the arms and the sanctuary in the centre of the long south wall. The interior has a plaster groin vault.[42]

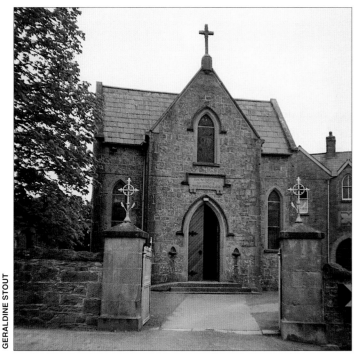

Fig. 24 Known as the Church of the Nativity of Mary Immaculate, this small church at Donore (built in 1838) is constructed of squared limestone rubble, with an unusual front.[43]

Fig. 25 The church at Monknewtown (built in 1837) has a simple T-plan.[44]

the current climate in Ireland which has seen the widespread replacement of this type of church in favour of large car parks with churches of incongruous styles attached. The nineteenth-century chapels reflect the strength of faith in post-Catholic Emancipation Ireland and are very important for their historical, aesthetic and architectural heritage. Appropriately, two of these churches, Monknewtown and Rossnaree, are listed in the County Meath Development Plan. Donore needs to be afforded similar protection.

Widows' House/Netterville Institute In 1826 the sixth Viscount Netterville bequeathed the castle at Dowth with the offices, garden and 60 acres (24ha) for the support of a charitable institution for 'poor desolate widows and orphans'.[45] The medieval towerhouse was modernised for their accommodation. This is the 'widows' house' on three acres (1 ha) at Dowth with a valuation of 150 shillings. There is a small Gothic-style chapel beside it with three pointed windows and a small porch. It is now roofless. This was associated with the widows' house. When the new institution was built it incorporated a chapel, replacing the earlier building which was allowed to fall into disrepair.

The widows' house was replaced by the Netterville Charitable Almshouse in 1877. The architect was the well-established George Ashlin. This imposing, forbidding building is a seven-bay, two-storey block, built of red brick with limestone and blue-brick trim.[46] A plaque records the building's erection resulting from 'provident management' of the Netterville Charities by the trustees. The institution was closed in the 1960s: after having a number of owners, it was converted into a guest house in 1998.[47]

Fig. 26 The Netterville Charitable Almshouse was built in 1867 to cater to the needs of Protestant widows and orphans.

Fig. 27 National school at Donore village built in 1870 to replace a mud-walled schoolhouse.

Fig. 28 This simple stone structure housed watchmen who protected the burials at Sheephouse graveyard at a time when grave-robbing was rife.

National schools *Griffith's Valuation* lists national schools in the parish centres within the Bend of the Boyne. These were established by the Education Act of 1831 which set up the national school system on a parish basis.[48] Listed are two national schools beside the church at Donore village in the townland of Cruicerath. They had valuations of 13 and 14 shillings, respectively. These were vernacular, mud-walled buildings which were replaced in 1870 by the present schoolhouse.[49] At Monknewtown the parish school and the master's house were valued at 30 shillings. The present buildings on the site appear to be late nineteenth century in date and must have replaced the buildings mentioned in the valuations. The schoolhouse at Dowth also had a valuation of 30 shillings. Roofless remains of this single-storey building with its pointed windows stand to the west of the towerhouse at Dowth. An impression of being a student at this school house at Dowth is evoked by John Boyle O'Reilly in his poem 'The old school clock'. The original clock hung on the wall of the Netterville schoolhouse at Dowth, where his father William David O'Reilly was the teacher.[50]

Watch-house Amongst the more unusual buildings listed in the 1854 valuation is a watch-house in the graveyard at Sheephouse with a rateable valuation of 10 shillings. This simple, single-roomed, stone-built structure was used by watchmen who protected the graves at Sheephouse from 'body-snatchers'. This was a major concern to people in the eighteenth and nineteenth centuries, when bodies were removed from graveyards to be sold on for medical dissection.[51] Watchmen were needed because the graveyard at Sheephouse, at the original Donore village, had become isolated from its parishioners, most of whom were living in the new chapel village of Donore in the townland of Cruicerath.

Mills *Griffith's Valuation* lists six mills in the area and the House Books provide detailed information on these mills. They have a wide range of valuations, from the old corn mill at Dowth mentioned in eighteenth-century deeds to the then modern mill at Monknewtown. Another impressive mill stood at Proudfootstown with a valuation of 600 shillings, but all that remains today are the storehouses. The mill at Rossnaree was valued at 400 shillings and a reference in the Ordnance Survey Field Books to it being 'unfinished' suggests that it was rebuilt on the site of the earlier eighteenth-century mill.[52]

The remaining mills are smaller, vernacular-style structures. The oat mill at Roughgrange was valued at 200 shillings. It was owned by William Norris and had three pairs of stones. It worked for about eight months of the year although the daily working time was uncertain. It was subject to backwater in flood.[53] The only indication of a mill at this site is the presence of a millstone by the riverside and traces of an artificial channel. At Stalleen the mill of Peter McCullagh was valued at 120 shillings. It also had three pairs of stones, two working constantly, and ground twenty-five barrels a day.[54] This mill is still partly standing and the kiln also survives. Lastly, the 'vacant corn mill' at Dowth had two pairs of stones for grinding corn and flour, one pair for shelling, another for grinding corn. In 1837–38 there were two water wheels with buckets present. The water mill was employed for seven months of the year and thirteen hours a day. Corn and flour could not be ground at the same time. There

Fig. 29 Monknewtown (1825) was the most impressive industrial mill in the area and, as a result, this complex had the highest valuation for a property in the Bend of the Boyne in the mid-nineteenth century (£134). The corn and flour mill of William Rogers had a constant supply of water for eight months of the year and a reasonable supply for the remainder. Steam was also used to power the mill when the water power was not sufficient. One-third of the work was effected by means of steam. The metal water wheel turned three pairs of stones for grinding flour. It was almost constantly employed. The principal block is a slate-roofed, seven-bay, four-storey structure of limestone with cut stone door and window surrounds. Flanking this is a red-brick chimney and a four-storey storehouse.[55]

was also a corn kiln. Twenty barrels were ground per day.[56] The only evidence on the ground today for this mill is the presence of a millstone at the site.

LAND TENURE

The factors which resulted in the very low rates of preservation, particularly in the lower-class housing, are related to the nature of land tenure in the nineteenth century. Thompson (1802) observed that in county Meath the house seldom lasted longer than the lease.[57] Although this is an exaggeration, it points to the fragility of the lowest class of housing in the Bend of the Boyne. Thompson also reasoned that it was in the tenant's interest to run the property down. The lease in Meath was twenty-one to thirty-one years or three named lives, which was considered good at the time for the stronger tenants.[58] The standard length of lease is confirmed in deeds and papers relating to the Rathmullan estate which quote a thirty-one-year lease or three lives.[59] Again, in a will dated 1816, Henry Coddington advised that his heirs should let the lands of Sheephouse and Donore for the terms of three lives or thirty-one years and the 'best improved rent that

Fig. 30 The ruins of the mill at Monknewtown. This picturesque pile on the banks of the Mattock is silent testimony to a time when the Irish rural landscape was greatly industrialised.

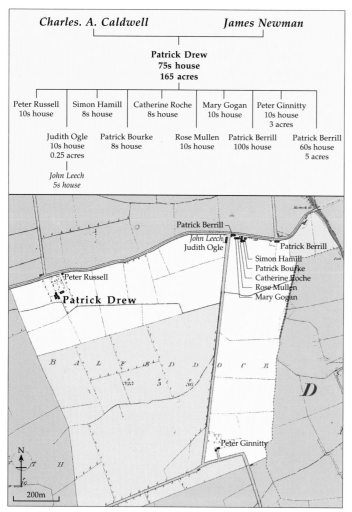

Fig. 31   The leasing structure in the Bend of the Boyne is exemplified in the hierarchy of buildings and landholdings in Balfeddock townland. Patrick Drew held 165 acres (67ha) of land from Charles Caldwell of Newgrange House and James Newman. A strong farmer, he lived in a house valued at 75 shillings. Drew sub-let ten houses and a small portion of his land to others on the margins of his property. The values of the houses varied considerably, from a 100-shilling house to 8 shilling 'cabins'. One of Drew's tenants (sub-tenants of Caldwell), Judith Ogle – who was herself housed in a dwelling with a value of only 10 shillings – sub-let a 5 shilling house to John Leech. The precarious and impoverished position of these sub-sub-tenants became totally unsustainable with the demise of the potato. Therefore, the leasehold structure recorded in *Griffith's Valuation* captured a society on the verge of crisis. With the breakdown of this system also came the deterioration of the housing stock.

can be reasonably had for the same should be reserved for the land'.[60] A condition of the rental was that the premises be kept in repair. However, the Field Books list the type of land tenure for each holding and in the majority of cases – the majority consisting of the very poor – it states that the land was held 'at will', i.e. on a yearly basis.[61] Rents were paid half-yearly on All Saints Day and May Day. Only 20% of tenants in Ireland had leases; however, the law recognised that in practice a yearly tenancy continued from one year to the next and did not expire at the end of each year. This could only be changed by mutual consent or by

litigation in the courts. The laws covering leasehold and descent were very much to the landlord's disadvantage as the landlord was often unaware of the number of sub-leases let by the middlemen. Long leases allowed middlemen to exploit the land, as landlords were reluctant to let good land to smallholders.[62]

The type of land tenure greatly influenced the agricultural situation in pre-Famine Meath.[63] Insecurity of tenure was detrimental to agricultural improvement. A class was allowed to accumulate on land which became non-productive in economic terms after the tillage boom came to an abrupt end in 1815. The baronies of east Meath carried an inordinately high cottier element in 1851.[64] The majority of the poor in county Meath, as in Leinster generally, were these landless who lived in the most wretched of dwellings.[65] Numerically they represented a substantial portion of the population, in what was in many ways one of Ireland's most affluent counties. Rural poverty was most in evidence in tillage areas, where there were large numbers of strong farmers as well as resident landlords.[66] The subdivision of agricultural holdings was regarded by 1830 as one of the chief causes of the troubled condition of Irish agriculture and the poverty of the smallholders. This subdivision of holdings was unsustainable. With a slump in agricultural prices, the small farmers were unable to switch to grazing, their ability to change being further hindered by the size of their holding.

POST-FAMINE POPULATION AND HOUSING DECLINE

The baronies of east Meath showed a demographic decline of 14% in the Famine decade.[67] This is relatively low when compared to figures of 20% for the whole of East Leinster and parts of north Meath where the population was halved in the period.[68] This decline was not universal within the Bend of the Boyne. Donore experienced growth in the 1870s, largely due to the input of local landlord Sharman Crawford of Stalleen. The number of houses in Donore increased by 50%, from twenty-one in 1851 to thirty-one in 1881.[69] For the most part, however, population decline continued into the twentieth century, as was the case nation-wide.[70] Some tenants emigrated to America in the years following the Famine, such as those on Chamney Grave's Rathmullan estate near Drogheda whose emigration was financed by the landlord.[71]

This population decline facilitated the consolidation of landholdings and resulted in increased prosperity and security amongst the stronger tenants whose dwellings have survived to the present day. It also facilitated the removal of the lower echelons of society, the cottiers/labourers whose dwellings have largely vanished.

Table 2
Population in the Bend of the Boyne 1841–1901[72]

Year	Population	Houses	Uninhabited houses
1841	2433	404	1
1851	2010	397	2
1861	1514	345	0
1871	1492	319	0
1881	1363	288	8
1891	1216	321	0
1901	897	289	0

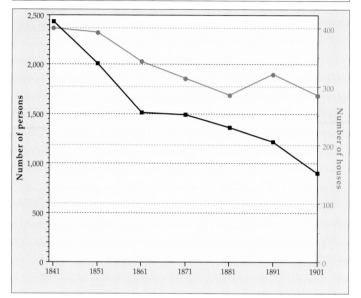

Fig. 32   The decennial census figures for the Bend of the Boyne indicates that the effect of the Famine (1845–48) on the Boyne population was immediate, beginning a downward trend in population figures and a corresponding decrease in house numbers for the area.

Generally speaking, the Great Famine did not affect the lower Boyne Valley as severely as other parts of the country. There are, however, indications of general depression and disease. A Parliamentary Report in 1846 describes a field in Oldbridge in which all the potatoes appeared to be rotting in pits.[73] An epidemic of cholera – one of the diseases associated with the Famine – took the life of a young parish priest in Rossnaree and a grave slab in Rossnaree church records this tragedy. Information contained in the Perambulation Books suggests that some of the landlords showed leniency about collecting rents during the Famine years. For instance, the Earl of Sheffield, landlord of Monknewtown, reduced rents from 1846.[74] Documentation relating to the Encumbered Estate at Rathmullan describes a 'temporary abatement' made to some of the tenants 'by reason of the depression of the times'.[75] Another symptom of the depression of the post-Famine years was that the large industrial mills such as Monknewtown, built in the boom time of the early century, became indebted and sought new investors.[76]

Landlords and tenants   From the 1860s there was growing tension between landlords and tenants. This manifested itself in the rise of the Fenian movement. Within the Bend of the Boyne it was evidenced by the rise to prominence of local patriot and leader John Boyle O'Reilly. O'Reilly, born at Dowth, was transported to Australia for his subversive activities. Before his exile, he had inscribed his initials into a stone at Dowth church. This later became a focus of commemoration by Fenians and 'Home Rulers', to the annoyance of the local gentry. So anxious were the local landlords that Richard Gradwell of Dowth Hall personally arranged for the removal of this stone to O'Reilly's grave in Holyhead cemetery in Brookline, Massachusetts.[77] A later monument erected to the memory of John Boyle O'Reilly is

ANCIENT MONUMENTS PROTECTION ACT, 1882.
45 & 46 Vic., Cap. 73.

ANCIENT MONUMENT, NEW GRANGE.

The Public are hereby informed that at the Petty Sessions held at Slane on the 30th day of May, 1899, on the proseoution of the Commissioners of Public Works in Ireland, a person was convicted and fined, with costs, for injuring or defacing this Monument.

By Order,

H. WILLIAMS,
Secretary.

Board of Public Works,
Custom House, Dublin,
11th July, 1899,

(1819.) Wt. 2211—7.50.11/18.A.T.&Co.,Ltd.

NATIONAL ARCHIVES

Fig. 33   Notice forbidding damage to the tomb at Newgrange.

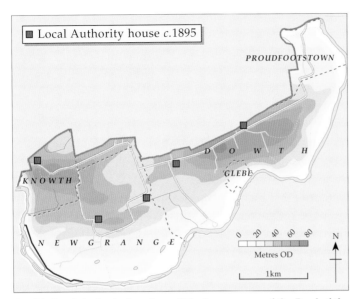

TOM BYRNE

Fig. 36 Local Authority house at Knowth.

Fig. 34 Local Authority housing within the core area of the Bend of the Boyne (after Higginbottom).

still a focus for commemoration and an attraction for visitors from both America and Australia.

A *cause celébrè* in the 1870s was the Dowth eviction case. In 1873 James Elcock, a local miller, began to build a wool store using stones from the passage tomb at Dowth. He was advised by Gradwell, the local landlord of Dowth Hall, to replace the stones or face eviction, which duly occurred in 1879. The Elcock family had a yearly tenancy permitting them to bring an action for disturbance. With the support of some members of Parliament, including Parnell, James Elcock was awarded the full amount claimed, with only a meagre £50 allowed to repair the injury to the mound going

TOM BYRNE

Fig. 35 Local Authority labourers' cottages form a distinct housing style within the Bend of the Boyne. They are detached dwellings, one and a half storeys high, with unplastered stone walls, dressed quoins and slated roofs. They have a brick finish on the windows and doors, in modern times customarily painted in bright colours.

to Gradwell.[78] The perception at the time was that Gradwell was using the destruction of the tomb as an excuse for evicting the Elcocks. It is more likely, however, that his motive was the preservation of the monument itself, because in September 1885 the tumulus of Dowth was vested in the State under the Ancient Monuments Protection Act (1882).[79] Negotiations to protect Newgrange also began in 1882. However, the eventual vesting of Newgrange was as a result of the owner being alarmed by a report of its deterioration. The Board of Works denounced any interference with the monuments. A defacement of a stone in the chamber of Newgrange in 1898 resulted in a succesful prosecution and notices were placed around the monument making the public aware of the offence.[80] The monument was taken into State care in that year.

Public housing   The enactment of the Labourers (Ireland) Acts from 1893 to 1919 resulted in the replacement of some of the fourth-class housing by stone cottages. This was part of a major public rehousing scheme in Ireland which sought to provide suitable dwellings and half-acre allotments for landless labourers who were inadequately housed.[81] In the Bend of the Boyne and elsewhere, these cottages were commonly known as 'Parnell Cottages' because Parnell lobbied for the improvement of the housing of this disadvantaged class in rural Irish society.[82] The housing programme was a joint venture between State and local authorities, and the earliest concerted public housing initiative in Britain and Ireland.

These labourers' cottages form a distinctive house style in the Bend of the Boyne. They were designed by a local architect, P. J. Dodd of Drogheda.[83] Their remarkable state of preservation is a tribute to their architect. The only exception is a pair of semi-detached houses in Newgrange townland which are in ruins. A fine terrace of nineteenth-century (post-1856) labourers' houses was built with stone and brick on the Oldbridge estate at the south-east corner of Sheephouse townland.

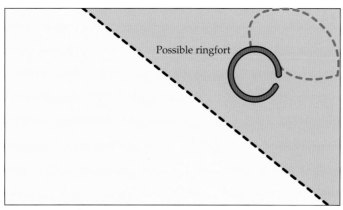

A) Prehistory

Some transient Late Bronze Age activity

Upland

Lowland

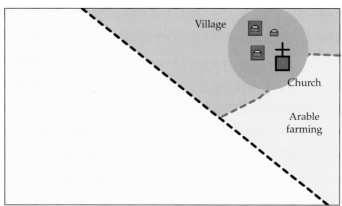

B) Iron Age / Early Christian

Possible ringfort

C) Medieval

Village

Church

Arable farming

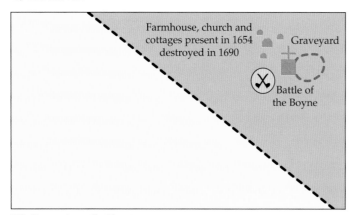

D) Seventeenth Century

Farmhouse, church and cottages present in 1654 destroyed in 1690

Graveyard

Battle of the Boyne

CASE STUDY 4:

LANDSCAPE DEVELOPMENT AT DONORE

Despite its proximity to the passage tomb cemeteries and its separation from the Bend of the Boyne by a fordable river, settlement on the south side of the Boyne took a distinctly different course. This is partly explained by the rugged hill topography south of the river. The old village of Donore lies on one of the higher elevations (over 80m) within the Boyne Valley Archaeological Park. This hill lay on the periphery of some Mid to Late Bronze Age transient settlement (A), but the early name for the place – *Dun Wabair* – suggests that its 'foundation' dates from the Early Christian period when a ringfort was probably built on the hill (B). In 1203 King John granted the lands at *Dun Wabair* to the Cistercian monastery at Mellifont; like much of the lower Boyne Valley, it became part of a large medieval estate. By 1539 there was a church on the site with two messuages and a cottage (C). This pattern of urban growth around a monastic core was also seen at Monknewtown. In 1622 the church at Donore was in reasonable repair but it was damaged in the 1641 rebellion. In 1654 there were three cottages and a farm house at Donore and in 1682 the church was repaired. Donore was the site of a major conflict in the Battle of the Boyne in 1690. Story's contemporary drawing shows that by this date the church, a turreted building, was in ruins. Another roofless building is depicted beside the church (D).

Donore Hill and chapel village *c.*1900.

The last remaining whitewashed cottage and thriving pub in Donore village *c*.2000.

A Catholic chapel was built at the bottom of the hill in 1727 on Lord Netterville's land at Cruicerath. This became a focus for new settlement and precipitated the further abandonment of the old village. A watch-house was built in the old graveyard at Donore because it had become isolated from its parishioners who were now living down the hill in the new village of Donore (E). By 1844 there were fifteen whitewashed cottages in the chapel village arranged on either side of the street opposite the village church and national schools. In the post-Famine period Donore underwent a building boom due to the intervention of the local landlord, Sharman Crawford of nearby Stalleen. The housing figures increased by a third between 1851 and 1870 (F). However, by the turn of the century the population had fallen in Donore and much of the nineteenth-century housing stock had been removed. All but a few of the 'whitewashed cottages' that remained on the north side of the street were demolished. One was demolished in the 1990s to make room for an extension to Daly's public house, recently renamed 'Brú na Bóinne' (G). This public house is enjoying new business brought into the area by the building of the Brú na Bóinne Visitor Centre near Donore.

In the future, as part of the development of the Battle of the Boyne battlefield site, the medieval church at old Donore will become more accessible to the public. The pressure for housing will probably result in building around the present church at Donore. The last nineteenth-century cottage may be preserved and used as a base for a local cultural society (H). Donore, a backwater throughout the millennia, will become not just the area's only true village but also the hub of the tourist trade attracted to the monuments north of the river.

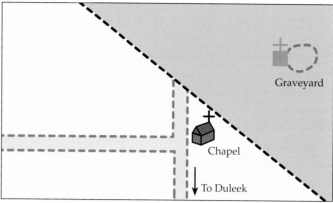

E) Eighteenth Century

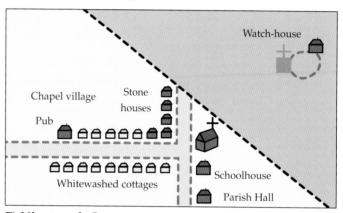

F) Nineteenth Century

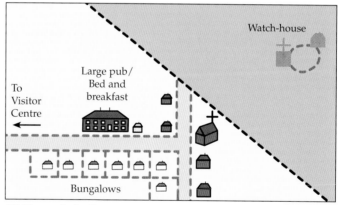

G) Twentieth Century

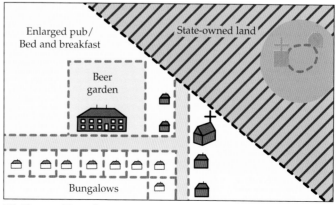

H) Future Trends

THE MODERN LANDSCAPE

The Bend of the Boyne is home today to what it has always been: a community of farmers. Only gradual change has occurred here in a climate of relative peace and prosperity. The area still practises a mixed farming economy and fewer residents commute to Dublin than is the norm for county Meath. No major new housing projects have taken place; there is no new industry, no new retail initiatives.

The world outside the Boyne has left only slight traces on the modern landscape. Given the economic and ideological policy of de Valera, many Irish speakers were transplanted to the area in the 1930s. Efforts to create an Irish-speaking community of small farmers were largely unsuccessful, however.

A recurring theme running through this study has been the strategic significance of the Boyne as a control on northern approaches to Dublin; this was apparent during the Anglo-Norman period, the 1641 rebellion and the Battle of the Boyne in 1690. Even today, large-scale security operations still include checkpoints on the bridges of the Boyne. Most recently, the Boyne was used as the line of defence against the spread of Foot and Mouth disease. The Boyne Valley's strategic importance was underlined during the Emergency, when the Boyne and Blackwater formed the planned main line of resistance, in effect the Irish Maginot line, in Ireland's defence against a threatened overland invasion by British forces. The legacy of World War II in Ireland was a line of defensive pillboxes.

Because farming is the main economic activity in the area, farmers have had the most profound effect on the modern landscape. State-aided farm improvement schemes, and after 1973 finance from Europe, dictated modernisation of farm buildings and a small amount of field clearance. Nonetheless, the rural landscape is not greatly altered and the most highly valued features have survived unscathed.

ALBERT KAHN

Fig. 1   The earliest colour photograph of a Boyne coracle maker taken in 1910 by a French photographer sponsored by Albert Kahn as part of his 'archive of the planet'. The craft of boat making, a millennia old tradition in decline, is recorded before its demise. The end of long-established folkways in the Bend of the Boyne marks the threshold of modern modes of living in the valley.

COLONY MIGRATION

The early years of the twentieth century witnessed the dismantling of the estate system and its replacement by the present owner/occupier system of landholding. This land reform was implemented through a series of land acts in which the British government encouraged Irish landlords to transfer land to their tenants.[1] Although revolutionary in its scope, this change in land tenure had few immediate landscape implications; it helped to maintain the *status quo* in the Bend of the Boyne.

Significant change was not to occur until the election of the populist Fianna Fáil government under the leadership of Eamon de Valera. From 1932, a scheme of state-assisted migration led to the transfer of Irish-speaking families from congested districts in the west of Ireland to five locations in county Meath, including the Bend of the Boyne. The availability of land in Meath was partly due to the Economic War of the 1930s, which had damaged the Meath graziers. This led to a dramatic upsurge in land purchase by the Land Commission between 1935 and 1940.[2] Architecturally, this impacted on the landscape in the form of a distinctively styled house built by the Land Commission for the migrants. The migrants were concentrated in the townlands of Newgrange and Dowth on land formerly held by the Gradwells of Dowth Hall. The houses were built on the roadside, mainly single-storey, with a porch, a tiled roof and roughcast walls. Although the migrants failed to establish a viable Irish-speaking community, they remain a distinctive cultural group within the population of the valley.

Fig. 2 A Land Commission house at Newgrange built in the 1930s. This is one of a number in the Bend of the Boyne built to house migrant families from county Mayo in the late 1930s and 1940s. It has recently been remodelled beyond all recognition.

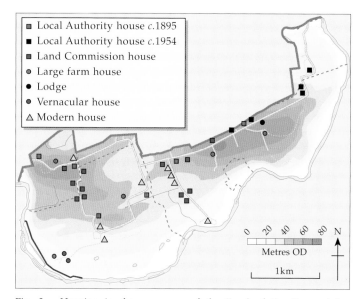

- ■ Local Authority house *c*.1895
- ■ Local Authority house *c*.1954
- ■ Land Commission house
- ● Large farm house
- ● Lodge
- ● Vernacular house
- △ Modern house

Fig. 3   Housing in the core area of the Bend of the Boyne (after Higginbottom).

THE EMERGENCY (1939–45) AND THE BEND OF THE BOYNE

The politics of Eamon de Valera had further landscape implications during World War II. As the major European powers prepared for war in the 1930s, Ireland made plans to defend its neutrality. In September 1936, the Irish government established a ministerial committee on national defence, chaired by de Valera, which agreed on a clear policy.[3] Ireland's recently won independence from Britain would not be surrendered lightly and its neutrality would be defended unless attacked by another country. The declaration of war in 1939, therefore, posed a major threat to Ireland's national security. With the fall of France and escalating German U-boat activity, there was concern that Ireland would be invaded by England so that it could take control of the deep water ports. The Emergency Powers Orders were enacted and preparations for the defence of the country were set in motion. The main landscape impact was a line of fortifications which comprised blockhouses and machine-gun pits concentrated along the river banks.

Defence plan   The Defence Forces produced plans detailing various operational procedures to deal with this perceived threat, the two main ones being an anti-German invasion plan and a plan to counter a British invasion.[4] This study concentrates on the defence plans for a British invasion because these had a direct bearing on the Boyne Valley.[5] It was proposed to place 'an infantry detachment along the line of the Boyne and Blackwater' which Major Tuohy (who devised the plan) referred to as the 'Main Line of Resistance'. The Boyne and Blackwater were considered a 'good line' because they acted as a 'tank obstacle'. All crossings were to be covered by blockhouses, and machine-gun pits 'were to be placed on the north side of Drogheda, Slane, Navan and Kells'. These proposals formed the basis for Operations Orders sent out from Portobello Barracks, Dublin, to its Eastern Command on 9 July 1940. According to these orders:

> Circumstances require the observation of the northern territory and the covering of routes from the border towards Dublin ... Provision will be made for ... prompt opposition to a hostile advance including delaying action by a small detachment between the border and a final line of defence. The final line of defence will be the general line of the rivers Boyne and Blackwater from the sea to Lough Ramor.[6]

This plan to counter a British offensive had two main elements: firstly, a defence of the ports and secondly, defensive operations against an overland assault along the east coast. Observation groups were to be placed on the frontier and coast. Behind the observers was the land frontier where a screen of cyclists and cavalry squadrons would operate as a covering force from the border back to the main line of resistance, with the task of providing information on the enemy and imposing the maximum amount of delay north of the line. This outpost line was assisted by the Local Defence Force (LDF), who had been established by the Emergency Powers Order 1940. The LDF was considered so important in the border areas that it was proposed that the army take over its training in the Garda Districts of Louth/Meath, Cavan/Monaghan and Sligo/Leitrim.[7] A 'cyclist' squadron (bicycles rather than motor-cycles) was located at Dundalk and another at Manorhamilton, while motor squadrons were located at Kingscourt, Cavan and Mohill. Three infantry battalions were to provide forces for a series of outposts forward of the main line of resistance. The main defence effort was to be concentrated along the line of the Boyne and Blackwater, extending to Lough Ramor, Lough Sheelin, Arvagh and Roosky, along the Shannon to Carrick-on-Shannon and then across to the Curlew Mountains. This was considered a good line of defence as the rivers acted as an obstacle to tank manoeuvres. This line was planned as a series of strong points covering main routes to the south.[8] All the crossings were to be covered by blockhouses, and machine-gun pits were to be constructed on the north side of Drogheda and at Slane, Navan and Kells.

Blockhouses on the Boyne   The blockhouses mentioned in the Strategic Defence Plan are reinforced concrete artillery emplacements and are usually referred to as 'pillboxes'.

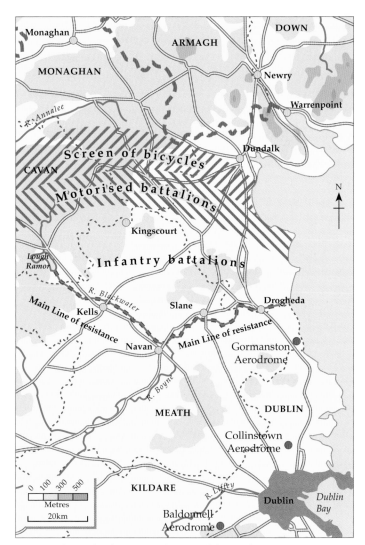

Fig. 4 Defence plan for Eastern Command during the Emergency.

They were first used by the Russians in the Russo-Japanese War. The concept was copied by the German army in World War I and later imitated by the British, who built them along the east coast of England during the Great War.[9] These blockhouses were circular in plan resembling the decorative boxes used to hold pills, hence the name 'pillbox'.[10] They are found across Europe and were used extensively on the Western Front during World War I.[11] During 1940, at the onset of World War II, more than 18,000 were built in Great Britain. However, by September 1941 all pillbox construction was stopped and subsequently forbidden in 1942 because these fortifications were deemed vulnerable to high velocity guns.[12] No such ban occurred in Ireland.

The basic structure is a squat, strong building, invariably of concrete, usually flat-topped, with one or two entrances protected by a covered porch or detached wall. Internally splayed horizontal slits, firing loops, loop holes and embrasures are a standard pillbox features. Most were designed to take rifle fire or light machine-gun fire and it was also *hoped* that the walls would resist anti-tank guns.[13]

There is little documentation on the works associated with the defence of the Boyne and Blackwater. A map of the Eastern Command identified only eight blockhouses along these rivers between Drogheda and Navan.[14] But field reconnaissance on the Boyne and Blackwater discovered of thirty-seven pillboxes between Baltray on the Boyne estuary and Navan. Another five pillboxes form a defensive ring around Gormanston Army camp. Thirteen of these pillboxes are in the Bend of the Boyne.

Location   The pillboxes are situated mainly on the south side of the Boyne close to the river bank, and tend to be grouped opposite major road junctions and bridging points. The greatest concentration, ironically, is at Oldbridge (site of the main conflict in the Battle of the Boyne 1690) and in the environs of Slane, an important junction on the Dublin–Derry road. Some of the pillboxes are so close to the river that they would have been prone to flooding. These have a limited and very localised field of cover. However, interspersed with these are more prominently positioned sites which provide a wider field of cover.[15] Those along the south side of the river are consistently aligned to the opposite bank of the river. They are occasionally incorporated into existing features such as the demesne wall at Oldbridge (11 and 12, see p. 174), a canal lock at Fennor (25) and a burial mound at Rossnaree (22).

Morphology   The Boyne pillboxes are squat, generally flat-topped, single entrance structures and vary in plan from square to trapezoidal. The hexagonal plan which was so widely used in Great Britain is not present on the Boyne.[16] They are *c*.4m in maximum width and length and are usually about 1.80m high. Wall thicknesses vary from 0.50m to 0.80m. In 1941 there was concern at the fragility of the walls and questions about their ability to withstand shell-fire. The Director of Engineers of the Irish Defence Forces suggested that in some cases it might be necessary to build shell-proof blockhouses which would have to have wall thickness increased to 0.90m. He observed that anti-tank 'two-point guns' would cut through walls 1.35m thick, and at that time most of the blockhouses had only 0.50m thick walls.[17] These dimensions indicate that the Boyne sites were not built to withstand shell-fire. In some cases the pillbox was further protected by a blast wall. An example of this type of detached wall is found at Oldbridge (9). Some pillboxes have a stepped entrance such as Mornington (2) and Rathmullan (10). Some, such as the site at Rossnaree (20), are partially sunken.

GERALDINE STOUT

Fig. 5   A typical pillbox at the mouth of the Boyne at Beaulieu. Unfortunately, the rubbish is also typical of many rural areas.

Pillboxes are invariably built of concrete. The concrete is distinctive by its relatively poor quality and the presence of pebbles and stones in the make-up. Traces of the planks used in the shuttering are apparent on the surface and in one case, sheets of corrugated iron were used for this purpose (the machine-gun pit in the canal at Fennor). The concrete shows signs of being reinforced with iron bars. Apparently bedsprings were universally used for this purpose in Great Britain, Slumberland being the chief supplier![18] Very few of the pillboxes have a concrete floor – Rossnaree is a rare exception. Some of the Boyne sites still have earthen mounds on the top suggesting that they were originally camouflaged and this is corroborated by guidelines given to the LDF which required them to ensure that the walls were reinforced by sod-covered banks of earth or stone.[19] Many have wide metal bands extending from their exterior at upper embrasure level. These enigmatic bands may have been

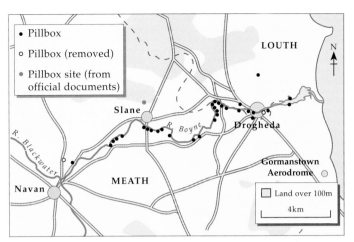

Fig. 6   Pillboxes on the Boyne and Blackwater, the main line of resistance during the Emergency.

used to camouflage the sites. The site at Mornington, the largest example identified, was painted black in the interior to embrasure level.

All the pillboxes have a series of horizontal slits or firing points which are usually internally splayed or parallel-sided. In some instances, like Oldbridge (13), there are smaller loop holes near the entrance. They provide cover of the immediate terrain. At Beauparc (27), a 'peephole' was present on the undefended side. The

openings slope up or down depending on the angle of elevation, depression and traverse required.[20] Most were designed to take rifle fire or light machinery fire. In general, the entrance side is undefended. There is no evidence for the use of steel shutters on the openings, as in some of the English pillboxes.[21] The entrances on the Boyne sites are rebated, indicating the former existence of steel shutters. One of the pillboxes at Gormanston Camp still has the steel shutters *in situ*.

The Military Archive throws light on the firing points which were used in the Boyne pillboxes. In July 1941, the Director of Engineers recommended that firing points should be wider on the inside than on the outside except where the gun was pivoted or where the walls were more than 0.90m thick.[22] His instructions included details regarding size of openings which in all cases depended on the angles of elevation, depression and traverse required. Three different firing ports were examined in detail: one with straight side, one with larger opening of the port to the inside, and one with larger opening of the port to the outside. A man with a rifle had better observation of the field when the embrasure had the larger port to the inside as he had more room to manipulate his weapon than in the other cases. On the other hand, if the sides of the firing port

GERALDINE STOUT

Fig. 7   The view from a pillbox along the Boyne. During the Emergency a volunteer member of the Local Defence Force was provided with a gun (and often a bottle of whiskey) and left to man these cold concrete bunkers through the night. The threat of a British invasion was real, and this is the perspective that would have greeted the volunteer at the end of his long night's vigil.

Fig. 8 In some cases the roof of a pillbox has an uneven external surface where the remains of the concrete used in its construction was apparently dumped (Oldbridge 18). This uneven roof feature also occurs on East Anglian pillboxes built in 1940 and German examples from World War I, where it was thought to be a conscious effort to camouflage the pillbox.[23] This is one of a tight group of eight pillboxes at Oldbridge. The most heavily defended crossing on the Boyne during this time was identical to the spot where William III (an earlier 'British' invader) crossed the Boyne in his passage to Dublin.

were made with a larger opening of port to the outside, better protection is afforded to the defender but observation of fire is reduced. Ultimately, it was decided that where defenders were armed with a rifle, the firing port should have the port opening to the inside. However, when using the Vickers MG there was thought to be no advantage in splaying the port as recommended for the rifle. In this case the gun rotates around an axis, so a square port opening was advisable. The openings in the Boyne sites are generally splayed internally, indicating that they were defended by rifle only.

Construction It is difficult to obtain specific information on the pillbox-building programme along the Boyne. Two of the sites, Roughgrange (21) and Mornington (2), have dates inscribed on their interiors; at Roughgrange '1942' was marked into the concrete at the

Fig. 9 Some of the pillboxes along the south side of the Boyne were prominently positioned to provide a wide field of cover. These protected the lower line of pillboxes near the river's edge.

time of construction and there are names in pencil on the walls of Mornington pillbox: 'N. Wall 1942' and 'Terry Skelly 1944'. This is the only precise dating evidence we have for the construction of the Boyne pillboxes. The procedure involved in the building of a pillbox saw the military authorities in Eastern Command issuing an Operations Order to district leaders which specified the situation of the blockhouses in the area and the tasks of the LDF.[24] Construction Corps, involved with mines, roads and pillboxes for the Eastern Command, were based at Gormanston Camp and they organised the construction of individual sites.[25] The LDF was then charged with the upkeep and protection of the blockhouses.

If an attack were pending or a training exercise was needed, a strong party within the local LDF was to be detached for the protection of the blockhouse. In advance of this, however, they were to prepare range cards for the different loop holes and armaments suitable for those ranges. They were to be acquainted with potential routes of approach likely to be used and measures necessary to protect these routes, with positions prepared outside the

Fig. 10 Some pillboxes were partially sunk in the ground to provide extra defence and to make them less visible. This is a feature of the cluster of pillboxes at Rossnaree.

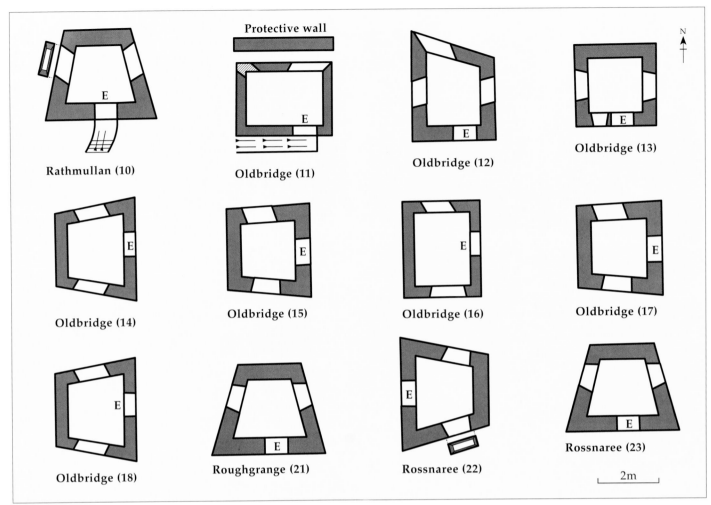

Fig. 11 Plans of pillboxes in the lower Boyne Valley. Numbering refers to map of pillboxes in the Bend of the Boyne on the opposite page.

blockhouse to assist its protection.[26] In Great Britain, the Army Command set up teams to survey the countryside and recommend suitable defence lines. They had the authority to enter private land and compensation was paid for any diminution to the value of land. Local contractors were used and even encouraged to provide original designs.[27] No such independence was afforded to local interests in the Irish case.

Strategy and tactics   The blockhouses on the Boyne were built as part of a larger defensive strategy. They were constructed along a strong defensive line formed by the Boyne but unevenly distributed at defensive strong points for defence in depth. Two or three were grouped close together in strategic places to provide mutual support.[28] The tactical use of the pillbox relied on it being hidden from sight until the enemy was in effective range. That is why so many of them were camouflaged. The concrete was a protection against bullets, shell splinters and the weather.[29] They were, however, vulnerable to a direct hit from heavy shells, they had the disadvantage of limiting the field of fire,

and their internal space restricted the amount of guns and personnel that could be used.[30] One of the problems in creating a line of pillboxes such as that along the Boyne is their fixed orientation and the inflexible siege consciousness or 'Maginot Mentality' which such a line creates.[31]

The Boyne pillboxes are artefacts of a world war, the faintest echo of the clash of nations which brought so much of Europe to its knees. They are a testimony to that troubled time and a physical reminder of the significant role played by the Boyne Valley in this period of Irish history. Because of the dearth of official information, these sites provide a local history of the Emergency.

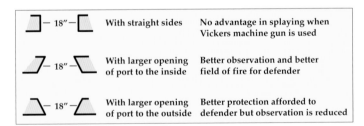

Fig. 12 Firing points for pillboxes as assessed by Major John Gleeson, Assistant Director of Engineers, 1941.

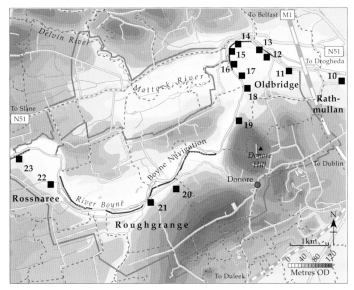

Fig. 13 Pillboxes within the Bend of the Boyne (numbering refers to pill box plans on the opposite page).

The Boyne sites are very well preserved, but there is, nontheless, ignorance of their historical significance. Emergency era defences receive no form of legal protection in Ireland. This is in stark contrast to Great Britain where they are a scheduled archaeological monument.

GRANT-AIDED LANDSCAPE CHANGE 1950–90

County Meath is widely perceived as a premier farming area with some of the best drained and most fertile soils in Ireland. The average farm size is 30% greater than the national average.[32] The historical strength of agriculture in Meath has been well attested in the preceding chapters. Farmers in the county have always shown a willingness to adapt to market needs, given their proximity to Dublin and European markets. In the last four decades there has been considerable restructuring of the landscape of the lower Boyne, with investment in both farms and farm buildings. Farmers in the valley are responding to the availability of financial incentives and demands from government for increased agricultural activity, with consequent profound environmental impacts. The setting for the Boyne monuments is being gradually transformed, as removal of field boundaries and construction of large farm buildings generated a new agricultural landscape. These changes have largely emanated from farm development schemes operated by the Department of Agriculture through the provision of grant-aid.[33]

Currently, farming comprises 97% of land use.[34] The study area features a mixture of both large and small farms. Fifty-eight per cent of the holdings are below 20ha and 10% are over 60ha. Many of the smaller holdings (below 20ha) are derived from Land Commission sub-divisions allocated to migrant families from Mayo in the late 1930s and 1940s.[35] The size of these farms proved inadequate and many are currently held in conacre, and used for dry stock. The larger farms practise intensive dairying, dry stock and tillage.

Farm development   Since 1950 there have been three principal farm development schemes available to farmers in the Boyne Valley. These were aimed directly at improving the structure of farms in order to increase agricultural production. The Land Rehabilitation Project was in operation after World War II and before Ireland's membership of the EEC.[36] Since EEC entry in 1973, the Farm Modernisation Scheme (1974–85) and the Farm Improvement Scheme (1986–present) have been co-financed by the EU and the Irish Government.[37]

The Land Rehabilitation Project (1949–74) operated in eight counties – Carlow, Kilkenny, Wicklow, Wexford, Louth, Monaghan, Sligo and Leitrim – and was extended to the remainder of the country (including Meath) in 1950.[38] It provided state grants towards the improvement of land on agricultural holdings, encompassing field drainage, fence removal, land reclamation and construction of watercourses. The stated objective of the project was the reclamation of 1.8 million hectares of unproductive land over ten years at a total estimated cost of forty million pounds, paid for by borrowings from America under the European Recovery Programme.[39] The grant represented two-thirds of the approved estimated cost of the work, subject to a maximum grant at the rate of £20 per statute acre. The works could be carried out by the applicant or arrangements could be made for the work to be carried out by the Department of Agriculture and the applicant would be required to pay 40% of the costs. The Land Reclamation Act (1949) authorised the Department to implement reclamation and other works on behalf of the occupier. Heavy machinery was used for the first time to undertake these works, such as high-powered crawler tractors with bulldozer equipment, drainage ploughs, excavators and calf dozers.

Within the Bend of the Boyne there was an immediate response to the Land Project Scheme in the year of its inception (1950), with six successful applications from the study area. Interest in the scheme remained steady, with the exception of the period 1957–61. In all, sixty-four applications for grant-aid were made under the scheme, representing 50% of grant-aided farm development in the Bend of the Boyne between 1950–90. A greater proportion of the smaller farmers in the area received grant-aid; 64% of take-up was from holdings below 20ha.

The development works consisted mainly of drainage improvement – reconditioning of watercourses, culvert construction, demolition of banks and clearing ditches of vegetation. A combination of stone drains and mole drainage was advised. In seven of the cases examined, the removal of field fences was included in the work. The scheme also extended to the removal of an 'unproductive orchard' at Ballyboy cottage (1973) and woodlands at Balfeddock (1968) and Dowth (1973). In only one instance did the works involve interference with an archaeological monument. Field banks which transected a probable medieval enclosure with an associated field system at Knowth were removed and culverts constructed (1962). This is in low-lying land with flood problems.

The Farm Modernisation Scheme (1974–85) was introduced in 1974, implementing an EEC directive which governs the payment of capital grants towards investment in agricultural development work on the farm.[40] It also regulated the type and levels of investment which could be given to farmers. The stated objective of this development

ORDNANCE SURVEY

Fig. 15   The impact of industrial-scale farming is shown in this photograph of recent field clearance and a large pig-fattening unit – catering for over 3,000 pigs.

work was to yield an income increase per labour unit to the level earned by non-agricultural workers. Development works could include land improvement, construction of farm buildings, farm roads and fencing. Capital grants of 50% or a 9% subsidy for up to fifteen years were offered. This EEC directive expired in September 1985 and the Farm Modernisation Scheme was terminated.[41]

The Farm Modernisation Scheme initiated a farm-building boom in the Bend of the Boyne. Of fifty-six applications to the scheme from the area, at least forty were for building aid. In contrast to earlier schemes, there was a tendency for the larger landholders to apply for this grant-aid. Little drainage or reclamation was undertaken during this period: only eighteen applications were received from the area for this work. There was a noticeable tailing off in applications to the Farm Modernisation Scheme in the early 1980s, possibly as a result of modifications made to the scheme. From 1983, grants for farm buildings and fixed assets were suspended.[42]

During this period, farmyards were remodelled and loose houses, silos and dungsteads were constructed. There was an emphasis on dairy-related projects in the mid-1970s to mid-1980s, at a period when milk production from the Irish dairy herd was growing at an annual rate of 5%.[43] Loose-houses were converted to cubicle houses and frequently further converted to slatted houses under the Farm Improvement Scheme. This period also witnessed the grant-aiding of industrial-scale production units. Pig fattening units catering for over 3,000 pigs were built at Proudfootstown during 1976–77.

The Farm Improvement Scheme (1986–present) implements the investment aid provision of the current EU

GERALDINE STOUT

Fig. 14   An American tractor brought into Dowth during the 1930s. Government grants aided the introduction of modern agricultural machinery, and the progressive farmers in the Boyne Valley were eager to avail of the incentives.

TOM BYRNE

Fig. 16 A portion of a prehistoric ceremonial enclosure had to be excavated in advance of the construction of this corn-drying kiln at Monknewtown. Built in the early 1970s during a period of intensive but short-sighted farm modernisation, the building now lies semi-derelict.

Council Regulation on improving the efficiency of agricultural structures.[44] This aid is administered by the Farm Development Service. Under this scheme the farmer undertakes a Farm Improvement Plan for at least two and not more than six years which must increase the farmer's income by 5% over that period. In the budget of March 1987 grant rates for buildings, fixed assets and land improvements were reduced by 10%. There has been a total of nine applications to the Farm Improvement Scheme from farmers in the Bend of the Boyne up to 1990, all for grant-aid towards farm buildings.

Impact of farming schemes   While public-funded farm development schemes have changed the face of the countryside in this part of the Boyne Valley, there have been no special planning arrangements to take account of their environmental impact. Planning permission is not needed for field drainage, as land improvement works are exempt from planning control. Reclamation presumably improved the economic viability of these holdings, but no attempt has been made to quantify this.[45] Agricultural structures were exempted developments until 1985 when some planning constraints were placed on them. Planning permission is now needed for agricultural structures which

exceed 300m^2. There is also a new principle of aggregation, placing an overall aggregation limit of 450m^2 for buildings within the same farmyard complex, after which planning permission is required.[46]

The construction of industrial-scale farm buildings, rather than hedgerow removal, has made the greatest visual impact. These conspicuous new farm buildings have a profound effect on the visual quality of the Bend of the Boyne area from the perspective of design, colour and materials used.[47] The use of galvanised tin, asbestos and cement sheets makes these buildings particularly conspicuous. There is no effort to screen them from view, nor is there the ordered layout and composition associated with the traditional Irish farms.[48] The location of piggeries and poultry units so close to the passage tombs is also undesirable. The new buildings appear as appendages to the old farmyard which is often left derelict. One can also see a gradual evolution of these buildings with the introduction of each new scheme.

Almost one-eighth (12%) of the land within the Bend of the Boyne underwent grant-aided reclamation between 1950 and 1990. This can be compared with an estimated figure of 25–30% of drained land in the county as a whole.[50] Less than 5% of the field boundaries in the Bend

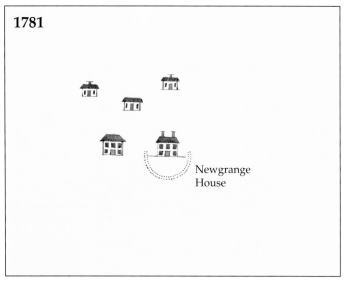

1781

Newgrange
House

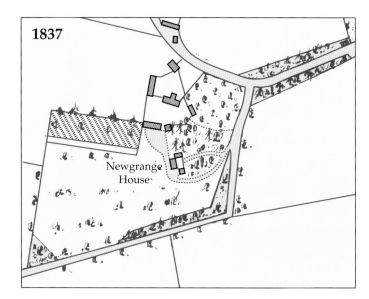

1837

Newgrange
House

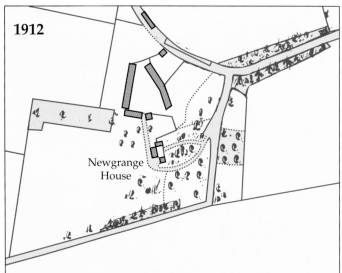

1912

Newgrange
House

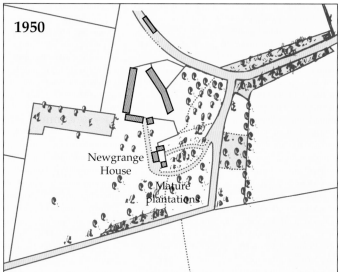

1950

Newgrange
House

Mature
plantations

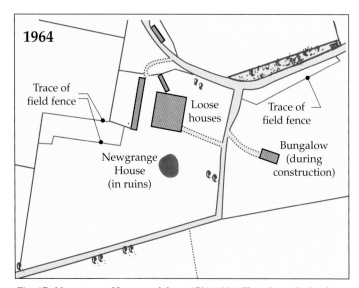

1964

Trace of
field fence

Loose
houses

Trace of
field fence

Bungalow
(during
construction)

Newgrange
House
(in ruins)

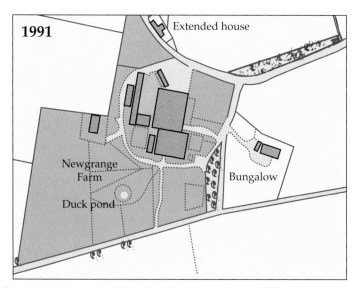

1991

Extended house

Newgrange
Farm

Duck pond

Bungalow

Fig. 17 Newgrange House and farm 1781–1991. This elegantly landscaped farm at Newgrange – with a triangular-shaped farmyard formed with fine stone outbuildings – has been modernised and the house levelled. Loose houses, silos and yards have been built over the last three decades with the help of grant-aid.[49]

DÚCHAS/CON BROGAN

Fig. 18 Considerable modernisation has taken place on this farm at Newgrange over the last three decades. Originally, it was an elegantly landscaped farm with a triangular yard formed by fine stone outbuildings. By 1964, the farm had been extensively modernised. Further changes occurred prior to 1991 when loose houses, silos and yards were constructed with the assistance of EU funding. Newgrange, the farm nearest to the most visited monument within the Bend of the Boyne, is now open to the public, introducing visitors to the workings of a modern farm.

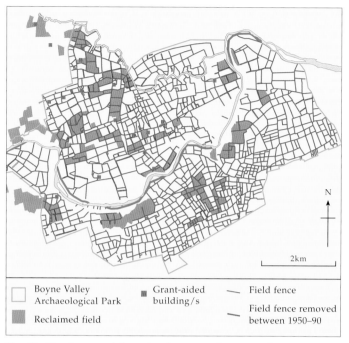

Boyne Valley Archaeological Park

Reclaimed field

Grant-aided building/s

Field fence

Field fence removed between 1950–90

Fig. 19 The impact of farm development schemes in the Bend of the Boyne, 1950–90. One-fifth of land in this archaeologically sensitive area underwent reclamation. In addition, state grants facilitated the removal of 5% of hedgerows. This is a low destruction rate in Irish terms, probably related to the large size of the fields to begin with. Grant-aided farm buildings include loose houses, silos, dungsteads, cubicle houses and slatted houses.

of the Boyne area have been removed in the years covered by these schemes. It is not possible to determine what proportion of this 5% was grant-aided, but field fence removal is documented in many files. The presence of machinery in the area encouraged further clearance. This is, however, a much lower figure than an estimated 14% removal rate for county Meath which is based on a preliminary survey undertaken in the early 1980s and a national removal rate estimated at 16%.[51] This is probably due to the fact that the area has maintained a pastoral bias and the fields were originally relatively large.

Digging drains and ditches in order to lower the water table and removing hedgerows cause environmental damage and habitat loss with an associated decline in aesthetic quality.[52] Hedges are habitats for woodland flora and fauna; nearly two-thirds of Ireland's bird species nest in hedges.[53] The partial removal of townland boundaries is also a historical loss. For instance, a section of townland boundary at Glebe marked a sunken way into the medieval parish church at Dowth. The removal of boundaries has also resulted in fragmentation of a distinctive eighteenth-century demesne at Dowth where much of the woodland has been removed and the field banks which enclosed the 'race course fields' have been

cleared. Overall though, while farming developments sometimes adversely altered the landscape context of archaeological monuments in the Bend of the Boyne, they have had minimal impact on the monuments themselves.[54] An encouraging feature of the last decade has been a dramatic fall in reclamation-related funding.

Since 1992 there have been structural changes in the agricultural industry and Common Agricultural Policy (CAP), with a move from market support and grant-aid for farm development to direct aid to farmers in the form of headage payments for livestock. The board of Meath Leader II (the EU initiative for rural development) examined the impact of these changes on farming in Meath.[55] The study concluded that the sector was in crisis with a great dependence on off-farm employment. Nonetheless, farmers still expressed a willingness to invest in infrastructural development. In contrast, there was a less than enthusiastic response towards investment in alternative enterprises like the tourism sector. They also expressed a reluctance to participate in the Rural Environmental Protection Scheme under its current parameters.

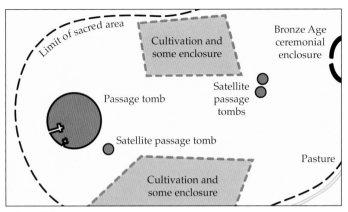

A) Prehistory

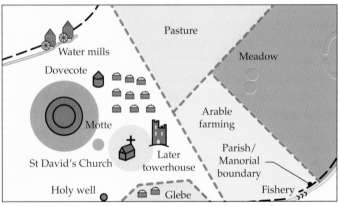

B) Iron Age / Early Christian

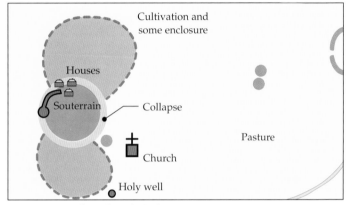

C) Medieval

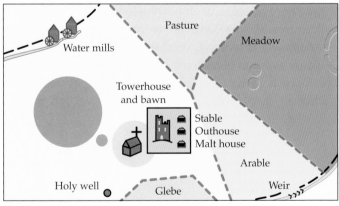

D) Seventeenth Century

CASE STUDY 5:
LANDSCAPE DEVELOPMENT AT DOWTH

Neolithic farming communities built communal passage tombs along the ridge above the Boyne, placing the largest of these tombs on the summit. These were built in cleared woodland and were surrounded by fields of corn and pasture. Following a period of consolidation and stability, Neolithic society adopted a simpler single burial tradition but continued to practise communal worship in large earthen enclosures (henges) erected within the sacred precincts of the passage tomb cemetery (A). This pattern (ridge-top passage tomb communities transferring religious practice to nearby 'henge' monuments) is replicated at Knowth, Newgrange and Monknewtown. In the Middle Bronze Age/Iron Age, Dowth lay on the periphery of ritual activity as the focus of activity continued at Newgrange, Knowth, Monknewtown and the south bank of the Boyne which began to be settled at this time. In the Early Christian period, however, a settlement grew up around Dowth mound, focused on a monastic site with a church and holy well associated with St Shengan. In the ninth century, this community attracted the attention of foreign raiding parties on the Boyne. The communities around Dowth built souterrains for their protection, making use of the original burial chambers. This monastic settlement became a parish and in the twelfth century remained independent from its Cistercian neighbours who held much of the lands outside the townlands of Dowth, Glebe and Proudfootstown (B). The Early Christian period also witnessed the similar transformation of Knowth – not around an ecclesiastical centre, but rather as a royal centre for the kings of northern Brega.

In 1172 Dowth became part of the kingdom of Meath, granted to the Anglo-Norman Hugh De Lacy, who brought it under military control through the construction of earthwork castles and the fortification of earlier earthworks such as Dowth and Knowth. Following successful consolidation, the church and part of the lands of Dowth parish were granted to the Augustinians. The church of St David's was established on the earlier monastic site in 1202 and its community lived close to the parish centre in cottages with yards on the glebeland. The medieval residents practised mixed farming. The remaining lands of the parish were granted to Fleming in Slane, who subsequently granted them for part of a knight's service to Ralph De Picheford in 1226. A manorial village developed around the fortified mound and by 1253 there were nine tenants on the manor which contained demesne land, two mills, a dovecote and a fishery. By the fourteenth century, Dowth manor was owned by the Netterville family, who

Dowth demesne *c*.2000.

built a towerhouse on the site in the late fourteenth or early fifteenth century (C). The Nettervilles remained at Dowth until the nineteenth century, demonstrating the tenacious hold by the 'Old English' Catholic aristocracy within the Pale on their estates. By 1654 a further stone house had been built at Dowth as had other ancillary buildings including a stable, outhouses and a malthouse (D).

In the eighteenth century the Netterville family abandoned the towerhouse and built a stylish mansion surrounded by parkland further east along the same ridge. This was separated physically from the medieval remains by a plantation and pleasure grounds that incorporated two of the prehistoric passage tombs and the henge. A summer-house was built on top of Dowth mound when it too was transformed into an ornamental landscape feature. A new road ran north of the passage tomb and the lands in its environs were enclosed for new tenants of the estate (E). Similar changes in land management were taking place at this time in Newgrange and Oldbridge. The estate system precipitated the demise of surviving nucleations in the area. In the nineteenth century Dowth mound was robbed of its stone for use in local building. The Netterville Trust was founded and in 1877 the Netterville Charitable Almshouse was built with a schoolhouse and chapel alongside. The surrounding fields were further subdivided, and cottages sprouted along the roadside as the population in the area continued to grow (F).

Today, cultural tourism needs have resulted in state acquisition of the land surrounding Dowth passage tomb; it has also purchased other properties at Knowth and Newgrange. Netterville Almshouse is now functioning as a guesthouse (G). In the future, Dowth will be opened to the public and the state will provide pathways to other sites in the townland. State ownership of land in the area is expected to increase (H).

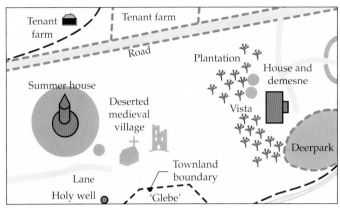

E) Eighteenth Century

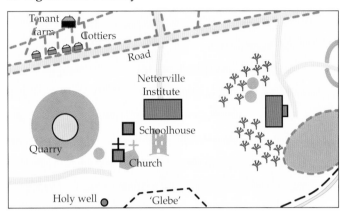

F) Nineteenth Century

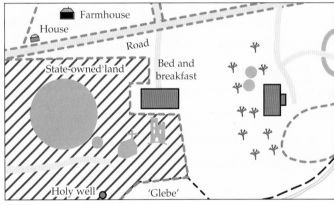

G) Twentieth Century

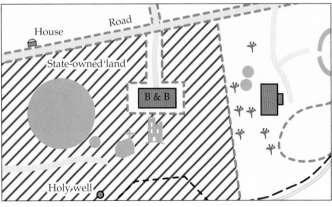

H) Future Trends

THE CHALLENGE OF CHANGE

The Bend of the Boyne is a dynamic rural landscape where the setting for its archaeological monuments will continue to evolve. The challenge is to minimise the impact of these changes on the highly valued features of its landscape. Developments which threaten the integrity of this protected area are multifaceted, involving land use practices, socio-economic issues, and cultural tourism needs. Farmers will continue to respond to financial incentives through various grant-aided schemes. Villages are being transformed with the current housing boom. Road improvements are making the area more accessible by car as the town invades the country and becomes more attractive as both recreational amenity and potential residence. Industrial development overshadows the south side of the river and poses a serious threat to the scenic quality of the valley.

Clearly the processes of change in this unique landscape need to be carefully guided if deterioration of its cultural and natural heritage is to be avoided and the area's visual quality maintained. An integrated approach to conservation is needed involving a partnership between State agencies and the local community, particularly farmers. Allied to conservation is the economic potential of cultural tourism. Employment in the tourist sector and related service industries has considerable potential for rural development in this area. Already, local initiatives have exploited the relocation of visitor facilities south of the river. Planners and architects can be encouraged to develop more visually sympathetic housing schemes incorporating ideas from the local built tradition. These opportunities are most likely to arise where the community feels included in heritage management. It should be possible to exploit the economic potential of Newgrange and the Bend of the Boyne without damaging monuments or inhibiting the quality of life of the local residents.

Fig. 1 Brú na Bóinne Visitor Centre (1997, designed by Tony O'Neill) near Donore acts as a gateway to the World Heritage Site. The decision to locate the Visitor Centre some distance away from the main monuments has successfully restored the rural character of Newgrange and its environs.[1]

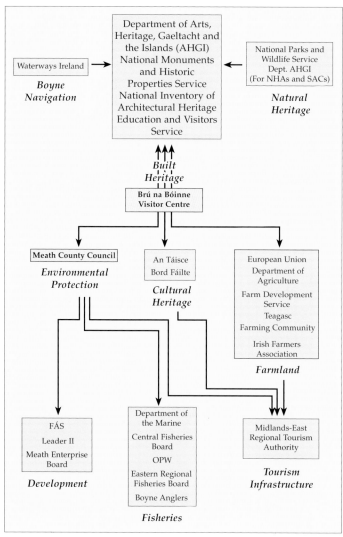

Fig. 2 The present management structure in the Bend of the Boyne encompasses a range of authorities and organisations each responsible for a different aspect of the landscape.

STATUTORY PROTECTION

In 1993 Newgrange and the Bend of the Boyne were listed by UNESCO as a World Heritage Site. This listing recognised the universal importance of this cultural landscape and legally obliged the State to protect the area to the highest international standards. The World Heritage Site is not covered by any statute specific to itself but it is legally protected through various statutes ranging from the *National Monuments Acts 1930–94* to the *Planning Act 2000*. There is also a wide body of Irish and international legislation applicable to World Heritage Sites. The Local Government Acts are aimed at preventing undesir-able development in the defined area. Meath Development Plan attaches three orders of protection to the area designated as the Boyne Valley Archaeological Park: it is an Area of High Natural Beauty; an Area of High Amenity; and an Area of Special Archaeological Interest. These protection orders

basically allow for a period of consultation in the monitoring of potential developments but they do not automatically freeze development.

The National Monuments Acts 1930–94 provide a strong legislative base for the protection of archaeological monuments regardless of an area's status and are regarded internationally as enlightened. The archaeological sites in the Boyne Valley Archaeological Park are listed in the *Record of Monuments and Places*.[2] Some are further covered by Preservation Orders, Guardianship or Registration Orders. However, limited resources make it difficult to monitor these sites on a daily basis. The *Architectural Heritage (National Inventory)* and *Historic*

Fig. 3 Management within the Bend of the Boyne involves a partnership between the local community and state authorities. When the Archaeological Park was first proposed, there was considerable concern that it would intefere with the right to privacy and control over property. As was feared, tourism on the north side of the Boyne has suffered as a direct result of relocating the visitor facilities. The spectre of compulsory purchase has waned with new efforts to negotiate with farmers over access to monuments.

Monuments (Miscellaneous Provisions) Act 1999 places the National Inventory of Architectural Heritage on a statutory basis.

The *Wildlife (Amendment) Act 2001* enables designation for protection of Natural Heritage Areas, Nature Reserves (State-owned), Refuges for Fauna and the making of Flora Protection Orders. The Act provides a legal basis for the designation of the NHA's in the vicinity of Brú na Bóinne, as well as the Boyne coast and estuary. It affords a level of protection broadly comparable to that provided for Special Areas of Conservation in the 1997 Habitats Regulations. The Boyne River Islands are further recognised as a Special Area of Conservation under the EU Habitats Directive (see pp 16-17).[3]

Environmental legislation relating to large-scale development requiring an Environmental Impact Assessment (EIS) is covered by *The European Communities (Amendment) Regulations 1999.* These restated and extended certain existing provisions and outlined the procedures to be followed in the case of a proposed development located in an environmentally sensitive area.[4]

The Meath County Development Plan 2001 (MCDP) contains a commitment by Meath County Council to the conservation of Brú na Bóinne as the prime archaeological site in the county. In addition the MCDP, administered by the Minister for Environment and Local Government, makes a commitment to 'Protected Structures' ranging from formal country houses to vernacular structures and industrial archaeological sites. These guidelines will protect areas of high amenity like the Boyne Valley and important 'views and prospects' within the Bend of the Boyne.

The Boyne Valley in general is managed by a range of authorities and organisations, each responsible for a different activity in the valley. These include local and regional authorities and various bodies at national level. Many voluntary and community organisations contribute to the overall management of the valley, generally working alongside the various statutory bodies. The wider Boyne catchment falls under the jurisdiction of Meath and Louth County Councils and within the Midlands-East Regional Authority whose function it is to co-ordinate the provision of public services at regional level.[5] The Office of Public Works (OPW) has responsibility for the design and execution of arterial drainage schemes and flood relief under the Arterial Drainage Act of 1945. The current *Brú na Bóinne, World Heritage Site, Draft Management Plan 2001* of the Department of Arts, Heritage, Gaeltacht and the Islands rightly recognises the need for closer co-operation with these bodies, working through a local liaison group to ensure the effectiveness of the Plan.

FARMING

A programme of landscape conservation in the Bend of the Boyne has to consider the impact of contemporary agricultural practices and anticipate the impact of new farming aid schemes in the area. Arable cultivation presents the most significant threat to the earthen monuments within the Bend of the Boyne. Burial mounds, embanked enclosures and ringforts are repeatedly eroded by the plough, and the more fragile, sub-surface remains of habitations and ritual sites are being destroyed because the prescribed generous fallow area around the perimeter of the monument is not being respected. Embanked enclosures or henge monuments, already much denuded, are particularly prone to plough damage. The National Monuments Act makes it unlawful 'to demolish or remove, wholly or in part, or to disfigure [or] deface' these monuments. Despite this, the henge monuments below Newgrange are ploughed annually.

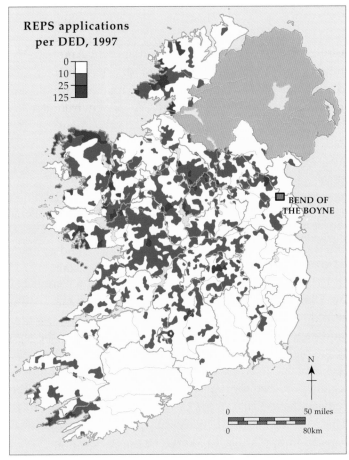

Fig. 4 REPS uptake 1997. The scale of participation in this scheme (23,000 by 1997) indicates the significance to landscape conservation of such an initiative. With an uptake of £100 million in 1997, the programme is one of the principal publicly funded schemes currently available to farmers. The highest uptake in this scheme has been in the small farm, non-dairying areas of the Midlands and the West; the two main farming groups that are not participating in this scheme are small drystock farms and intensive dairy farmers.[6] There is a very low uptake in the Boyne Valley.

LEO SWAN

Fig. 5 The henge monument at Newgrange will only survive if ploughing activity is stopped.

Much remedial work can be implemented, and preservation maintained, by working in collaboration with farmers and their agricultural advisers through such conservation schemes as the Rural Environment Protection Scheme (REPS). Launched in 1994, it is the Republic of Ireland's Agri-Environmental Programme, implemented pursuant to EU Council Regulations.[7] Amongst its fundamental aims is the promotion of active maintenance of features in the landscape. Participating farmers are required to manage their farms in an environmentally friendly manner. The farmer must implement a wide range of measures: those of most relevance to this study are the preservation of field boundaries on the farm, the protection of historical and archaeological features and the upkeep of the aesthetic appearance of the farmyard and farm. A supplementary measure gives the farmer an extra 20% on the standard grant if public access is provided to the land for environmentally friendly leisure and sporting activities. These farming activities must be sustained over a five-year period in accordance with an agri-environmental plan, which is specific to each farm. Unfortunately, the larger, more intensive developing farmers in the protected area are precisely the ones least likely to join agri-environmental schemes such as REPS and Set-Aside, under which it is compulsory to protect archaeological sites. Until this sector of the farming community becomes fully involved in agri-environmental schemes, the protection of archaeological landscapes will be dangerously incomplete. The recent publication of *Good Farming Practice* by the Department of Agriculture and Food provides welcome advice on the care of the natural and built heritage and should assist in the promotion of sustainable farming practices in Brú na Bóinne.

The *Brú na Bóinne Draft Management Plan* acknowledges the need to work closely with the farming community and

their agricultural advisers to encourage farming practices that respect and preserve the cultural and natural resources of the area. Management agreements and promotion of agri-environmental protection schemes are the preferred option for landscape management. The Department of Arts, Heritage, Gaeltacht and the Islands will shortly review the condition and vulnerability of all archaeological sites and monuments in Brú na Bóinne and prepare a management plan for each site. Regardless of future legislation, the Bend of the Boyne has no future as an amenity without the co-operation of the farming community

EXTRACTIVE INDUSTRIES

Quarrying poses a real threat to landscape quality, particularly south of the river. The shale ridge, which creates such a dramatic setting for the passage tombs at Knowth, Dowth and Newgrange and continues south of the river, is a major target for extraction. The strong pressure from commercial interests to develop these geological resources was highlighted in 1989 when permission was given to quarry part of Donore Hill, and three separate Local Authority orders of protection failed to ensure its integrity. Permission was given by Meath County Council to Irish Cement for a shale quarry and settling ponds in Donore which lay within the buffer zone of the Boyne Valley Archaeological Park. This went ahead despite the fact that the Meath County Development Plan identified this zone as an area of high amenity, an area of natural beauty and a special area of historic importance. In a further planning appeal, An Bord Pleanála considered the proposed site marginal in terms of its visual quality and its amenity value, which was narrowly identified as the passage tombs of Knowth, Dowth and Newgrange only.[8] The significance of this ruling for landscape conservation is

DÚCHAS/CON BROGAN

Fig. 6 Quarrying at Donore threatens the scenic quality of the valley and has already defaced part of the Jacobite Camp associated with the Battle of the Boyne.

that the Meath County Development Plan did not set out to limit development in those areas identified as protected, and that a precedent has now been set to allow quarrying in the Park area. There are sufficient shale deposits for at least twenty-five years of quarrying at Donore. It is important that there are no further extensions in any direction when this intrusive quarry is exhausted.

In order to avoid any further visual scarring of this landscape, it is also imperative that no existing quarries or gravel-pits be re-activated, or new gravel workings opened. Mining exploration licences for lead and zinc have been taken out at various times for large areas in Meath, including the Bend of the Boyne. Fortunately none have been activated, nor should they ever be allowed without serious consideration of their environmental impact.

HOUSING

The housing boom over the last few years is changing the face of the Meath countryside and its villages. In the Bend of the Boyne, planning regulations have kept at bay some of the worst excesses of house building experienced elsewhere in the county, in particular the disastrous planning decisions inflicted on east Meath. Paradoxically, the recent economic boom that created a strong demand for housing has encouraged the renovation of the old housing stock. Where these buildings were listed, owners were assisted in rebuilding by grant-aid from schemes operated by the Local Authority.[9] A planned programme of preservation is being implemented, using a combination of legislative safeguards and financial incentives.

The visual impact of new housing schemes would be minimised if they were built to harmonise with older traditional buildings. Characteristic features in local building styles should, therefore, be used as a model for further developments. Many of the features of the small farmers' or cottiers' houses could be duplicated to produce a sympathetic design for modern housing in the valley. Traditionally, cottages in the Bend of the Boyne were set low and inconspicuously in the landscape. They are frequently aligned at right angles to the road (in contrast with most modern bungalows), which immediately creates a safe space in front of the house for children. Traditional houses were built on the central-hearth, lobby-entrance plan characteristic of eastern Ireland and are very long in proportion to their width; this emphasises the horizontal. However, there is a vertical emphasis in detailing with windows that are long and narrow. Usually, a central porch is present with a slated, pitched roof. In the Bend of the Boyne, traditional houses were usually painted white or with an orange wash. 'Starter homes' could be built on this

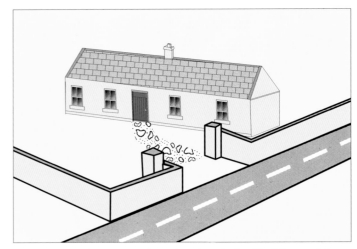

Fig. 7   Proposed new starter home based on the local building tradition.

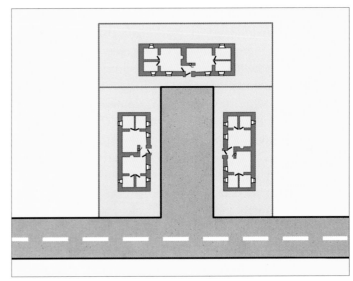

Fig. 8   Proposed layout of new housing developments based on local cottage clusters.

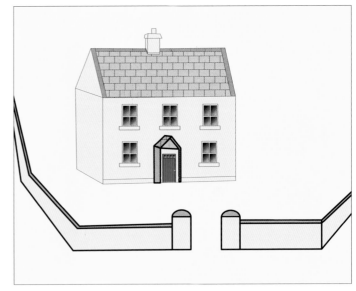

Fig. 9   Proposed new family home based on the local building tradition. Architects could learn much from observing traditional building styles.

Fig. 10   The house at Roughgrange before (A) and after (B) its sensitive restoration. Property values and the difficulty in getting planning permission for new structures have led to the renovation of many such buildings, in landscape terms perhaps the only benefit of the recent 'Celtic Tiger' economy.

model. Strong farmers' houses in the valley have vernacular roots and retain the traditional central-hearth, lobby-entrance plan. The slated porch is also a regular feature of these larger houses. Houses in this style either fronted the road (set back at some distance) or were built at right angles to it. These features could be replicated today in larger family homes. For larger housing developments, architects desiring to build in harmony with traditional styles may like to emulate the arrangement for eighteenth-century house clusters. In the Bend of the Boyne, these houses were built around the open space of a short cul-de-sac.

CULTURAL TOURISM

Employment in the tourist sector and related service industries has considerable potential to provide a living for those who live in this rural area. These opportunities are most likely to arise where the community feels included in heritage management through talks, farm visits and local community schemes in heritage management. It should be possible to exploit the economic potential of cultural tourism without damaging monuments or the quality of life of the local residents once the local community is given proper support, Conservation can go hand in hand with rural development.

There are already a number of encouraging local initiatives. The West Ferrard Rural Development Group (with the support of Leader and FÁS) has been involved in the restoration of a nature trail at Townleyhall and interpretation of the Battle of the Boyne site. Elsewhere in the Bend of the Boyne festivals and events are held annually which heighten an awareness of its history and folk traditions. These include the *salmon of knowledge*

Fig. 11   The Brú na Bóinne Visitor Centre is a beautiful building internally and externally and was designed to almost disappear into the landscape. Visitors cross the new suspension bridge and are brought by bus to Knowth and Newgrange.

Fig. 12   This interpretation facility at the site of the Battle of the Boyne at Oldbridge is a local initiative by the West Ferrard Rural Development Group. Local guides bring visitors from the north and south of Ireland around the battlefield site.

Fig. 13   The village of Donore has enjoyed the economic benefits which came with the siting of the Brú na Bóinne Visitor Centre on the south side of the Boyne. One of the last remaining nineteenth-century cottages in Donore village was knocked down to make way for an extension to a public house benefiting from the growth in the tourist trade. Unfortunately, the presentation of heritage in one area can impact on the heritage of another.

competition (a fishing festival) and the Celtic Festival at Rossnaree which re-enacts *Cath Ros na Righ* (the battle of Rossnaree). A number of local artists involved in the Meath Craft Trail include Seamus Cassidy, a wood turner based in Lougher, and Clive Ó Gibne, a wood carver and basket maker. Clive has revived the craft of Boyne coracle making and is teaching these crafts to local schoolchildren and adults. The Ó Gibne's organise the annual *Imran* or trip downriver on the Boyne which brings together coracle makers from Ireland and Wales.

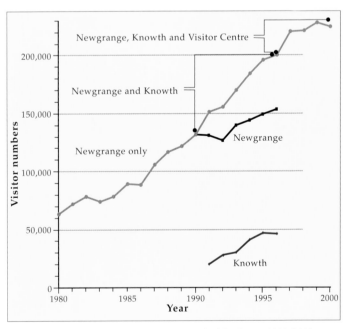

Fig. 14   Visitor numbers to sites in the Bend of the Boyne 1980–2000.

Fig. 15   Guide service in action at Newgrange.

RECREATIONAL AND EDUCATIONAL AMENITY

The recreational value of protected landscapes is becoming more apparent in Europe. As leisure time increases, public enjoyment of the countryside grows in importance. This is recreation in a physical sense but also 're-creation' in terms of inspirational and spiritual values.[10] With the improvement of roads in the Boyne Valley there is now great potential for growth in the tourist industry. Within the Bend of the Boyne and its environs, Dúchas provides much of the

Fig. 16   Clive Ó Gibne and his wife Sinéad have established the National Currach Centre at Roughgrange on the south side of the river opposite Newgrange.

Fig. 17   Currach enthusiasts meet for their 2001 annual *Imran*.

Fig. 18 The participants in the 2001 charity walk from Drogheda to Navan along the Boyne. The Boyne Canal towpath passes through the heart of the Boyne providing access to both archaeological and natural heritage sites. Both organised and unorganised walks take place regularly between Drogheda and Navan.

archaeological heritage interpretation, meeting the needs of most visitors to the area. Information is available in the Brú na Bóinne Visitor Centre, the Mellifont Visitor Centre and through the guide service at Knowth, Newgrange and Mellifont. Information is also presented in a range of pamphlets and brochures produced by Dúchas, the Heritage Service. Under the enthusiastic care of Clare Tuffy, the Visitor Centre also provides support for local community events, festivals and exhibitions, which raise awareness of the history and traditions of the area.

There is great potential for combining the discovery of the Bend of the Boyne with recreation through the development of walking routes. The current restoration of the canal towpath will enhance the existing heritage value of the Boyne and increase access. 'The Boyne Way' (the towpath for the Boyne Navigation) is an ideally situated and non-invasive way of channelling the public though the area. The fact that it goes by the Visitor Centre is an additional bonus. The Department of Arts, Heritage, Gaeltacht and the Islands is co-operating with the Steering Committee for the Boyne Valley Integrated Development Plan in the promotion of long-distance walking routes, with priority being given to circular walking routes in the core area of the park. The *Boyne Valley Management Plan 2002* states the objective of improving access to other monuments in Brú na Bóinne by building stiles and fenced walkways to field monuments, in consultation with the landowners and the local community.

There are many features of interest directly accessible from 'The Boyne Way' including the Natural Heritage Areas and Emergency fortifications on which a 'War Walk' could be developed. These pillboxes could also be used by walkers for bird-watching or shelter. Further thematic walks could be developed using the present lane system.

For instance, a 'Monk's Trail' could exploit the old laneway which connects Mellifont Abbey with her medieval church and grange at Monknewtown. A network of lanes connects Dowth with Rossin, past sites of nineteenth-century settlements and mills on which a 'Famine Trail' could be based. The area also has a number of fossil-rich quarries, disused quarries and gravel pits, which could be a useful resource for fieldwork in geology and geomorphology.

Clearly, protected landscapes such as the Bend of the Boyne have considerable educational value. The visitor is exposed to an elective education and gains first-hand experience of the landscape itself. As the great park interpreter Freeman Tilden reminds us, 'here … the visitor meets the thing itself'.[11] Interpretation and promotion are a powerful means of raising public awareness of landscape. The provision of a guide service, a wide range of literature, and site signage are effective in the interpretation of the cultural and natural wealth of this World Heritage Site. Use of the park for educational purposes by universities and schools is encouraged. Amongst the key objectives of the

Fig. 19 Bed and breakfast accommodation will benefit from developments in cultural tourism.

Boyne Valley Management Plan is to encourage a programme of third level research focused on knowledge gaps to improve understanding and the subsequent presentation of the area.

Prehistoric sites in the Boyne Valley have been the main focal point of archaeological research. Excavation programmes have increased our knowledge of prehistoric land use in the valley and the results have been published in numerous archaeological papers and books. This detailed appreciation of the Neolithic now forms the basis of the presentation in the Brú na Bóinne Visitor Centre. It has justifiably been awarded the 'Interpret Ireland Award' and Interpret Ireland's 'Special Judges Award' for 1999.[12] However, sites from a later date have only been dealt with where they have impinged on the prehistoric sites under excavation. There are knowledge gaps in the broader settlement history of the area which need to be bridged. The World Heritage Site listing acknowledges the continuity of human activity at Brú na Bóinne evident in its broad range of archaeological monuments of prehistoric and historic date. In order to decipher these for the public a multi-disciplinary research programme is needed with a clear set of priorities. A study framework can be formulated which is more problem-orientated and will combine excavation and field survey with palynology, plough soil archaeology, remote sensing, underwater archaeology and aerial photography. Historical research also has great potential for enhancing our awareness of the landscape history of the area, particularly in the early historic and medieval periods. A detailed examination of relevant proto-historical sources could be initiated by scholars with a comprehension of Early Irish and structured in a similar way to the Discovery Programme project at Tara.[13]

CONCLUSIONS

The passage tombs of Newgrange, Knowth and Dowth have conferred global fame on the Bend of the Boyne and form the basis of the World Heritage Site designation. After the Neolithic, the Bend of the Boyne was never again to the fore of international technological or artistic developments. Nonetheless, it periodically featured prominently in historic events within Ireland and wider European affairs. These include the arrival of Christianity to Ireland, the establishment of the first European-style monastery in Ireland, and the Battle of the Boyne. This study has embraced the physical and cultural history of this exceptional part of the Irish countryside and shown how the landscape can speak for all periods. The great challenge will be to preserve this prized cultural landscape within the wealthy and environmentally favoured east so that William Wilde's assertion can become a living reality: 'the history of Ireland might be written in tracing the banks of the Boyne'.[14]

grange and the River Boyne from the air.

BOYNE VALLEY ENVISIONED

The Boyne Valley has remained an enduring inspiration ever since the first Neolithic artists inscribed the passage tombs five millennia ago. Poets, painters, philosophers, musicians and scholars have explored the complex meanings of Brú na Bóinne, with its graceful interplay of river, ridge and megalith. Through thousands of years, the Boyne has flowed through the same enfolding bend: the same sun, the same moon, the same stars have persisted in the same sky above it. While the original inspiration for Europe's most assured assemblage of Neolithic art has inevitably faded from the cultural memory of Meath, these enigmatic and moving symbols have continued to captivate and inspire.[1]

At the same time, scholars have introduced hard-headed observation and critical investigation to the more free-wheeling speculations of those who believe that the tombs and their symbols encode profound mystical, spiritual and astrological knowledge. Above all, the last half-century has witnessed sustained archaeological excavation and research, backed by increasingly sophisticated scientific techniques. The two Boyne Valleys – one scientific and secular, the other mystical and spiritual – coexist, sometimes amicably, more often fractiously. And in recent years, as the world

historic significance of these magnificent megaliths has become increasingly appreciated, tourists have descended in their thousands, creating a further tension between demands for democratic access and the necessity for conservation of a vulnerable heritage. This has created the need for professional management of visitor flows, sometimes in opposition to the wishes of the local community. A further two Boyne Valleys are that of visitors, on a fleeting tour, and that of the locals – those for whom the Bend of the Boyne is home and for whom the tombs are familiarly referred to as 'the caves', where many spent long summers digging for 'Dr Eogan' alongside ephemeral collections of exotic students.

For some, the excavations have lessened rather than enhanced the attraction of the tombs. The painter Nano Reid, for example, stopped painting them after the excavations began in the 1960s. When asked why she had stopped painting in the Boyne Valley, she replied:

> Somehow the place isn't the same since they've started all that excavation. To me the mounds were interesting when you didn't know what was inside them. All the digging reminds me of a curious child who has to tear open a doll to see what's inside and then all the saw dust comes pouring out.[2]

Fig. 1 *Ros-na-Ri* by Nano Reid. Her distinctive modernist style evokes the majesty of the swirling river, while absorbing symbols from Newgrange. Modern artists have been drawn to the decorated stones, attracted by their cubist clarity and symbolic density. The mighty river itself has proved an enduring constant in the artistic imagination of the region from the Neolithic to the new millennium.

Fig. 2 *View of Fennor Rock, on the Boyne* by James George O'Brien, *c*.1811. This picturesque view of a wild landscape untouched by human endeavour is typical of early Romanticism. The artist has dramatically heightened the rock, making it tower over the river in fashionably sublime style. These paintings should not be read as a direct transcript of the actual landscape but rather as revelations of the perceptual environment.

ULSTER MUSEUM

PIONEERING WILDERNESS

Edmund Spenser used just three words – 'the pleasant Boyne' – to describe the river in his *Faerie Queene* of 1590.[3] For the embattled Spenser, on the front line of colonial strife deep in Munster, the peaceful Boyne rolling serenely through the settled landscape of the Pale must indeed have seemed 'pleasant'. Meath of the pastures has long conveyed images of pastoral tranquillity, superb grassland and overwhelming greenness. In thrall to the fashions of the age, eighteenth-century artists imbued the Boyne with Gothic sublimity as a turbulent river of dangerous rapids, racing through overhanging precipices. They often juxtaposed this savage force of nature with the civilised nurture of the surrounding landscape of enlightened landlordism, with their manicured parklands, elegant demesnes and reassuringly solid, neo-classical Big Houses.

The Boyne's turbulence remained as a last reminder of the primitive world which they had eclipsed through their civility. This is well seen in the series of views of Fennor Rock by James George O'Brien (fl. 1779–1819). The rock face towers precipitously above the river, shrouded in dense foliage and ferns. The cliff face dwarfs two tiny figures at the foot of the rock. O'Brien's view chimed with contemporary romantic sensibility, and the painting was engraved for Francis Grose's *Antiquities of Ireland*.[4] This defile is also the subject of Henry Jones's poem 'On the Boyn Rock' (1735) which laments the demise of a tavern that stood by it on the banks of the Boyne.[5]

> Near that place, a Pile appears,
> Disguis'd with Age and Gray with Years;
> Its nodding Summit seems to peep,
> And view its shadow in the deep…

Behind the closed eye
by Francis Ledwidge

I walk the old frequented ways
    That wind around the tangled braes,
I live again the sunny days
    Ere I the city knew.

And scenes of old again are born,
    The woodbine lassoing the thorn,
And drooping Ruth-like in the corn
    The poppies weep the dew.

Above me in their hundred schools
    The magpies bend their young to rules,
And like an apron full of jewels
    The dewy cobweb swings.

And frisking in the stream below
    The troutlets make the circles flow,
And the hungry crane doth watch them grow
    As a smoker does his rings.

Above me smokes the little town,
    With its whitewashed walls and roofs of brown
And its octagon spire toned smoothly down
    As the holy minds within.

And wondrous impudently sweet,
    Half of him passion, half conceit,
The blackbird calls adown the street
    Like the Piper of Hamelin.

I hear him, and I feel the lure
    Drawing me back to the homely moor,
I'll go and close the mountains' door
    On the city's strife and din.

Thomas McDonagh
by Francis Ledwidge

He shall not hear the bittern cry
In the wild sky, where he is lain,
Nor voices of the sweeter birds
Above the wailing of the rain.

Nor shall he know when loud March blows
Thro' slanting snows her fanfare shrill,
Blowing to flame the golden cup
Of many an upstart daffodil.

And when the Dark Cow leaves the moor,
And pastures poor with greedy weeds,
Perhaps he'll hear her low at morn
Lifting her horn in pleasant meads.

LEDWIDGE COUNTRY

As the Victorian era set in, the old perceptions of the Boyne as a raging torrent of sublimity passed and the river was increasingly viewed as a quiet adornment to a pastoral setting. This is the view enshrined in the lyric poetry of Francis Ledwidge (1887–1917), the best-known laureate of the valley. He was born and reared just outside Slane village and came from the agricultural labourer class (he is commemorated by a plaque on the bridge over the Boyne at Slane and in the restored labourer's cottage outside the village). This area has been branded *Ledwidge Country* in an effort to capitalise on the poet's fame. Taken up by Lord Dunsany (a local landlord and minor figure of the literary revival), Ledwidge came to prominence as a lyric poet of sensitivity. His first poem, 'Behind the closed eye', was written while he was a young grocery apprentice in Dublin.[6]

The poem deploys the conventional contrast between the city and the fondly remembered natural world of the Boyne Valley. The valley is a maternal landscape of 'hilly swollen plain[s]', 'homely moor[s]' and 'coloured wood[s]', with 'ferny turnings of the woodbine on the lane'.[7] His poetry depicts a vibrant and ever-changing countryside, filled with bird song 'upon the tops of dusty hedges' and splashing trout 'frisking in the stream below'.[8] The contrast between city and country was to be heightened by Ledwidge's early death in the trenches of Yprés (Belgium), blown to bits by an exploding shell. Like Rupert Brooke (1887–1915) and others of that tragic generation, his poems acquired resonance from the contrast between the senseless imperial carnage of World War I, and the earlier innocent pastoral world from which it seemed to irrevocably sever European culture. The small, knowable, intimate community in harmony with nature and continuous with the past had been horribly extinguished by the intrusion of larger, more imperial and brutal forces. The innocent fields around Slane had mutated into the murderous intensity of the killing fields of the Great War.[9] Ledwidge's best poem commemorates Thomas McDonagh, one of the martyrs of the 1916 rising. When he was seeking an image for this tragedy, Ledwidge reached back to the sound of the bittern, a bird of the Boyne, and an image of Ireland drawn from the Gaelic tradition as 'a dark cow' resplendent in Meath meadows

A second poet of the Boyne Valley was Fred Higgins (1896–1941). He had been born in county Mayo but was introduced at an early age to county Meath via his grandparents home of Higginsbrook near Bective on the Boyne.[10] Looked at through western eyes, Meath seemed impossibly lush and fertile, but also culturally impoverished and money-grubbing. Higgins's 'Auction'

GERALDINE STOUT

Fig. 3 John Boyle O'Reilly memorial at Dowth erected in 1903. Placed close to his boyhood home on the river, the monument is festooned with the prevalent nationalist iconography of the late nineteenth century – wolfhounds, shamrocks, round towers, pikes, etc. These symbols have now been relegated to the level of *kitsch,* but in their day they were enormously vibrant in creating a public iconography of nationalism where none had existed previously. In 1890 when O'Reilly died, he was considered to be the most distinguished Irishman in America. He was buried in Holyhead cemetery, Brookline, Massachusetts. There is also a memorial to him at Belvedere, in Western Australia. His fellow poet Francis Ledwidge was present at the unveiling ceremony of the O'Reilly monument beside the medieval ruins of Dowth church at the spot where he wished to be buried.

describes 'men of stealth, gentlemen jobbers, heavy in dung, beef belted, pea-eyed men of Meath'.[11] But he too succumbed to the innate fertility of the region, symbolised for him by the teeming fecundity of the Boyne:

> Here, drowned within their dewy deeps of June,
> The fields for graziers, gather evening silver,
> And while each isle becomes a bush in tune,
> The Boyne flows into airy stillness.

> Yet by the weirs, that shiver with dark eels,
> Dusk breaks in leaps of light, and salmon snarers,
> Are nightly snaring fish in sally creels,
> That merely seem a dream to Clare-men.

A third poet of the Boyne Valley was John Boyle O'Reilly (1844–90), destined to look back on his native region with an emigrant's eye, like so many Irish people of the post-Famine period.[12] He had been born on the eve of the Famine to Elisa and David O'Reilly, a schoolteacher at Dowth. He spent his childhood acquiring knowledge in a Wordsworthian way, as he describes it in his poem 'At school':[13]

> He knows not he is learning;
>   He thinks nor writes a word;
> But in the soul discerning
>   A living spring is stirred.

O'Reilly enlisted as a British soldier, but became a Fenian in England and then set about infiltrating the British army back in Ireland. He was arrested in 1866, court-martialled and sentenced to death. This was commuted (on grounds of age) to twenty years of hard labour. By 1868 he had been transported on the convict ship the *Hougomont* to Fremantle penal colony in Australia. In 1869 he staged a spectacular escape on an American whaler, the *Gazelle*, and eventually reached Boston in 1870, where he settled into a spectacularly successful newspaper career. O'Reilly became editor of the *Boston Pilot* and rose to prominence as a political conciliator, a cross-cultural communicator, an advocate for Irish America and a link between Brahmin Boston and the increasingly Irish Catholic city. The University of Notre Dame conferred him with a doctorate in 1881. A democrat, O'Reilly preached the message of brotherhood across racial, class and religious divides. He was also a popular inspirational poet to the extent that he was commissioned to write the dedicatory verses on the Pilgrim Fathers' monument at Plymouth Rock.

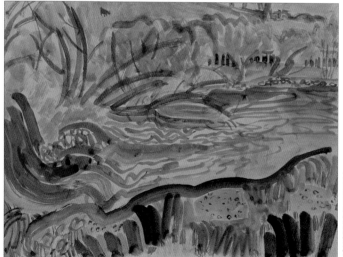

PRIVATE COLLECTION

Fig. 4 *Fallen tree in the river* by Nano Reid. 'I would fly to the woods' low rustle/And the meadows' kindly page' (John Boyle O'Reilly).

But while he scaled the pinnacle of American society, he never forgot Dowth and the Boyne of his childhood. In the crowded schedule of an incredibly busy professional and public career, he often longed to be back beside the 'dear old river':[14]

> I am tired of planning and toiling
> In the crowded hives of men;
> Heart-weary of building and spoiling,
> And spoiling and building again.
> And I long for the dear old river,
> Where I dreamed my youth away;
> For a dreamer lives forever,
> And a toiler dies in a day.
>
> No, no! from the street's rude bustle,
> From trophies of mart and stage,
> I would fly to the woods' low rustle
> And the meadows' kindly page.
> Let me dream as of old by the river,
> And be loved for the dream away;
> For a dreamer lives forever,
> And a toiler dies in a day.

The beauty of the Boyne also inspired the artist Nano Reid (1900–81). A pioneering modernist painter, she was drawn to the kinetic intensity of the Boyne, alive with water, wildlife and vegetation. The sheer variety of natural profusion remained a constant stimulus, even as she sought to capture it in a non-representational and minimalist style. Reid was an artist of movement, of energy, of the ever-changing kaleidoscope of nature. Domiciled at Drogheda, the Boyne Valley released her inner vision onto an outer landscape: subject matter and technique fused into an

GERALDINE STOUT

Fig. 5 *Reeds* by Nano Reid. Reid was a painter fascinated by the dynamism of life forms. This watercolour captures the fluid interface between water, land and air, vibrant with vegetation and wildlife.

PRIVATE COLLECTION

Fig. 6 *Ancient landscape* by Nano Reid *c.*1962. Reid was equally fascinated by the interplay between past and present, and the way that ancient forms lived on in the modern landscape. Here she shows the Bend of the Boyne, dense with mythological and historical resonance. The resurgence of scholarship about Irish mythology released an enormous cornucopia for artists. The precise association of the ancient sagas with specific sites represented a major enhancement of the Irish landscape. Reid celebrated the linkage between the mythological Aengus and Newgrange, which conferred an ancient aura on the tomb.

intensely perceived, flowing evocation of the Boyne.[15] Her work inspired a fine book – the historian Elizabeth Hickey's *I send my love along the Boyne* – which is woven around a portfolio of Reid's drawings.[16]

CELTIC ALLURE

Until the late nineteenth century, the ancient Boyne of legend and mythology survived as a vernacular wisdom enshrined in tales, poems and legends. The linguistic transition from Irish to English impoverished but did not entirely obliterate that knowledge, as can be seen in Ledwidge's poetry. It is clear that he imbibed much of his knowledge at his mother's knee,[17] as for example, in his poems 'At Currabwee' and 'The dead kings'. But for many the tombs remained inert mounds of earth and stone, a useful quarry for road-fill, field walls and outbuildings. However, in the second half of the nineteenth century, the seemingly arcane researches of philologists and antiquarians gradually shone a new light on the Boyne. The work of John O'Donovan, Eugene Curry and Edmund Hogan, among others, produced accessible translations of the magnificent Irish manuscripts, while simultaneously identifying their place names with specific sites in the Irish countryside. Suddenly, decrepit old mounds and mouldy ruins achieved a new glamour; here were the Irish sacred places, *lieux de mémoire* with a historic pedigree which

The Dead Kings
by Francis Ledwidge

All the dead kings came to me
At Rossnaree, where I was dreaming,
A few stars glimmered through the morn,
And down the thorn the dews were streaming.

And every dead king had a story
Of ancient glory, sweetly told.
It was too early for the lark
But the starry dark had tints of gold.

I listened to the sorrows three
Of that Eire passed into song.
A cock crowed near a hazel croft,
And up aloft dim larks winged strong.

And I, too, told the kings a story
Of later glory, her fourth sorrow:
There was a sound like moving shields
In high green fields and the lowland furrow.

And one said: "We who yet are kings
Have heard these things lamenting inly."
Sweet music flowed from many a bill
And on the hill the morn stood queenly.

And one said: "Over is the singing,
And the bell bough ringing, whence we come;
With heavy hearts we'll thread the shadows,
In honey meadows birds are dumb."

And one said: "Since the poets perished
And all they cherished in the way,
Their thoughts unsung, like petal showers
Inflame the hours of blue and grey."

And one said: "A loud tramp of men,
We'll hear again at Rosnaree."
A bomb burst near me where I lay.
I woke, 'twas day in Picardy.

The spot within the first circle is earth, and the first circle is the sea, the second circle is the heavens, and the third circle is the infinite Lir, the God over all Gods, the great fate that surrounds mankind and Godkind.[18]

Russell – 'the hairy fairy' – can be regarded as the progenitor of the New Age tradition of the Boyne Valley.[19] He popularised the concept of the valley as steeped in spiritual *numen* which modern sceptics could tune into if only they dropped their shield of rationalism:

The palace of Aengus remains to this day at Newgrange, wrought over with symbol of the Astral Fire and the Great Serpentine Power … The action of this power was symbolised in many ways, notably by the passage of the sun through zodiacal signs.[20]

He believed that the megalithic art concerned an ancient cult in which the serpent was a potent symbol; it was these symbolic serpents of the old religion that the Christian St Patrick had banished from Ireland.[21] But Russell was not just some dreamy mystic wrapped in Celtic drapery. Long before the celebrated discovery of the Newgrange roof box by the archaeologist M. J. O'Kelly, Russell was aware of the annual solstice phenomenon at Newgrange, and described it in *A dream of Aengus Oge* in 1897.[22]

Unencumbered by modern archaeology, which can provide scientifically derived precise dates, the rediscovery of the Boyne in the late nineteenth century promoted a wealth of speculative interpretation. Because racial theory was still an accepted science, concepts of a Celtic underlay

Fig. 7   Irish postage stamp (1983) celebrating the winter solstice at Newgrange. Louis Le Brocquy often depicted aspects of the megalithic art from the Boyne tombs in his graphics. Some of his freehand drawings made in the 1940s were later adapted for fabric designs in Dublin's Brown Thomas department store (1952) and large murals at Tulse Hill Comprehensive School, London (1954).

stretched back over astonishingly long periods of time to the very origins of European civilisation. The scale of the revelations inspired the Irish Literary Revival, one of whose foundation texts was the *Heroic history of Ireland* by Standish Hayes O'Grady, which strongly featured the Boyne Valley. The excitement of these discoveries is brilliantly captured in George Moore's sardonic description in *Ave Atque Vale* of the mystically minded A. E. (George Russell) entering the passage at Dowth fully expecting to meet there the great pre-Christian god of love Aengus. Russell claimed that Aengus was more real to him than Christ. Asked to decipher the strange symbols on the wall of the tomb, he explained to a sceptical Moore:

J.F. HUNTER

JIM FITZPATRICK

Fig. 9 Page from a 'Celtic Calendar' illustrated by Jim Fitzpatrick (2001). Fitzpatrick, heavily influenced by American pop-culture, comic book illustration and the Celtic Revival, fused them into a new 'Celtic'-style visual vocabulary, much used as album covers by rock artists like Thin Lizzy. This type of illustration perpetuates the misconception that the Boyne tombs are Celtic monuments.

Fig. 8 'The bier of King Cormac at the river for burial at Pagan Brugh-na-Bóinne or Christian Ross-na-Ri' by J. F. Hunter (1926). This woodcut was commissioned by the Belfast antiquarian F. J. Bigger, who had a celebrated collection of archaeological objects. Hunter tries to provide his Celtic warriors with authentic spears, shields and jewellery based on actual examples. Cormac Mac Airt is a well-known mythological figure associated with Newgrange. Cormac, pseudo-historical high king of Ireland, anticipating the coming of St Patrick, did not wish to be buried in the pagan tombs at Newgrange.[23]

to Irish culture had enormous credibility. This was largely derived from Matthew Arnold (1822–88) and his *On the study of Celtic literature* (1867) and *Irish essays* of 1882. For Arnold the Celt was naturally imaginative, spiritual, mystic as opposed to the solid, sober, pragmatic Anglo-Saxon. Yeats seized on those distinctions to claim special privileges for the Celtic dimension in Irish culture which had preserved it from the errors of Saxon England – a culture which had elevated getting and spending at the expense of wisdom and insight, and which had produced a dreadful middle-class world of grimy industrial cities, the yellow press, and a shallow derivative mass culture that crushed individuality and creativity. Yeats argued that Celtic Ireland had remained in touch with its deeper past: imagination still flourished amongst the Irish country

people who had never been detached by industrialisation from their ancient landscapes. That enduring 'peasant' wisdom could now be enjoyed by all through the scholarly work of translation and critical transformation of these raw materials into a pure art. The Irish, denizens of a Celtic twilight world, had access to spiritual and cultural insights denied to the materially richer but spiritually blind English who lived in the plain light of the Saxon day.[24]

As Ireland sought a distinctive cultural identity, the siren call of the Celtic note was irresistible. It proved especially seductive in the Boyne Valley where the spirals and whorls of the art seemed indubitably Celtic in style: not for the Celts the linear Lockean art of the Enlightenment. The superimposition of this Celtic overlay on the Boyne tombs has been so overwhelmingly powerful that it has resisted the best efforts of modern archaeology to provide credible dates and contexts. Radiocarbon dates, palynology and painstaking excavation lack the emotional Celtic resonance. To the great frustration of scientifically minded archaeologists, in the popular imagination Celtic mystery still haunts the Boyne. Astringent scholarly efforts to fumigate Newgrange, Dowth and Knowth of their Celtic allure have proved remarkably ineffectual.

STARS AND STONES

The Boyne attracts many in search of spiritual consolation, healing and renewal. Practitioners of New Age philosophy are attracted to the 'good energy' of the tombs.[25] Once derided as hippies, 'New Agers' subscribe to the belief that we are on the threshold of a new spiritual age in which humans will develop a closer, more nurturing relationship with the life force embedded in nature. This

Solstice
by Susan Connolly

Outside the mound   a flametide
a trail of footprints   kept rising,
had frozen   creeping —
in the grass;   till I sensed
but along,   in a beam of light
its inner walls   my spirit-world
   revealed.

DÚCHAS/CON BROGAN

Fig. 10 The winter sunrise lights up the passage and inner chamber at Newgrange. This has been a source of inspiration to artists since its discovery in 1963.

life force is felt with special intensity at some key sites identified by ancient people who were still spiritually bonded to their environment. New Agers believe that by visiting the Boyne Valley in the proper spirit, travellers can re-energise their spirits jaded by the materially full but spiritually depleted modern world. They can renew their creative vitality by reconnecting with the life force whose aura is especially potent at these ancient sites of spiritual wisdom. The New Age quest for spiritual knowledge embraces the symbols, myths and rites of pre-technical civilisations, which they believe encode age-old spiritual

wisdom denied to the modern technocratic/rationalist world. New Age philosophy is syncretic and polytheistic, believing that different cultures produced variants of one great natural spiritual sensibility. New Age is therefore tolerant and hospitable to many different strands of religious practice – ecological, eastern, druidic, pagan.[26] In Ireland there has been some continuity from the hermetic and theosophical traditions of the Literary Revival, and the movement has gained ground as the quality of the environment looms larger as an issue in Irish life. There is also the persistent Celtic note, where everything from Enya's music to tree-hugging is believed to flower from the Celtic roots of the Irish people. New Age in Ireland has also a particular fascination with the druids, priests of the pre-Christian religion.

The power of natural energy is a central tenet of the New Age philosophy and the mapping of flows of this energy is a constant preoccupation.[27] Energy is believed to flow with special intensity along 'ley lines' – zones of accelerated or concentrated energy flow. These ley lines can be discovered by the spiritually adept, using natural techniques such as 'dowsing' and 'water-tuning'. A major ley line has been identified running from Anglesey to St Patrick's Island on the east coast of Ireland, via Newgrange, and then on to Carrowmore on the west

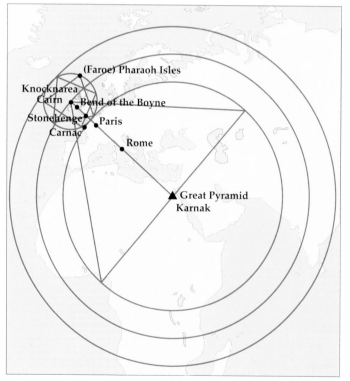

Fig. 11 The Boyne has proved greatly inspirational to New Age philosophy. Some believe that a ley line (a conduit of heightened natural energy) called *Hyperborea* runs from the Great Pyramid of Cheops, through Stonehenge and across Newgrange to the Neolithic settlements at Carrowmore overlooking Sligo Bay.[28]

SEÁN HILLEN

SEÁN HILLEN

Fig. 12   Imagery from *Irelantis* by Seán Hillen (Dublin, 1999). A) The queen of Heaven appears at Newgrange, Irelantis. B) The island of Newgrange, county Meath, Irelantis. The *Sunday Times* referred to these illustrations as being 'bigger than anything [Dúchas] could invent'.

coast.[29] It has been suggested that a mega ley line connects the Boyne tombs with the Pyramids of Egypt. The argument is that prehistoric communities had already discovered these ley lines and had deliberately aligned their sacred sites along them. Ley lines are therefore punctuated by standing stones, stone circles and burial mounds, and these are power points along a vast grid of natural energy. Newgrange is one of the most potent points within this massive matrix.[30]

Most archaeologists are scornful of these claims, on the grounds that a hotchpotch of monuments of different ages and purposes have been arbitrarily shoe-horned into a reductive concept. New Agers, they argue, credulously accept any major structure as a point along a projected alignment. Archaeologists point to the New Age claim that the stone circle at Newgrange pre-dated the tomb and was incorporated into the later passage tomb at Newgrange. According to the archaeological evidence, the outer stone circle is actually 1,000 years younger than the inner passage grave. New Agers retort that human culture continuously rediscovers the power of the ley line, hence the continuity of the site. As the late Bean Uí Chairbre of

Drogheda often said: "the problem with archaeologists is that they have no imagination!"

New Age philosophy also embraces feminist perspectives. Because nature is coded as feminine and because the ancient world religion is believed to be focussed on an earth-centred, matriarchal divinity, the earth goddess is a symbolic and ritual focus of New Age practitioners, the embodiment of spiritual power and at-one-ness with nature.[31] The 'mother earth' philosophy also appeals to some environmental thinkers who argue that human nature can only protect itself from the threat of global warming, the destruction of rain forests, the extinction of fossil fuels and exorbitant modern energy use by embracing the concept of sustainability. This focus on Gaia as a symbol of the sustainable earth with humans and nature in harmonic balance can coexist quite easily with a belief that the pre-modern world had been a peaceful, creative, woman-centred civilisation. The Boyne megaliths had been built by such a society, a 'Utopian Megalithic Matriarchy', which was later to be obliterated by aggressive war-mongering invaders, who brought with them metallurgy, dominant males and a patriarchal division of labour.[32]

The discovery of female figures at Neolithic sites was used as evidence for ancient goddess worship, a theory especially associated with the California-based Maria Gimbutas. Her academic status gave renewed credibility to the feminist reading of the Neolithic tombs. Currently, the Boyne Valley megaliths attract many followers of the female goddess. These gatherings aim to re-energise women with a vision of their age-old identity as both mother and goddess. Specific Boyne Valley tours now cater to this spiritual quest which has proved especially attractive to New Age lesbians. The local tutelary deity Boánn, associated with the origin legend of the Boyne, has been particularly significant to those pursuing this version of New Age spirituality. Boánn played a central role in Celtic religious ritual.[33] The modern Boyne poet Susan Connolly has invoked her in 'Boánn'.[34] For her, the river and goddess are one. Boánn soothes, supports and calms; the ebb and flow of the great river responds to her mood swings:

> o Boánn Boánn fertile
> and plentiful
>
> draw near
>
> do something
> to relieve this desire
> this emptiness
>
> be the one stable thing
> as you rush by
>
> clear rapid water
>
> I feel you the way
> I feel my own blood
> turn hot turn cold

The New Age calendar embraces a seasonal cycle of eight rituals (Sabbats), occurring at the solstices, equinoxes and the four quarter days. Some of these correspond to ritual highpoints of vernacular calendar custom:[35] Imbolg, Bealtaine, John's Eve (midsummer), Lughnasa and Samhain.[36] By far the most significant ritual at the Boyne occurs at the winter solstice. This Newgrange event is now of equal significance in the New Age religious calendar with the celebration of the summer solstice at Stonehenge. As the Boyne Valley declines into the grey grip of winter, the warm honey-light of the winter solstice penetrates the inner core of the megalith, offering a reassuring affirmation that the advent of spring will soon overthrow the reign of winter.

Not surprisingly, the solstice phenomenon has been celebrated by leading contemporary poets, including Seamus Heaney, Richard Murphy and John F. Deane.[37] They focus on the solstice as an emblem of spiritual solace,

Fig. 13 *The solstice at Newgrange* by Adam Woolfitt. Candles and crystals play an important part in the spiritual ceremonies attached to solstice celebrations.

ROBERT HARDING PICTURE LIBRARY

a sentiment believed to chime with the original intentions of the tomb builders. Being present at the solstice generates a deeply satisfying sense of the long-running continuity of Irish history, and a real sense of communion with a millennia-old cultural force which penetrates to the heart of human history on this island. This theme is also present in Susan Connolly's poem 'Solstice',[38] which inspired *A beam of light*, composed by local man Michael Holohan in 1997.[39]

A further interpretative layer was added to the Boyne megaliths by the American graphic artist Martin Brennan in 1983. He confidently argued that the tombs of the Boyne Valley were complex constructs, carefully aligned to the rising and setting sun at pivotal moments in the year's turning.[40] Brennan also sought to read the megalithic art as directly related to the astronomical function of the mounds. Indeed, Brennan claimed that they were in the first instance constructed solely for astronomical purposes

RICHARD MOORE

RAYMOND BALFE

Fig. 14   A) *The cyngus configuration of stars over Newgrange on the winter solstice* by Richard Moore (2000).   B) *Solstice at Dowth* by Raymond Balfe (2001). The 1960s' discovery that the tombs were astronomically aligned has stimulated artists' imaginations. One of its benefits has been to draw attention to the startling beauty of the night sky and the continuity that it offers between past and present. When we look at the sky over Newgrange, we are gazing at a view that would also have been available to our Neolithic ancestors, a direct link with the past unmediated by text of interpretation.

and that they were not tombs at all. Brennan certainly discovered for the first time a significant astronomical event at Knowth.[41] At sunset on the summer equinox, the standing stone outside the entrance to the west tomb casts a shadow on the entrance stone along the vertical line of the megalithic art. Brennan was also the first to record that the setting sun lights up the south chamber at Dowth on the winter solstice.[42] These observations have been confirmed by subsequent fieldwork.[43]

Brennan also attacked archaeologists for their neglect of the crucial astronomical importance of the tombs, which he described as 'the greatest blunder of Irish archaeology'.[44] Archaeologists were not at all impressed by his dismissal of the burial evidence which they had painstakingly assembled from major excavations at Newgrange and Knowth. Neither did they appreciate Brennan's lack of emphasis on M. J. O'Kelly's discovery of the purpose of the roof box at Newgrange back in the 1960s.

It is undoubtedly the case that these tombs are susceptible to many different interpretations. We can learn something from all of them. For example, artists drawn to the tombs have been able to record subtle gradations of colour which the impassive camera misses. As such they

have made significant contributions to our understanding of the Boyne monuments.

It is equally true that the tombs also attract a riot of interpretations which do not fit well with the more sober scientific record. Untethered from the actual, these interpretations soar into speculative realms which belong to a mystical dimension of the human spirit. At regular intervals, too, fabulous new keys to unlock the ancient megalithic code are announced – and just as regularly dismissed by the archaeologists. One theory proposes that the circles focused on sunburst images in the Boyne Valley megalithic art are based on the pattern of halos over the sun and moon, caused by the refraction of light through floating ice crystals (the 'cascading comets' theory).[45] A Canadian cartographer has argued that the art is in fact a map of the moon, with specific symbols closely corresponding to lunar geography observable by the naked eye.[46] There are even fictional treatments as in Tom Richards's *The lost scrolls of Newgrange*, where the secrets of Newgrange are revealed not by the archaeologists but by an enterprising maths teacher and his students.[47]

LAND OF RESISTANCE

While the tombs exert their palpable fascination, the association with the Battle of the Boyne in 1690 is another indelible aspect of the valley. Fifty years after the battle it was commemorated with the construction of a massive monument which soon after its construction was painted by Joseph Tudor (1695–1759).[48] 'The obelisk in memory of the Battle of the Boyne' (*c.*1746) dominates the view, a

PRIVATE COLLECTION

Fig. 15 *The obelisk, in memory of the Battle of the Boyne* (*c*.1746). This towering monument built in 1736 indicated the significance of the Williamite victory at the Boyne in underpinning 'Protestant Ascendancy' in eighteenth-century Ireland. The relationship is symbolised visually by the manicured demesne of the Oldbridge estate, the reassuring landscape equivalent of the iconography of the obelisk. The obelisk was blown-up in 1923 shortly after the advent of the Irish Free State. The inscription on the north side of the obelisk read: *Sacred to the Glorious Memory of King William III who on the 1st July 1690 passed the river near this place to attack James II at the head of a popish army advantageously posted on the south side of it and did on that day by a successful battle secure to us and to our posterity our liberties and our religion. In consequence of this action James II left this Kingdom and fled to France. This memorial of our deliverance was erected in the 9th year of the Reign of King George II, the first stone being laid by Lionel Sackville, Duke of Dorset, Lord Lieutenant of the Kingdom of Ireland, MDCCXXXVI [1736].* The inscription on the south side read: *Marshal the Duke of Schomberg in passing this river died bravely fighting.* The inscription on the east side read: *In defence of Liberty, July 1st MDCLXXXX [1690].* The inscription on the west side read: *This monument was erected by the grateful contributions of several protestants of Great Britain and Ireland.*

powerful reminder of the triumph of 'the Protestant Ascendancy' intimately, if inaccurately (Aughrim was the decisive battle of the campaign) associated with the Williamite victory at the Battle of the Boyne on 1 July 1690. It must have seemed all the more reassuring in 1746 after the recent Jacobite scare in Scotland in 1745 which threatened the stability of the Hanoverian regime. The painting also depicts Oldbridge demesne, whose neo-classical symmetry symbolised the highly regulated, hierarchical world of the cultivated Protestant gentry.

Every 12 July (the date of commemoration was changed with the introduction of the 'new' calendar), the battle is commemorated with incredible fervour within the Unionist tradition in Ulster. Until recently, there was little interest within the Republic in recognising the battle site, but in response to the Peace Process, the southern state has

finally moved to acknowledge it. In 2003 a major Battle of the Boyne Visitor Centre will be opened. Yet the battle itself survived in popular memory, as can be seen in the traditions collected in the Schools Manuscripts of the late 1930s. These remain the most important collection of folklore for the Bend of the Boyne.[49] A child from Oldbridge National School referred to a local man, Burke the Gunner, a Jacobite soldier who was killed in the battle and buried in Tullyallen church. Another story tells how a distraught King James retreated to Drogheda and beseeched a local wine merchant to help him escape. The dealer promptly immersed him in a barrel labelled 'pickled pork' and got local sailors to carry him overseas. Other stories record the inevitable buried treasure at Oldbridge, while weapons were buried after the battle at a place called The Buildings. Incredibly, on 6 January 1839,

DÚCHAS/CON BROGAN

Fig. 16   A concrete plaque erected on Mattock Bridge (Slane–Drogheda road) honours the memory of local man Philip Clarke 'who died for Ireland' in the Easter rising at Dublin, 1916. The culture of commemorating the dead has a long pedigree in the Boyne.

the 'Night of the Big Wind', bones of soldiers buried after the Battle of the Boyne were once more exposed by the severity of the storm.

Some local place names are also explained. *Pass if you can* at Drybridge is a point on the river where the Jacobites taunted the Williamites to cross the Boyne. Dogget's Hill is named for James and Richard Dogget of Toberfinn, who participated in the Cromwellian wars. Later in the Penal times, Mass was celebrated furtively on Dogget's Hill.

Many songs on both sides commemorated the battle.[50] In the Irish language tradition the battle was called *Briseadh na Bóinne* ('the Break of the Boyne'). This tradition was unforgiving to King James – *Séamas an Chaca* (James the shit);

> Séamas an Cháca a chaill Éirinn
> lena leathbhróg ghallda is a leathbhróg Ghaelach.[51]

Another poem exhorted the Meath farmers not to be downhearted by the defeat:

> A scológaí na Mí, ná goilleadh oraibh an fómhar
> nó an mórchloí fuaramar ag briseadh na Bóinne;
> tá an Sáirséalach láidir is a thrúpaí aighe in ordú
> le gunnaíbh is dromaíbh leis na bodaigh a chur as
> Fódla.
>
> Achainím ar Mhuire is ar Rí na féile,
> go bhfeicead na Sacsanaigh ag stealladh na déirce,
> a rámhainne ar a nguaillibh ag tuilleamh pá lae leo,
> is a mbróga lán d'uisce mar bhíos ar Ghael bocht …[52]

The battle also entered the English language song traditions. An early one celebrates William's victory:

> July the first, in Oldbridge town,
>   there was a grievous battle,

> Where many a man lay on the ground,
>   by the cannons that did rattle;
> King James he pitched his tents between
>   the lines for to retire,
> but King William threw his bomb-balls in,
>   and set them all on fire…[53]

The celebrated *Lilliburlero* by Thomas Wharton also relates to the battle; the catchy tune was so popular that Jonathan Swift, in 1712, claimed that the song 'whistled a king out of three kingdoms.' The tune was later used for other Orange songs such as *The Protestant Boys*. These songs, and the other stalwart, *The Boyne Water*, denigrated the Jacobites as a Popish rabble bent on massacre and plunder:

> July the First, of a morning clear, one thousand,
>   six hundred and ninety,
> King William did his men prepare, of thousands
>   he had thirty;
> To fight King James and all his foes, encamped
>   near the Boyne Water,
> He little feared, though two to one, their
>   multitudes to scatter.
>
> So praise God, all true Protestants, and I will say
>   no further,
> But had the Papists gained the day, there would
>   have been open murder,
> Although King James and many more, were ne'er
>   that way inclined,
> It was not in their power to stop what the rabble
>   they designed.

As late as 1905, Lady Gregory had *The White Cockade* staged at the Abbey Theatre – a tragi-comedy which features Patrick Sarsfield, James II and King William.[54]

THE CAVES

The Boyne megaliths mean different things to different people. In the Slane area they are colloquially referred to as 'the caves', where most local families have participated in the excavations over four decades. Some families have had more than one generation work at Knowth. Here they rubbed shoulders and trowels with exotic students from universities all over the world – French, German, English, Australian and American. Side by side they unravelled the mysteries of these monuments, slowly and painstakingly stripping it back 'layer by layer like the skin of an onion'.[55] Many locals can recall personal stories of discovery and funny incidents that never made it into the official records of the site. Love blossomed and some found a husband here. The ceremonial macehead at Knowth was discovered by Liam O'Connor; Taoiseach Charles Haughey rushed

The Knowth Troweller
by Tom Delaney
Sung to the tune of *The Bard of Armagh*.

Come list to the lay of the mound-disemboweller,
'Tis of the Knowth troweler the legend I tell,
Cut down in his beauty while doing his duty,
To serve his director he strove and he fell.

The passage was shaking, the orthostats quaking,
An evacuation was ordered in haste.
But some fool left the level 'mid all the upheaval,
And only remembered when it seemed too late.

George lost his good humour when he heard the rumour
Of the terrible bloomer the youth had performed.
He rushed to the passage when he got the message,
His passion to assuage he strutted and stormed.

Back in the fool scrambled, 'neath lintel he ambled
While orthostats trembled, the level to get.
He knew it was risky but swallowed his whiskey
And his footstep was frisky as he strode to his death.

For a boulder came crashing, a megalith mashed him
When up through the entrance the level he threw.
His corpse out we carried while life it yet tarried,
To hear his last words we lined up in a queue.

"Oh send my expenses back home to my mother,
Tell her I died with a trowel in my hand.
Assure her my sections will need no corrections,
Send her some soil from the sites I have planned.

Oh make me a 'secondary crouched inhumation',
Put my knees to my nose and my arse to my heels.
With a beaker of Guinness to hearten my finish,
At last I'll know how a cist-burial feels.

Or else raise a pyre and set it on fire,
The future can date me by dating the fuel.
I'd hoped to be famous but fate often shames us,
The past is misleading and fortune cruel."

From the passage we scraped him, with trowels re-
    shaped him
And taped up his face till it seemed that he smiled.
And the very last words that the Knowth troweler spoke us
Were, "Mother!", "Director!" and "Vere Gordon Childe".

Then half we cremated and half inhumated
Where the grass waves above and the Boyne wanders by.
Now with a new level he surveys the heavens,
His celestial trowel scrapes a hole in the sky.

He lies 'neath the spoil-heap beside the new office,
Each barrow-load added increases his name.
And sorrowing maidens with soil and tears laden,
Diminish their grief as they add to his fame.

So if ever you wander from Slane to Drogheda,
Consider this youth and the mound where he sagged.
The whole of creation's a vast excavation,
By his duty he's labelled, by God he's been bagged.

George Eogan
by Tom Delaney
Sung to the tune of *Tooralooralooralooraloo*.

Archaeologists are a funny lot its true
Tooralooralooralooraloo
Always looking for new ways each other to outdo
Tooralooralooralooraloo
So I'll tell you of the race they held
To see whose showmanship excelled
And I'll tell you of the man who won it, too —

Chorus: So come all you excavators and dustbin
    ruminators
    And celebrate George Eogan, Tooraloo.

O'Kelly had Americans half-naked at Newgrange,
And Herity had television watch him excavate,
But George Eogan won the race,
He put a passage grave in space,
Eogan used his dynamite and blew!

Some archaeologists used politics and bribes,
Others sat on sidelines with inconsequential jibes,
But Dr Eogan won the fight,
When he used his dynamite
And decorated stones blew into view!

Now R——y and N—-a were doin' a strong line,
Behind the Rock of Cashel they managed to entwine,
But Dr Eogan keeps his place,
None can escape his interlace,
The gripping beast called Eogan has his due!

There came to Knowth Glyn Daniel, the famous
    Cambridge cook,
At the battleaxe motifs there he just had to cock a
    snook,
But he's condemned by his own mouth,
His theories are destroyed at Knowth
And Eogan's cooking he must learn to chew!

Now Townley Hall palatial is and beauteous for to see,
And beverages there are served in pots of Trickter-
    becker 'B',
There Dr Eogan is the host,
Of all the guests he eats the most!
They say his thirst is megalithic too!

When Pearly Gates are opened to allay the digger's
    thirst,
As at Knowth Dr Eogan through the passage will be
    first.
St Peter will say "What's your name?"
The other saints will all exclaim
"'Tis the Patron Saint of Knowth and of Lough Crew!"

GERALDINE STOUT

Fig. 17 The recently thatched *Tourist's Rest* public house at Rossin. This has been the favourite haunt of 'Knowth trowellers' for four decades.

down to see it and gave Liam money for a few celebratory jars. The fun and camraderie of the site are still vividly recalled by those that work there: the twinkle in the eye of Jimmy Morgan; Tommy Dixon's humourous escapades like dancing on the spoil heap; the sudden silence that would descend over the site when George Eogan clambered up the ladder to take site photographs with Bernie Heston and Frank Taffe holding on for dear life – 'the loss to mankind would be too great' if they let go; of the rainy lunches in the site hut which were never complete without 'the Hellman's'.

Two buildings in the Bend of the Boyne are intimately associated with the 'Knowth Trowellers' as the cohorts of student diggers at Knowth came to be known: Townley Hall (a Georgian mansion owned by the late Frank Mitchell), where the volunteers were accommodated during the summer campaigns; and 'Lev Mitchell's pub (now the *Tourist's Rest*), where the events of the day's digging would be dissected over a few libations. The annual celebration of the discovery of the eastern tomb at Knowth on 31 July 1968 always began at Knowth but ended well into the night at Lev's. Davy, a local aficionado of the Scotish bagpipes, loudly featured in the night's revelry. It was in this warm, convivial atmosphere that two popular songs by the archaeologist Tom Delaney,

Knowth Troweller and *George Eogan,* were invariably sung.[56] Distinguished visitors like the debonair Leo Swan would make star appearances on these special nights. In a corner of the lounge at the *Tourist's Rest,* a photograph of 'the Doctor' (George Eogan) still hangs, a nook known to many as 'the shrine'. It remains a place of quiet pilgrimage for those of us who were privileged, at one time or another, to excavate in Brú na Bóinne.

As the new millennium beckoned, it was celebrated on Irish television with a reading by Seamus Heaney of his 'A Dream of Solstice'. It seemed appropriate that the Irish people should mark the millennium moment by once again turning to the mighty megaliths which have sentinelled the Boyne Valley for over 5,000 years. Heaney approaches the 'tonsured' Newgrange as the modern world flew overhead or met him in headlights on the Belfast road. But once he enters the mound, he is drawn back to the roots of culture in agriculture, back beyond Dante to ancient rituals of sowing and seeding, and back beyond that again to the cosmic origins of life, death and the universe. As the kindly light penetrates the cold chamber, Heaney feels released into a world which precedes speech, at the very origins of the European tradition. Theories come and go; so do archaeologists, scholars and poets; so have hundreds of generations; but the tombs endure.

A Dream of Solstice
by Seamus Heaney

Qual è colüi che sognando vede,
che dopo 'l sogno la passione impressa
rimane, e l'altro a la mente non riede,
cotal son io…
        Dante, *Paradiso*, Canto xxxiii

Like somebody who sees things when he's dreaming
And after the dream lives with the aftermath
Of what he felt, no other trace remaining,

So I live now, for what I saw departs
And is almost lost, although a distilled sweetness
Still drops from it into my inner heart.

It is the same when snow the sun releases,
The same as when in wind, the hurried leaves
Swirl round your ankles and the shaking hedges

That had flopped their catkin cuff-lace and green sleeves
Are sleet-whipped bare. Dawn light began stealing
Through the cold universe to County Meath,

Over weirs where the Boyne water, fulgent, darkling,
Turns its thick axle, over rick-sized stones
Millennia deep in their own unmoving

And unmoved alignment. And now the planet turns
Earth brow and templed earth, the corbelled rock
And unsunned tonsure of the burial mounds,

I stand with pilgrims, tourists, media folk
And all admitted to the wired-off hill.
Headlights of juggernauts heading for Dundalk,

Flight 104 from New York audible
As it descends on schedule into Dublin,
Boyne Valley Centre Car Park already full,

Waiting for seedling light on roof and windscreen.
And as *in illo tempore* people marked
The king's gold dagger when he plunged it in

To the hilt in unsown ground, to start the work
Of the world again, to speed the plough
And plant the riddled grain, we watch through murk

And overboiling cloud for the milted glow
Of sunrise, for an eastern dazzle
To send forth light like share-shine in a furrow

Steadily deeper, farther available,
Creeping along the floor of the passage grave
To backstone and capstone, to hold its candle

Inside the cosmic hill. Who dares say "love"
At this cold coming? Who would not dare say it?
Is this the moved wheel that the poet spoke of,

The star pivot? Life's perseid in the ashpit
Of the dead? Like his, my speech cannot
Tell what the mind needs told: *an infant tongue*

Milky with breast milk would be more articulate.

APPENDIX 1: MID-NINTEENTH-CENTURY HOUSES AND HOLDINGS

Key – C = Caretaker, CFM = Corn/flour mill, CH = Chapel, CM = Corn mill, CO = Coachman, D = Destroyed (house), F= Forge, FI = Fishery, G = Garden, GL = Gate lodge, GR = Graveyard, H = House, HE = Herd, K = Kiln, L = Land, LH = Lock house, MD = Master's dwelling, NS = National school, O = Office/s, P = Present (house), PA = Parish, PL = Ploughman, Q = Quarry, S = School, SM = Small, SR = Stores, ST = Steward, W = Widow, WA = Watchhouse, WO = Workman, WR = Woodranger, Y = Yard

No.	Townland	Occupier	Lessor	Description	Area	Land Value	Building Value	Current Status
1a	Balfeddock	Patrick Drew	C.A. Caldwell	C H, O, L.	84	122	75	P
1b	Balfeddock	Peter Russell	Patrick Drew	H			10	D
1c	Balfeddock	Judith Ogle	Patrick Drew	H, O, G	0.25	5	15	D
1d	Balfeddock	John Leech	Judith Ogle	H			5	
2	Balfeddock	Patrick Drew	James Newman	L	73	152		
2a	Balfeddock	Simon Hamill	Patrick Drew	H			8	D
2b	Balfeddock	Patrick Bourke	Patrick Drew	H			8	D
2c	Balfeddock	Catherine Roche	Patrick Drew	H			8	D
2d	Balfeddock	Rose Mullen	Patrick Drew	H			10	D
2e	Balfeddock	Mary Gogan	Patrick Drew	H			10	D
2f	Balfeddock	Patrick Berrill	Patrick Drew	H, O			10	D
3a	Balfeddock	Patrick Ginnitty	Patrick Drew	H, O, L	3	60	10	D
4a	Balfeddock	Patrick Berrill	Patrick Drew	H, O, L	5	90	60	P
5a	Balfeddock	Francis Maguire	C.A. Caldwell	HE H, O, L	152	3000	15	P
5b	Balfeddock	Michael Hall	Francis Maguire	H			5	D
6	Balfeddock	John Gorman	C.A. Caldwell	H, O, L	3	62	18	D
7a	Balfeddock	Bryan Heaney	C.A. Caldwell	H, O, L	4	62	18	D
7b	Balfeddock	Michael Bryan	Bryan Heaney	H, G			5	D
1a	Corballis	Laurence Gogarty	Reps. Ths. McDermot	H, O, L	193	2240	100	P
3Aa	Corballis	Michael Moore	Reps. Ths. McDermot	O, L	21	360	15	D
4a	Corballis	Patrick Gogan	Reps. Ths. McDermot	H, O, L	34	430	15	D
5a	Corballis	Richard Walsh	Reps. Ths. McDermot	H, O, L	40	492	13	D
5b	Corballis	Michael Mooney	Richard Walsh	H			5	D
6a	Corballis	Nicholas Fitzsimons	Reps. Ths. McDermot	H, O, L	49	535	55	
8Aa	Corballis	William Pentony	St George W. Smith	O, L	32	445	13	D
9a	Corballis	William Pentony	William Blackburne	H, O, L	47	725	60	P
2a	Crewbane	Thomas McGuire	C.A. Caldwell	HE H, O, L	178	3240	15	D
1a	Cruicerath	Peter Connolly	Arthur J. Netterville	HE H, O, L	102	1640	20	D
1b	Cruicerath	Board of Education	In fee	NS-H			13	D
1c	Cruicerath	Board of Education	Peter Connolly	NS-H			14	P
1d	Cruicerath	—	—	R.C. CH, Y	0.25		200	P
2a	Cruicerath	Thomas Bellew	Arthur J Netterville	HE, H. O, L	35	640	20	P
3Aa	Cruicerath	John Mulvany	Arthur J Netterville	H, O, L	29	405	25	P
1Aa	Donore	James Dogot	E.H. Coddington	H, O, L	15	245	35	P
1B	Donore	James Dogot	E.H. Coddington	L	19	220		
2a	Donore	Peter Connolly	E.H. Coddington	H, O, L	57	940	300	D
2b	Donore	Silvester McGinn	Peter Connolly	H			7	D
2c	Donore	Vacant	Peter Connolly	H			7	D
3a	Donore	Catherine Reid	E.H. Coddington	H, O, L	17	212	13	P
3b	Donore	Patrick Reid	E.H. Coddington	H, O, L		105	15	P
3c	Donore	Christopher Reid	Patrick Reid	H, SM G			7	D
3d	Donore	John Reid	Patrick Reid	H			5	D
3e	Donore	Mary Mulligan	Patrick Reid	H			6	D
3f	Donore	Michael Preston	Catherine Reid	H			6	D
4Aa	Donore	John Owens	E.H. Coddington	H, O, L	30	443	17	D
4Ab	Donore	Garrett Dinning	John Owens	H			5	D
4Ac	Donore	Richard Rooney	John Owens	H		5		D
4B	Donore	John Owens	E.H. Coddington	L	22	300		
5Aa	Donore	Patrick Moonan	E.H. Coddington	H, O, L	7	135	10	P
5Ba	Donore	Patrick Moonan	E.H. Coddington	O, L	17	265	10	
6a	Donore	Catherine Fullam	E.H. Coddington	H, O, L	95	1590	110	P
7a	Donore	Thomas Hammond	E.H. Coddington	HE H, O, L	36	710	20	D
7b	Donore	Peter Madden	Thomas Hammond	H			12	D
8a	Donore	James Monaghan	Eleanor King	H, O, L	94	1460	50	P
8b	Donore	Patrick Campbell	Eleanor King	H, G		1	5	D
8c	Donore	Margaret Conroy	Eleanor King	H, G		1	5	D
9Aa	Donore	Boyle Simpson	E.H. Coddington	H, O, L	20	285	30	P
9B	Donore	Boyle Simpson	E.H. Coddington	L	43	805		
10a	Donore	James Green	James Doolan	H			8	
1	Dowth	John Gorman	Edmond Wynne	L	8	130		
1a	Dowth	Michael Murphy	John Gorman	H, SM G			10	D
3a	Dowth	Margaret Smith	Edmond Wynne	H, O, L	12	217	13	D
4a	Dowth	John Ogle	Edmond Wynne	H, O, L	35	640	30	P
4b	Dowth	Anne Doonen	John Ogle	H			10	D

No.	Townland	Occupier	Lessor	Description	Area	Land Value	Building Value	Status
5a	Dowth	Nicholas Smith	Edmond Wynne	H, O, L	4	60	10	D
6	Dowth	Bryan Heaney	Edmond Wynne	L	18	320		
6a	Dowth	John Mathews	Bryan Heaney	H			5	D
6b	Dowth	Robert Moore	Bryan Heaney	H			5	D
6c	Dowth	Owen Johnston	Bryan Heaney	H			5	D
6d	Dowth	John Bock	Bryan Heaney	H			5	D
7a	Dowth	Michael Conway	Edmond Wynne	C H, O, L	24	440	15	D
7b	Dowth	George Puigh	Michael Conway	H			5	D
8Aa	Dowth	Mary Elcock	Edmond Wynne	H, O, L	22	430	50	D
8Ab	Dowth	Vacant	Mary Elcock	CM			20	D
8B	Dowth	Mary Elcock	Edmond Wynne	L	15	320		
9Aa	Dowth	James Farrell	Edmond Wynne	H, O, L	9	180	20	P
9B	Dowth	James Farrell	Edmond Wynne	L	6	120		
10a	Dowth	Thomas Devine	Edmond Wynne	H, O, L	11	230	30	P
11a	Dowth	James Drew	Edmond Wynne	H, L	13	260	10	D
11b	Dowth	Mary Gorman	James Drew	H			5	D
11c	Dowth	Eliza Reynolds	James Drew	H			5	D
11d	Dowth	John Magrane	Netterville Trustees	H, SM G	1		10	D
11e	Dowth	Peter Heany	Netterville Trustees	H, O, G	1	10	15	D
12a	Dowth	Nicholas Smith Jnr	Edmond Wynne	H, L	2	25	5	D
13	Dowth	Michael Elcock	G.W. Monsell	L	14	220		D
14Aa	Dowth	G.W. Monsell	In fee	C H, O, L	52	850	50	P
14Ab	Dowth	James Elcock	G.W. Monsell	H, O, SM G			20	D
14Ac	Dowth	Michael Elcock	G.W. Monsell	H, O, G	1	10	30	D
14Ad	Dowth	Laurence Hey	G.W. Monsell	H			8	D
14Ae	Dowth	Michael Connor	G.W. Monsell	H, O, G	1	12	13	D
14B	Dowth	G.W. Monsell	In fee	L	5	90		
14C	Dowth	G.W. Monsell	In fee	L	6	130		
15	Dowth	Michael Connor	G.W. Monsell	L	15	300		
16	Dowth	Laurence Hey	G.W. Monsell	L	5	92		
17	Dowth	Michael Elcock	G.W. Monsell	L	12	230		
17a	Dowth	James Boylan	G.W. Monsell	H, O, G	0.25	5	15	D
18	Dowth	Mary Brien	G.W. Monsell	L	4	80		
17b	Dowth	Alice Elcock	Michael Elcock	H, O			10	D
19A	Dowth	Cornelius Brien	G.W. Monsell	L	4	80		
19B	Dowth	Cornelius Brien	G.W. Monsell	L	4	80		
20a	Dowth	Hugh Brien	G.W. Monsell	H, O, L	18	345	15	D
20b	Dowth	Mary Brien	G.W. Monsell	H, O, SM G			10	D
20c	Dowth	Cornelius Brien	G.W. Monsell	H, O, SM G			10	D
20d	Dowth	James Carolan	G.W. Monsell	H, G		2	10	D
21	Dowth	James Boylan	G.W. Monsell	L	1	10		
22a	Dowth	James McCormack	G.W. Monsell	C H, O, L	14	240	10	P
23a	Dowth	Richard Maguire	G.W. Monsell	HE H, O, L	275	5460	140	P
24	Dowth	Richard Maguire	G.W. Monsell	L	14	240		
25a	Dowth	William Rogers	William Wynne	H, O, L	53	1030	70	P
25b	Dowth	Vacant	William Rogers	H			10	D
26a	Dowth	Robert Bredon	In fee	HE H, L	105	2000	10	P
27	Dowth	Peter Heany	Netterville Trustees	L	1	25		
28A	Dowth	Thomas Devine	Netterville Trustees	L	3	50		
28B	Dowth	Thomas Devine	Netterville Trustees	L	39	660		
28Ba	Dowth	Charles Puigh	Peter McCullagh	H, G		4	6	D
28Bb	Dowth	Patrick Mathews	Charles Puigh	H			5	D
28Bc	Dowth	Mary Martin	Charles Puigh	H			5	D
28Bd	Dowth	—	—	GR	0.5	5		
29	Dowth	James Elcock	Netterville Trustees	L	17	320		
30	Dowth	James Boylan	Netterville Trustees	L	3	50		
31	Dowth	Richard Gradwell	Netterville Trustees	L	11	220		
2a	Dowth	James Stafford	Edmond Wynne	H, O, L	10	160	10	P
32a	Dowth	Netterville Trustees	In fee	W H, O, L	3	50	150	P
32b	Dowth	Comsrs. Nat. Education	Trustees Netterville	S-H			30	P
33	Dowth	James Elcock	William Rogers	L	12	240		
34	Dowth	Peter McCullough	Richard Maguire	L	4	60		
35a	Dowth	Richard Gradwell	In fee	H, O, ST H, GL, L	314	5600	700	P
35b	Dowth	Patrick Heany	Richard Gradwell	H			10	
35c	Dowth	Mary Roche	Richard Gradwell	H			1	
36	Dowth	James Drew	Ambrose Cox	L	1	3		
1a	Gilltown	Thomas Garrigan	Andrew Colwell	H, O, L	133	1850	90	P
1b	Gilltown	James Rooney	Thomas Garrigan	H, O, G	1	17	13	P
6	Gilltown	Joseph Boylan	Andrew Colwell	L	17	200		
1a	Glebe	Peter McCullagh	Rev Edward Batty	L	31	600		
1a	Knowth	Patrick Sullivan	C.A. Caldwell	H, O, L	118	2250	110	P
1b	Knowth	Owen Farrell	Patrick Sullivan	H, G		3	12	D
1c	Knowth	Thomas Russell	Patrick Sullivan	H			10	D

No.	Townland	Occupier	Lessor	Description	Area	Land Value	Building Value	Status
2a	Knowth	Anne Maguire	C.A. Caldwell	H, O, L	191	3840	120	P
1	Littlegrange	Peter Roache	James Tyrell	H, O, L	90	1600	100	P
2	Littlegrange	Peter Roache	James Tyrell	L	49	960		
2a	Littlegrange	Vacant	Peter Roche	H			10	D
3a	Littlegrange	James White	Nicholas Tierney	H, L	3	60	5	D
4A	Littlegrange	Thomas Cheavers	Nicholas Tierney	L	5	100		
4Ba	Littlegrange	Thomas Cheavers	Nicholas Tierney	H, O, G		5	15	D
5a	Littlegrange	Patrick Stafford	Nicholas Tierney	H, O, L	10	220	30	D
6	Littlegrange	Patrick Stafford	Nicholas Tierney	L	12	230		
7a	Littlegrange	Nicholas stafford	Nicholas Tierney	H, L	14	250	10	D
8a	Littlegrange	Patrick Marron	Ambrose Cox	H, O, L	167	3530	70	P
8b	Littlegrange	Patrick Lynes	Patrick Marron	H, G		3	12	P
8c	Littlegrange	Thomas McGrane	Patrick Marron	H, G	0	3	12	P
8d	Littlegrange	Owen Matthews	Patrick Marron	H			10	D
7a	Monknewtown	Vacant	Earl of Sheffield	H			5	D
7b	Monknewtown	Henry White	Earl of Sheffield	H, O			10	D
8	Monknewtown	Patrick Moonan	Earl of Sheffield	L	34	480		
9a	Monknewtown	Thomas Warde	Earl of Sheffield	H, O, L	59	950	50	P
10Aa	Monknewtown	Patrick Drew	Earl of Sheffield	WO H, O, L	58	1120	5	D
10Ab	Monknewtown	Patrick Drew	Earl of Sheffield	R.C. CH			200	P
10Ac	Monknewtown	Patrick Drew	Earl of Sheffield	PA S, H, MD			30	P
10Ba	Monknewtown	Patrick Drew	Earl of Sheffield	H, O, L	92	2060	105	P
10Bb	Monknewtown	James Hanly	Patrick Drew	H			10	D
10Bc	Monknewtown	Bryan Cunningham	Patrick Drew	H			10	D
11a	Monknewtown	Richard R. Hill	William Rogers	H, O, CFM, SR, L	9	120	2680	P
11b	Monknewtown	Richard R. Hill	Earl of Sheffield	GR	0.25	2		
12a	Monknewtown	John Reynolds	Patrick Drew	H, O, L	8	170	20	D
12b	Monknewtown	Matthew Smith	John Reynolds	H			8	D
13A	Monknewtown	James Drew	Earl of Sheffield	L	90	2000		
13Ba	Monknewtown	James Drew	Earl of Sheffield	H, O, GL, L.	181	3060	300	P
13Bb	Monknewtown	John Gorman	James Drew	H			10	D
14a	Monknewtown	Archibold Malcolm	Earl of Sheffield	H, O, L	104	1530	70	D
14b	Monknewtown	Vacant	Archibold Malcolm	H			7	D
14c	Monknewtown	Michael Leech	Archibold Malcolm	H			5	D
14d	Monknewtown	Catherine McDonnell	Archibold Malcolm	H			5	D
14e	Monknewtown	Hugh McGuinness	Archibold Malcolm	H			5	D
14f	Monknewtown	John Flynn	Archibold Malcolm	H			5	D
14g	Monknewtown	Thomas Taffe	Archibold Malcolm	H, G	0.25	8	7	D
17B	Monknewtown	Margaret Curry	Earl of Sheffield	L	9	115		
18A	Monknewtown	Thomas Curry	Earl of Sheffield	L	8	160		
18Ba	Monknewtown	Thomas Curry	Earl of Sheffield	H, O, L	54	640	60	
19Aa	Monknewtown	Nicholas Curry	Earl of Sheffield	CH, O, L	30	420	15	
19B	Monknewtown	Nicholas Curry	Earl of Sheffield	L	12	155		
1Aa	Newgrange	Thomas Maguire	C.A. Caldwell	H, O, L.	193	4260	200	P
1B	Newgrange	Thomas Maguire	C.A. Caldwell	L	18	240		
1Bb	Newgrange	Patrick Reilly	Thomas Maguire	H			5	D
2a	Newgrange	Richard Kirk	C.A. Caldwell	H, O, HE H, L	197	4000	160	P
3	Newgrange	Francis Maguire	C.A. Caldwell	L	8	120		
3a	Newgrange	Patrick Fitzpatrick	Francis Maguire	H, SM G			10	D
4a	Newgrange	Francis Berrill	C.A. Caldwell	H, O, L	9	160	20	D
5a	Newgrange	Richard Maguire	C.A. Caldwell	H, O, L	325	8000	400	D
5b	Newgrange	Patrick Fowler	Boyne Navigation	L H			20	P
6	Newgrange	Patrick Fowler	Boyne Navigation	L (marsh)	2	5		
7	Newgrange	Boyne Navigation	In fee	Canal	6			
1Aa	Oldbridge	H.B. Coddington	In fee	H, O, L	586	13040	1300	P
1Ab	Oldbridge	B.T. Balfour	H.B. Coddington	H, O,			700	P
1Ac	Oldbridge	H.B.Coddington	In Fee	PL H, O,			75	P
1Ad	Oldbridge	Thomas McCullagh	H.B. Coddington	H			16	P
1Ae	Oldbridge	Nicholas Craven	H.B. Coddington	H			16	P
1Af	Oldbridge	Laurence McDonnell	H.B. Coddington	H			16	P
1Ag	Oldbridge	Mary Hallahan	H.B. Coddington	H, G		3	17	P
1Ah	Oldbridge	H.B. Coddington	In fee	WR H, O, G		5	25	P
1Ai	Oldbridge	Thomas Marry	H.B. Coddington	H		25		P
1Aj	Oldbridge	John Magrane	H.B. Coddington	H, O, G		3	13	P
1Ak	Oldbridge	Thomas McDonnell	H.B. Coddington	H, O, G		3	20	P
1Al	Oldbridge	Francis White	H.B. Coddington	H, O, G		3	20	P
1Am	Oldbridge	Patrick Murphy	H.B. Coddington	H, O, G		3	20	P
1An	Oldbridge	John Reilly	H.B. Coddington	H			25	P
1Ao	Oldbridge	Patrick Closkey	H.B. Coddington	H			20	P
1B	Oldbridge	H.B. Coddington	In fee	L	15	348		
1C	Oldbridge	H.B. Coddington	In fee	L	2	12		
2	Oldbridge	B.T. Balfour	H.B. Coddington	G	4	240		
3a	Oldbridge	John Murray	H.B. Coddington	Q	1	160		

No.	Townland	Occupier	Lessor	Description	Area	Land Value	Building Value	Status
3a	Oldbridge	John Murray	H.B. Coddington	L	2	45		
4a	Oldbridge	Matthew Clarke	H.B. Coddington	H, O, F, L	8	190	20	P
5a	Oldbridge	John Mullins	H.B. Coddington	H, O, G	1	20	22	P
5b	Oldbridge	William Reynolds	H.B. Coddington	H, O, G	1	28	22	P
5c	Oldbridge	James Nugent	H.B. Coddington	H, O, G	1	20	20	P
5d	Oldbridge	William Malone	H.B. Coddington	H, O, G	2	55	45	D
5e	Oldbridge	Thomas Magennis	H.B. Coddington	H, G	1	26	16	D
5f	Oldbridge	Owen Magrane	H.B. Coddington	H, O, G	1	26	16	D
5g	Oldbridge	James Lynch	H.B. Coddington	H, O, G	1	24	16	D
5h	Oldbridge	Thomas McCullagh	H.B. Coddington	G	0.25	12		
5i	Oldbridge	Laurence McDonnell	H.B. Coddington	G	0.25	12		
6a	Oldbridge	James Kelly	H.B. Coddington	H, G	1	62	28	D
6b	Oldbridge	Thomas Brien	H.B. Coddington	H			15	D
6c	Oldbridge	Patrick McNally	H.B. Coddington	H			15	D
8a	Oldbridge	Boyne Navigation	In fee	L H, Canal	20		50	P
6a	Platin	John Brian	Michael Doherty	H			10	D
9a	Platin	Patrick Greene	Boyle Simpson	H, O, L	5	110	15	D
11a	Platin	Michael Gibney	Frederick Medcalf	H, L	1	38	12	P
11b	Platin	Henry Smith	Michael Gibney	H			8	P
11c	Platin	Vacant	Michael Gibney	H			6	P
11f	Platin	Michael Cawlin	Michael Cawlin	H, Os			12	P
11g	Platin	Francis Markey	Michael Gibney	H, G			8	P
12a	Platin	John McKeon	Frederick Medcalf	H, L	1	36	12	D
12b	Platin	Michael Doherty	Frederick Medcalf	H, G			12	D
12c	Platin	Margaret McCormick	John McKeon	H			5	D
12d	Platin	Patrick Birle	John McKeon	H			5	D
13a	Platin	Thomas Gibney	Frederick Medcalf	H, L	1	36	12	P
13b	Platin	Rose Birle	Thomas Gibney	H			8	P
14a	Platin	William Gibney	Frederick Medcalf	H, O, L	2	43	12	D
16Aa	Platin	Thomas White	Edward Atkinson	HE H	10	165	15	P
1a	Proudfootstown	James Drew	Ambrose Cox	H, O, CM, L	43	800	600	P
1b	Proudfootstown	James Drew	Richard Gradwell	L	1	20		D
1c	Proudfootstown	Richard Drew	James Drew	H			14	D
1d	Proudfootstown	Michael Pentony	James Drew	H			10	D
1e	Proudfootstown	Bryan Gorman	James Drew	H			10	D
2	Proudfootstown	Richard Gradwell	In fee	L	40	740		
3a	Proudfootstown	Matthew Crinnion	Richard Gradwell	H, O, L	60	1210	40	P
4	Proudfootstown	Thomas Drew	Richard Gradwell	L	17	360		
5a	Proudfootstown	Michael Conway	Richard Gradwell	H, O, L	42	880	30	P
5b	Proudfootstown	Thomas Drew	Richard Gradwell	H, O, G		5	15	D
5c	Proudfootstown	Anne Gerratty	Michael Conway	H			8	D
5d	Proudfootstown	James Bristle	Michael Conway	H			8	D
6a	Proudfootstown	Barthlomew Halpin	Richard Gradwell	H, L	1	60	10	D
31a	Rathmullan	Vacant	Robert Cathcart	H, O, L			7	D
32a	Rathmullan	John Duff	Robert Cathcart	H, G			90	P
1a	Redmountain	Mary Sampson	Henry Kemmis	H, Os, L	6	75	10	P
2a	Redmountain	Thomas Sampson	Henry Kemmis	H, Os, L	6	80	10	P
3a	Redmountain	Patrick Gogan	Henry Kemmis	H, Os, L	87	1160	60	P
3b	Redmountain	Patrick Mooney	Patrick Gogan	H			8	D
3c	Redmountain	Patrick Barnett	Patrick Gogan	H			7	D
1a	Rossnaree	Andrew Tiernan	Rev. Charles Osborne	Os, L	233	4395	85	P
1b	Rossnaree	John Geoghegan	Andrew Tiernan	H			10	P
1c	Rossnaree	Charles Moran	Andrew Tiernan	H			10	P
1d	Rossnaree	Vacant	Andrew Tiernan	H			14	P
1e	Rossnaree	Luke Brodigan	Andrew Tiernan	H			14	P
2a	Rossnaree	Rev. Charles Osborne	Marquis of Drogheda	Os, L	217	387	105	P
3Aa	Rossnaree	Peter Tiernan	Rev Charles Osborne	H, O, L	5	100	130	P
3B	Rossnaree	Peter Tiernan	Rev Charles Osborne	L	3	45		
3Bab	Rossnaree	William Loughran	Rev Charles Osborne	H, G		1	9	P
4Aa	Rossnaree	Michael Drew	Rev Charles Osborne	H, O, L	25	360	60	P
4B	Rossnaree	Michael Drew	Rev Charles Osborne	L	9	120		
5Aa	Rossnaree	James Swift	Rev Charles Osborne	H, O, L	8	150	80	P
5B	Rossnaree	James Swift	Rev Charles Osborne	L	9	170		
6	Rossnaree	James Swift	Rev Charles Osborne	L	5	85		
7a	Rossnaree	Patrick Garagan	Rev Charles Osborne	H, O, L	85	1165	75	P
7b	Rossnaree	—	—	R.C. CH, Y	1		200	P
8a	Rossnaree	Walter Johnston	Rev Charles Osborne	H, O, CM, K, L	41	570	400	P
8b	Rossnaree	Margaret Brodigan	Walter Johnston	H, SM G, O, L			7	D
9Aa	Rossnaree	Thomas Johnston	Rev Charles Osborne	Os, L	24	330	105	P
9B	Rossnaree	Thomas Johnston	Rev Charles Osborne	L	2	5		
10a	Rossnaree	Hugh Morgan	Boyne Navigation	LH, O, Canal	31	20	25	P
11	Rossnaree	Boyne Navigation	In fee	Canal	2			
1A	Roughgrange	Michael Moore	William Brabazon	L	2	33		

No.	Townland	Occupier	Lessor	Description	Area	Land Value	Building Value	Status
1B	Roughgrange	Michael Moore	William Brabazon	L	2	28		
1C	Roughgrange	Michael Moore	William Brabazon	L	3	26		
1D	Roughgrange	Michael Moore	William Brabazon	L	6	15		
1E	Roughgrange	Michael Moore	William Brabazon	L	2	33		
2A	Roughgrange	Michael Moore	Reps. T. McDermot	L	37	465		
2Ba	Roughgrange	Michael Moore	Reps. T. McDermot	H, Os, L	118	1345	50	P
2Bb	Roughgrange	John McCormack	Michael Moore	H			10	D
2Bc	Roughgrange	James Donegan	Michael Moore	H			7	D
3A	Roughgrange	Michael Moore	William Brabazon	L	0.25	5		
3AB	Roughgrange	N. Madden, P. McCullagh	Reps. T. McDermot	L	176	2265		
3Ba	Roughgrange	N. Madden, P. McCullagh	Reps. T. McDermot	H, O			105	P
3Bb	Roughgrange	John Murray	Peter McCullagh	H, O, G	0.25	5	10	D
3Bc	Roughgrange	Matthew Monaghan	Peter McCullagh	H			8	D
3Bd	Roughgrange	Vacant	—	H			7	D
3Be	Roughgrange	Patrick Carlon	Peter McCullagh	H			7	D
4a	Roughgrange	Michael Boyle	Reps. T. McDermot	H, Os, L	90	1150	55	D
5	Roughgrange	Michael Boyle	Reps. T. McDermot	L	15	195		
6a	Roughgrange	Michael Gogan	Reps. T. McDermot	H, Os, L	17	180	55	D
7	Roughgrange	Laurence Gogarty	Reps. T. McDermot	L	42	550		
8A	Roughgrange	William Norris	Reps. T. McDermot	FI		160		
8Aa	Roughgrange	William Norris	Reps. T. McDermot	H, O, CM, L	8	145	200	P
8B	Roughgrange	William Norris	Reps. T. McDermot	L	30	545		
9a	Roughgrange	James McDonnell	Reps. T. McDermot	H, O, L	64	870	40	P
-	Roughgrange	William Norris	Reps. T. McDermot	GR	0.25	5		
10a	Roughgrange	Patrick Gogan	Reps. T. McDermot	H, L	84	1065	25	D
11	Roughgrange	Richard Moore	Reps. T. McDermot	L	30	410		
11a	Roughgrange	Thomas Walsh	Richard Moore	H			6	D
11b	Roughgrange	John Devine	Richard Moore	H			5	D
12a	Roughgrange	Peter Moore	Reps. T. McDermot	H, O, L	8	140	30	
13	Roughgrange	Reps. T. McDermot	In fee	R. Boyne	18			
14	Roughgrange	Boyne Navigation	In fee	Canal	10	15		
1a	Sheephouse	Thomas Hammond	E.H. Coddington	H, O, L	8	185	310	P
1b	Sheephouse	Patrick Bellew	Thomas Hammond	H			11	
1c	Sheephouse	Michael Tiernan	Thomas Hammond	H			10	D
1d	Sheephouse	William Finegan	Thomas Hammond	H, G			15	
2a	Sheephouse	Thomas Hammond	W.S. Crawford	Q	1			
2b	Sheephouse	Thomas Hammond	E.H. Coddington	CO H			20	P
3a	Sheephouse	Henry Coddington	E.H. Coddington	Os, L	91	79	80	P
4	Sheephouse	James Dogat	E.H. Coddington	L	81	1240		
5a	Sheephouse	Hugh Connell	E.H. Coddington	H, O, L	70	152	200	P
6b	Sheephouse	William Moran	William Malone	H			12	D
6c	Sheephouse	William Malone	E.H. Coddington	PL H			12	P
6d	Sheephouse	—	E.H. Coddington	WH, GR	0.5	10	10	P
1Aa	Stalleen	Richard Moore	W.S. Crawford	H, Os, L	15	180	20	P
1B	Stalleen	Richard Moore	W.S. Crawford	L	9	85		
1Ba	Stalleen	Patrick Barron	W.S. Crawford	H, G		4	8	D
2a	Stalleen	Patrick Boyle	W.S. Crawford	H, O, L	27	320	15	D
3a	Stalleen	Patrick Kirwan	W.S. Crawford	H, O, L	9	120	10	D
4a	Stalleen	Catherine Barron	W.S. Crawford	H, Os, L	65	775	30	P
5a	Stalleen	John C. Sheiler	W.S. Crawford	H, Os, L	40	545	60	P
6a	Stalleen	William Bellew	W.S. Crawford	H, Os, L	29	390	40	D
7Aa	Stalleen	John Moore	W.S. Crawford	H, O, L	79	955	40	P
7Ab	Stalleen	John Crogan	John Moore	H		7	7	D
7B	Stalleen	John Moore	W.S. Crawford	L	2	20		
7Ba	Stalleen	Henry Kirwan	W.S. Crawford	H		10	10	D
7Bb	Stalleen	Bridget Sheeran	W.S. Crawford	H		5		D
8A	Stalleen	Patrick Bellew	W.S. Crawford	L	2	23		
8Ba	Stalleen	Patrick Bellew	W.S. Crawford	H, O, L	5	60		D
9Aa	Stalleen	James Reilly	W.S. Crawford	C H, L	4	50	10	D
9B	Stalleen	James Reilly	W.S. Crawford	L	13	195		
—	Stalleen	Peter McCullagh	—	FI		150		
10	Stalleen	Christopher Callaghan	W.S. Crawford	L	12	135		
11a	Stalleen	Patrick Callan	W.S. Crawford	H, O, L	10	140	15	D
12a	Stalleen	Margaret Byrne	W.S. Crawford	H, O, L	4	60	10	D
13a	Stalleen	James Murray	W.S. Crawford	H, O, L	3	35	15	P
14	Stalleen	Mary Hammil	W.S. Crawford	L	3	35		
15a	Stalleen	Peter Quinn	W.S. Crawford	H, O, L	4	55	10	P
15b	Stalleen	Mary Hammill	W.S. Crawford	H			10	P
16	Stalleen	Eliza Murphy	W.S. Crawford	L	23	520		
16a	Stalleen	John Moore	Eliza Murphy	H			13	D
17Aa	Stalleen	James McEntaggart	W.S. Crawford	H, O, L	3	47	15	D
17Ab	Stalleen	Matthew Clarke	James McEntaggart	H, F			25	D
17Ac	Stalleen	Charles McGinn	James McEntaggart	H			7	D

No.	Townland	Occupier	Lessor	Description	Area	Land Value	Building Value	Status
17Ad	Stalleen	Thomas Dowdall	Charles McGinn	H, G		1	7	D
17Ae	Stalleen	Andrew Barry	Thomas Dagot	H		6		
17Af	Stalleen	James Fay	Thomas Dagot	H		10		D
17Ag	Stalleen	John Green	Thomas Dagot	H			12	P
17Ah	Stalleen	Richard Magenniss	Julia Moore	H			7	D
17Ai	Stalleen	Eliza Burns	James McEntaggart	H, G		6	7	D
17Aj	Stalleen	Judith Moore	Eliza Burns	H			8	D
17Ak	Stalleen	James Reilly	James McEntaggart	H, O, G		2	25	D
17Al	Stalleen	John Campbell	James McEntaggart	H, G		2	10	D
17Am	Stalleen	Bryan Donnell	James McEntaggart	H, G		6	9	D
17An	Stalleen	George Gill	Bryan Donnelly	H			6	D
17Ao	Stalleen	James McKeon	Bryan Donnelly	H			6	D
17B	Stalleen	James McEntaggart	W.S. Crawford	L	5	63		
18a	Stalleen	Christopher Waters	W.S. Crawford	H, L	2	20	6	
18b	Stalleen	Patrick Bellew	W.S. Crawford	H, O			10	P
18c	Stalleen	Margaret Stairs	Patrick Bellew	H		6		
19a	Stalleen	Mary Hall	W.S. Crawford	H, O, L	5	73	12	D
20	Stalleen	Patrick Bellew	W.S. Crawford	L	2	22		
21a	Stalleen	Jane Murray	W.S. Crawford	H, O, L	9	185	20	D
22a	Stalleen	Valentine Clinch	W.S. Crawford	H, Os, L	10	198	17	P
23a	Stalleen	James Martin	W.S. Crawford	H, L	5	70	15	D
23b	Stalleen	William Connolly	James Martin	H			6	D
23c	Stalleen	Thomas Martin	James Martin	H			8	D
24Aa	Stalleen	Laurence Bellew	W.S. Crawford	H, Os, L	1	10	30	P
24B	Stalleen	Laurence Bellew	W.S. Crawford	L	4	45		
25Aa	Stalleen	Thomas Bellew	W.S. Crawford	H, Os, L	30	525	80	D
25Ab	Stalleen	Margaret Corrigan	W.S. Crawford	H, G	0.25	11	13	D
25B	Stalleen	Thomas Bellew	W.S. Crawford	L	34	505		
25Ba	Stalleen	Vacant	Thomas Bellew	H, Os			30	P
25C	Stalleen	Thomas Bellew	W.S. Crawford	L	49	675		
25D	Stalleen	Thomas Bellew	W.S. Crawford	L	11	245		
26a	Stalleen	John Bellew	W.S. Crawford	H, L	7	100	15	P
27a	Stalleen	Thomas Bellew Jnr	W.S. Crawford	H, Os, L	9	125	25	P
28a	Stalleen	James McCann	W.S. Crawford	H, Os, L	81	1140	700	P
29	Stalleen	W.S. Crawford	In fee	L	42	775		
29a	Stalleen	Vacant	W.S. Crawford	H.Os			10	D
30Aa	Stalleen	Peter McCullagh	W.S. Crawford	H, O, K, L	41	730	90	P
30Ab	Stalleen	Mary Dagot	Peter McCullagh	H			11	D
30Ac	Stalleen	Patrick Johnston	Peter McCullagh	H, G		2	8	D
30Ad	Stalleen	John Johnston	Peter McCullagh	H			13	D
30Ba	Stalleen	Peter McCullagh	W.S. Crawford	CM, L	2	5	120	P
31	Stalleen	Peter McCullagh	W.S. Crawford	L	45	685		
31a	Stalleen	Vacant	Peter McCullagh	H, Os		90		
32	Stalleen	Patrick & Catherine Reid	W.S. Crawford	L	15	140		
33a	Stalleen	Boyne Navigation	In fee	LH	9	15	30	P

ENDNOTES AND BIBLIOGRAPHY

The abbreviations listed here are used for sources that occur frequently; other sources are given in full.

AFM	Annals of the Four Masters	**N.L.I.**	National Library of Ireland
Ann. Tig.	Annals of Tigernach	**O.P.W.**	Office of Public Works
Arch. Ir.	Archaeology Ireland	**O.S.**	Ordnance Survey of Ireland
AU	Annals of Ulster	**P.R.O.N.I.**	Public Records Office, Northern Ireland
C.D.I.	Calendar of Documents relating to Ireland	*R.I.A. Proc.*	*Proceedings of the Royal Irish Academy*
C.U.C.A.P.	Cambridge University Committee on Aerial Photography	*R.S.A.I. Jn.*	*Journal of the Royal Society of Antiquaries of Ireland*
Ir. Geog.	*Irish Geography*	**SMR**	Sites and Monuments Records, Dublin and Belfast
N.A.I.	National Archives of Ireland		

THE BEND OF THE BOYNE

1. R. Meehan and W. Warren, *The Boyne valley in the Ice Age; a field guide to some of the valley's most impressive glacial geological features* (Dublin, 1999); see preface.

2. F. Aalen, 'The Irish rural landscape: synthesis of habitat and history' in F. Aalen, K. Whelan and M. Stout (ed.), *Atlas of the Irish rural landscape* (Cork, 1997), pp 4–30, see pp 10–12; G. Herries Davies and N. Stephens, *Ireland* (London, 1978), see pp 17–24, 97.

3. M. Gardiner, T. Finch, M. Conry and T. Radford, 'Over one–third of Meath land has a drainage problem' in *Farm and Food Research*, vi (1975), p. 15.

4. J. Andrews, 'A geographer's view of Irish history' in T. Moody and F. Martin (ed.), *The course of Irish history* (Cork, 1967), pp 17–29, see p. 21.

5. G. Mitchell, 'The landscape' in G. Eogan, *Excavations at Knowth I* (Dublin, 1984), pp 9–11; G. Mitchell, 'The geology of the Bend of the Boyne' in *Brú na Bóinne; A supplement to Arch. Ir.*, xi (1997), pp 5–6.

6. A. Bowden, 'The Carboniferous geology of P.L. 1039 and P.L. 1040 and adjoining application areas near Drogheda, county Louth' (unpublished GSI report AB1/71, 1971), pp 1–30.

7. A. O'Neill, *National Archaeological Park: Boyne Valley* (unpublished consultancy report, 1989), pp 15–16.

8. Andrews, 'A geographer's view', pp 19–21.

9. A. McCabe, 'Directions of late-Pleistocene ice-flows in eastern counties Meath and Louth, Ireland' in *Ir. Geog.*, xx (1972), pp 443–61, see p. 443.

10. Bowden, 'Carboniferous geology', pp 11–12.

11. S. Matthews, 'Under the hill of Donore' in *Journal of the Old Drogheda Society*, ix (1994), pp 118–28, see p. 126.

12. S. Matthews, *Place and people: a family exploration* (unpublished family history, 1980), p. 16.

13. Geological Survey of Ireland, 'Explanatory memoir to accompany Sheets 91 and 92' (unpublished memoir, 1871), p. 22.

14. W. Neville, 'The Carboniferous knoll-reefs of east central Leinster' in *R.I.A. Proc.*, B, lix (1957–9), pp 285–303.

15. Geological Survey of Ireland, 'Explanatory memoir', p. 22.

16. *Ibid.*

17. G. Stout, 'Embanked enclosures of the Boyne region' in *R.I.A. Proc.*, xci (1991), C, pp 245–84, p. 253, fig 5; G. Cole, *Memoir and map of localities and minerals of economic importance and metaliferous mines in Ireland* (2nd ed., Dublin, 1956); J. Jackson, 'Metallic ores in Irish prehistory: copper and tin' in M. Ryan (ed.), *The origins of metallurgy in Atlantic Europe* (Hojberg, 1978), pp 107–25.

18. Quoted in C. Ellison, *The waters of the Boyne and Blackwater* (Dublin, 1983), p. 58.

19. Geological Survey of Ireland, 'Explanatory memoir', p. 42.

20. Meehan and Warren, *The Boyne valley in the Ice Age*.

21. McCabe, 'Directions of late-Pleistocene ice-flows', p. 448.

22. Meehan and Warren, *The Boyne valley in the Ice Age*, p. 6.

23. A. McCabe, 'Directions of late-Pleistocene ice-flows', p. 448.

24. T. Finch, M. Gardiner, M. Conry and T. Radford, *Soils of county Meath* (Dublin, 1983), p. 12.

25. F. Synge, 'The coasts of Leinster' in C. Kidson and M. Tooley (ed.), *The quaternary history of the Irish sea* (Liverpool, 1977), pp 199–222, see pp 212–15.

26. F. Synge, *Field Handbook: Annual field meeting 1979* (Irish Quaternary Association, Dublin, 1979), pp 12–13.

27. Meehan and Warren, *The Boyne valley in the Ice Age*, p. 6.

28. G. Mitchell, 'Did the tide once flow as far as Newgrange?' in *Living Heritage*, xii (1995), p. 34.

29. Geological Survey of Ireland, 'Explanatory memoir', p. 13.

30. Bowden, 'Carboniferous geology', p. 3.

31. Mitchell, 'Tide', p. 34.

32. E. Kelly, 'Investigation of ancient fords on the river Suck' in *Inland Waterways News*, xx (1993), pp 4–5.

33. Meehan and Warren, *The Boyne valley in the Ice Age*, p. 6.

34. A. McCabe, 'The glacial stratigraphy of Meath and Louth' in *R.I.A. Proc.*, C, lxxiii (1973), pp 355–82, see pp 356–7, 377.

35. Finch, *et al.*, *Soils of County Meath*, p. 54.

36. *Ibid.*, preface.

37. *Ibid.*, p. 30.

38. *Ibid.*, p. 54.

39. *Ibid.*, p. 53.

40. *Ibid.*, pp 40–2.

41. *Ibid.*, p. 5.

42. J. Haughton (ed.), *Atlas of Ireland* (Dublin, 1978), p. 32.

43. P. Rohan, *The climate of Ireland* (Dublin, 1986), p. 18.

44. Finch, *et al.*, *Soils of county Meath*, p. 8.

45. *Ibid.*, p. 7.

46. *Ibid.*, p. 6.

47. Haughton (ed.), *Atlas of Ireland*, p. 32.

48. Brady, Shipman and Martin, *Boyne Valley Integrated Development Plan* (Dublin, 1996), pp 16–17; 78/659/EEC, SI 293. Three official bodies are involved in administration of the Fisheries on the Boyne: the Department of Marine, Central Fisheries Board and the Eastern Regional Fisheries Board (ERFB).

49. R. Lunnon, 'Ireland: the last stronghold of the European otter' in P. Nugent (ed.), *Natural Heritage* (Longford, 1991), pp 117–19; See also Nano Reid's drawing of 'waterhens at the river's edge' in E. Hickey, *I send my love along the Boyne* (Dublin, 1966), p. 11.

50. P. Lack, *The atlas of wintering birds in Britain and Ireland* (Catton, Staffordshire, 1986), p. 66; G. Atkinson–Willes, 'The numerical distribution and the conservation requirements of swans in north–west Europe' in Anon., *Second International Swan Symposium* (Japan, 1980), pp 40–8.

51. A. Went, 'Material for a history of the fisheries of the river Boyne' in *R.S.A.I. Jn.*, xiii (1953), pp 18–33; G. Stout, 'Fishing at Brú na Bóinne' in *Brú na Bóinne*, pp 34–5.

52. J. Reynolds, *A life on the Boyne* (Trim, 1984).

53. Information provided by the National Parks and Wildlife Service, 51 St Stephen's Green, Dublin 2.

Boyne Valley Fossils

Fossils from the locality collected in the last century and mentioned in the Geological Survey Memoirs are now part of a National Collection held in the Geological Survey of Ireland. Resident palaeontologist Matthew Parkes has established a detailed database for the collection of *c*.25.000 fossils. Illustrated are Brachiopoda from *circa* two miles north of Duleek at Cruicerath: GSI:F20137, F20138, F20139, F20140, F20141, F20143, F20145, F20146; Bivalve Mullusca: GSI:F16805, F16817, F16885; Orthocone Mollusca: GSI: F20162, F20113, F20113.

THE PREHISTORIC LANDSCAPE

1. D. Lehane, 'The flint work' in M. O'Kelly, R. Cleary and D. Lehane (ed.), *Newgrange, county Meath, Ireland* (Oxford, 1983), pp 150–3.

2. V. Buckley and P. Sweetman, *Archaeological survey of county Louth* (Dublin, 1991), pp 15–16; G. Stout and M. Stout, 'Patterns in the past: county Dublin 5000BC–1000AD in F. Aalen and K. Whelan (ed.), *Dublin from prehistory to present – studies in honour of J. H. Andrews* (Dublin, 1992), pp 5–25, see pp 5–6; G. Cooney, 'The Red Mountain transect: the results of a pilot fieldwalking study in the Boyne Valley area' (unpublished Dúchas report, Dublin, 1998).

3. P. Woodman and E. Anderson, 'The Irish Later Mesolithic: a partial picture' in P. Vermeersch and P. Van Peer (ed.), *Contributions to the Mesolithic in Europe* (Leuven, 1990), pp 377–87, see p. 387.

4. M. O'Kelly, Cleary and Lehane, 'Newgrange', pp 118–70, see pp 144–6.

5. G. Cooney and E. Grogan, *Irish prehistory: a social perspective* (Dublin, 1994), p. 13.

6. M. O'Kelly, 'Surface collected flints from two sites in the Boyne valley, county Meath' in *Journal of the Cork Historical and Archaeological Society*, lxxiii (1968), pp 114–19; C. Brady, 'Surface collected flint from Site A, Newgrange, county Meath' in *Trowel*, vii (1996), pp 41–5.

7. W. Groenman–van–Waateringe and J. Pals, 'Pollen and seed analyses' in G. Eogan, *Excavations at Knowth I* (Dublin, 1984), pp 325–8.

8. L. van Wijngaarden–Bakker, 'The animal bones from the Beaker settlement at Newgrange, county Meath: first report' in *R.I.A. Proc.*, C, lxxiv (1974), pp 313–83, see pp 353–4.

9. L. van Wijngaarden–Bakker, *An archaeological study of the Beaker settlement at Newgrange, Ireland* (Amsterdam, 1980), p. 185.

10. L. van Wijngaarden–Bakker, 'The animal remains from the Beaker settlement at Newgrange, county Meath: final report' in *R.I.A. Proc.*, C, lxxxvi (1986), pp 2–111, see p. 80.

11. Wijngaarden–Bakker, 'Animal bones from the beaker settlement', p. 344.

12. Cooney, 'Red Mountain transect'.

13. *Ibid.*, for Clonlusk, see pp 31–36; for Oldbridge, see pp 55–60.

14. A. Schofield (ed.) *Interpreting artefact scatters: contributions to ploughzone archaeology* (Oxford, 1991); J. Steinberg, 'Ploughzone sampling in Denmark: site signatures from disturbed contexts' in *Antiquity*, lxx (1996), pp 368–92. For Ballylough, see M. Zvelebil, M. Moore, J. Green and D. Henson, 'Regional survey and the analysis of lithic scatters: a case study from south–east Ireland' in R. Conway, M. Zvelibil and H. Blankholm (ed.), *Mesolithic north–west Europe: recent trends* (Sheffield, 1987), pp 9-23; for the Barrow Valley, see M. Zvelibil, M. Mackin, M. Passmore and P. Ramsden, 'Alluvial archaeology in the Barrow valley, south–east Ireland: the Riverford culture re–visited' in *Journal of Irish Archaeology*, vii (1996), pp 13–40; for Salterstown, see D. Hodgers, 'The Salterstown surface collection project' in *Louth Archaeological and Historical Society Journal*, xxiii (1994), pp 240–68; for Mount Oriel, see G. Cooney, 'The Mount Oriel project: an introduction' in *Louth Archaeological and Historical Society Journal*, xxix (1990), pp 125–33. For Fourknocks, see S. Cross, 'An intensive survey of the early prehistoric archaeology in the environs of Fourknocks, county Meath' (unpublished MA thesis, Department of Archaeology, NUI Dublin, 1991); for Barnageera, see B. Guinan, 'Fieldwalking in Irish archaeology' in *Trowel*, iii (1992), pp 4–8; for Greystones, see S. Cafferkey, 'Prehistory of the ploughzone in north–east county Wicklow' (unpublished MA thesis, Department of Archaeology, NUI Dublin, 1996).

15. G. Eogan, 'Prehistoric and early historic culture change at Brugh na Bóinne' in *R.I.A. Proc.*, C, xci (1991), pp 105–32, see pp 107–8.

16. Cooney, 'Red Mountain transect', p. 16.

17. E. Grogan, 'Appendix: radiocarbon dates from Brugh na Bóinne' in G. Eogan, 'Prehistoric and early historic culture change at Brugh na Bóinne' in *R.I.A. Proc.*, C, xci (1991), pp 126–7.

18. H. Roche, 'Prehistoric settlement in Brú na Bóinne' in *Brú na Bóinne*; supplement to *Arch. Ir.*, xi (1997), pp 28–9; G. Eogan and H. Roche, *Excavations at Knowth II* (Dublin, 1997), pp 7–16.

19. B. Collins, 'Appendix 3: plant remains' in Eogan and Roche, *Excavations at Knowth II*, pp 295–300.

20. G. Eogan, *Excavations at Knowth I* (Dublin, 1984), pp 211–44; G. Eogan and H. Roche, 'Pre–tomb Neolithic house discovered at Knowth' in *Arch. Ir.*, xi (1997), p. 31.

21. M. O'Kelly, F. Lynch and C. O'Kelly, 'Three passage graves at Newgrange, county Meath' in *R.I.A. Proc.*, C, lxxviii (1978), pp 249–352, see pp 263–9.

22. *Ibid.*, pp 293–7.

23. [G.]F. Mitchell and M. Ryan, *Reading the Irish landscape* (Dublin, 1997), pp 155–60.

24. M. Gowan, 'A Neolithic house at Newtown' in *Arch. Ir.*, vi (1992), pp 25–7.

25. [G.]F. Mitchell, *The Irish landscape* (Cork, 1976), p. 104.

26. Eogan and Roche, *Excavations at Knowth II*, pp 25, 42.

27. Dúchas, 'Record of Monuments and Places, county Meath' (unpublished Dúchas report, 1997); G. Cooney, 'The place of megalithic tomb cemeteries in Ireland' in *Antiquity*, lxiv (1990), pp 741–53.

28. This figure does not include the passage tombs

Townleyhall I and II which are just outside the designated area.

29. M. O'Kelly, *Newgrange: archaeology, art and legend* (2nd ed., London, 1994), p. 122.

30. M. O'Kelly and C. O'Kelly, 'The tumulus of Dowth, county Meath' in *R.I.A. Proc.*, C, lxxxiii (1983), pp 136–90, see p. 148; C. O'Kelly, *Illustrated guide to Newgrange and the other Boyne monuments* (3rd ed., Cork, 1978), p. 59.

31. O'Kelly, Lynch and O'Kelly, 'Three passage graves', p. 276.

32. M. O'Kelly, *Newgrange,* pp 22, 113.

33. G. Eogan, *Knowth and the passage–tombs of Ireland* (London, 1986), p. 44.

34. Eogan, *Excavations at Knowth I*, p. 68.

35. *Ibid.*, p. 102.

36. G. Eogan, 'A neolithic habitation–site and megalithic tomb in Townleyhall townland, county Louth' in *R.S.A.I. Jn.*, xciii (1963), pp 37–81, see pp 68–9.

37. O'Kelly and O'Kelly 'Tumulus of Dowth', p. 149.

38. O'Kelly, Lynch and O'Kelly, 'Three passage graves', pp 289–93.

39. M. O'Kelly, *Newgrange*, p. 92.

40. O'Kelly and O'Kelly, 'Tumulus of Dowth', p. 148.

41. M. O'Kelly, *Newgrange*, p. 73.

42. Eogan, 'Townleyhall', pp 75–6.

43. Eogan, *Knowth*, p. 45.

44. Eogan, *Excavations at Knowth I*, p. 36.

45. *Ibid.*, pp 57, 124–5.

46. *Ibid.*, p. 96.

47. Eogan, *Knowth*, p. 96.

48. Eogan, *Excavations at Knowth I*, p. 198.

49. *Ibid.*, p. 199.

50. *Ibid.*, p. 200.

51. O'Kelly, Lynch and O'Kelly, 'Three passage graves', pp 276–7; Eogan, *Knowth*, p. 43.

52. Eogan, *Knowth*, p. 35; Eogan, *Excavations at Knowth I*, p. 134.

53. *Ibid.*, p. 194.

54. O'Kelly, Lynch and O'Kelly, 'Three passage graves', p. 291; Eogan, *Knowth*, p. 43.

55. F. Prendergast, 'Shadow casting phenomena at Newgrange' in *Survey Ireland*, ix (1991), pp 9–18, see p. 9; M. O'Kelly, *Newgrange*, pp 123–6.

56. K. O'Sullivan, 'Canadian cartographer uncovers the hidden secret of Knowth moon carvings' in *The Irish Times*, 28 April 1999, p. 5; reports the alleged discovery by Dr Philip Stooke of the University of Western Ontario.

57. *Ibid.*, p. 179.

58. M. O'Sullivan, *Megalithic art in Ireland* (Dublin, 1993), p. 10.

59. Eogan, *Knowth*, p. 168.

60. *Ibid.*, p. 149.

61. O'Sullivan, *Megalithic art*, p. 17.

62. Eogan, *Knowth*, pp 183–4.

63. *Ibid.*, p. 151.

64. Eogan, *Excavations at Knowth I*, pp 114–15.

65. G. Eogan, 'The passage tombs of Brú na Bóinne' in *Brú na Bóinne*; supplement to *Arch. Ir.*, xi (1997) pp 9–11, see p. 11; Eogan, *Knowth*, p. 135.

66. M. O'Kelly, *Newgrange*, pp 197–214; O'Kelly, Lynch and O'Kelly, 'Three passage graves', p. 291.

67. *Ibid.*, p. 261.

68. Eogan, *Knowth*, pp 39–40.

69. Eogan, *Excavations at Knowth I*, p. 115.

70. *Ibid.*, pp 57–8.

71. Eogan, *Knowth*, pp 40–3.

72. *Ibid.*, p. 112; I. Meighan, D. Simpson and B. Hartwell, 'Newgrange: Sourcing of its granitic cobbles' in *Arch. Ir.*, xvi (2002), pp 32–5.

73. *Ibid.*

74. *Ibid.*, pp 113–14.

75. M. O'Kelly, *Newgrange*, p. 117.

76. J.–P. Mohen, *The world of megaliths* (New York, 1990), pp 158–68.

77. G.F. Mitchell, 'Notes on some non–local cobbles at the entrance to the passage–graves at Newgrange and Knowth, county Meath' in *R.S.A.I. Jn.*, cxxii (1992), pp 128–45.

78. *Ibid.*

79. G. Cooney, 'Irish Neolithic landscapes and land use systems: the implications of field systems' in *Rural History*, ii (1991), pp 123–9.

80. W. Groenman–van Watteringe and J. Pals, 'Pollen and seed analysis' in M. O'Kelly, *Newgrange*, pp 219–23; W. Groenman–van Watteringe and J. Pals 'Pollen and seed analysis' in Eogan, *Excavations at Knowth I*, pp 325–8.

81. M. Monk, 'Macroscopic plant remains' in M. O'Kelly, *Newgrange*, pp 219–23.

82. Collins, 'Plant remains', pp 295–7.

83. F. McCormick, 'Animal bone analysis from Neolithic and Beaker complexes' in Eogan and Roche, *Excavations at Knowth II*, pp 301–6. It is difficult to distinguish sheep and goat from one another in the faunal record.

84. Eogan, 'Townleyhall', pp 38–9.

85. *Ibid.*, p. 42.

86. Cooney, 'Irish Neolithic landscapes', pp 123–9.

87. Eogan and Roche, *Excavations at Knowth II*, p. 88.

88. *Ibid.*, pp 51–71.

89. Cooney and Grogan, *Irish prehistory*, p. 48.

90. Eogan and Roche, *Excavations at Knowth II*, p. 52.

91. F. Dillon, 'Lithic assemblage' in Eogan and Roche, *Excavations at Knowth II*, p. 81.

92. G. Liversage, 'A neolithic site at Townleyhall, county Louth' in *R.S.A.I. Jn.*, xc (1960), pp 49–60; Eogan 'Townleyhall', pp 40–64.

93. M. O'Kelly, *Newgrange*, pp 76–7.

94. C. Mount, 'Aspects of ritual deposition in the Late Neolithic and Beaker periods at Newgrange, county Meath' in *Proceedings of the Prehistoric Society* (lx) (1994), pp 433–43.

95. G. Eogan and H. Roche, 'A Grooved Ware wooden structure at Knowth, Boyne Valley, Ireland' in *Antiquity*, lxviii (1994), pp 322–30.

96. D. Sweetman, 'A Late Neolithic/Early Bronze Age pit circle at Newgrange, county Meath' in *R.I.A. Proc.*, C, lxxxv (1985), pp 195–221; D. Sweetman, 'Excavations of a Late Neolithic/Early Bronze Age site at Newgrange, county Meath' in *R.I.A. Proc.*, C, lxxxvii (1987), pp 283–98.

97. T. Condit, 'The Newgrange cursus and the theatre of ritual' in *Brú na Bóinne,* supplement to *Arch. Ir.*, xi (1997), pp 26–7.

98. G. Stout, 'Embanked enclosures of the Boyne region' in *R.I.A. Proc.*, C, xci (1991), pp 245–85.

99. The historiography of this monument type can be traced in the following papers: S. Ó Ríordáin, *Antiquities of the Irish countryside* (London, 1953), pp 21, 93; G. Wainwright, 'A review of henges in the light of recent research' in *Proceedings of the Prehistoric Society*, xxxv (1969), pp 112–33, see pp 114–16; H. Burl, 'Henges: internal features and regional groups' in *Archaeological Journal*, cxxvi (1969), pp 1–26, see pp 10, 17–18; R. Hicks, 'Some henges and hengiform earthworks in Ireland: form, distribution, astronomical correlations and associated mythology' (unpublished PhD thesis, University of Pennsylvania, 1975). For an assessment of the Irish henges in their 'Irish Sea' context, see T. Clare, 'Towards a re–appraisal of henge monuments' in *Proceedings of the Prehistoric Society*, lii (1986), pp 281–316, see pp 287, 291; T. Clare, 'Towards a re–appraisal of henge monuments: origins, evolution and hierarchies' in *Proceedings of the Prehistoric Society*, liii (1987), pp 457–77, see pp 468–9. See also A. Harding and G. Lee, *Henge monuments and related sites of Great Britain* (Oxford, 1987); G. Wainwright, *The henge monuments* (London, 1989), p. 14.

100. D. Sweetman, 'An earthen enclosure at Monknewtown, Slane, county Meath' in *R.I.A. Proc., C,* lxxvi (1976), pp 25–72, see pp 26–7, fig. 1.

101. CUCAP AYM 70.

102. Sweetman, 'Earthen enclosure at Monknewtown', pp 25–72.

103. Sweetman, 'Pit circle at Newgrange', pp 195–221.

104. *Ibid.,* appendix I, pp 219–20.

105. G. Stout, 'Embanked enclosures', p. 252.

106. Sweetman, 'Pit circle at Newgrange', p. 212.

107. *Ibid.,* pp 283–98.

108. Eogan and Roche, *Excavations at Knowth II,* pp 101–222.

109. F. Prendergast, 'New data on Newgrange' in *Technology Ireland,* xxii (1991), pp 22–5; Prendergast, 'Shadow casting phenomena at Newgrange', pp 9–18.

110. M. O'Kelly, *Newgrange,* pp 79–84.

111. Sweetman, 'Pit circle at Newgrange', pp 208–9.

112. Lehane, 'The flint work' in M. O'Kelly, Cleary and Lehane, *Newgrange, county Meath,* pp 118–67.

113. Dillon, 'Lithic assemblage' in Eogan and Roche, *Excavations at Knowth II,* p. 162.

114. M. O'Kelly and C. Shell, 'Some objects and a bronze axe from Newgrange, county Meath' in M. Ryan (ed.), *Origins of metallurgy in Atlantic Europe* (Dublin 1979), pp 127–44.

115. G. Stout, 'Embanked enclosures', pp 252–3.

116. R. Cleary, 'The ceramic assemblage' in M. O'Kelly, Cleary and Lehane, *Newgrange, county Meath,* pp 58–117, see p. 62.

117. *Ibid.*

118. Cooney, 'Irish Neolithic landscapes', pp 123–9.

119. Mc Cormick, 'Animal bone analysis' in Eogan and Roche, *Excavations at Knowth II,* pp 301–6.

120. F. McCormick, 'appendix I' in Sweetman, 'Pit circle at Newgrange', pp 219–20.

121. Collins, 'Plant remains', pp 295–7.

122. Groenman–van Waateringe, 'Pollen and seed analyses' in Eogan, *Excavations at Knowth I,* pp 325–9.

123. M. O'Kelly, Cleary and Lehane, *Newgrange, county Meath,* pp 1–2.

124. T. Darvill, *Prehistoric Britain* (London, 1987), pp 75–107.

125. G. Eogan, 'The M1 motorway and its archaeology: Introduction' in *Ríocht na Midhe,* xiii (2002), pp 1–6.

126. T. Bolger, 'Three sites on the M1 motorway at Rathmullan, Co. Meath' in *Ríocht na Midhe,* xiii (2002), pp 8–17.

NEWGRANGE PASSAGE TOMB

1. Lhywd's Irish notes were destroyed by fire at a bookbinders in London but much detail is contained in several letters written by him at the time. Copies of these letters, including his detailed drawing of the chamber, are held at Trinity College Dublin, Ms. 883 ff 10, ff 285–6; Ms 888/2 ff 312–3. Further letters are published in R. Gunther, *Life and letters of Edward Lhwyd* (Oxford, 1945), pp 421–3, 429. See also J. Campbell, 'The tour of Edward Lhwyd in Ireland in 1699 and 1700' in *Celtica,* v (1960–3), pp 218–28.

2. Gunther, *Edward Lhwyd,* pp 421–3.

3. E. Ledwich, *Antiquities of Ireland* (2nd ed., London, 1804).

4. R.C. Hoare, *A journal of a tour in Ireland in AD 1806* (London, 1807).

5. G. Coffey, *New Grange (Brugh na Bóinne) and other incised tumuli in Ireland* (Dublin, 1912).

6. T. Molyneaux, 'A discourse concerning the Danish mounts, forts and towers in Ireland' in G. Boate (ed.), *A natural history of Ireland* (London, 1725), p. 206.

7. T. Pownall, 'A description of the sepulchral monument at Newgrange, near Drogheda, in the county of Meath, in Ireland' in *Archaeologia,* ii (1773), pp 236–75.

8. C. Vallancey, *Collectanea de rebus Hibernicus* (Dublin, 1786), vol. iv.

KNOWTH PASSAGE TOMB

1. Thomas Molyneaux, 'A discourse concerning the Danish mounts, forts and towers in Ireland' in G. Boate (ed.), *A natural history of Ireland* (London, 1725).

2. W.F. Wakeman, *Archaeologia Hibernica: A handbook of Irish antiquities* (3rd ed., Dublin, 1891); W. Wilde, *The beauties of the Boyne and Blackwater* (Dublin, 1849).

3. W. Wilde, *The Beauties of the Boyne and its tributary, the Blackwater* (Dublin, 1849), p. 189

4. G. Coffey, *New Grange (Brugh na Bóinne) and other incised tumuli in Ireland* (Dublin, 1912).

5. Molyneaux, 'A discourse'.

6. W.F. Wakeman, *Archaeologia Hibernica: A handbook of Irish Antiquities* (Dublin, 1848).

7. R.A.S. Macalister, 'A preliminary report on the excavation of Knowth' in *R.I.A. Proc.,* il (1943), C, pp 131–66.

DOWTH PASSAGE TOMB

1. An invaluable and comprehensive account of the history and archaeology of Dowth passage tomb is contained in M. O'Kelly and C. O'Kelly, 'The tumulus of Dowth, county Meath' in *R.I.A. Proc,* lxxxiii (1983), C, pp 136–90.

2. T. Pownall, 'A description of the sepulchral monuments at Newgrange' in *Archaeologia,* ii (1773), pp 236–75.

3. G. Petrie, 'An essay on military architecture in Ireland previous to the English invasion (with notes and explanatory appendix by D.J.S. O'Malley' in *R.I.A. Proc.,* lxxii (1972), C, pp 219–69.

4. S. Lewis, *A topographical dictionary of Ireland* (2 vols., Dublin, 1837).

5. W.F. Wakeman, *Archaeologia Hibernica: A handbook of Irish antiquities* (Dublin, 1848), p. 31.

6. O'Kelly and O'Kelly, 'Dowth', pp 141–4.

7. *Ibid.,* pp 144–7.

NEWGRANGE PIT CIRCLE

1. P.D. Sweetman, 'A Late Neolithic/Early Bronze Age pit circle at Newgrange, county Meath' in *R.I.A. Proc., C,* lxxxv (1985), pp 195–221; P.D. Sweetman, 'Excavations of a Late Neolithic/Early Bronze Age site at Newgrange, county Meath' in *R.I.A. Proc.,* lxxxvii (1987), C, pp 283–98.

2. M. O'Kelly, *Newgrange: archaeology art and legend* (2nd ed., London, 1994), p. 67.

MONKNEWTOWN HENGE

1. P.D. Sweetman, 'An earthen enclosure at Monknewtown, Slane, county Meath' in *R.I.A. Proc.,* lxxvi (1976), C, pp 25–72.

HEROES AND SAINTS: THE EARLY HISTORIC LANDSCAPE

1. W. Hennessy and B. McCarthy (ed. and trans.) *Annala Uladh, Annals of Ulster, otherwise, Annala Senait, Annals of Senat: A chronicle of Irish Affairs from AD 431 to AD 1540* (4 vols, Dublin, 1887–1901); S. MacAirt and G. Mac Niocaill, *The Annals of Ulster (to AD 1131)* (Dublin, 1983). Dates from these two sources are prefixed by AU; J. O'Donovan, *Annala Riogachta Eireann. Annals of the kingdom of Ireland by the Four Masters from the earliest period to the year 1616* (seven vols, Dublin, 1848–51). Dates from this source are prefixed by AFM.

2. AFM 5160 – years after creation.

3. D. Weir, 'A palynological study of landscape and agricultural development in county Louth from the second millennium BC to the first millennium AD' in *Discovery Programme project results 2* (Dublin, 1995), pp 77–126.

4. *Ibid.,* p. 106; G. Stout and M. Stout, 'Early landscapes: from prehistory to plantation' in F. Aalen, K. Whelan and M. Stout (ed.), *Atlas of the Irish rural landscape* (Cork, 1997), pp 31–63, see p. 45, fig. 39.

5. Weir, 'Palynological study', p. 108.

6. S. Caulfield, 'The beehive quern in Ireland' in *R.S.A.I. Jn.,* cvii (1977), pp 104–38.

7. E. Kelly, 'Two quernstones from county Meath' in *Ríocht na Midhe,* vii (1984), pp 104 –111, see p. 104.

8. C. Bowen, 'An historical inventory of the Dind–shenchas' in *Studia Celtica,* x–xi (1975–6), pp 113–37; E. Bhreathnach, *Tara: a select bibliography* (Dublin, 1995), p. 27.

9. C. Newman, *Tara: an archaeological survey* (Dublin, 1997), p. 2; Bhreathnach, *Tara,* p. 27.

10. E. Hickey, 'The house of Cleitech' in *Ríocht na Midhe,* iii (1965), pp 181–5; M. O'Kelly, F. Lynch and C. O'Kelly, 'Three passage graves at Newgrange, county Meath' in *R.I.A. Proc., C,* lxxviii (1978), pp 249–352, see p. 332.

11. E. Gwynn (ed. and trans.), *The Metrical Dindshenchas, part iv* (Dublin, 1924), pp 11–17.

12. *Ibid.,* pp 18–25.

13. *Ibid.,* p. 10–11.

14. Quoted in G. Petrie, *The ecclesiastical architecture of Ireland anterior to the Anglo–Norman period* (Dublin, 1845), pp 102–3.

15. Gwynn, *Metrical Dindshenchas,* pp 10–11. It is necessary to rely on Gwynn's Victorian–style translation as no more recent edition exists.

16. *Ibid.,* pp 12–15.

17. *Ibid.,* pp 18–19.

18. Royal Irish Academy, *Dictionary of the Irish language* (Dublin, 1913–76).

19. Gwynn, *Metrical Dindshenchas,* p. 11.

20. S. O'Grady (ed. and trans.), *Silva Gaedelica, (i.–xxxi): A collection of tales in Irish with extracts illustrating persons and places* (London, 1892), p. 103.

21. Quoted in O'Donovan, *Annals of the Four Masters,* i, p. 22.

22. Gwynn, *Metrical Dindshenchas,* pp 18–19.

23. *Ibid.,* pp 20–21.

24. *Ibid.,* pp 12–15; Petrie, *Ecclesiastical architecture,* p. 100.

25. J. Laverty, 'Miscellanea: Newgrange still called by its ancient name, Brugh na Bóinne' in *R.S.A.I. Jn.,* xxii (1892), p. 430; T. Westropp, 'Ancient place–names, Brugh of the Boyne and others' in *R.S.A.I. Jn.,* xxxvi (1906), pp 82–3.

26. W. Wilde, *The beauties of the Boyne and Blackwater* (Dublin, 1847), p. 184.

27. Gwynn, *Metrical Dindshenchas,* pp 42–7.

28. T. Ó Cathasaigh, 'The Eponym of Cnogba' in *Eigse,* v (1989–90), pp 27–38.

29. Gwynn, *Metrical Dindshenchas,* pp 42–7, line 34.

30. *Ibid.,* pp 40–1.

31. *Ibid.,* pp 272–3.

32. *Ibid.,* p. 42; M. O'Kelly and C. O'Kelly, 'The tumulus of Dowth, county Meath' in *R.I.A. Proc., C,* lxxxiii (1983), pp 136–90, see pp 143–7.

33. Gwynn, *Metrical Dindshenchas,* pp 42–7.

34. *Ibid.,* p. 200.

35. B. Raftery, *Pagan Celtic Ireland* (2nd ed., London, 1997), pp 112–13.

36. *Ibid.,* p. 113.

37. Hickey, 'The house of Cleitech'.

38. G. Eogan, 'Iron Age and Early Christian settlement' in V. Markotic (ed.), *Ancient Europe and the Mediterranean: studies in honour of Hugh Hencken* (Warminster, Wiltshire, 1977), pp 69–76; G. Eogan, 'The archaeology of Brugh na Bóinne during the early centuries AD' in *Seanchas Ard Mhacha,* v (1990), pp 20–34, see pp 24–5.

39. G. Eogan, 'Prehistoric and early historic culture change at Brugh na Bóinne' in *R.I.A. Proc., C,* xci (1991), pp 105–32, see p. 118.

40. Raftery, *Pagan Celtic Ireland,* pp 73–4.

41. E. Hogan (ed. and trans.), *Cath Ruis na Rig for Boinn,* (Dublin, 1892), p. 33.

43. Raftery, *Pagan Celtic Ireland*, p. 196, fig. 121; G. Eogan, 'Report on the excavations of some passage graves, unprotected inhumation burials and a settlement site at Knowth, county Meath' in *R.I.A. Proc.*, C, lxxiv (1974), pp 2–112, see p. 70; Eogan, 'Brugh na Bóinne', p. 24.

44. G. Eogan, 'Excavations at Knowth, county Meath' in *R.I.A. Proc.*, C, lxvi (1966), pp 199–382, see 365–73; Eogan, 'Some passage graves', pp 68–87.

45. Raftery, *Pagan Celtic Ireland*, p. 195.

46. Eogan, 'Some passage graves', pp 73–8; Raftery, *Pagan Celtic Ireland*, p. 157.

47. Hogan, *Cath Ruis na Rig for Boinn*, p. xiii.

48. *Ibid.*, p. xiii.

49. For all quotes see *ibid.*, p. 35.

50. J. O'Donovan (ed. and trans.), *The banquet of Dun na n–Gedh: and The battle of Magh Rath: an ancient historical tale now first published from a manuscript in the Library of Trinity College, Dublin* (Dublin, 1842); C. Marstrander, 'A new version of the Battle of Mag Rath' in *Ériú*, v (1911), pp 226–9. O'Donovan believed this referred to the embanked enclosure at Dowth. However, I have shown (chapter 3) that this is a prehistoric ceremonial enclosure, see W. Wilde, *The beauties of the Boyne and Blackwater* (Dublin, 1849), p. 211.

51. Quoted in Raftery, *Pagan Celtic Ireland*, p. 204.

52. J. Bateson, 'Roman material from Ireland: a re–consideration' in *R.I.A. Proc.*, C, lxxv (1973), pp 21–97, see p. 36.

53. G. Orpen, 'Ptolemy's map of Ireland' in *R.S.A.I. Jn.*, xxiv (1894), pp 115–28; J. Andrews, *Shapes of Ireland* (Dublin, 1997), pp 26–9.

54. A. Brindley and J. Lanting, 'A Roman boat in Ireland' in *Arch. Ir.*, iv, (1990), pp 10–11; Raftery, *Pagan Celtic Ireland*, pp 208–9.

55. Bateson, 'Roman material', p. 80; Eogan, 'Brugh na Bóinne', p. 24.

56. R. Carson and C. O'Kelly, 'A catalogue of the Roman coins from Newgrange, county Meath' in *R.I.A. Proc.*, C, lxxvii (1977), pp 35–55, see p. 45.

57. *Ibid.*

58. C. Thomas, *Christianity in Roman Britain to AD 500* (London, 1982), p. 297.

59. Raftery, *Pagan Celtic Ireland*, pp 47.

60. C. Swift, 'Pagan monuments and Christian legal centres in early Meath' in *Riocht na Midhe*, ix (1996), pp 1–26, see pp 6–7.

61. S. Piggott, *The West Kennet Long Barrow* (London, 1962), pp 55–6.

62. M. O'Kelly, *Newgrange: archaeology, art and legend* (2nd ed., London, 1994), p. 47.

63. This interpretation is at odds with views expressed in C. Ó Lochlainn, 'Roadways in ancient Ireland' in J. Ryan (ed.), *Essays and studies presented to Professor Eoin Mac Néill* (Dublin, 1940), pp 465–74. Ó Lochlainn, influenced by the modern road system, incorrectly placed Dublin at the focal point of the road network; see G. Stout and M. Stout, 'Patterns in the past: county Dublin 5000BC–1000AD' in F. Aalen and K. Whelan (ed.), *Dublin from prehistory to present – studies in honour of J.H. Andrews* (Dublin, 1992), pp 5–25, see p. 15.

64. M. Dobbs, 'Some ancient placenames' in *R.S.A.I. Jn.*, lvi (1926), pp 106–18, see p. 108.

65. Eogan, 'Some passage graves', p. 76.

66. L. Bieler, *The Patrician texts in the book of Armagh* (Dublin, 1979).

67. *Ibid.*, p. 85.

68. Swift, 'Pagan monuments', p. 11.

69. Eogan, 'Brugh na Bóinne', pp 9–13.

70. Eogan, 'Brugh na Bóinne', p. 119.

71. Less tenable is Swift's suggestion that the site could be near Trim. Trim is more than a day's walk west of the Colpe. Swift also incorrectly locates *Lind Feic* near Navan rather than Rossnaree (see chapter 4Bv) undermining her claims for this far western location; see Swift, 'Pagan monuments', pp 9–13.

72. But not necessarily Knowth as was rather parochially suggested in Eogan, 'Brugh na Bóinne', p. 119.

73. Petrie, *Ecclesiastical architecture*, p. 103.

74. Gwynn, *Metrical Dindshenchas*, p. 447.

75. 'Repose of Erc, Bishop of Slane'.

76. One of these shrines was recently excavated on Illaunloughan, county Kerry. It covered two small stone–lined, stone–covered cists, which contained human long bones exhumed from a burial; see J. White–Marshall and C. Walsh, 'Illaunloughan: life and death on a small early monastic site' in *Arch. Ir.*, viii (1994), pp 24–8.

77. AFM 784 'Feadach, son of Cormac… of Slaine died'; AU 814 AD 'Son of Maenach, steward of Slane, and Gormgal, son of Niall son of Fergal, who died'. Its international contacts are highlighted in AU 824 'Colman, son of Ailill, abbot of Slaine and of other monasteries in France and Ireland, died', AFM 847 'Onchu, bishop and anchorite of Slaine… Robhartach, son of Colgan, Abbot of Slane… died', AFM 854 'Sodhomna, Bishop of Slane, received martyrdom from the Norsemen', AU 869 'The death of Niallan, bishop of Slane', AU 938 'Fedach, superior of Slane, died', AU 948 'Colman, son of Mael Patraic, superior of Slane was taken prisoner by the foreigners and died on their hands', AU 950 'The bell house of Slaine was burned by the foreigners of Ath Cliath'. The founder's episcopal staff, and the best of all bells, the lector of Caenchair, and a large number with him, were all burned', AU 956 'Mael Patraic, son of Cu Bretan, superior of Slane, died', AU 1028 'The wooden church of Slane fell down', AFM 1170 'Slane was burned'.

78. AFM 847.

79. P. Harbison, 'A shaft–fragment from Slane, county Meath, and other recent high cross discoveries' in C. Manning (ed.), *Dublin and beyond the Pale* (Dublin, 1998), pp 173–6.

80. T. Westropp, 'Slane in Bregia, county Meath: its friary and hermitage' in *R.S.A.I. Jn.*, xxxiii (1901), pp 405–30.

81. W. O'Sullivan, 'Medieval Meath manuscripts' in *Riocht na Midhe*, vii (1985–6), pp 3–21, see p. 17; T.C.D. Ms. 786, f. 23V.

82. C. Plummer, *Vitae Sanctorum Hiberniae* (Oxford, 1910), p. cxxxvi.

83. Irish Tourist Association records in Dúchas.

84. Wilde, *Boyne and Blackwater*, p. 210; this stone–lined well is accessed through a metal grate.

85. Ordnance Survey Letters, county Meath (unpublished typescript, Royal Irish Academy, Dublin, 1836), p. 137. This reference indicates bilingualism in the Bend of the Boyne at this date.

86. J. Raftery, 'Long stone cists of the Early Iron Age' in *R.I.A. Proc.*, C, xlvi (1941), pp 299–315, see p. 303.

87. Letters, Meath, pp 93, 183.

88. Anon, 'Early silver ear ring found at Rossnaree' in *County Louth Archaeological and Historical Society Journal*, x (1942), p. 157; Pers. comm. Raghnaill Ó Floinn, National Museum of Ireland.

89. W. Stokes (ed. and trans.), *Martyrology of Oengus, the Culdee* (London, 1905).

90. F. Byrne, *Irish kings and high kings* (London, 1987), p. 87.

91. *Ibid.*, p. 395.

92. F. Byrne, 'Historical note on Cnogba (Knowth)' in G. Eogan, 'Excavations at Knowth, county Meath, 1962–5' in *R.I.A. Proc.*, lxvi (1967), C, pp 383–400, see p. 383.

93. *Ibid.*

94. M. Stout, *The Irish ringfort* (Dublin, 1997).

95. Lord Netterville to Kelly 1750, R.D., 142, p. 297, 95575.

96. G. Stout, *Archaeological survey of the barony of Ikerrin* (Roscrea, 1984), pp 16–17.

97. M. Moore (comp.), *Archaeological inventory of county Meath* (Dublin, 1987), pp 56–93.

98. Eogan, 'Brugh na Bóinne', p. 120.

99. *Ibid.*

100. Eogan, 'Some passage graves', pp 102–3.

101. *Ibid.*, pp 88, 103, 110.

102. *Ibid.*, p. 110.

103. F. McCormick, 'Exchange of livestock in Early Christian Ireland, AD 450–1150' in *Anthropozoological Journal*, xvi (1992), pp 31–6, p. 31.

104. Eogan, 'Some passage graves', p. 88.

105. E. Hickey and E. Rynne, 'Two souterrains on the lower slopes of Tara' in *Journal of the Kildare Archaeological Society*, xiii (1953), pp 220–1. I am grateful to Dr Mark Clinton for this reference and information regarding souterrains in Ireland.

106. M. Gowen, 'Excavation of two souterrain complexes at Marshes Upper, Dundalk, county Louth' in *R.I.A. Proc.*, C, xcii (1992), pp 55–120.

107. M. Clinton, 'Two recently discovered souterrains in county Meath' in *Riocht na Midhe*, ix (1996), pp 30–3.

108. T. Reid, *Travel in Ireland in the year 1822* (London, 1823), pp 7–8; Meath SMR 19:48.

109. Moore (comp.), *Archaeological inventory Meath*, p. 53; Meath SMR 20:7.

110. *Ibid.*, p. 53; Meath SMR 20:4.

111. *Irish Times*, 3 August 1991, p. 1.

112. *Lusca* = Underground chamber, crypt, vault; see T. De Bhaldraithe (ed.), *Foclóir Gaeilge–Béarla* (Dublin, 1977), p. 812.

113. A. Lucas, 'Souterrains: the literary evidence' in *Bealoideas*, xxxix–xliv (1971–3), pp 39–41.

114. V. Buckley, 'Meath souterrains: some thoughts on Early Christian distribution patterns' in *Riocht na Midhe*, viii (1988–9), pp 64–7, see p. 65.

115. M. Clinton, 'Structural aspects of souterrain in Ireland' (unpublished PhD thesis, NUI Galway, 1998), pp 246–8. M. Clinton, *The souterrains of Ireland* (Dublin, 2001), see p. 64.

116. Byrne, 'Historical note on Cnogba', p. 398.

117. *Ibid.*, p. 389.

118. This may account for the presence of five Anglo–Saxon pennies from Knowth which can be attributed to contact with Viking Dublin; see Eogan, 'Brugh na Bóinne', p. 121.

MONKS AND KNIGHTS: THE MEDIEVAL LANDSCAPE

1. R. Stalley, *The Cistercian monasteries of Ireland* (London, 1987), pp 7–16.

2. Fr Colmcille, 'Seven documents from the old abbey of Mellifont' in *County Louth Archaeological and Historical Journal*, xiii (1953), pp 35–67, see p. 39.

3. F. Byrne, *Irish kings and high kings* (London, 1987), p. 89; P. Ó Riain, 'Boundary association in Early Irish society' in *Studia Celtica*, vii (1972), pp 12–29.

4. B. Smith, *Colonisation and conquest in medieval Ireland: the English in Louth 1170–1330* (Cambridge, 1999), p. 20.

5. Fr Colmcille, *The story of Mellifont* (Dublin, 1958), p. 38.

6. Colmcille, 'Seven documents', p. 41.

7. *Ibid.*, pp 36–7.

8. Colmcille, *Mellifont*, p. 105.

9. *Ibid.*, p. 171.

10. *Calendar of Irish patent rolls of James 1* (Dublin, 1966); see patent roll 10 James 1, part 2, p. 130.

11. C. Platt, *The monastic grange in medieval England* (London, 1969), p. 15.

12. Stalley, *Cistercian monasteries*, pp 45–6.

13. Colmcille, 'Seven documents', p. 41.

14. G. Eogan, *Knowth: 21 years on* (Guide to exhibition, NUI Dublin, 1984), pp 20–1.

15. Smith, *Colonisation and conquest*, p. 108.

16. C. Ellison, 'Bishop Dopping's Visitation Book 1682–1685' in *Riocht na Midhe*, v (1973), p. 6.

17 Stalley, *Cistercian monasteries*, p. 176.

18. Colmcille, *Mellifont*, p. xxviii.

19. M. O'Kelly, 'Plough pebbles from the Boyne Valley' in C. Ó Danachair (ed.), *Folk and farm: essays in honour of A.T. Lucas* (Dublin 1976), pp 165–75, see p. 169, fig. 18.

20. W. Horn and E. Born, *The barns of the abbey of Beaulieu at its granges of Great Coxwell and Beaulieu–St. Leonards* (Berkeley, 1965).

21. H. Sweetman, *Calendar of documents relating to Ireland 1171–1251* (Dublin, 1875), p. 189, 11 April 1245.

22. L. Van Wijngaarden–Bakker, 'The animal bones from the Beaker settlement at Newgrange, county Meath: First report' in *R.I.A. Proc.,* lxxiv (1974), pp 313–83, see pp 367–8.

23. G. Carville, 'The Cistercians in Ireland and their economy: 1142–1541' (unpublished MA thesis, The Queens University of Belfast, 1969), p. 25; Colmcille, *Mellifont,* pp xxvii–xxix.

24. N. Brady, 'The plough in early historic and Medieval Ireland' (unpublished MA thesis, NUI Dublin, 1986).

25. Fr Colmcille, 'Seven documents', pp 57–61.

26. N.B. White (ed.), *Extents of Irish monastic possessions, 1540–1541, from manuscripts in the Public Record Office, London* (London, 1943).

27. *Ibid.*

28. *Ibid.,* p. 218.

29. *Ibid.*

30. Colmcille 'Seven documents', pp 37, 41; White (ed), *Extents,* Rossnaree, p. 258; Stalleen. p. 253; Browe's mill, p. 257.

31. *Ibid.,* pp 216–19: this may be the same mill at Broe which appears on a Caldwell estate map from 1760; only the mill race is visible on the ground today. N.A. 1095/2/56, Caldwell Papers. 'A map of that part of Newgrange wasted and lost by the navigation with a draft of the old and new canal made near the river Boyne in the Barony of Slane and County Meath being part of the estate of Andrew Caldwell Esq. taken and surveyed by order and appointment of Mr. Robert Berrill the 25th day of January 1781. Patrick Frain.'

32. A. Lucas, 'The horizontal mill in Ireland' in *R.S.A.I. Jn.,* vol. lxxxiii (1953), pp 1–36.

33. G. Stout, 'Fishing at Brú na Bóinne' in *Brú na Bóinne;* supplement to *Arch. Ir.,* xi (1997), pp 34–5.

34. *C.D.I.* 1203; Colmcille 'Seven documents' pp 36–7.

35. *Ibid.,* pp 46–7.

36. A. Went, 'Material for a history of the fisheries of the river Boyne' in *County Louth Archaeological and Historical Journal,* xiii (1953), pp 18–33, see p. 22.

37. White (ed.), *Extents,* pp 217–18.

38. Colmcille, *Mellifont,* p. 253.

39. Went, 'The fisheries', pp 30–3.

40. *Ibid.*

41. Pers. comm. Pauline Fulham, Stalleen.

42. Went, 'The fisheries', p. 39.

43. White (ed.), *Extents,* p. 253.

44. Colmcille, *Mellifont,* p. xxxiii.

45. Colmcille, 'Seven documents', pp 58, 61; Colmcille, *Mellifont,* p. 149.

46. *Ibid.,* pp xxxiv.

47. J. Hornell, *British coracles and Irish curraghs* (London, 1938), pp 154–61.

48. T. Jones Hughes, *'Town* and *Baile* in Irish place–names' in N. Stephens and R. Glasscock (ed.), *Irish geographical studies in honour of E. Estyn Evans* (Belfast, 1970), pp 244–58.

49. W. Wilde, *The beauties of the Boyne and Blackwater* (2nd ed., Dublin, 1850), p. 243.

50. C. Ellison, 'Bishop Dopping's visitations: 1682–85' in *Riocht na Midhe,* iv (1971) pp 28–39, see pp 36–7.

51. M. Moore (comp.), *The archaeological inventory of county Meath* (Dublin, 1987), p. 144.

52. White (ed.), *Extents,* Tullyallen, Monknewtown, Donore and Knockcommon, p. 219; Dowth, p. 316.

53. C. Elrington, *The whole works of Most Rev. James Ussher, Lord Archbishop and Primate of Ireland, i* (Dublin, 1864), p. 57.

54. N.A., Tithe Applotment Books: parish of Knockcommon, f.17.

55. Moore (comp.), *Meath,* p. 144.

56. J. Mills and J. Mc Enery (ed.), *Calendar of the Gormanston Register* (Dublin, 1916), p. 177.

57. *Ibid.,* p. 140.

58. H. Roe, *The medieval fonts of Meath* (Dublin, 1968), pp 124–5.

59. H. Carey, 'The kingdom and lordship of Meath: 1100–c.1215' (unpublished MLitt thesis, Trinity College Dublin, 1998).

60. A. Scott and F. Martin (ed. and trans.), *Expugnatio Hibernica; the conquest of Ireland by Giraldus Cambrensis* (Dublin, 1978), pp 191, 195; A. Otway–Ruthven, *A history of medieval Ireland* (2nd ed., New York, 1980), p. 63.

61. Moore (comp.), *Meath,* pp 156–61; Dúchas, 'Recorded monuments and places, county Westmeath' (Dublin, 1996); Graham put the figure at ninety–four, eighty–four surviving mottes and ten destroyed mottes. See B. Graham, 'The mottes of the Norman Liberty of Meath' in H. Murtagh (ed.), *Irish Midland Studies* (Athlone, 1980), pp 39–56.

62. *Ibid.*

63. B. Graham, 'Anglo–Norman settlement in county Meath' in *R.I.A. Proc.,* C, lxxv (1975), pp 223–49, see p. 230.

64. Graham, 'Mottes of Meath', p. 45.

65. Graham, 'Anglo–Norman settlement', p. 225.

66. *Misc. Ir. Annals,* 1176 recte 1175. This entry was placed under the year 1176 but is accompanied by a reference to the death of Magnus Ua Maelechlainn which is known to have taken place in 1175.

67. Carey, *Meath,* p. 77.

68. G. Orpen (ed. and trans.), *The song of Dermot and the Earl* (Oxford, 1892); Graham, 'Anglo–Norman settlement', pp 223–49.

69. J. Dimock (ed. and trans.), *Expugnatio Hibernica Giraldi Cambrensis Opera, v* (Rolls Series, Dublin, 1967), p. 139.

70. *Misc. Ir. Annals,* Ann. Tig., 1175, see also A.U. 1176.

71. *Misc. Ir. Annals,* Ann. Tig. 1176.

72. B. Graham, 'Medieval settlements in county Meath' in *Riocht na Midhe,* v (1974), pp 40–59, see pp 42–3; Graham, 'Mottes of the Norman Liberty of Meath', p. 48.

73. Graham, 'Medieval settlements in county Meath', p. 46. This motte was cleared away for gravel in the eighteenth century.

74. *Ibid.,* p. 51.

76. J. D'Alton, *History of Drogheda* (Dublin, 1844), ii, p. 432.

77. M. O'Kelly and C. O'Kelly, 'The tumulus of Dowth, county Meath' in *R.I.A. Proc.,* C, lxxxiii (1983), pp 135–90; see plate ii.

78. *Ibid.,* p. 149.

79. Graham, 'Mottes of Meath', p. 54.

80. Smith, *Colonisation and conquest,* p. 40.

81. *Ibid.,* p. 38.

82. B. Smith, 'The de Pitchford family in thirteenth–century Ireland' in *Studia Hibernica,* xxvii (1993) pp 29–43.

83. *C.D.I.,* 1226, no.1440, p. 217; no. 283, p. 42; 1234, no. 2208, p. 327.

84. *C.D.I.,* 1253, no. 179, p. 27.

85. Smith, *Colonisation and conquest,* p. 42.

86. *C.D.I.,* 1244, no. 2724, p. 406.

87. *Ibid.,* 1253, no. 283.

88. E. Brooks (ed.), *The Irish cartularies of Llanthony Prima and Secunda* (Dublin, 1953), p. 238.

89. C.U.C.A.P. AHJ 76–9; AJO 101, 103; AYM 85.

90. Dúchas, SMR file 20:18.

91. Moore (comp.), *Meath,* p. 170.

92. Smith, *Colonisation and conquest,* p. 42.

93. *C.D.I.,* 1253, no. 179; for Dunethe [Dowth] see Otway–Ruthven, *Medieval Ireland,* p. 114.

94. F. Galway, 'Meath towerhouses' in *Riocht na Midhe,* vii (1985–6), pp 28–200, see p. 81.

95. E. Hickey, *Skryne and the early Normans* (Dublin, 1994), pp 177–18, 212–3. It has been stated that John Netterville was resident at Dowth in the mid–thirteenth century but historical sources have never been provided to corroborate this statement; T. Sadleir, *Georgian mansions in Ireland* (Dublin, 1915).

96. *Chancery of Judiciary Rolls of Ireland* (London, 1914), 33 Edward I, Membrane 17d.

97. D'Alton, *Drogheda,* p. 432.

98. *Ibid.,* p. 433.

99. W. O'Sullivan, 'Medieval Meath manuscripts' in *Riocht na Midhe,* vii (1985–86), pp 3–21, see pp 5, 17.

100. B. Balfour, 'Round tower at Proudfootstown' in *R.S.A.I. Jn.,* xxi (1890), pp 247–8. For further work on rural medieval settlement see: K. O'Conor, *The archaeology of medieval rural settlement in rural Ireland* (Dublin, 1998), p. 44; D. Hall, M. Hennessy and T. O'Keefe, 'Medieval agriculture and settlement in Oughterard and Castlewarden, county Kildare' in *Ir. Geog.,* xviii (1985), pp 16–25.

101. White (ed.), *Extents.*

102. Brooks (ed.), *Llanthony Prima and Secunda;* E. Brooks, 'Fourteenth–century monastic estates in Meath' in *R.S.A.I. Jn.,* lxxxiii (1953), pp 140–9.

103. Brooks (ed.), *Llanthony Prima and Secunda,* p. 231.

104. *Ibid.,* p. 299; This is from Platt's partial translation, see Platt, *Monastic grange,* p. 35.

105. Roe, *Medieval fonts,* pp 124–5.

106. Brooks (ed.), *Llanthony Prima and Secunda,* pp 111, 238.

107. D'Alton, *Drogheda,* p. 432.

108. *Ibid.,* p. 433.

109. *Ibid.,* pp 297–8.

110. *Ibid.,* p. 297.

111. *Ibid.*

112. *Ibid.,* pp. 308–10.

113. O. Davies, I.T.A. Survey, Dúchas, SMR file 20:19; Moore (comp.), *Meath,* p. 134.

114. Brooks (ed.), *Llanthony Prima and Secunda,* p. 300; For partial translation see Brooks, 'Fourteenth–century monastic estates in Meath', p. 146.

115. Brooks (ed.), *Llanthony Prima and Secunda,* pp 116–17.

116. *Ibid.,* p. 296.

117. Moore (comp.), *Meath,* p. 142.

118. *Ibid.,* p. 142.

119. *Ibid.,* p. 296.

120. White (ed.), *Extents.*

121. T. O'Keefe, 'Medieval frontiers and fortifications: the Pale and its evolution' in F. Aalen and K. Whelan (ed.), *Dublin from prehistory to present – studies in honour of J. H. Andrews* (Dublin, 1992), pp 57–77.

122. Colmcille 'Seven documents', pp 57–61.

123. Colmcille, *Mellifont,* p. 198; B. Bradshaw, *The dissolution of the monastic properties of Ireland under Henry VIII* (Cambridge 1974), p. 114.

124. H. O'Sullivan, 'Northern Motorway environmental impact study, Stamullin to Monasterboice: report on cultural and heritage aspects' (unpublished EIS, Louth County Council, no date) pp 12–3.

'BRISEADH NA BÓINNE': BATTLES ON THE BOYNE

1. G. Stout and M. Stout, 'Early landscapes: from prehistory to plantation' in F. Aalen, K. Whelan and M. Stout (ed.), *Atlas of the Irish rural landscape* (Cork, 1997), pp 31–63, see p. 62.

2. In 1660, over 40% of families had Old English names in this region; W. Smyth, 'Society and settlement in seventeenth–century Ireland: the evidence of the "1659 Census"' in W. Smyth and K. Whelan (ed.), *Common ground: essays on the historical geography of Ireland* (Cork,

1988), pp 55–83, see p. 61, fig. 4.2.

3. A. Clarke, 'The colonisation of Ulster and the rebellion of 1641' in T. Moody and F. Martin (ed.) *The course of Irish history* (Cork, 1967), pp 189–203, see p. 198–9.

4. M. Ó Siochrú, *Confederate Ireland 1642–1649: a constitutional and political analysis* (Dublin, 1999), p. 225.

5. J. D'Alton, *The history of Drogheda with its environs and an introductory memoir of the Dublin and Drogheda railway*, ii (1844), p. 224.

6. Clarke, 'Colonisation of Ulster', pp 189–98.

7. H. O'Sullivan, 'Northern Motorway environmental impact study, Stamullin to Monasterboice: report on cultural and heritage aspects' (unpublished EIS, Louth County Council, no date) pp 12–13.

8. Depositions of 1641, Examination of Richard Streete, TCD Ms. 816.F.2.9, pp 24–5. The depositions by witnesses of these events of 1641 pinpoint properties in the lower Boyne Valley where events in the rising took place. These depositions provide vivid accounts of 'treacheries' on the part of the rebels and their supporters among old established families in the Bend of the Boyne. Topographical information is disappointingly slight.

9. TCD Ms. 816.F.2r; Bríd McGrath, 'County Meath from the Depositions' in *Riocht na Midhe*, ix (1994–5), pp 24–41, see p. 30.

10. *Ibid.*, pp 32–2.

11. D'Alton, *Drogheda*, pp 230–2.

12. Depositions 1641, Examination of Thomas Charles, TCD Ms. 816.F.2.9, pp 189–90.

13. D'Alton, *Drogheda*, p. 246.

14. *Ibid.*, p. 251; J. Gilbert, *History of the Irish Confederation and the war in Ireland* (Dublin, 1882), p. 51.

15. N. Barnard, *The whole proceedings of the siege of Drogheda* (London, 1642), p. 71.

16. J. Gilbert, *A contemporary history of affairs in Ireland from 1641–1652, vol. ii, part ii* (Dublin, 1980), p. 248.

17. D'Alton, *Drogheda*, p. 247.

18. C. Ellison, 'Bishop Dopping's Visitation Book 1682–1685' in *Riocht na Midhe*, iv (1971), pp 28–39, see p. 36; C. Ellison, 'Bishop Dopping's Visitation Book 1682–1685' in *Riocht na Midhe*, v (1973), pp 2–11, Slane, p. 4; Dowth, p. 5; Knowth, p. 6; Monknewtown, p. 7.

19. D'Alton, *Drogheda*, p. 254.

20. S. Barnwall, 'Darcys of Plattin, county Meath' in *Ir. Geneal.*, vi (1983), pp 419–22.

21. L. Arnold, *The Restoration land settlement in county Dublin, 1660–1688: a history of the administration of the acts of settlement and explanation* (Dublin, 1993), p. 28; Ó Siochrú, *Confederate Ireland*, pp 222–5.

22. C. Casey and A. Rowan, *The buildings of Ireland: north Leinster* (London, 1993), pp 154–6.

23. D. Murphy, *Cromwell in Ireland: a history of Cromwell's Irish campaign* (Dublin, 1883), p. 84.

24. J. Simms, 'Cromwell at Drogheda' in *Irish Sword*, xi (1974) pp 212–21; T. Reilly, *Cromwell at Drogheda* (Drogheda 1993).

25. Gilbert, *Affairs in Ireland*, pp 248–9; Murphy, *Cromwell*, p. 91.

26. Smyth, 'Evidence of the '1659 Census'', p. 56.

27. *Ibid.*, p. 61, fig. 4.2.

28. S. Pender (ed.), *A census of Ireland circa 1659, with supplementary material from the poll money ordinances (1660–1661)* (Dublin, 1939), pp 471, 480.

29. Gilbert, *Affairs in Ireland*, pp 250–1; Simms, 'Cromwell at Drogheda', pp 212–21.

30. Gilbert, *Affairs in Ireland*, pp 247–8.

31. R. Simington (ed.), *The Civil Survey: county of Meath 1654–56*, v (Dublin, 1940).

32. W. Nolan, *Tracing the past: sources for local studies in the Republic of Ireland* (Dublin, 1982), pp 50–3.

33. Simington (ed.), *Civil Survey: Meath*.

34. *Ibid.*, p. 2.

35. *Ibid.*, p. 342.

36. W. Smyth, 'Exploring the social and cultural geographies of sixteenth and seventeenth–century county Dublin' in F. Aalen and K. Whelan (ed.), *Dublin from prehistory to present – studies in honour of J.H. Andrews* (Dublin, 1992), pp 121–79, see p. 126.

37. *Ibid.*, p. 351.

38. Nolan, *Tracing the past*, pp 53–5.

39. Simington, *Civil Survey: Meath*.

40. *Ibid.*, p. 250.

41. J. Hyland, 'The battle of the Boyne' in *Command Magazine*, xliii (1997), pp 30–46.

42. J. Simms, *A Jacobite narrative of the war in Ireland: 1688–1691* (Shannon, 1971), p. 98. The term 'rubicon' is defined in the Oxford dictionary as a pass or cross; to take the step that commits one to an undertaking. It was the boundary stream of ancient Italy crossed by Hannibal in his famous traverse of the Alps, and represented the point of no return.

43. D. O'Carroll, 'An indifferent good post: the battlefield of the Boyne' in *Irish Sword*, xviii (1992), pp 49–56, see p. 49.

44. A. Crookshank and Knight of Glin, *The painters of Ireland c.1600–1920* (London, 1978), p. 58; *Victoire remportée par le Roy Guillaume III par le defaite entiére de l'armee de Jacques II en Irlande, l'Ile de Juillet, 1690*.

45. O'Carroll, 'An indifferent good post', p. 49.

46. G. Story, *An impartial history of the wars of Ireland* (London, 1693).

47. P. Beresford–Ellis, *The Boyne Water* (Belfast, 1976), p. 103.

48. Hyland, 'The battle of the Boyne', p. 33.

49. O'Carroll, 'An indifferent good post: the battlefield of the Boyne', p. 54; Hyland, 'The battle of the Boyne', p. 33.

50. *Ibid.*

51. R. Murray (ed.), *The journal of John Stevens* (Oxford, 1912).

52. O'Carroll, 'An indifferent good post', pp 49–56.

53. P. Harrington, 'Images of the Boyne' in *Irish Sword*, xviii (1992), pp 57–61, see p. 57; *Victoire rememportée par le Roy Guillaume sur les Irlandaise a la riviere de Boyne en Irlande, le ler Juillet, 1690*. Original in the Rijksmuseum-Stichting, Amsterdam, engraving sold in London by E. Cooper. Maes was born in Haarlem, and was one of the leading battle artists in late seventeenth-century Holland.

54. *Designe sur le lieu, le I Juillet 1690, par Theodor Maas, peintre du Roy Guillaume*; Crookshank and Knight of Glin, *The painters of Ireland*, p. 54, plate 36.

55. [G. S.], 'Two unpublished diaries related to the battle of the Boyne' in *Ulster Journal of Archaeology*, iv (1856), pp 77–95, see Bonnivert's journal.

56. Hyland, 'Battle of the Boyne', p. 44.

57. C. Brady and E. Byrnes, 'A pilot archaeological survey for the site of the Battle of the Boyne, Oldbridge Estate, county Meath' in *Second Irish Post-Medieval Archaeology Group Conference, Paper abstracts* (Dublin, 2002).

58. N. Gregory, 'River Boyne, Stalleen townland, county Meath: excavation report' in *County Louth Archaeological and Historical Journal*, xxiii (1995), pp 329–35.

59. Beresford-Ellis, *Boyne Water*, p. 56.

60. [G. S.], 'Two unpublished diaries', p. 81.

61. Story, *Impartial history*, p. 55.

62. Murray (ed.), *John Stevens*.

63. Story, *Impartial history*, p. 75.

64. Quoted in Beresford-Ellis, *Boyne Water*, p. 82

65. Story, *Impartial history*, p. 83.

66. Ordnance Survey, first edition 1:10,560 map (1840).

67. D'Alton, *Drogheda*, p. 43.

68. S. Matthews, 'Under the hill of Donore' in *Journal of the Old Drogheda Society*, ix (1994), 118–28, see p. 125.

69. Beresford-Ellis, *Boyne Water*, p. 109.

70. Story, *Impartial history*, p. 78

71. Brady and Byrnes, 'A pilot survey of Oldbridge'.

72. A. Hewitson (ed.), *Diary of Thomas Bellingham: an officer under William III* (Preston, 1908), p. 129.

73. Story, *Impartial history*, p. 74.

74. Quoted in Beresford-Ellis, *Boyne Water*, p. 26.

75. *Ibid.*, pp 83, 106–7; Story, *Impartial history*, p. 83.

76. Harrington, 'Images of the Boyne', p. 59.

77. Quoted in Beresford-Ellis, *Boyne Water*, p. 26.

78. Sir Robert to the Earl of Nottingham, 1 and 2 July 1690 (HMC Finch MSS, ii 326, 329).

79. Beresford-Ellis, *Boyne Water*, pp 74, 81–2.

80. G. Stout, *The bend of the Boyne: an archaeological landscape* (Dublin, 1997), p. 30.

80. Gregory, 'River Boyne', pp 329–35.

EIGHTEENTH-CENTURY ECONOMIC BOOM

1. L. Cullen, 'Man, landscape and roads: the changing eighteenth-century landscape' in W. Nolan (ed.), *The shaping of Ireland* (Dublin, 1988), pp 123–36, see p. 124.

2. R. Buchanan, 'Field systems of Ireland' in A. Baker and R. Butlin (ed.), *Studies of field systems in the British Isles* (London, 1973), pp 580–618.

3. J. Andrews, 'Land and people, c.1780' in T. Moody and W. Vaughan (ed.), *A new history of Ireland iv, the eighteenth century: 1691-1800* (Oxford, 1986), pp 236–64, see p. 257.

4. T. Reeves-Smith, 'Demesnes' in F. Aalen, K. Whelan and M. Stout (ed.), *Atlas of the Irish rural landscape* (Cork, 1997), pp 197–205.

5. R. Tomlinson, 'Tree planting by tenants in county Down during the eighteenth and nineteenth centuries' in *Ir. Geog.*, xxix (1996), pp 83–95, see pp 83–4; E. McCracken, 'Tree planting by tenants in Meath 1800–1850' in *Riocht na Midhe*, viii (1987–93), pp 3–20.

6. W. Smyth, 'Estate records and the making of the Irish landscape; an example from county Tipperary' in *Ir. Geog.*, ix (1976), pp 29–47.

7. W. Nolan, *Tracing the past: sources for local studies in the Republic of Ireland* (Dublin, 1982), p. 69.

8. Enrolled in a convert roll dated 12 November, 1728, see E. O'Byrne (ed.), *The convert rolls* (Dublin, 1981), p. 211.

9. T. Sadleir, *Georgian mansions in Ireland* (Dublin, 1915), p. 63.

10. Lord Netterville to Samuel Burton 1731, R.D. vol. 69, p. 199, deed 47900.

11. C. Casey and A. Rowan, *The buildings of north Leinster* (London, 1993), pp 228–30.

12. Patrick Evers to Matthew Warren 1734, R.D., 82-530-58890.

13. Lord Netterville to John Farrell 1736, R.D., 86-64-59336.

14. Lord Netterville to Sarah Walsh 1750, R.D., 144-11-96241.

15. Lord Netterville to Dunan 1732, R.D., 82-249-57710. Lord Netterville and Patrick Dunan.

16. Lord Netterville to Kindelan 1736, R.D., 83-347-59215.

17. Lord Netterville to Walsh 1750, R.D., 144-11-96241. Did demise and set unto all that and those of the townland of Proudfootstown then in the possession of Sarah Walsh … 74 acres mearing and bounding on the east with the river Boyne south with the paddock wall of Dowth and the new walk ditch leading to the river Boyne on the west with Henry Smith's farm on the north with Littlegrange as also the park or close commonly called or known by the Miller's meadow and joining the river Boyne 2 acres formerly held by Ita Kelly was on two parks or parcels of land adjoining the lands of Proudfootstown in the west lately held by the widow Smith now in the possession of Sarah Walsh containing 22 acres … one acre of bog on the lands of Ballyboy joining all that farm formerly held by Luke Smith … 58 acres … with 16 acres in Ballyboy; Lord Netterville to Hall 1749, R.D., 136-503-92249. Lands of Ballynacrade and part of the bog of Ballyboy formerly in the possession of Thomas Cunningham containing 12 acres … mearing on the east to James Dungan's holding on

the south to the cabbins and gardens in the possession of Kindelan and Dungan … 31 years for yearly rent of £6.

18. Lord Netterville to Dunan 1732, R.D., 82-249-57710. Lord Netterville and Patrick Dunan; Lord Netterville to Kindelan 1736, R.D., 83-347-59215.

19. Lord Netterville to Dunan 1732, R.D., 82-249-57710; Lord Netterville to Smith 1734, R.D., 82-530-58890. Susanna Smith of the mill of Dowth … all that part of the parcel of land now or lately in possession of Elizabeth Smith, widow containing … 25 acres together with dwelling house wherein the said Smith now dwells, the barn, cow house, stable and orchard thereunto belonging as also two other houses or tenements on the said premises, one of which joins Nicholas Hillock's mill and the other the said orchard with stang of turf bog on the bog of Ballyboy … mearing on the north with Littlegrange, on the east with a part of Dowth land formerly in possession of Henry Smith on the west with part of the land of Dowth aforesaid now in the possession of Mr. Anthony Walsh and on the south with Pat Dunan's farm together with all and singular appurtenances to hold to Susanna Smith during the term of 31 years … under the yearly rent of 7s per acre together.

20. Lord Netterville to Dunan 1732, R.D., 82-249-57710; Lord Netterville to Kelly 1748, R.D., 130-314-89197. Those parcell lands commonly called the paddock and Dremsale containing 38 acres as also the pieces or parcels of lands commonly called the Strevade containing 5 acres being all part of the lands of Dowth … for 10 years at a yearly rent of £9-6s; Lord Netterville to Kelly 1750, R.D., 142-297-95575. The cornmill of Proudfootstown and 14 acres with the house … improvements … belongings to the old tuck mill in the parcel of land called Listiveran adjoining and there to two weyres … fishery together with the parcel of land called the paddock and demesne and the field called the Strevade.

21. Lord Netterville to John Farrell 1736, R.D., 86-69-59336. That farm or parcel of land commonly called Coleman's farm with the houses, tenements and garden thereon belonging with one house and garden in the village of Ballynacraide, an acre of Curraghboy containing turf and marl … then in the possession of John Farrell … containing 170 acres … being in the manor of Dowth. Its mear and boundary on the east with Nicholas, Lord Netterville's new lane, grove and the land called Glebe land, on the river Boyne and on the north with the Great Avenue leading through Dowth, to the lands of Newgrange, on the west with Newgrange; Lord Netterville to Kindelan 1736, R.D., 83-347-59215; Lord Netterville to Hall 1749, R.D., 136-503-92249.

22. Lord Netterville to Smith 1734, R.D., 82-530-58890.

23. Ibid., Lord Netterville to Kelly 1750, R.D., 142-297-95575.

24. N.A., TAB 22/48 for Dowth parish.

25. N.A., Caldwell Papers, M1095/2/2:7.

26. N.A., Caldwell Papers, M1095/2/8 and M1095/2/2 iii.

27. Trinity College Dublin, Ms 883.ii, p. 10.

28. Earl of Drogheda to Charles Campbell 1721, R.D., 33-264-20275.

29. Burton to Netterville 1734, R.D., 77-448-54314.

30. N.L.I., Manuscript map, 21 F78 (63), A survey of part of the estate of Charles Caldwell in the counties of Meath and Louth with names of tenants, by Bernard Scalé, 1766.

31. Quoted in C. Ellison, The waters of the Boyne and Blackwater (Navan, 1983), p.102.

32. N.A., Caldwell Papers, Manuscript map, 10952/2/56, A map of that part of Newgrange wasted and lost by navigation with a draft of the old and new canal made near the river Boyne … being part of the estate of Andrew Caldwell Esq. taken and surveyed by order and appointment of Mr. Robert Berrill the 21st day of January, 1781.

33. Charles Campbell to Francis Berrill 1724, R.D., 42-435-26956. 215 acres … of the town and lands of

Newgrange now in the possession and tenure of Frances Berrill and his undertenants together with the rectorial tithes … 31 years for the yearly rent of £9-10s payable half yearly. Incidentally, this is the earliest reference to the placename 'Rossin' which is still in use but is not a local townland name; Charles Campbell to Peter Evers, 1724, R.D., 42-432-26923. Set and farm let unto the said Peter Evers all that part and parcel of the said town and lands of Balfaddock now in his possession containing 152 acres … 31 years under yearly rent of £6.10s; Charles Campbell to Edmund Hall 1724, R.D., 40-517-27194. All that part or parcell of the town lands of Ballfaddock, containing 20 acres … in his possession on the south side of the highway leading from Mattock bridge to Slane and partly enclosed by a new ditch adjoining to the ditch on the highway … 20 acres at £8.10s p.a.

34. Charles Campbell to Henry Smith 1723, R.D., 42-432-24711. Henry Smith, carpenter in 1723 farm lett two houses on the north side of the street of the town of Balfaddock, in one of the houses John Hall now dwells and in the other of which said houses Patrick Hall lately dwells with the outhouses and garden there belonging except the little ash grove and the ground between it and the street and the house joining Peter Evers garden … on the lands of Balfaddock and the east side of the ditch lately made beginning at the highway leading from Mattock Bridge to Slane and ending in the little bridge lately made … near Peter Evers garden in the town and lands of Balfeddock and held by the Patrick Hall then in possession of Henry Smith and of the said Hall his undertenant containing 48 acres … for the term of three lives at an annual rent of £28; Campbell to Edmund Hall 1724, R.D., 40-517-27194.

35. Campbell to Henry Smith 1723, R.D., 42-432-24711.

36. Peter Evers to Frances Farrell 1733, R.D., 79-91-54734; Edward Hall to Edward Norris 1727, R.D., 86-142-59685.

37. Campbell to Henry Smith 1723, R.D., 42-432-24711.

38. N.A., Caldwell papers; M 10951/2/2vi.

39. Burton to Netterville 1734, R.D., 77-448-54314; Wesley to Campbell 1722, R.D., 33-370-20581.

40. Edward, Earl of Drogheda to Andrew Caldwell 1729, R.D., 62-410-43431.

41. Caldwell to Cooper 1806, R.D., 604-369-415265.

42. McCracken, 'Tree planting', p. 7.

43. Campbell to Frances Berrill 1724, R.D., 42-435-26956; Burton to Berrill 1737, R.D., 88-390-63015. The inconsistencies in the spelling of this surname arise from inconsistencies in the sources.

44. Genealogical Office, Ms no. 182, N.L.I. mic. p. 8309.

45. Charles Campbell to Edmund Hall 1724, R.D., 40-517-27194.

46. Campbell to Henry Smith 1723, R.D., 42-432-24711.

47. N.L.I., Reports on Private Collections, ii, Report 21; pp 18–36.

48. N.L.I., Drogheda Papers, Ms 13024.

49. The architect is thought to be Hugh Darley. See Casey and Rowan, Buildings of North Leinster, pp 446–7.

50. A. Crookshank and Knight of Glin, The painters of Ireland c.1600-1920 (London, 1978), p. 65, fig. 11.

51. Peter Evers to Frances Farrell 1733, R.D., 79-91-54734; Edward Hall to Edward Norris 1727, R.D., 86-142-59685.

52. K. Whelan, 'The modern landscape: from plantation to present', in Aalen, Whelan and Stout (ed.), Atlas, pp 67–103, see 72–3.

53. L. Cullen, 'Economic development: 1691–1750' in T. Moody and W. Vaughan (ed.), A new history of Ireland iv, the eighteenth century: 1691–1800 (Oxford, 1986), pp 123–58, see pp 134–5.

54. Andrews, 'Land and people, c.1780', pp 247–8.

55. L. Cullen, 'Eighteenth-century flour milling in Ireland' in Ir. Ec. Soc. Hist., iv (1977), pp 5–25, see p. 9.

56. Whelan, 'Modern landscape', pp 85–8.

57. Ibid., p. 79.

58. See, for example, J. Holroyd, Observations on the manufacturing trade and present state of Ireland (Dublin,

1785).

59. W. Smyth, 'The greening of Ireland – tenant tree-planting in the eighteenth and nineteenth centuries' in Irish Forester, liv (1997), pp 55–72, see p. 59.

60. A. Young, Tour of Ireland (London, 1780, reprinted Shannon, 1970), i, pp 37–49; Ibid. for subsequent text.

61. Cullen, 'Eighteenth-century flour milling', pp 5–25.

62. R. Simington (ed.), The Civil Survey: county Meath 1654–56, v (Dublin, 1940).

63. Cullen, 'Eighteenth-century flour milling', pp 8–9, 15.

64. N.A., M 3725, Abstract of Covenant between John Chamney and William Sharman Crawford 1775.

65. Young, Tour of Ireland, i, pp 44–6; N.A., 16954, deed of lease, David Jebb of Slane to the lands of Crewbane.

66. Viscount Netterville to Susanna Smith 1734, R.D., 82-530-58890.

67. Evers to Warren 1734, R.D., 82-542-58940.

68. Lord Netterville to Osborne, R.D., 310-78-2055980.

69. Viscount Netterville to Susanna Smith 1734, R.D., 82-530-58890.

70. Lord Netterville to Patrick Kindelan 1736, R.D., 83-347-59215.

71. Nicholas, Lord Viscount Netterville to Kelly 1750, R.D., 142-297-95575.

72. Lord Netterville to Sarah Walsh 1750, R.D., 144-11-96241.

73. Lord Netterville to Thomas Lunn to Earl of Drogheda 1721, R.D., 62-278-42867.

74. N.L.I., A survey of part of the estate of Charles Caldwell Esq. in the counties of Meath and Louth by Bernard Scalé, 1766.

75. Simington (ed.), Civil Survey: Meath, p. 26; Down Survey map of the barony of Duleek.

76. Earl of Drogheda to Stewart 1732, R.D., 89, pp 343-5-48655.

77. N.A., Caldwell Papers, Manuscript map, 10952/2/56.

78. N.A., Caldwell Papers (1095/2/36).

79. N.A., Caldwell Papers (1095/2/2xi).

80. W. Smyth, 'Locational patterns and trends within the pre-famine linen industry' in Ir. Geog., viii (1978), pp 97–110, see p. 100, fig. 1.

81. W. Smyth, 'Flax cultivation in Ireland: the development and demise of a regional staple' in W. Smyth and K. Whelan (ed.), Common ground: essays on the historical geography of Ireland (Cork, 1981), pp 234–52, see p. 238.

82. Ibid., pp 234–52.

83. Young, Tour of Ireland, i, p. 38.

84. Ellison, Boyne and Blackwater, p.71.

85. J. Killen, 'Communications' in Aalen, Whelan and Stout (ed.), Atlas, pp 206–19, p. 207

86. Young, Tour of Ireland, i, p. 49.

87. Andrews, 'Land and people', p. 257.

88. N.A., Grand Jury Query Book, county Meath 1761–1776, Query no. 110.

89. N.A., Grand Jury Query Book, county Meath 1761–1776, Query no. 113; N.A., Grand Jury Presentment Book 1809-1814, 1C/33/30, nos 8, 29, 122.

90. Young, Tour of Ireland, i, p. 37.

91. Brady, Shipman and Martin, 'National canals and waterways strategy' (unpublished report, Office of Public Works, Dublin, 1992), p. 1.

92. N.L.I., Ms. 500, 'A scheme of navigation of the noble river Boyne'.

93. Ellison, Boyne and Blackwater, p. 12.

94. N.L.I., D 14917.

95. Ibid., p. 13.

96. N.A., manuscript map, Caldwell Papers (1095/2/56).

97. Ibid.

98. N.L.I., Ms 7352, Minutes and Proceedings of the

Boyne Navigation Commissioners, pp 41, 47.

99. J. McCracken, 'The ecclesiastical structure, 1714–60' in Moody and Vaughan (ed.), *A new history of Ireland iv*, pp 84–104, see pp 87–98.

100. *Ibid.*, p. 96.

101. K. Whelan, 'The regional impact of Irish catholicism: 1700–1850' in Smyth and Whelan (ed.), *Common ground*, pp 257–77, see pp 257–8.

102. P. Corish, *The catholic community in the seventeenth and eighteenth centuries* (Dublin, 1981), p. 49; McCracken, 'Ecclesiastical structure', p. 96.

103. Quoted in S. Matthews, 'Under the hill of Donore' in *Journal of the Old Drogheda Society*, ix (1994), pp 118–28, see pp 118–19, 125–6.

104. *Ibid.*, p. 125.

105. *Ibid.*, p. 125.

106. O. Curran, *History of the Diocese of Meath 1860–1993*, i (reprint, Dublin, 1995), p. 306.

107. *Ibid.*, p. 338.

108. Quoted in S. Matthews, 'Place and People: a family exploration' (unpublished family history, 1987), see p. 18–19 and accompanying map.

109. A. Day (ed.), *Letters from Georgian Ireland: The correspondence of Mary Delany, 1731–68* (Belfast, 1991).

BUILDINGS IN THE NINETEENTH–CENTURY LANDSCAPE

1. T. Jones Hughes, 'Landholding and settlement in counties Meath and Cavan in the nineteenth century' in P. O'Flanagan, P. Ferguson and K. Whelan (ed.), *Rural Ireland: modernisation and change 1600–1900* (Cork, 1987), pp 104–46, see p. 105.

2. W. Vaughan, *Landlords and tenants in mid–Victorian Ireland* (Oxford, 1994), p. 6.

3. R. Griffith, *General valuation of rateable property in Ireland: county Meath* (Dublin, 1854); *General valuation of rateable property in Ireland: county Louth* (Dublin, 1854); *Census of Ireland 1851*: County of Meath, pp 92–3, 98–9; *Census of Ireland 1881*: County of Meath, pp 668–9, 708–9; *Census of Ireland 1911*: County of Meath, pp 1–9, 34.

4. R. Thompson, *Statistical survey of county Meath* (Dublin, 1802). These surveys were undertaken by the Royal Dublin Society in order to make recommendations on the improvement of agriculture.

5. *Ibid.*, p. 3.

6. *Ibid.*, p. 45.

7. S. Lewis, *Topographical dictionary of Ireland* (London, 1837), see for Duleek i, p. 566; for Monknewtown, ii, p. 389.

8. N.A., Field Books, Donore parish N.A.4.1334, Dowth Parish N.A.4.1461, Duleek Parish N.A.4.1335, Knockcommon Parish N.A.4.1340, Monknewtown Parish N.A.4.1464. The Field Books are held in the National Archives, Dublin. They are original returns made by Valuers in the field in preparation for the *Primary Valuation of Property*. Compiled for the study area between 1838 and 1839, their emphasis is on soil quality and type of farming practised. The information is presented in tabulated form, organised on a parish and townland basis. It lists the number of areas where soil was sampled in the townland, the farming practice observed (arable, pasture, meadow), occupants and their buildings. Each entry concludes with a recommended valuation.

9. Jones Hughes, 'Meath and Cavan', p. 124.

10. T. Jones Hughes, 'East Leinster in the mid–nineteenth century' in *Ir. Geog.*, iii (1958), pp 227–41, see p 231.

11. J. D'Alton, *History of Drogheda* (Dublin, 1844), p. 4.

12. Jones Hughes, 'East Leinster', p. 231.

13. Lewis, *Topographical dictionary*, i, p. 481.

14. *Ibid.*, ii, p. 657.

15. D'Alton, *History of Drogheda*, p. 384.

16. C. Ellison, *The waters of the Boyne and Blackwater* (Dublin, 1983), p. 53.

17. Lewis, *Topographical dictionary*, i, p. 481.

18. Thompson, *Statistical survey*, pp 62–77.

19. The 'Tithe Applotment Books' were examined as a potential source of information on housing and land holdings in the study area. These are generally considered an important pre-*Valuation* source. However, they were only available for a small portion of the study area and were not accompanied by maps, making precise location of properties difficult. The 'Tithe Applotment Books' (TAB) are held in the National Archives. See TAB 2748, Dowth parish 1833; TAB 22/64 (2), part of Duleek parish 1830; TAB 22/64, Lougher townland 1853; TAB 22/63, Knockcommon parish 1830.

20. The 'House Books' are held in the Valuation Office, Irish Life Centre, Dublin 1. They are the original returns made by valuers in the field in preparation for the publication of the *Primary Valuation*.

21. Only seventy-six houses are listed in these 'House Books', comprising just 26% of the dwellings listed in the 1854 *Valuation*. No fourth-class houses are described. Most entries relate to houses and industrial buildings valued at more than £5 but some houses as low as £3 valuation were inspected. In the study area, thirty-five first-class houses, twenty-six second-class houses and fifteen third-class houses are listed. Within the first-class housing, the various ancillary buildings are also given their rateable valuation. Nevertheless, the published figures and the 1851 Census indicate that fourth-class houses were present in considerable numbers in the area. The values listed in the manuscripts contrast markedly with the figures published for the same property in the 1854 *Valuation*, showing both increases and decreases in rateable valuation for particular properties. The numeration of holdings also differs from the final valuation, making comparison of holdings between both sources problematic. This is further complicated by the apparent change in occupier on many of the properties in the years between 1838 and 1854. These discrepancies make it difficult to obtain more detailed information on levelled buildings. See also W. Nolan, *Tracing the past: sources for local studies in the Republic of Ireland* (Dublin, 1982), p. 87.

22. C. Casey and A. Rowan, *The buildings of Ireland: north Leinster* (London, 1993), pp 446–8.

23. T. Wilson 'The great landowners of Meath, 1789' in *Riocht na Midhe*, vii (1980–86), pp 99–110, see p. 109.

24. Valuations Office, House Books, Monknewtown parish, p. 20.

25. *Ibid.*, p. 15.

26. *Ibid.*, p. 20.

27. F. Aalen, 'Buildings', in F.H.A. Aalen, K. Whelan and M. Stout (ed.), *Atlas of the Irish rural landscape* (Cork, 1997), pp 145–79, see pp 159–61.

28. Valuations Office, House Books, Monknewtown parish, p. 18. The house and part of its land have recently been purchased by the state.

29. *Ibid.*, Duleek parish, pp 31–2.

30. *Ibid.*, p. 48.

31. Aalen, 'Buildings', pp 156–9.

32. *Ibid.*, p. 152.

33. Rev. M. O'Flanagan, 'Letters containing information relating to the antiquities of county Meath collected during the progress of the survey in 1836'.

34. P. Shaffrey and M. Shaffrey, *Irish countryside buildings* (Dublin, 1985), p. 22.

35. D'Alton, *History of Drogheda*, p. 464.

36. For an example of a similar attitude towards strong farmers, see M. Stout, 'The geography and implications of Post-Famine population decline in Baltyboys, County Wicklow' in C. Morash and R. Hayes (ed.), '*Fearful realities': New perspectives on the Famine* (Dublin, 1992), pp 15–34, see pp 21–2.

37. K. Whelan, 'The Catholic church, the Catholic chapel and village development in Ireland' in *Ir. Geog.*, xvi (1983), pp 1–15.

38. O. Curran, *History of the Diocese of Meath 1860–1993, i* (reprint, Dublin, 1995), p. 336.

39. *Ibid.*, p. 388.

40. S. Matthews, 'Under the hill of Donore' in *Journal of the Old Drogheda Society*, ix (1994), pp 118–28; see p. 126.

41. Curran, *Diocese of Meath*, i , see pp. 832–3.

42. Casey and Rowan, *Buildings: North Leinster*, p. 447.

43. *Ibid.*, pp 65, 448.

44. *Ibid.*, p. 448.

45. T. Sadleir, *Georgian mansions in Ireland* (Dublin, 1915), p. 64.

46. Casey and Rowan, *Buildings: North Leinster*, p. 230.

47. P. Synnott, 'The Netterville monument and family: formerly of Dowth, county Meath' (unpublished family history), pp 16–17.

48. Shaffrey and Shaffrey, *Irish Countryside Buildings*, p. 78.

49. Matthews, 'Donore', p. 124.

50. P. O'Reilly and B. Tuite (ed.), *The cry of the dreamer and other poems* (Drogheda, n.d.) pp 15–16.

51. J. Fleetwood, *The Irish body snatchers: a history of body snatching in Ireland* (Dublin, 1988).

52. N.A., Ordnance Survey Field Books, Donore parish N.A.4.1334.

53. Valuation Office, House Books, Duleek parish, p. 31.

54. *Ibid.*, Donore parish, p. 17.

55. *Ibid.*, Monknewtown parish, p. 17.

56. *Ibid.*, Dowth parish, p. 8.

57. Thompson, *Statistical survey*, p. 65.

58. *Ibid.*, *Statistical survey*, pp 96–101.

59. N.L.I., Encumbered Estates, xliii, 19 May 1854.

60. N.A., T11692, Copy of will and codicil of Henry Coddington Esq. 1816, pp 5–6.

61. Valuation Office, Perambulation Books. This source lists the types of tenure arrangement.

62. Vaughan, *Landlords*, p. 7.

63. M. Kenny 'Land Tenure in east Westmeath and its influence upon the state of agriculture, 1820–1840' in *Riocht na Midhe*, vi (1978–79), pp 33–48.

64. Jones Hughes, 'East Leinster', p. 239.

65. Jones Hughes, 'Meath and Cavan', p. 125.

66. *Ibid.*, p. 129.

67. Jones Hughes, 'East Leinster', p. 239.

68. *Ibid.*

69 *Census of Ireland 1881*, county Meath, i , 8 (Dublin 1881), p. 668.

70. C. O'Grada, *Ireland: a new economic history 1780–1939* (Oxford, 1994), p. 213.

71. N.L.I., Encumbered estates, xliii, 19 May 1854.

72 *Census of Ireland*, 1841, 1851, 1861, 1871, 1881, 1891, 1901. The discrepancy between the figures for the total number of houses within the Bend of the Boyne and the number in the censuses is due to the fact that the area takes in portions of many townlands and the census gives total figures for those townlands. It is not known why 1891 records a rise in house numbers despite the fall in population.

73. British Parliamentary Papers, Famine Ireland, 8, 1846, 3, see p. 9.

74. Valuation Office, Perambulation Books.

75. N.L.I., Encumbered estates, xliii, 19 May 1854.

76. M. Lyons, *Illustrated incumbered estates: Ireland, 1850–1905* (Whitegate, Clare, 1993), pp 168–9.

77. M. Conway, 'The Boyle O'Reilly stone' in *Journal of the Old Drogheda Society*, iv (1968), pp 3–7.

78. M. O'Kelly and C. O'Kelly, 'The tumulus of Dowth, county Meath' in *R.I.A. Proc.*, C, lxxxiii (1983), pp 188–90; Rev. J. Graves, 'The Dowth eviction case' in *R.S.A.I. Jn.*, cx (1980), pp 205–9.

79. N.A. OPW 7148/96.

80. N.A. OPW 7724/99.

81. F. Aalen, 'The re-housing of rural labourers in Ireland under the Labourers (Ireland) Act, 1883–1919' in *Journal of Historical Geography*, xii (1986), pp 287–306.

82. F. Aalen, 'Public housing in Ireland' in *Planning Perspectives*, ii (1987), pp 175–93, see p. 179.

83. J. Geraghty, 'P.J. Dodd of Drogheda: architect and

civil engineer' in *Journal of the Old Drogheda Society*, ix (1994), pp 7–37, see pp 24–5.

THE MODERN LANDSCAPE

1. K. Whelan, 'The modern landscape: from plantation to present', in Aalen, Whelan and Stout (ed.), *Atlas*, pp 67–103, see 97–8.

2. W. Nolan, 'New farms and fields: migration policies of state land agencies 1891–1980' in W. Smyth and K. Whelan (ed.), *Common ground: essays on the historical geography of Ireland* (Cork, 1981), pp 296–319.

3. E. O'Halpin, 'The army in independent Ireland' in T. Bartlett and K. Jefferey (ed.), *A military history of Ireland* (Cambridge, 1996), pp 407–30, see p. 420.

4. C. Mangan, 'Plans and operations' in *Irish Sword*, xix (1993–95), pp 47–56, see p. 47.

5. Military Archive, Cathal Brugha Barracks, Dublin, EDP/E/3/5. A transcript of a lecture given by Major Tuohy (Eastern Command) dated 24 March 1941 and held in the Military Archive outlines the security problem faced by the defence forces in 1941 and their proposals to deal with them: 'In the eastern command the defence problem is twofold ... they had to prepare to meet British and German aggression … in the event of British aggression the main effort will be made in Eastern Command. Because Britain has forces in the Six Counties invasion overland is much easier. The British want to secure harbour facilities and airports, in the west and south west and to prevent this country being used as a base for operations against Britain.' In order to meet this threat Major Tuohy identified a need to: 'Provide observation groups on the frontier and coast. Behind the observants is the land frontier… We have a screen of cyclists from Dundalk to Cavan whose mission is to delay the advance of the enemy by every and any means in order to gain time to enable us to bring our main forces against him ... assisted by the Local Defence Forces' (LDF). This he refers to as the 'Outpost Line' (OL).

6. Military Archive, EDP/E/3/1, Operations Order No. 20.

7. Mangan, 'Plans and operations', see p. 51.

8. *Ibid*.

9. I. Brown, *Twentieth century defences in Britain: an introductory guide* (London, 1995), p. 79.

10. H. Willis, *Pillboxes: a study of UK defences 1940* (London, 1985), p. 2.

11. P. Oldham, *A guide to the design, construction and use of concrete pillboxes in 1914–1918* (London, 1995).

12. A. Saunders, *Fortress Britain: artillery fortifications in the British Isles and Ireland* (London, 1989), p. 219.

13. Brown, *Twentieth century defences*, pp 79–84.

14. Military Archive, Blockhouses: Eastern Command, EDP/1/6; DD/C/364D/24/2/41; Willis, *Pillboxes*. A similar dearth of official information was experienced in Great Britain where pillbox research is at an advanced stage. When Henry Willis, pioneer of pillbox studies, undertook his survey in the 1970s, moved by a concern for the rapidity with which pillboxes were being demolished, he was advised unofficially to go out and count them as no details of design or accurate maps of the many miles of defences were in official records. He did just that and has recorded a staggering 18,000 sites.

15. Mangan, 'Plans and operations', p. 53. An example of a prominent pillbox is that at Highfield (31). There were two pillboxes covering the Boyne Viaduct which was considered a prime target: one at Weirhope, the other in the yard of the Drogheda Railway station which was recently demolished.

16. Willis, *Pillboxes*, p. 23.

17. Military Archive, Minutes of conference re engineering matters held at Plans and Operations Branch, 31/7/41, EDP2/8.

18. Willis, *Pillboxes*, pp 56–7.

19. Anon., 'Things umpires should look for' in *An Cosantoir*, i (1941), pp 12–16, see p. 13.

20. Brown, *Twentieth century defences*, pp 79–84.

21. Willis, *Pillboxes*, p. 7.

22. Military Archive, Minutes of conference re engineering matters held at Plans and Operations Branch, 31/7/41, EDP2/8. The British had their firing points narrow on the inside and widening in a 'zig–zag' fashion to the outer wall. Subsequently, the assistant Director of Engineers sent instructions to the Chief of Staff regarding this matter: Firing ports or embrasures had to give an adequate field of fire and adequate observation to the defenders. The maximum protection to the defenders must be given consistent with this; Military Archive, 1941, EDP8/4.

23. Willis, *Pillboxes*, pp 56–7.

24. Anon.. 'Umpires', pp 12–16.

25. D. O'Carroll, 'The emergency army' in *Irish Sword*, xix (1993–95), pp 19–46, see p. 33; Military Archive, EDP1/6/CC 25, Blockhouse Correspondence.

26. Anon., 'Umpires', pp 12–3.

27. Willis, *Pillboxes*, p. 46.

28. Saunders, *Fortress Britain*, p. 219; Willis, *Pillboxes*. The potential of systematic mapping of these features is underlined in Great Britain, where the national defence strategy has been reconstructed in detail on the basis of a systematic mapping of pillboxes. There it has been possible to identify main defence lines – similar to that along the Boyne – which followed the course of rivers and canals and employed these pre–existing features as ready–made, anti–tank obstacles defended by a line of pillboxes and manned by a Home Guard that was similar to the LDF.

29. *Ibid*., p. 65.

30. *Ibid*., pp 58, 65.

31. Saunders, *Fortress Britain*, p. 214. The Maginot Line was a line of strongly protected underground forts encased in concrete built on the Franco–German border in the 1930s to defend France against Germany. The position of these forts depended upon an alliance with Belgium because the Franco–Belgian border was poorly defended. However, Belgium fell to the Germans who then attacked the Maginot Line from the rear.

32. Meath Leader II, *Meath's farming future; facing challenge*, (Kells, 1999).

33. A. O'Neill, National Archaeological Park: Boyne Valley (unpublished consultancy report, Dublin, 1989).

34. *Ibid*., p. 5.

35. Nolan, 'New farms and fields', pp 309, 314.

36. Department of Agriculture, *Nineteenth annual report of the Minister of Agriculture 1949–50* (Dublin, 1950), pp 133–4.

37. Department of Agriculture and Fisheries, *Annual report of the Minister for Agriculture and Fisheries 1973–1974* (Dublin, 1974), pp 102–5; Department of Agriculture, *Annual Report of the Minister for Agriculture 1986 Ireland* (Dublin, 1987), p 79–80.

38. Department of Agriculture, *Nineteenth report*, pp 133–4.

39. Data sources: In the Department of Agriculture Annual Reports, response to their schemes is presented on a nationwide basis with a corresponding breakdown of figures by county. However, more specific information is held in regional offices. Records for the East Meath region are held by the Farm Development Service in Navan. The process involved in obtaining grant–aid for farm development is as follows. In general, the farmer initiates the proposal and an officer inspects the site to determine the land's suitability for agriculture and that the development will represent a reasonable increase in productivity. Specifications are then drawn up for the project and approved for a grant. For the period up to 1974 the documentation available is limited. A General Register and a Reclamation Register provide basic information on each application and whether or not the grant was successful. Both registers refer to separate files which contain detailed information on the development work and include a section of the relevant 6 inch or 25 inch OS map. There is also a working set of annotated 6 inch maps held in the Navan office which refer to the works undertaken. Information on the Farm Modernisation and the Farm Improvement Schemes are held on a card

index which refers to individual files. These files contain details of the works with guidelines as to how they should be carried out. The cartographic record included under the latter schemes is more schematic than that with the Land Rehabilitation Project which causes difficulties when attempting to plot the precise location of various works.

40. Department of Agriculture and Fisheries, *Annual Report 1973–1974*, pp 102–7; R. Alexander and S. Gahan, 'A review of sites protected for conservation in the Republic of Ireland' in *Ir. Geog.*, xx (1987), pp 82–8. In 1987 the National parks represented 71% of all protected land in the State.

41. Department of Agriculture, *Annual Report of the Minister for Agriculture 1985 Ireland* (Dublin, 1986), p. 76.

42. D. Baldock, *Wetland drainage in Europe: the effects of agricultural policy in four EEC countries* (London, 1984), p. 81.

43. *Ibid*., p. 81.

44. Department of Agriculture, *Annual report 1986*, p. 79–80.

45. Baldock, *Wetland drainage*, p. 67.

46. Local Government (Planning and Development) Exempted Development and Amendment Regulations 1984.

47. P. Tuite, 'New farm buildings' in F. Aalen (ed.), *The future of the Irish rural landscape* (Dublin, 1985), pp 46–55.

48. P. Shaffrey and M. Shaffrey, *Irish countryside buildings: everyday architecture in the rural landscape* (Dublin, 1985), p. 2.

49. O.S. 1:10.560 first and third editions, Irish Army Air Corps circa 1950, C.U.C.A.P. AJY 22 1964, O.S. Aerial Photograph 1991.

50. R. Bruton and F. Convery, *Land drainage policy in Ireland* (Dublin, 1982), p. 24.

51. R. Webb, 'The status of hedgerow field margins in Ireland' in J. Park (ed.), *Environmental management in agriculture – European perspective* (London, 1988), pp 125–43, see p. 127.

52. *Ibid*., p. 130; D. Gillmor, 'Agricultural development' in R. Carter and A. Parker (ed.), *Ireland: a contemporary geographical perspective on a land and its people* (London, 1989), see p. 192–3.

53. *Ibid*.

54. Recent field fence removal in the townland of Littlegrange exposed a hitherto unknown souterrain and there have been many similar discoveries during reclamation works throughout the country.

55. Meath Leader II, *Meath's farming future*.

THE CHALLENGE OF CHANGE

1. E. Keane, 'The Visitor Centre: gateway to Bru na Bóinne' in *Brú na Bóinne*, supplement to *Arch. Ir.*, xi, 36–7.

2. Dúchas, *Record of Monuments and Places, County Meath*, 1997).

3. Site Code 1862; Directive 92/43/EEC.

4. Statutory Instrument (S.I.) No. 93 of 1999.

5. Brady, Shipman and Martin, *Boyne Valley Integrated Development Plan* (Dublin, 1995), pp 9, 15.

6. Department of Agriculture, Food and Forestry, *Rural Environment Protection Scheme* (Dublin, 1994).

7. T. Leavy and B. Coulter, 'REPS: Highest uptake in Midlands and West' in *Today's Farm*, vii (1997), p. 42.

8. Meath County Council, PL 17/5/74394.

9. Department of Arts, Culture and the Gaeltacht, *Protecting our architectural heritage* (Dublin, 1998).

10. P. Lucas, *Protected landscapes, A guide for Policy makers and planners* (London, 1992), p. 29.

11. F. Tilden, *Interpreting our heritage* (Chapel Hill, 1977), p. 3.

12. D. Ó Ríordáin, 'Interpreting the interpretation' in *Arch. Ir.*, xiii (1999), pp 8–9.

13. E. Bhreathnach, *Tara: A select bibliography. Discovery Programme Reports 3* (Dublin, 1995).

14. W. Wilde, *The beauties of the Boyne and Blackwater* (Dublin 1849), p. 4.

BOYNE VALLEY ENVISIONED

1. J. Westwood, *Sacred Journeys: Paths for the new Pilgrim*, (London, 1997). This is 'A Sacred land book', one of a series of books dealing with New Age travel destinations.

2. D. Mallon, *Nano Reid: 1900–1981* (Drogheda, 1994), p. 111.

3. E. Spenser, *The Faerie Queen* (London, 1590), book iv, canto xi, stanza 40.

4. A. Crookshank, The *watercolours of Ireland: Works on paper in pencil, pastel and pen* c. *1600–1914* (London, 1994), p. 92.

5. H. Jones, *Poems on several occasions* (Dublin, 1735), pp 29–33.

6. F. Ledwidge, *Selected poems* (Dublin, 1992), edited by D. Bolger with a introduction by S. Heaney.

7. *Ibid.*, 'To a linnet in a cage', p. 34; 'homely moors', p. 26 ; 'The hills', p. 32.

8. *Ibid.*, 'Desire in Spring', p. 28; 'Behind the closed eye', p. 25.

9. A. Curtayne, *Francis Ledwidge: a life of the poet* (London, 1972).

10. F.R. Higgins, *The 39 poems* (Dublin, 1992), edited by R.D. Clarke, p. 7.

11. *Ibid.*, p. 60.

12. L. Barry (ed.), *Selected poems, speeches, dedications, and letters of John Boyle O'Reilly 1844–1890* (Australind, Western Australia, 1994). For what follows see S. Ashton, 'John Boyle O'Reilly and Moondyne' in *History Ireland*, x (2002) pp 38–42.

13. Barry (ed.), *Selected poems of John Boyle O'Reilly*, pp 312–3.

14. *Ibid.*, p. 31.

15. Mallon, *Nano Reid*, p. 62.

16. E. Hickey, *I send my love along the Boyne* (Dublin, 1966).

17. Ledwidge, *Selected poems*, p. 60.

18. G. Moore, *Hail and farewell* (1911, 5th ed. by R. Cave, Gerrards Cross, Buckinghamshire, 1985).

19. R. Iyer and N. Iyer, *The descent of Gods* (Gerrards Cross, Buckinghamshire, 1988), pp 163, 395.

20. *Ibid.*, pp 132, 342.

21. *Ibid.*, p. 345.

22. Quoted in *Ibid.*, p. 525, first published in *The Internationalist*, October 1897.

23. F.J. Bigger, *Crossing the bar* (Belfast, 1926), p. 19.

24. S. Deane, *Celtic revivals: Essays in modern Irish literature 1880–1980* (London, 1985, p. 17.

25. *Ibid.*

26. J. Watson, *A guide to the New Age for confused Christians* (Bramcote Grove, 1991).

27. D. Sullivan, *Ley Lines: A comprehensive guide to alignments* (London, 1999), p. 61.

28. M. Poynder, *Pi in the sky: A revelation of the ancient wisdom tradition* (London, 1992), p. 177.

29. *Ibid.*, p. 86.

30. *Ibid.*, p. 83.

31. P. Shallcrass, 'A priest of the goddess' in J. Pearson, R. Roberts and G. Samuel (ed.), *Nature religion today; paganism in the modern world* (Edinburgh, 1998), pp 158–69, see p. 167.

32. R. Hutton, 'The discovery of the mother goddess' in Pearson, Roberts and Samuel (ed.), *Nature religion today*, pp 89–100, see pp 93–4.

33. M. Green, *Celtic goddesses* (London, 1995).

34. S. Connolly, *How high the moon: Boann and other poems* (Dublin, 1991), p. 4-6.

35. G. Samuel, 'Paganism and Tibetan Buddhism: contemporary western religions and the question of nature' in Pearson, Roberts and Samuel (ed.), *Nature religion today*, pp 123–42, see p. 132.

36. K. Danaher, *The year in Ireland* (Cork, 1972).

37. J.F. Deane, *Winter in Meath* (Dublin, 1985), p. 28; S. Heaney, 'A dream of solstice', *The Irish Times*, 21 December 2000, p. 1.

38. S. Connolly, *For the stranger* (Dublin, 1993), 'Solstice', p. 29.

39. *A beam of light; the music of Michael Holohan* (1997) Drogheda Arts Centre/Hugh Lane Gallery of Modern Art. The piece included 'Solstice', 'Newgrange', 'The Dream of Aenghus' and 'Dowth'.

40. M. Brennan, *The stars and the stones: ancient art and astronomy in Ireland* (London, 1983).

41. *Ibid.*, p. 101.

42. *Ibid.*, p. 82.

43. A. Moroney, *Dowth: winter sunsets* (Drogheda, 1999).

44. Brennan, *The stars and the stones*, p. 28.

45. L. Cyr, *Cascading comets: The key to ancient mysteries* (Santa Barbara, California, 1998). The publishers of this book call themselves 'Stonehenge Viewpoint'.

46. K. O'Sullivan, 'Canadian cartographer uncovers the hidden secret of Knowth moon carvings' in *The Irish Times*, 28 April 1999, p. 5, reports the alleged discovery by Dr Philip Stooke of the University of Western Ontario. See also W. Antpohler, *Newgrange, Dowth and Knowth: A visit to Ireland's Valley of the Kings* (Dublin, 2000).

47. T. Richards, *The lost scrolls of Newgrange* (Dublin, 1994).

48. A. Crookshank and Knight of Glin, *The painters of Ireland c.1660–1920* (London, 1978), pp 61–5.

49. Information based on a lecture given by Bairbe Ni Floinn, Folklore Department, University College Dublin, Drogheda, 14 September 1997.

50. B. Ó Buachalla, *Aisling Ghéar* (Dublin, 1996), p. 169.

51. *Ibid.*, p. 174.

52. *Ibid.*, p. 168.

53. I would like to acknowledge information received from the Irish Traditional Music Archive, Merrion Square, Dublin, and song collector Sean Corcoran, Drogheda.

54. Lady Gregory, *Our Irish theatre*, (New York, 1914).

55. A comment often made by Professor George Eogan, Director of the Knowth excavations.

56. *Home on the page: Songs by Tom Delaney* (Dublin, no date) 'George Eogan', pp 32–3, 'Knowth trowler', pp 40–1.

BIBLIOGRAPHY

Aalen, F. (ed.) 1985 *The future of the Irish rural landscape*, Dublin.

Aalen, F. 1985 'The rural landscape: change, conservation and planning' in Aalen (ed.), *Future of the Irish rural landscape*, pp 1–25.

Aalen, F. 1986 'The re–housing of rural labourers in Ireland under the Labourers (Ireland) Act, 1883–1919' in *Journal of Historical Geography*, xii, pp 287–306.

Aalen, F. 1987 'Public housing in Ireland' in *Planning Perspectives*, ii, pp 175–93.

Aalen, F. (ed.) 1996 *Landscape study and management*, Dublin.

Aalen, F. 1996 'Approaches to the study and management of the landscape' in Aalen (ed.), *Landscape study*, pp 1–12.

Aalen, F. 1997 'Buildings', in Aalen, Whelan and M. Stout (ed.), *Atlas*, pp 145–79.

Aalen, F. 1997 'The Irish rural landscape: synthesis of habitat and history' in Aalen, Whelan and M. Stout (ed.), *Atlas*, pp 4–30.

Aalen, F. 1997 'Management of the landscape' in Aalen, Whelan and M. Stout (ed.), *Atlas*, pp 255–59.

Aalen, F. and Whelan, K. (ed.) 1992 *Dublin from prehistory to present – studies in honour of J. H. Andrews*, Dublin.

Aalen, F., Whelan, K. and Stout, M. (ed.) 1997 *Atlas of the Irish rural landscape*, Cork.

Aitchison, J. 1996 'The World Heritage Convention: cultural sites and landscapes' in Aalen (ed.), *Landscape study*, pp 183–93.

Albright, H. 1985 *The birth of the National Park Service: the founding years, 1913–33*, Salt Lake City, Utah.

Alexander, R. and Gahan, S. 1987 'A review of sites protected for conservation in the Republic of Ireland', *Ir. Geog.*, xx, pp 82–8

Andrews, J. 1967 'A geographer's view of Irish history' in Moody and Martin (ed.), *Course of Irish history*, pp 17–29.

Andrews, J. 1986 'Land and people, c. 1780' in Moody and Vaughan (ed.), *New history of Ireland iv, eighteenth century*, pp 236–64.

Andrews, J. 1997 *Shapes of Ireland*, Dublin.

Anon., 1941 'Things umpires should look for' in *An Cosantóir*, i, pp 12–16.

Anon., 1942 'Early silver ear ring found at Rossnaree' in *County Louth Archaeological and Historical Society Journal*, x, p. 157.

Antpohler, W. 2000 *Newgrange, Dowth and Knowth: A visit to Ireland's Valley of the Kings*, Dublin.

Arnold, L. 1993 *The restoration land settlement in county Dublin, 1660–1688: a history of the administration of the acts of settlement and explanation*, Dublin.

Ashton, S. 2002 'John Boyle O'Reilly and Moondyne' in *History Ireland*, x, pp 38–42.

Atkinson–Willes, G. 1980 'The numerical distribution and the conservation requirements of swans in north–west Europe' in Anon., *Second International Swan Symposium*, Japan, pp 40–8.

Baldock, D. 1984 *Wetland drainage in Europe: the effects of agricultural policy in four EEC countries*. International Institute for Environment and Development and the Institute for European Environmental Policy, London.

Balfour, B. 1890 'Round tower at Proudfootstown' in *R.S.A.I. Jn.*, xxi, pp 247–8.

Balfour, J. 1984 *A new look at the Northern Ireland countryside*, Belfast.

Bangor–Jones, M. 1993 'The incorporation of documentary evidence and other historical sources into preservation and management strategies' in R. Hingley (ed.), *Medieval or later rural settlement in Scotland*, Edinburgh, pp 36–42.

Barnard, N. 1642 *The whole proceedings of the siege of Drogheda*, London.

Barnwall, S. 1983 'Darcys of Plattin, county Meath' in the *Irish Genealogist*, vi, pp 419–22.12.

Barry, L. (ed.) 1994 *Selected poems, speeches, dedications, and letters of John Boyle O'Reilly 1844–1890*, Australind, Western Australia.

Bateson, J. 1973 'Roman material from Ireland: a re–consideration' in *R.I.A. Proc.*, C, lxxv, pp 21–97.

Beresford-Ellis, P. 1976 *The Boyne Water*, Belfast.

De Bhaldraithe, T. (ed.) 1977 *Foclóir Gaeilge–Béarla*, Dublin.

Bhreathnach, E. 1995 *Tara: a select bibliography*, Dublin.

Bieler, L. 1979 *The Patrician texts in the book of Armagh,* Dublin.

Birks, H. 1988 'Introduction' in H. Birks, P. Kaland, M. Dagfinn (ed.), *The cultural landscape: past, present, future*, Cambridge, pp 7–8.

Bolger, T. 2002 'Three sites on the M1 motorway at Rathmullan, Co. Meath' in *Ríocht na Midhe*, xiii, pp 8–17.

Bord Failte–Cóspoir n.d. *Walking in Ireland*, Dublin.

Bowden, A. 1971 'The Carboniferous geology of P.L. 1039 and P.L. 1040 and adjoining application areas near Drogheda, county Louth', unpublished GSI report AB1/71.

Bowen, C. 1975–6 'An historical inventory of the Dindshenchas' in *Studia Celtica*, x–xi, pp 113–37.

Bradley, K., Skehan, C. and Walsh, G. (ed.) 1991 *Environmental impact assessment: a technical approach*, Dublin.

Bradshaw, B. 1974 *The dissolution of the monastic properties of Ireland under Henry VIII,* Cambridge.

Brady, Shipman and Martin 1992 National canals and waterways strategy, unpublished report, Office of Public Works, Dublin.

Brady, Shipman and Martin 1996 Boyne valley integrated development plan, unpublished report, Office of Public Works, Dublin.

Brady, C. 1996 'Surface collected flint from Site A, Newgrange, county Meath' in *Trowel* , vii, pp 41–5.

Brady, C. and Byrnes, E. 2002 'A pilot archaeological survey for the site of the Battle of the Boyne, Oldbridge Estate, county Meath' in *Second Irish Post–Medieval Archaeology Group Conference, Paper abstracts*, Dublin.

Brady, N. 1986 The plough in early historic and medieval Ireland, unpublished MA thesis, NUI Dublin.

Brennan, E. (ed.) 1990 *Heritage: a visitor's guide*, Dublin.

Brennan, M. 1983 *The stars and the stones: ancient art and astronomy in Ireland*, London.

Brindley, A. and Lanting, J. 1990 'A Roman boat in Ireland' in *Arch. Ir.*, iv, pp 10–11.

British Parliamentary Papers, Famine Ireland, 8, 1846, 3.

Brooks, E. (ed.) 1953 *The Irish cartularies of Llanthony Prima and Secunda*, Dublin.

Brooks, E. 1953 'Fourteenth–century monastic estates in Meath' in *R.S.A.I. Jn.*, lxxxiii, pp 140–9.

Brown, I. 1995 *Twentieth century defences in Britain: an introductory guide*, London.

Bruton, R. and Convery, F. 1982 *Land drainage policy in Ireland*, Dublin.

Buchanan, R. 1973 'Field systems of Ireland' in A. Baker and R. Butlin (ed.), *Studies of field systems in the British Isles*, London, pp 580–618.

Buchanan, R. 1982 'Landscape' in J. Cruickshank and D. Wilcock (ed.), *Northern Ireland: environment and natural resources*, Belfast, pp 265–89.

Buckley, V. 1988–9 'Meath souterrains: some thoughts on Early Christian distribution patterns' in *Ríocht na Midhe*, viii, pp 64–7.

Buckley, V. and Sweetman, P. 1991 *Archaeological survey of county Louth*, Dublin.

Burl, H. 1969 'Henges: internal features and regional groups' in *Archaeological Journal*, cxxvi, pp 1–26.

Byrne, F. 1967 'Historical note on Cnogba (Knowth)' in G. Eogan, 'Excavations at Knowth, county Meath, 1962–5' in *R.I.A. Proc.*, lxvi, C, pp 383–400.

Byrne, F. 1987 *Irish kings and high kings*, London.

Cafferkey, S. 1996 Prehistory of the ploughzone in north–east county Wicklow, unpublished MA thesis, Department of Archaeology, NUI Dublin.

Calendar of Irish patent rolls of James 1 1966 Dublin.

Campbell, J. 1960–3 'The tour of Edward Lhwyd in Ireland in 1699 and 1700' in *Celtica*, v, pp 218–28.

Carey, H. 1998 The kingdom and lordship of Meath: 1100–c.1215, unpublished MLitt thesis, Trinity College Dublin.

Carson, R. and O'Kelly, C. 1977 'A catalogue of the Roman coins from Newgrange, county Meath' in *R.I.A. Proc.*, C, lxxvii, pp 35–55.

Carville, G. 1969 The Cistercians in Ireland and their economy: 1142–1541, unpublished MA thesis, The Queens University of Belfast.

Casey, C. and Rowan, A. 1993 *The buildings of Ireland; North Leinster*, Dublin.

Caulfield, S. 1977 'The beehive quern in Ireland' in *R.S.A.I. Jn.*, cvii, pp 104–38.

Census of Ireland, 1841, 1851, 1861, 1871, 1881, 1891, 1901.

Chancery of Judiary Rolls of Ireland 1914 London.

Clare, T. 1986 'Towards a re–appraisal of henge monuments' in *Proceedings of the Prehistoric Society*, lii, pp 281–316.

Clare, T. 1987 'Towards a re–appraisal of henge monuments: origins, evolution and hierarchies' in *Proceedings of the Prehistoric Society*, liii, pp 457–77.

Clarke, A. 1967 'The colonisation of Ulster and the rebellion of 1641' in Moody and Martin (ed.), *The course of Irish history*, Cork, pp 189–203.

Cleary, R. 1983 'The ceramic assemblage' in M. O'Kelly, Cleary and Lehane, *Newgrange, county Meath*, pp 58–117.

Cleere, H. 1995 'Cultural landscapes as world heritage' in *Conservation and management of archaeological sites*, i, pp 65–8.

Clinton, M. 1996 'Two recently discovered souterrains in county Meath' in *Ríocht na Midhe*, ix, pp 30–3.

Clinton, M. 1998 Structural aspects of souterrain in Ireland, unpublished PhD thesis, NUI Galway.

Clinton, M. 2001 *The souterrains of Ireland*. Dublin.

Coffey, G. 1912 *New Grange (Brugh na Bóinne) and other incised tumuli in Ireland*, Dublin.

Cole, G. 1956 *Memoir and map of localities and minerals of economic importance and metaliferous mines in Ireland*, 2nd ed., Dublin.

Collins, B. 1997 'Appendix 3: plant remains' in Eogan and Roche, *Excavations at Knowth II*, pp 295–300.

Colmcille, Fr 1953 'Seven documents from the old abbey of Mellifont' in *County Louth Archaeological and Historical Journal*, xiii, pp 35–67.

Colmcille, Fr 1958 *The story of Mellifont*, Dublin.

Commission of the European Communities Com (91) 100 Fund 1991 'The development and future of the CAP', reflections paper of the Commission, Brussels.

Condit, T. 1997 'The Newgrange cursus and the theatre of ritual ' in *Brú na Bóinne;* supplement to *Arch. Ir.*, xi, pp 26–7.

Condit, T. 1991 'Archaeology' in Bradley, Skehan and Walsh (ed.), *Environmental impact assessment*, pp 111–5.

Connolly, S. 1991 *How high the moon: Boann and other poems*, Dublin.

Connolly, S. 1993 *For the stranger*, Dublin.

Conway, M. 1968 'The Boyle O'Reilly stone' in *Journal of the Old Drogheda Society*, iv, pp 3–7.

Convery, F and Flanagan, S. 1991 *Tourism in County Meath: a strategy for the 90s*, Dublin.

Cooney, G. 1990 'The Mount Oriel project: an introduction in *Louth Archaeological and Historical Society Journal*, xxix, pp 125–33

Cooney, G. 1990 'The place of megalithic tomb cemeteries in Ireland' in *Antiquity*, lxiv, pp 741–53.

Cooney, G. 1991 'Irish Neolithic landscapes and land use systems: the implications of field systems' in *Rural History*, ii, pp 123–9.

Cooney, G. 1992 'The archaeological endowment' in J. Feehan (ed.), *Environment and development in Ireland*, pp 70–80.

Cooney, G. 1998 The Red Mountain transect: the results of a pilot fieldwalking study in the Boyne Valley area, unpublished Dúchas report, Dublin.

Cooney G. and Grogan, E. 1994 *Irish prehistory: a social perspective*, Dublin.

Coones, P. 1992 'The unity of landscape' in Macinnes and Wickham–Jones (ed.), *All natural things: archaeology and the green debate*, pp 22–40.

Corish, P. 1981 *The Catholic community in the seventeenth and eighteenth centuries*, Dublin.

Council of Europe 1966 *European Convention on the Protection of the Archaeological Heritage*, Strasbourg.

Council of Europe 1985 *Convention for the protection of the architectural heritage of Europe*, Granada.

Council of Europe 1992 *European Convention on the Protection of the Archaeological Heritage*, Valetta.

Council of Europe 1995 *Recommendation of the committee of ministers to member states on the integrated conservation of cultural landscape areas as part of landscape policies*, Strasbourg.

Countryside Commission 1983 *Management agreements: policy statements and grants,*, CCP 156, Cheltenham.

Countryside Commission 1986 *Heritage landscapes: management plans*, CCP206, Cheltenham.

Countryside Commission 1986 *Management plans: a guide to their preparation and use*, CCP205, Cheltenham.

Countryside Commission 1990 *Countryside and nature conservation issues in district local plans: guidance notes for district councils*, CCP 317, Cheltenham.

Countryside Commission 1992 *Protected landscapes in the United Kingdom*, CCP 326, Cheltenham.

Countryside Commission 1993 *Landscape assessment guidance*, CCP423, Cheltenham.

Cregan, M. 1996 'Landscape architecture: a view of the profession' in Aalen (ed.), *Landscape study*, pp 55–80.

Crookshank, A. 1994 The w*atercolours of Ireland: Works on paper in pencil, pastel and pen c.1600–1914*, London.

Crookshank A. and Knight of Glin 1978 *The painters of Ireland c.1600–1920*, London.

Cross, S. 1991 An intensive survey of the early prehistoric archaeology in the environs of Fourknocks, county Meath, unpublished MA thesis, Department of Archaeology, NUI Dublin.

Cullen, L. 1977 'Eighteenth-century flour milling in Ireland' in *Ir. Ec. Soc. Hist.*, iv, pp 5–25.

Cullen, L. 1986 'Economic development: 1691–1750' in Moody and Vaughan (ed.), *New history of Ireland iv, eighteenth century*, Oxford, pp 123–58.

Cullen, L. 1988 'Man, landscape and roads: the changing eighteenth–century landscape' in Nolan (ed.), *The shaping of Ireland*, Dublin, pp 123–36.

Curran, O. 1995 *History of the Diocese of Meath 1860–1993*, reprint, Dublin.

Curtayne, A. 1972 *Francis Ledwidge: A life of the Poet*, London.

Cyr, L. 1998 *Cascading comets: The key to ancient mysteries*, Santa Barbara, California.

D'Alton, J. 1844 *The history of Drogheda with its environs and an introductory memoir of the Dublin and Drogheda railway*, 2 vols, Dublin.

Danaher, K. 1972 *The year in Ireland*, Cork.

Darvill, T. 1987 *Prehistoric Britain*, London.

Darvill, T. 1996 'European heritage and the recognition of cultural landscape areas' in Aalen (ed.), *Landscape study*, pp 173–81.

Darvill, T., Gerrard, C. and Startin, B. 1993 'Identifying and protecting historic landscapes ' in *Antiquity*, lxvii, pp 563–74.

Davies, O. I.T.A. Survey, Dúchas.

Day, A. (ed.) 1991 *Letters from Georgian Ireland: The correspondence of Mary Delany, 1731–68*, Belfast.

Deane, J.F. 1985 *Winter in Meath*, Dublin.

Deane, S. 1985 *Celtic revivals: Essays in modern Irish literature 1880–1980*, London.

Delaney, T. n.d. *Home on the page: Songs by Tom Delaney*, Dublin.

Department of Agriculture 1932 First annual report of the Minister for Agriculture 1931–1932, Dublin.

Department of Agriculture 1941 Tenth annual report of the Minister for Agriculture 1940–41, Dublin.

Department of Agriculture 1942 Eleventh annual report of the Minister for Agriculture 1941–42, Dublin.

Department of Agriculture 1950 Nineteenth annual report of the Minister of Agriculture 1949–50, Dublin

Department of Agriculture 1953 Twenty–second annual report of the Minister of Agriculture 1952–53, Dublin

Department of Agriculture and Fisheries 1974 Annual Report of the Minister for Agriculture and Fisheries 1973–1974, Dublin.

Department of Agriculture and Fisheries 1975 Annual Report of the Minister for Agriculture and Fisheries 1974 Ireland, Dublin.

Department of Agriculture and Fisheries 1977 Annual Report of the Minister for Agriculture and Fisheries 1976 Ireland, Dublin.

Department of Agriculture 1982 Annual Report of the Minister for Agriculture 1981 Ireland, Dublin.

Department of Agriculture 1984 Annual Report of the Minister for Agriculture 1983 Ireland, Dublin.

Department of Agriculture 1986 Annual Report of the Minister for Agriculture 1985 Ireland, Dublin.

Department of Agriculture 1987 Annual Report of the Minister for Agriculture 1986 Ireland, Dublin.

Department of Agriculture and Food 1988 Annual Report of the Minister of Agriculture and Food 1988 Ireland, Dublin.

Department of Agriculture and Food 1989 Annual Report of the Minister of Agriculture and Food 1988 Ireland, Dublin.

Department of Agriculture, Food and Forestry 1994 *Rural Environment Protection Scheme*, Dublin.

Department of Agriculture, Food and Forestry 1996 *Schemes and services 1996*, Dublin.

Department of Arts, Culture and the Gaeltacht 1996 *Strengthening the protection of the architectural heritage*, Dublin.

Department of Arts, Culture and the Gaeltacht 1998 *Protecting our architectural heritage*, Dublin.

Department of Local Government 1963 *Planning and Development Act, 1963*, No. 28, Dublin.

Devine–Wright, P. and Lyons, E. 1997 'Remembering pasts and representing places: the construction of national identities in Ireland' in *Journal of Environmental Psychology*, xvii, pp 33–45.

Dillon, F. 1997 'Lithic assemblage' in Eogan and Roche, *Excavations at Knowth II*, p. 81.

Dimock, J. (ed. and trans.) 1967 *Expugnatio Hibernica Giraldi Cambrensis Opera*, Dublin.

Dobbs, M. 1926 'Some ancient placenames' in *R.S.A.I. Jn.*, lvi, pp 106–18.

Dúchas 1996 Record of monuments and places, county Westmeath, unpublished report, Dublin.

Dúchas 1997 Record of monuments and places, county Louth, unpublished report, Dublin.

Dúchas 1997 Record of monuments and places, county Meath, unpublished report, Dublin.

Duffy, P. 1998 'Locality and changing landscape: geography and local history' in Gillespie and Hill (ed.), *Doing Irish local history: pursuit and practice*, Belfast, pp 24–46.

Dyson–Bruce, L. 1999 *Historic Landscape Assessment*, Edinburgh.

Ellison, C. 1971 'Bishop Dopping's visitation book 1682–1685' in *Riocht na Midhe*, iv, pp 28–39.

Ellison, C. 1973 'Bishop Dopping's visitation book 1682–1685' in *Riocht na Midhe*, v, pp 2–11.

Ellison, C. 1983 *The waters of the Boyne and Blackwater*, Navan.

Elrington, C. 1864 *The whole works of Most Rev. James Ussher, Lord Archbishop and Primate of Ireland*, 2 vols, Dublin.

Environmental Impact Services Ltd. 1992 'Environmental Impact study for Oldbridge House golf and leisure development', unpublished report, Dublin.

Eogan, G. 1963 'A neolithic habitation–site and megalithic tomb in Townleyhall townland, county Louth' in *R.S.A.I. Jn.*, xciii, pp 37–81.

Eogan, G. 1966 'Excavations at Knowth, county Meath' in *R.I.A. Proc.*, C, lxvi, pp 199–382.

Eogan, G. 1974 'Report on the excavations of some passage graves, unprotected inhumation burials and a settlement site at Knowth, county Meath' in *R.I.A. Proc.*, C, lxxiv, pp 2–112.

Eogan, G. 1977 'Iron Age and Early Christian settlement' in V. Markotic (ed.), *Ancient Europe and the Mediterranean: studies in honour of Hugh Hencken*, Warminster, Wiltshire, pp 69–76.

Eogan, G. 1984 *Knowth: 21 years on*, guide to exhibition, NUI Dublin.

Eogan, G. 1984 *Excavations at Knowth I*, Dublin.

Eogan, G. 1986 *Knowth and the passage–tombs of Ireland*, London.

Eogan, G. 1990 'The archaeology of Brugh na Bóinne during the early centuries AD' in *Seanchas ard Mhacha*, v, pp 20–34.

Eogan, G. 1991 'Prehistoric and early historic culture change at Brugh na Bóinne' in *R.I.A. Proc.*, C, xci, pp 105–32.

Eogan, G. 1997 'The passage tombs of Brú na Bóinne' in *Brú na Bóinne*; supplement to *Arch. Ir.*, xi, pp 9–11.

Eogan, G. 2002 'The M1 motorway and its archaeology: Introduction' in *Ríocht na Midhe*, xiii, pp 1–6.

Eogan, G. and Roche, H. 1994 'A Grooved Ware wooden structure at Knowth, Boyne Valley, Ireland' in *Antiquity*, lxviii, pp 322–30.

Eogan, G. and Roche, H. 1997 *Excavations at Knowth II*, Dublin.

Eogan, G. and Roche, H. 1997 'Pre–tomb Neolithic house discovered at Knowth' in *Arch. Ir.*, xi, p. 31.

Feehan, J. (ed.) 1992 *Environment and development in Ireland*, Dublin.

Feehan, J. 1992 'A direction for rural tourism on the farm' in Feehan (ed.), *Environment and development in Ireland*, pp 577–82.

Finch, T., Gardiner, M., Conry, M. and Radford, T. 1983 *Soils of county Meath*, Dublin.

Fleetwood, J. 1988 *The Irish body snatchers: a history of body snatching in Ireland*, Dublin.

Fleming, A. 1996 'Total landscape archaeology – dream or necessity' in Aalen (ed.), *Landscape study*, pp 81–92.

Fox, R. 1993 *Archaeology, history and Custers last battle*, Norman, Oklahoma.

Galway, F.   1985–6   'Meath towerhouses' in *Riocht na Midhe*, vii, pp 28–200.

Gardiner, M., Finch, T., Conry, M. and Radford, T.   1975   'Over one–third of Meath land has a drainage problem' in *Farm and Food Research*, vi, p. 15.

Geological Survey of Ireland   1871   'Explanatory memoir to accompany Sheets 91 and 92', unpublished memoir, Dublin.

Geraghty, J.   1994   'P.J. Dodd of Drogheda: architect and civil engineer' in *Journal of the Old Drogheda Society*, ix, pp 7–37.

Gilbert, D.   1992   'Appropriate rural development for social and environmental sustainability' in J. Feehan (ed.), *Environment and development in Ireland*, Dublin, pp 568–76.

Gilbert, J.   1882   *History of the Irish Confederation and the war in Ireland*, Dublin.

Gilbert, J.   1980   *A contemporary history of affairs in Ireland from 1641–1652*, 2 vols, Dublin.

Gillespie, R. and Hill, M. (ed.)   1998   *Doing Irish local history: pursuit and practice*, Belfast.

Gillmor, D.   1989   'Agricultural development', in R. Carter and A. Parker (eds.), *Ireland: a contemporary geographical perspective on a land and its people*, London, pp 192-3.

Gillmor, D.   1991   'Agricultural impacts and the Irish environment' in *Geographical Viewpoint*, xx, 5–22.

Gosling, P.   1987   'An interim measure' in *Arch. Ir.*, i, pp 23–27.

Gowen, M.   1992   'Excavation of two souterrain complexes at Marshes Upper, Dundalk, county Louth' in *R.I.A. Proc.*, C, xcii, pp 55–120.

Gowan, M.   1992   'A Neolithic house at Newtown' in *Arch. Ir.*, vi, pp 25–7.

Graham, B.   1974   'Medieval settlements in County Meath' in *Riocht na Midhe*, v, pp 40–59.

Graham, B.   1975   'Anglo–Norman settlement in county Meath' in *R.I.A. Proc.*, C, lxxv, pp 223–49.

Graham, B.   1980   'The mottes of the Norman Liberty of Meath' in H. Murtagh (ed.), *Irish Midland Studies*, Athlone, pp 39–56.

Graves, Rev. J.   1980   'The Dowth eviction case' in *Journal of the Royal Society of Antiquaries*, cx, pp 205–9.

Green, B.   1985   *Countryside conservation: the protection and management of amenity ecosystems*, 2nd ed., London.

Green, B.   1996   'Landscape conservation or landscape preservation' in Aalen (ed.), *Landscape study*, pp 161–72.

Green, M.   1995   *Celtic goddesses*, London.

Greeves, T.   1992   'Reclaiming the land: why archaeology is green' in Macinnes and Wickham–Jones (ed.), *All natural things*, pp 14–21.

Gregory, N.   1995   'River Boyne, Stalleen townland, county Meath: excavation report' in *County Louth Archaeological and Historical Journal*, xxiii, pp 329–35.

Griffith, R.   1854   *General valuation of rateable property in Ireland: county Meath*, Dublin.

Griffith, R.   1854   *General valuation of rateable property in Ireland: county Louth*, Dublin.

Groenman–van Watteringe, W. and Pals, J.   1984   'Pollen and seed analysis' in Eogan, *Newgrange*, pp 219–23.

Groenman–van Watteringe, W. and Pals, J.   1994   'Pollen and seed analysis' in Eogan, *Excavations at Knowth I*, pp 325–8.

Grogan, E.   1991   'Appendix: radiocarbon dates from Brugh na Bóinne' in G. Eogan, 'Prehistoric and early historic culture change at Brugh na Bóinne' in *R.I.A. Proc.*, C, xci, pp 126–7.

Guinan, B.   1992   'Fieldwalking in Irish archaeology' in *Trowel*, iii, pp 4–8.

Gunther, R.   1945   *Life and letters of Edward Lhwyd*, Oxford.

Gwynn, E. (ed. and trans.)   1924   *The Metrical Dindshenchas*, 5 vols, Dublin.

D. Hall, M. Hennessy and T. O'Keefe,   1985   'Medieval agriculture and settlement in Oughterard and Castlewarden, county Kildare' in *Ir. Geog.*, xviii, pp 16–25.

Harbison, P.   1998   'A shaft–fragment from Slane, county Meath, and other recent high cross discoveries' in C. Manning (ed.), *Dublin and beyond the Pale*, Dublin, pp 173–6.

Harding A. and Lee, G.   1987   *Henge monuments and related sites of Great Britain*, Oxford.

Harrington, P.   1992   'Images of the Boyne' in *Irish Sword*, xviii, pp 57–61.

Heaney, S.   2000   'A dream of solstice', in *The Irish Times*, 21 December, p. 1.

Hennessy, W. and McCarthy B. (ed. and trans.)   1887–1901   *Annals Uladh, Annals of Ulster, otherwise, Annala Senait, Annals of Senat: A chronicle of Irish Affairs from AD 431 to AD 1540*, 4 vols, Dublin.

Herity, M.   1967   'From Lhuyd to Coffey: new information from unpublished descriptions of the Boyne valley tombs' in *Studia Hibernica*, vii, pp 127–45.

Herries Davies, G. and Stephens, N.   1978   *Ireland*, London.

Hewitt, S.   1992   'European policy and management at European level' in J. Feehan (ed.), *Environment and development in Ireland*, pp 259–70.

Hewitson, A. (ed.)   1908   *Diary of Thomas Bellingham: an officer under William III*, Preston.

Hickey, E.   1965   'The house of Cleitech' in *Riocht na Midhe*, iii, pp 181–5.

Hickey, E.   1966   *I send my love along the Boyne*, Dublin.

Hickey, E.   1994   *Skryne and the early Normans*, Dublin.

Hickey, E. and Rynne, E.   1953   'Two souterrains on the lower slopes of Tara' in *Journal of the Kildare Archaeological Society*, xiii, pp 220–1.

Hicks, R.   1975   Some henges and hengiform earthworks in Ireland: form, distribution, astronomical correlations and associated mythology, unpublished PhD thesis, University of Pennsylvania.

Higgins, F.R.   1992   *The 39 poems*, Dublin, edited by R.D. Clarke.

Hoare, R.C.   1807   *A journal of a tour in Ireland in AD 1806*, London.

Hodgers, D.   1994   'The Salterstown surface collection project' in *Louth Archaeological and Historical Society Journal*, xxiii, pp 240–68.

Hogan, E. (ed. and trans.)   1892   *Cath Ruis na Rig for Boinn*, Dublin.

Holroyd, J.   1785   *Observations on the manufacturing trade and present state of Ireland*, Dublin.

Horn, W. and Born, E.   1965   *The barns of the abbey of Beaulieu at its granges of Great Coxwell and Beaulieu–St. Leonards*, Berkeley.

Hornell, J.   1938   *British coracles and Irish curraghs*, London.

Hossack, H.   1993   *Buildings at risk*, Belfast.

Haughton, J. (ed.)   1978   *Atlas of Ireland*, Dublin.

Hughes, J. and Huntley, B.   1988   'Upland hay meadows in Britain: their vegetation, management and future' in Birks, Kaland and Dagfinn (ed.), *Cultural landscape: past, present, future*, Cambridge, pp 91–110.

Hutton, R.   1998   'The discovery of the mother goddess' in Pearson, Roberts and Samuel (ed.), *Nature religion today*, pp 89–100.

Hyde, D.   1993   *Building on the past: urban change and archaeology*, Dublin.

Hyland, J.   1997   'The battle of the Boyne' in *Command Magazine*, xliii, pp 30–46.

Iyer, R. and Iyer, N.   1988   *The descent of Gods*, Gerrards Cross, Buckinghamshire.

Jackson, J.   1978   'Metallic ores in Irish prehistory: copper and tin' in M. Ryan (ed.), *The origins of metallurgy in Atlantic Europe*, Hojberg, pp 107–25.

Jones, H.   1735   *Poems on several occasions*, Dublin.

Jones Hughes, T.   1958   'East Leinster in the mid–nineteenth century' in *Ir. Geog.*, iii, pp 227–41.

Jones Hughes, T.   1970   *'Town* and *Baile* in Irish place–names' in N. Stephens and R. Glasscock (ed.), *Irish geographical studies in honour of E. Estyn Evans*, Belfast, pp 244–58.

Jones Hughes, T.   1987   'Landholding and settlement in counties Meath and Cavan in the nineteenth century' in P. O'Flanagan, P. Ferguson and K. Whelan (ed.), *Rural Ireland: modernisation and change 1600–1900*, Cork, pp 104–46.

Keane, E.   1995   'Interpreting, preserving and managing ritual landscapes', unpublished abstract from the 60th anniversary conference of the Prehistoric Society, Dublin.

Keane, E.   1997   'The visitor centre: gateway to Brú na Bóinne' in *Brú na Bóinne*; supplement to *Arch. Ir.*, xi, pp 36–7.

Kelly, E.   1984   'Two quernstones from county Meath' in *Riocht na Midhe*, vii, pp 104–11.

Kelly, E.   1993   'Investigation of ancient fords on the river Suck' in *Inland Waterways News*, xx, pp 4–5.

Kenny, M.   1978–79   'Land Tenure in east Westmeath and its influence upon the state of agriculture, 1820–1840' in *Riocht na Midhe*, vi, pp 33–48.

Killen, J.   1997   'Communications' in Aalen, Whelan and M. Stout (ed.), *Atlas*, pp 206–19.

Kirby, K.   1988   'Conservation in British woodland' in Birks, Kaland and Dagfinn (ed.), *Cultural landscape*, pp 79–89.

Lack, P.   1986   *The atlas of wintering birds in Britain and Ireland*, Catton, Staffordshire.

Lady Gregory   1914   *Our Irish theatre*, New York.

Lambrick, G.   1992   'The importance of cultural heritage in a green world: towards the development of landscape integrity assessment' in Macinnes and Wickham–Jones (ed.), *All natural things*, pp 105–26.

Laux, L.   1997   'National Parks and education' in F. O'Gorman, T. Bryson and B. Green (ed.), *Tourism and protected areas; final report of the fifth European training seminar for managers of protected areas*, Dublin, p. 3.

Laverty, J. 1892 'Miscellanea: Newgrange still called by its ancient name, Brugh na Bóinne' in *R.S.A.I. Jn.*, xxii, p. 430.

Leavy, T. and Coulter, B. 1997 'REPS: Highest uptake in Midlands and West' in *Today's Farm*, vii, p. 42.

Ledwich, E. 1804 *Antiquities of Ireland*, 2nd ed., London.

Ledwidge, F. 1992 *Selected poems*, Dublin, edited by D. Bolger with an introduction by S. Heaney.

Lehane, D. 1983 'The flint work' in M. O'Kelly, Cleary and Lehane (ed.), *Newgrange, county Meath, Ireland*, Oxford, pp 118–70.

Leopold, A. 1989 *A Sand County almanac*, 3rd ed., Oxford.

Lewis, S. 1837 *Topographical dictionary of Ireland*, 2 vols, London.

Lindsay, A. 1992 'Architectural heritage inventory post–1700' in Feehan (ed.), *Environment and development in Ireland*, p. 113.

Liversage G. 1960 'A neolithic site at Townleyhall, county Louth' in *R.S.A.I. Jn.*, xc, pp 49–60.

Loeber, R. 1991 *The geography and practise of English colonisation in Ireland, 1534–1609*, Athlone.

Lucas, A. 1953 'The horizontal mill in Ireland' in *R.S.A.I. Jn.*, lxxxiii, pp 1–36.

Lucas, A 1971–73 'Souterrains: the literary evidence' in *Bealoideas*, xxxix–xliv, pp 39–41.

Lucas, P. 1992 *Protected landscapes: a guide for policy–makers and planners*, London.

Lunnon, R. 1991 'Ireland: the last stronghold of the European otter' in P. Nugent (ed.), *Natural Heritage*, Longford, pp 117–9.

Lyons, M. 1993 *Illustrated incumbered estates: Ireland, 1850–1905*, Whitegate, Clare.

MacAirt, S. and MacNiocaill, G. (ed. and trans.) 1983 *The Annals of Ulster (to AD 1131)*, Dublin.

McCabe, A. 1972 'Directions of late–Pleistocene ice–flows in eastern counties Meath and Louth' Ireland', in *Ir. Geog.*, vi, pp 443–61.

McCabe, A. 1973 'The glacial stratigraphy of Meath and Louth' in *R.I.A. Proc.*, C, lxxiii, pp 355–82.

McCormick, F. 1985 'appendix I' in Sweetman, 'Pit circle at Newgrange', pp 219–20.

McCormick, F. 1992 'Exchange of livestock in Early Christian Ireland, AD 450–1150' in *Anthropozoological Journal*, xvi, pp 31–6.

McCormick, F. 1997 'Animal bone analysis from Neolithic and Beaker complexes' in Eogan and Roche, *Excavations at Knowth II*, pp 301–6.

McCracken, E. 1987–93 'Tree planting by tenants in Meath 1800–1850' in *Riocht na Midhe*, viii, pp 3–20.

McCracken, J. 1986 'The ecclesiastical structure, 1714–60' in Moody and Vaughan (ed.), *A new history of Ireland iv*, pp 84–104.

McGrath, B. 1994–5 'County Meath from the Depositions' in *Riocht na Midhe*, ix, pp 24–41.

Macalister, R.A.S. 1943 'A preliminary report on the excavation of Knowth' in *R.I.A. Proc.*, il, C, pp 131–66.

Macinnes, L. and Wickham–Jones, C. (ed.) 1992 *All natural things: archaeology and the green debate*, Edinburgh.

Macinnes, L. 1996 'Between idea and reality: integrating landscapes in practice' in Aalen (ed.), *Landscape study*, pp 135–50.

Mackay, D. 1993 'Scottish rural highland settlement: preserving a people's past' in R. Hingley (ed.), *Medieval or later rural settlement in Scotland: management and preservation*, Edinburgh, pp 43–51.

Mallon, D. 1994 *Nano Reid: 1900–1981*, Drogheda.

Mangan, C. 1993–95 'Plans and operations' in *Irish Sword*, xix, pp 47–56.

Mansergh, N. 1991 'Housing and conservation' in J. Feehan (ed.), *Environment and Development in Ireland*, Dublin, pp 109–13.

Marstrander, C. 1911 'A new version of the Battle of Mag Rath' in *Ériu*, v, pp 226–9.

Matthews, S. 1987 'Place and People: a family exploration', unpublished family history.

Matthews, S. 1994 'Under the hill of Donore' in *Journal of the Old Drogheda Society*, ix, pp 118–28.

Mawhinney, K. 1979 'Recreation' in D. Gillmor (ed.), *Irish resources and land use*, Dublin, pp 196–225.

Meath County Council 1994 *County Meath Development Plan*, Navan.

Meath Leader II 1999 *Meath's farming future; facing challenge*, Kells.

Meehan, R. and Warren, W. 1999 *The Boyne valley in the Ice Age; a field guide to some of the valley's most impressive glacial geological features*, Dublin.

Meeus, J., Wijermans, M. and Vroom, M. 1990 'Agricultural landscapes in Europe and their transformation' in *Landscape and Urban Planning*, xviii, pp 289–352.

Meighan, I., Simpson, D. and Hartwell, B. 2002 'Newgrange: Sourcing of its granitic cobbles' in *Arch. Ir.*, xvi, pp 32–5.

Mercer, I. 1979 *Buildings in the Dartmoor National Park*, Dartmoor.

J. Mills and J. Mc Enery (ed.) 1916 *Calendar of the Gormanston Register*, Dublin.

Mitchell and Associates 1992 *Environmental impact statement, Park Centre Building for Boyne Valley Archaeological Park: non–technical summary*, Dublin.

Mitchell, G.F. 1976 *The Irish landscape*, Cork.

Mitchell, G.F. 1984 'The landscape' in G. Eogan, *Excavations at Knowth I*, pp 9–11.

Mitchell, G.F. 1992 'Notes on some non–local cobbles at the entrance to the passage–graves at Newgrange and Knowth, county Meath' in *R.S.A.I. Jn.*, cxxii, pp 128–45.

Mitchell, G.F. 1995 'Did the tide once flow as far as Newgrange?' in *Living Heritage*, xii, p. 34.

Mitchell, G.F 1997 'The geology of the Bend of the Boyne' in *Brú na Bóinne*; supplement to *Arch. Ir.*, xi, pp 5–6.

Mitchell, G.F. and Ryan, M. 1997 *Reading the Irish landscape*, Dublin.

Molyneaux, T. 1725 'A discourse concerning the Danish mounts, forts and towers in Ireland' in G. Boate (ed.), *A natural history of Ireland*, London.

Mohen, J.–P. 1990 *The world of megaliths*, New York.

Monk, M. 1994 Macroscopic plant remains' in M. O'Kelly, *Newgrange*, pp 219–23.

Moody, T. and Martin, F. (ed.) 1967 *The course of Irish history*, Cork.

Moody, T. and Vaughan, W. (ed.) 1986 *A new history of Ireland iv, the eighteenth century: 1691–1800*, Oxford.

Moore, G. 1985 *Hail and farewell*, 5th ed. by R. Cave, first published in 1911, Gerrards Cross, Buckinghamshire.

Moore, M. (comp.) 1987 *The archaeological inventory of county Meath*, Dublin.

Moroney, A. 1999 *Dowth: winter sunsets*, Drogheda.

Mount, C. 1994 'Aspects of ritual deposition in the Late Neolithic and Beaker periods at Newgrange, county Meath' in *Proceedings of the Prehistoric Society*, lx, pp 433–43.

Murphy, D. 1883 *Cromwell in Ireland: a history of Cromwell's Irish campaign*, Dublin.

Murray, M. and Greer, J. 1990 'Prized landscapes and recreation policy in Northern Ireland: the Mournes exemplar' in *Ir. Geog.*, xxiii, pp 43–9.

Murray, R. (ed.) 1912 *The journal of John Stevens*, Oxford.

National Park Service 1975 Interpretative prospectus: Little Bighorn Battlefield National Monument, unpublished United States Department of the Interior report.

National Park Service 1995 Final general management plan and development concept plans: Little Bighorn National Monument, unpublished United States Department of the Interior report.

Neville, W. 1957–59 'The Carboniferous knoll-reefs of east central Leinster' in *R.I.A. Proc.*, B, lix, pp 285–303.

Newman, C. 1997 *Tara: an archaeological survey*, Dublin.

Newman, C. and Bhreathnach, E. 1993 'Tara project' in *Discovery Programme reports: 1, project results 1992*, Dublin, pp 69–103.

Nolan, W. 1982 *Tracing the past: sources for local studies in the Republic of Ireland*, Dublin.

Nolan, W. 1988 'New farms and fields: migration policies of state land agencies, 1891–1980' in W. Smyth and K. Whelan (ed.) *Common ground: essays on the historical geography of Ireland*, Cork, pp 296–319.

Nolan, W. (ed.) 1988 *The shaping of Ireland*, Dublin.

Ó Buachalla, B. 1996 *Aisling Ghéar*, Dublin, 1996.

O'Byrne, E. (ed.) 1981 *The convert rolls*, Dublin.

O'Carroll, D. 1992 'An indifferent good post: the battlefield of the Boyne' in *Irish Sword*, xviii, pp 49–56.

O'Carroll, D. 1993–95 'The emergency army' in *The Irish Sword*, xix, pp 19–46.

Ó Cathasaigh, T. 1989–90 'The Eponym of Cnogba' in *Eigse*, v, pp 27–38.

O'Connor–Nash, P. 1992 'The great houses: how to breastfeed a dinosaur in the late 20th century' in J. Feehan (ed.), *Environment and development in Ireland*, pp 114–7.

O'Conor, K. 1998 *The archaeology of medieval rural settlement in rural Ireland*, Dublin.

O'Donovan, J. (ed. and trans.) 1842 *The banquet of Dun na n-Gedh: and The battle of Magh Rath: an ancient historical tale now first published from a manuscript in the Library of Trinity College, Dublin*, Dublin.

O'Donovan, J. 1848–51 *Annala Riogachta Eireann. Annals of the kingdom of*

Ireland by the Four Masters from the earliest period to the year 1616, 7 vols, Dublin.

Office of Public Works 1995 *Establishment and Exhibition of Record of Monuments and Places under Section 12 National Monuments (Amendment) Act 1994,* Dublin.

O'Grada, C. 1994 *Ireland: a new economic history 1780–1939,* Oxford.

O'Grady, S. (ed. and trans.) 1892 *Silva Gadelica, (i–xxxi): A collection of tales in Irish with extracts illustrating persons and places,* London.

O'Halpin, E. 1996 'The army in independent Ireland' in T. Bartlett and K. Jefferey (ed.), *A military history of Ireland,* Cambridge, pp 407–30.

O'Keefe, T. 1992 'Medieval frontiers and fortifications: the Pale and its evolution' in F. Aalen and K. Whelan (ed.), *Dublin from prehistory to present – studies in honour of J. H. Andrews,* Dublin, pp 57–77.

O'Kelly, C. 1978 *Illustrated guide to Newgrange and the other Boyne monuments,* 3rd ed., Cork.

O'Kelly, M. 1968 'Surface collected flints from two sites in the Boyne valley, county Meath' in *Journal of the Cork Historical and Archaeological Society,* lxxiii, pp 114–9.

O'Kelly, M. 1976 'Plough pebbles from the Boyne Valley' in C. Ó Danachair (ed.), *Folk and farm: essays in honour of A.T. Lucas,* Dublin, pp 165–75.

O'Kelly, M. 1994 *Newgrange: archaeology art and legend,* 2nd ed., London.

O'Kelly, M., Cleary, R. and Lehane, D. (ed.) 1983 *Newgrange, county Meath, Ireland,* Oxford.

O'Kelly, M., Lynch, F. and O'Kelly, C. 1978 'Three passage graves at Newgrange, county Meath' in *R.I.A. Proc.,* C, lxxviii, pp 249–352.

O'Kelly, M. and O'Kelly, C. 1983 'The tumulus of Dowth, county Meath' in *R.I.A. Proc.,* C, lxxxiii, pp 136–90.

O'Kelly, M. and Shell, C. 1979 'Some objects and a bronze axe from Newgrange, county Meath in M. Ryan (ed.), *Origins of metallurgy in Atlantic Europe,* Dublin, pp 127–44.

Ó Lochlainn, C. 1940 'Roadways in ancient Ireland' in J. Ryan (ed.) *Essays and studies presented to Professor Eoin Mac Néill,* Dublin, pp 465–74

Oldham, P. 1995 *A guide to the design, construction and use of concrete pillboxes in 1914–1918,* London.

O'Neill, A. 1989 *National Archaeological Park: Boyne Valley,* unpublished consultancy report, Dublin.

Ordnance Survey 1836 *Letters, county Meath,* unpublished typescript, Royal Irish Academy, Dublin.

O'Reilly, P. and Tuite, B. (ed.) n.d. *The cry of the dreamer and other poems,* Drogheda.

Ó Riain, P. 1972 'Boundary association in Early Irish society' in *Studia Celtica,* vii, pp 12–29.

Ó Ríordáin, D. 1999 'Interpreting the interpretation' in *Arch. Ir.,* xiii, pp 8–9.

Ó Ríordáin, S. 1953 *Antiquities of the Irish countryside,* London.

Orpen, G. (ed. and trans.) 1892 *The song of Dermot and the Earl,* Oxford.

Orpen, G. 1894 'Ptolemy's map of Ireland' in *R.S.A.I. Jn.,* xxiv, pp 115–28.

Ó Siochrú, M. 1999 *Confederate Ireland 1642–1649: a constitutional and political analysis,* Dublin.

O'Sullivan, H. n.d. Northern Motorway environmental impact study, Stamullin to Monasterboice: report on cultural and heritage aspects, unpublished EIS, Louth County Council.

O'Sullivan, K. 1999 'Canadian cartographer uncovers the hidden secret of Knowth moon carvings' in *The Irish Times,* 28 April, p. 5.

O'Sullivan, M. 1993 *Megalithic art in Ireland,* Dublin.

O'Sullivan, M. and Kennedy, L. 1998 'The survival of archaeological monuments: trends and attributes' in *Ir. Geog.,* xxxi, pp 88–99.

O'Sullivan, W. 1985–86 'Medieval Meath manuscripts' in *Riocht na Midhe,* vii, pp 3–21.

Otway–Ruthven, A. 1980 *A history of medieval Ireland,* 2nd ed., New York.

Park, J. (ed.) 1988 *Environmental management in agriculture: European perspectives,* Environmental Unit, Agricultural Development and Advisory Service, Ministry of Agriculture, Fisheries and Food (UK), London.

Pearson, J., Roberts, R. and Samuel, G. (ed.) 1998 *Nature religion today: paganism in the modern world,* Edinburgh.

Pender, S. (ed.) 1939 *A census of Ireland* circa 1659, *with supplementary material from the poll money ordinances (1660–1661),* Dublin.

Petrie, G. 1845 *The ecclesiastical architecture of Ireland anterior to the Anglo–Norman period,* Dublin.

Petrie, G. 1972 'An essay on military architecture in Ireland previous to the English invasion (with notes and explanatory appendix by D.J.S. O'Malley)' in *R.I.A. Proc.,* lxxii, C, pp 219–69.

Piggot, S. 1962 *The West Kennet Long Barrow,* London.

Plachter, H. and Rossler, M. 1995 'Cultural landscapes: reconnecting culture and nature' in B. Droste, H. Plachter and M. Rossler (ed.), *Cultural landscapes of universal value,* Stuttgart, pp 15–18.

Platt, C. 1969 *The monastic grange in medieval England,* London.

Plummer, C. 1910 *Vitae Sanctorum Hiberniae,* Oxford.

Power, D. (comp.) 1992 *Archaeological inventory of county Cork, i, West Cork,* Dublin.

Pownall, T. 1773 'A description of the sepulchral monument at Newgrange, near Drogheda, in the county of Meath, in Ireland' in *Archaeologia,* ii, pp 236–75.

Poynder, M. 1992 *Pi in the sky: A revelation of the ancient wisdom tradition,* London.

Prendergast, F. 1991 'New data on Newgrange' in *Technology Ireland,* xxii, pp 22–5.

Prendergast, F. 1991 'Shadow casting phenomena at Newgrange' in *Survey Ireland,* ix, pp 9–18.

Quigley, M 1997 'The effects of EC policy on the rural landscape and environment of Ireland' in M. Blacksell and A. Williams (ed.), *The European challenge,* London.

Raftery, B. 1997 *Pagan Celtic Ireland,* 2nd ed., London.

Raftery, J. 1941 'Long stone cists of the Early Iron Age' in *R.I.A. Proc.,* C, xlvi, pp 299–315.

Reilly, T. 1993 *Cromwell at Drogheda,* Drogheda.

Reeves–Smith, T. 1997 'Demesnes' in Aalen, Whelan and M. Stout (ed.), *Atlas,* Cork, pp 197–205.

Reid, T. 1823 *Travel in Ireland in the year 1822,* London.

Reidy, K. 1989 'Farmers attitudes to countryside protection' in *Farm and Food Research,* xx, pp 13–14.

Reynolds, J. 1984 *A life on the Boyne,* Trim.

Richards, T. 1994 *The lost scrolls of Newgrange,* Dublin.

Roche, H. 1997 'Prehistoric settlement in Brú na Bóinne' in *Brú na Bóinne;* supplement to *Arch. Ir.,* xi, pp 28–9.

Roe, H. 1968 *The medieval fonts of Meath,* Dublin.

Rohan, P. 1986 *The climate of Ireland,* Dublin.

Royal Irish Academy 1913–76 *Dictionary of the Irish language,* Dublin.

Sadleir, T. 1915 *Georgian mansions in Ireland,* Dublin.

[G. S.], 1856 'Two unpublished diaries related to the battle of the Boyne' in *Ulster Journal of Archaeology,* iv, pp 77–95.

Samuel, G. 1998 'Paganism and Tibetan Buddhism: contemporary western religions and the question of nature' in Pearson, Roberts and Samuel (ed.), *Nature religion today,* pp 123–42.

Sauer, C. 1925 'The morphology of landscape' in *Publications in Geography,* ii, pp 11–54.

Saunders, A. 1989 *Fortress Britain: artillery fortifications in the British Isles and Ireland,* London.

Scannell, Y. 1991 'The European Community Directive on Environmental Impact Assessment and its implementation in Ireland' in K. Bradley, C. Skehan and G. Walsh (ed.), *Environmental impact assessment: a technical approach,* Dublin, pp 7–20.

Schofield, A. (ed.) 1991 *Interpreting artefact scatters: contributions to ploughzone archaeology,* Oxford.

Scott, A. and Martin, F. (ed. and trans.) 1978 *Expugnatio Hibernica; the conquest of Ireland by Giraldus Cambrensis,* Dublin.

Scott, D., Fox, R., O'Connor, M. and Harmon, D. 1989 *Archaeological perspectives on the Battle of Little Big Horn,* Norman, Oklahoma.

Shaffrey, P. and Shaffrey, M. 1985 *Irish countryside buildings: everyday architecture in the rural landscape,* Dublin.

Shallcrass, P. 1998 'A priest of the goddess' in Pearson, Roberts and Samuel (ed.), *Nature religion today; paganism in the modern world,* pp 158–69.

Shine, J. 1985 'Rural landscape and the planner' in Aalen (ed.), *Future of the Irish rural landscape,* pp 73–201.

Simington, R. (ed.) 1940 *The Civil Survey: county of Meath 1654–56,* v, Dublin.

Simms, J. 1971 *A Jacobite narrative of the war in Ireland: 1688–1691,* Shannon.

Simms, J. 1974 'Cromwell at Drogheda' in *Irish Sword,* xi, pp 212–21.

Smith, B. 1993 'The de Pitchford family in thirteenth–century Ireland' in *Studia Hibernica,* xxvii, pp 29–43.

Smith, B. 1999 *Colonisation and conquest in medieval Ireland: the English in Louth 1170–1330,* Cambridge.

Smith, K. 1992 'Protected landscapes: integrated approaches to conservation management' in Macinnes and Wickham–Jones (ed.) *All natural things*, pp 127–33.

Smyth, W. 1976 'Estate records and the making of the Irish landscape; an example from county Tipperary' in *Ir. Geog.*, ix, pp 29–47.

Smyth, W. 1978 'Locational patterns and trends within the pre–famine linen industry' in *Ir. Geog.*, viii, pp 97–110.

Smyth, W. 1988 'Flax cultivation in Ireland: the development and demise of a regional staple' in Smyth and Whelan (ed.), *Common ground*, Cork, pp 234–52.

Smyth, W. 1988 'Society and settlement in seventeenth century Ireland: the evidence of the '1659 Census'' in Smyth and Whelan (ed.), *Common ground*, Cork, pp 55–83.

Smyth, W. 1992 'Exploring the social and cultural geographies of sixteenth and seventeenth–century county Dublin' in Aalen and Whelan (ed.), *Dublin from prehistory to present*, pp 121–79.

Smyth, W. 1997 'The greening of Ireland – tenant tree–planting in the eighteenth and nineteenth centuries' in *Irish Forester*, liv, pp 55–72.

Smyth, W. and Whelan, K. (ed.) 1988 *Common ground: essays on the historical geography of Ireland*, Cork.

Stalley, R. 1987 *The Cistercian monasteries of Ireland*, London.

Steinberg, J. 1996 'Ploughzone sampling in Denmark: site signatures from disturbed contexts' in *Antiquity*, lxx, pp 368–92.

Stokes, W. (ed. and trans.) 1905 *Martyrology of Oengus, the Culdee*, London.

Streeten, A. 1994 'Managing ancient earthworks: diagnosis, cure and prevention of erosion' in A. Berry and I. Brown (ed.), *Erosion on archaeological earthworks: its prevention, control and repair*, Clwyd, pp 5–15.

Story, G. 1693 *An impartial history of the wars of Ireland*, London.

Stout, G. 1984 *Archaeological survey of the barony of Ikerrin*, Roscrea.

Stout, G. 1991 'Embanked enclosures of the Boyne region' in *R.I.A. Proc.*, xci, C, pp 245–84.

Stout, G. 1993 'Grant–aided change in the Boyne Valley Archaeological Park: agricultural grants 1950–1990' in *Ir. Geog.*, xxvi, pp 79–88.

Stout, G. 1997 *The bend of the Boyne: an archaeological landscape*, Dublin.

Stout, G. 1997 'Fishing at Brú na Bóinne' in *Brú na Bóinne*; supplement to *Arch. Ir.*, xi, pp 34–5.

Stout, G. and Keane, M. 1997 *Farming and the ancient countryside*, Dublin.

Stout, G. and Stout, M. 1992 'Patterns in the past: county Dublin 5000BC–1000AD in Aalen and Whelan (ed.), *Dublin from prehistory to present*, pp 5–25.

Stout, G. and Stout, M. 1997 'Early landscapes: from prehistory to plantation' in Aalen, Whelan and Stout (ed.), *Atlas*, pp 31–63.

Stout, M. 1992 'The geography and implications of Post–Famine population decline in Baltyboys, county Wicklow' in C. Morash and R. Hayes (ed.), *'Fearful realities': new perspectives on the Famine*, Dublin, pp 15–34.

Stout, M. 1997 *The Irish ringfort*, Dublin.

Sullivan, D. 1999 *Ley Lines: A comprehensive guide to alignments*, London.

Sweetman, H. 1875 *Calendar of documents relating to Ireland 1171–1251*, Dublin.

Sweetman, P.D. 1976 'An earthen enclosure at Monknewtown, Slane, county Meath' in *R.I.A. Proc.*, C, lxxvi, pp 25–72.

Sweetman, P.D. 1985 'A Late Neolithic/Early Bronze Age pit circle at Newgrange, county Meath' in *R.I.A. Proc.*, C, lxxxv, pp 195–221.

Sweetman, P.D. 1987 'Excavations of a Late Neolithic/Early Bronze Age site at Newgrange, county Meath' in *R.I.A. Proc.*, C, lxxxvii, pp 283–98.

Swift, C. 1996 'Pagan monuments and Christian legal centres in early Meath' in *Riocht na Midhe*, ix, pp 1–26.

Synge, F. 1977 'The coasts of Leinster' in C. Kidson and M. Tooley (ed.), *The quaternary history of the Irish sea*, Liverpool, pp 199–222.

Synge, F. 1979 *IQUA field handbook: annual field meeting 1979*, Dublin.

Synnott, P. n.d. The Netterville monument and family: formerly of Dowth, county Meath, unpublished family history.

Thomas, C. 1982 *Christianity in Roman Britain to AD 500*, London.

Thompson, R. 1802 *Statistical survey of county Meath*, Dublin.

Tictchen, S. 1996 'On the construction of outstanding universal value' in *Conservation and management of archaeological Sites*, i, pp 235–42.

Tilden, F. 1977 *Interpreting our heritage*, 3rd ed., Chapel Hill.

Tomlinson, R. 1996 'Tree planting by tenants in county Down during the eighteenth and nineteenth centuries' in *Ir. Geog.*, xxix, pp 83–95.

Tuite, P. 1985 'New farm buildings' in Aalen (ed.), *The future of the Irish rural landscape*, pp 46–55.

UNESCO 1994 *Intergovernmental committee for the protection of the world cultural and nature heritage operational guidelines for the implementation of the World Heritage Convention*, WHC/2, Paris.

Vallancey, C. 1786 *Collectanea de rebus Hibernicus*, Dublin.

Vaughan, W. 1994 *Landlords and tenants in mid–Victorian Ireland*, Oxford.

Vervloet, J., Renes, J. and Spek, T. 1996 'Historical geography and integrated landscape research' in Aalen (ed.), *Landscape study*, pp 112–22.

Wainwright, G. 1969 'A review of henges in the light of recent research' in *Proceedings of the Prehistoric Society*, xxxv, pp 112–33.

Wainwright, G. 1989 *The henge monuments*, London.

Wakeman, W.F. 1848 *Archaeologia Hibernica: A handbook of Irish Antiquities*, Dublin.

Wakeman, W.F. 1891 *Archaeologia Hibernica: A handbook of Irish Antiquities*, 3rd ed., Dublin.

Walsh, J. 1986 'Uneven development in agriculture in Ireland' in *Geographical Viewpoint*, xiv, pp 37–65.

Watson, J. 1991 *A guide to the New Age for confused Christians*, Bramcote Grove.

Webb, R. 1988 'The status of hedgerow field margins in Ireland' in J. Park (ed.), *Environmental management in agriculture – European perspective*, London, pp 125–43.

Weir, D. 1995 'A palynological study of landscape and agricultural development in county Louth from the second millenium BC to the first millennium AD' in *Discovery Programme project results 2*, Dublin, pp 77–126.

Went, A. 1953 'Material for a history of the fisheries of the river Boyne' in *County Louth Archaeological and Historical Journal*, xiii, pp 18–33.

Westwood, J. 1997 *Sacred Journeys: Paths for the new Pilgrim*, London.

Westropp, T. 1901 'Slane in Bregia, county Meath: its friary and hermitage' in *R.S.A.I. Jn.*, xxxiii, pp 405–30.

Westropp, T. 1906 'Ancient place–names, Brugh of the Boyne and others' in *R.S.A.I. Jn.*, xxxvi, pp 82–3.

Wheeler, H. 1985 'The national monuments of Ireland' in *Archaeologia Cambrensis.*, cxxxiv, pp 1–10.

Whelan, K. 1983 'The Catholic church, the Catholic chapel and village development in Ireland' in *Ir. Geog.*, xvi, pp 1–15.

Whelan, K. 1988 'The regional impact of Irish catholicism: 1700–1850' in Smyth and Whelan (ed.), *Common ground*, pp 257–77.

Whelan, K. 1995 'Review' in *History Ireland*, iii, pp 61.

Whelan, K. 1997 'The modern landscape: from plantation to present', in Aalen, Whelan and M. Stout (ed.), *Atlas*, Cork, pp 67–103.

White, N.B. (ed.), *Extents of Irish monastic possessions, 1540–1541, from manuscripts in the Public Record Office, London*, London.

White–Marshall, J. and Walsh, C. 1994 'Illaun–loughan: life and death on a small early monastic site' in *Arch. Ir.*, viii, pp 24–8.

Wijngaarden–Bakker, L. van 1974' The animal bones from the Beaker settlement at Newgrange, county Meath: first report' in *R.I.A. Proc.*, C, lxxiv, pp 313–83.

Wijngaarden–Bakker, L. van 1980 *An archaeological study of the Beaker settlement at Newgrange, Ireland*, Amsterdam, p. 185.

Wijngaarden–Bakker, L. van 1986 'The animal remains from the Beaker settlement at Newgrange, county Meath: final report' in *R.I.A. Proc.*, C, lxxxvi, pp 2–111.

Wild, P. 1979 *Pioneer conservationists of western America*, Missoula, Montana.

Wilde, W. 1849 *The beauties of the Boyne and Blackwater*, Dublin.

Wilde, W. 1850 *The beauties of the Boyne and Blackwater*, 2nd ed., Dublin.

Williams, M. 1994 'The relations of environmental history and historical geography' in *Jn. Hist. Geog.*, xx, pp 3–21.

Willis, H. 1985 *Pillboxes: a study of UK defences 1940*, London.

Wilson, T. 1980–86 'The great landowners of Meath, 1789' in *Riocht na Midhe*, vii, pp 99–110.

Woodman, P. and Anderson, E. 1990 'The Irish Later Mesolithic: a partial picture' in P. Vermeersch and P. Van Peer (ed.), *Contributions to the Mesolithic in Europe*, Leuven, pp 377–87.

Young, A. 1970 *Tour of Ireland*, 2 vols., reprinted Shannon, pp 37–49.

Zvelebil, M., Moore, M., Green, J. and Henson, D. 1987 'Regional survey and the analysis of lithic scatters: a case study from south–east Ireland' in R. Conway, M. Zvelebil and H. Blankholm (ed.), *Mesolithic north–west Europe: recent trends*, Sheffield, pp 9-23.

Zvelebil, M., Mackin, M., Passmore, M. and Ramsden, P. 1996 'Alluvial archaeology in the Barrow valley, south-east Ireland: the Riverford culture re-visited' in *Jn. Ir. Arch*, vii, pp 13–40.

INDEX

Page numbers in italics refer to illustrations and captions

CASHEL MONKNEWTOWN

Crewbane Bog

Earthen enclosure

Ritual pond

Passage tomb

CREWBANE

BUFFER ZONE

Monknewtown Chur

Medieval chu

Crewbane Marsh NHA

Ring ditch

BALFEDDOCK

Rossin

D-shaped enclosure

Large circular enclosure 'M'

The Tourist's R Public House

ROSSNAREE

KNOWTH

Knowth House

Ballyboy Lake

Knowth passage tombs and archaeological complex

Ringfort 'N'

Pillbox 22 (site of 'Cormac's Grave)

CORE AREA

Craud

D O

D-shaped enclosure

Ringfort

Passage tombs 'K' and 'L' circle

Pit

Ice house

Passage tomb and stone circle

Passage tombs 'Z', Z

Breo House

Cursus

Newgrange Farm

Timber circle

Johnson's mill

'Ford of Brow'

NEWGRANGE

Passage tomb 'E'

Passage tomb 'F'

Rossnaree River Bank NHA

Passage tomb 'U'

Passage tomb 'H'

Passage tomb and Earthen Enclosure 'A'

Standing stone 'D'

Newgrange 'P' Earthen Enclosure

Standing stone 'C'

LOUGHER

GILLTOWN

Passage tomb 'B'

Brú na Bóinne Visitor Centre

BUFFER ZONE

River Boyne

National Currach Centre

Ringfort site

ROUGHGRANGE

EPGRANGE

TOWNLEYHALL

Townley Hall

Townleyhall
passage tomb

Barrow

ck Bridge

ITTLEGRANGE

Mattock River

Oldbridge
House

Site of
Oldbridge
Village 1690

Mill

Caillemote's
memorial
stone

LESTIVERAN

PROUDFOOTSTOWN

Ringfort site

W   T   H

Battlefield
1690

mb,
n

Deserted
Medieval
village   'Fort'

Site of
Cloghalea
stone circle

Dowth
Wetland
NHA   OLDBRIDGE

Passage
tomb 'I'

Church and
towerhouse   Netterville
Institute   Dowth Hall   Earthen
enclosure
'Q'

Passage
tomb 'J'

LEBE

Glenmore
House

Farmhouse (Jacobite
rallying point)

Boyne Navigation

Mill   Miller's
House

SHEEPHOUSE

Donore
Medieval